Praise for *The Kedumah E*

MW00528183

"This book is a treasure of the most profound Jewish mysticism from very ancient sources which predate the Kabbalah, and which also, through Zvi Ish-Shalom's expert presentation, is made available for people of our time of all religious traditions."

—Father Thomas Keating, founding teacher of the Centering Prayer movement and author of *Open Mind, Open Heart*

"An exciting, inspiring, and ground breaking book. Zvi lays bare the ultimate, primordial spirituality of the "Torah," what is finally real and true in Judaism. In these pages, Zvi frees the Torah from its social and cultural limitations so that, with him, we may see and appreciate the full measure of its sacred and universal truth.

In Zvi's reading, the Torah, over the millennia so faithfully honored and protected in Judaic tradition, can now be discovered not only as the innermost, animating force of Judaism but as the spiritual inheritance of all people, no matter their time or place.

Zvi's impeccable training and experience as an Orthodox Rabbi positions him to show us the true, spiritual meaning of "orthodoxy" in Judaism, that is, utter fidelity to the infinite depth and wisdom of the Torah. The very nature of the Torah itself requires, in his view, that the Torah be freed for all humanity.

This book is important both for Jews, "practicing" and otherwise, and also for all people who are engaged in the spiritual quest."

—Reginald A. Ray, University Professor, Naropa University and Co-founder of Dharma Ocean Foundation. Author of *Secrets of the Vajra World* and *Touching Enlightenment*.

"I am delighted that my friend, Rabbi Zvi Ish-Shalom, is sharing his captivating and touching reflections on the profound tradition of Jewish mysticism and other contemplative paths in *The Kedumah Experience: The Primordial Torah*. As a follower of the Vajrayana tradition of Buddhism, I have always valued a wide variety of spiritual approaches to awakening the heart and mind and discovering new insights about ourselves and our world. I am confident that readers from all backgrounds will find in this beautiful book a compelling invitation to explore the nature of their experience."

"Zvi Ish-Shalom's experience with a variety of therapies and meditation has given him a deep psychological sophistication. He is not only conceptually involved in the teachings; he is an adept in applying them experientially, with introspective awareness."

"*The Kedumah Experience* is an innovative and creative examination of the potential of Kabbalah to move beyond the confines of normative Judaism and speak to the world about the nature and depth of human consciousness through the lens of the Jewish esoteric tradition. Combining learned expositions of mystical lore with a practical guide to its adaptation through conversation and practice, Ish-Shalom's book will inspire both beginner and expert alike. His extensive end-notes give the adept a clear sense of the depth of his learning while the book itself is a lucid journey through the portals of human consciousness via a sparkling synthesis of Kabbalah and other forms of mystical praxis. A masterful combination of theory and practice."

"Among the prerequisites for prophets and teachers of the emerging paradigm are direct knowledge of Reality, mastery of the language and practices of a particular historical tradition, and a vast command and familiarity with many other forms of inquiry, conceptualization, and methods of awakening. When it comes to the manifestation of this fully planetary light in a form that is rooted in the ancient Torah tradition, there are as yet very few who can embody these requisite qualities. Zvi Ish-Shalom is one such person and I cannot adequately express how much I respect him. One could, of course, list some of his many accomplishments, and skills, languages, and fields of knowledge that Zvi has mastered, but when it comes to the genius of real mastery the whole is always so much greater than the sum of its parts. Because Zvi has had the capacity and merit to do the work required in order to qualify for direct knowledge that is independent of any intermediate authority and has an extremely high level of facility in all major aspects and stages of the Torah tradition, he can express a mode of Primordial Torah that is authentic yet really new. I marvel at how clearly Zvi has been able to conceptualize the entire field of Torah, to diagnose what needs to be transcended and how skillfully he can perform the transformations that actually make the fourth turning of Torah manifest. With humility and admiration, I am honored to fully endorse his work."

—Rabbi Dr. Miles Krassen, author of *Steps towards a World-that-is-Coming*, founder of Planetary Judaism (formerly "Rain of Blessings"), former Associate Professor of Religious Studies and Contemplative Judaism at Naropa University and Oberlin College

The Kedumah Experience

The Primordial Torah

The Kedumah Experience

The Primordial Torah

Zvi Ish-Shalom

The Kedumah Series

Albion
Andalus
Boulder, Colorado
2017

"The old shall be renewed,
and the new shall be made holy."
— Rabbi Avraham Yitzhak Kook

Albion-Andalus, Inc.
P. O. Box 19852
Boulder, CO 80308
www.albionandalus.com

Cover design by Sari Wisenthal-Shore
Design and layout by Albion-Andalus Books

Manufactured in the United States of America

ISBN-13: 978-0692764213 (Albion-Andalus Books)
ISBN-10: 0692764216

Dedicated to:

The Masters of Kedumah

Contents

Acknowledgments

THANK YOU TO the following friends for reviewing all or parts of the manuscript and for offering helpful feedback (in alphabetical order): A. H. Almaas, Gaylon Ferguson, Oleg Gorelik, Shaya Ish-Shalom, Shaul Magid, Zarina Maiwandi, Netanel Miles-Yépez, Leslie Potter, and Gil Shalit. I am particularly grateful to A.H. Almaas for his careful reading of the manuscript and for his invaluable insights, thoughtful advice, and detailed suggestions; the Diamond Approach teachings I learned from him contribute richly to Kedumah. Special thanks to my brother Shaya Ish-Shalom for his heartfelt engagement with the material, his insightful and generous feedback, and for his skillful editing of key sections of the manuscript. Oleg Gorelik encouraged me to offer the first series of Kedumah talks upon which this book is based, and this book is therefore an expression of his foresight. I am especially grateful to him for his wise counsel, his important feedback on key segments of the book, and for his ongoing support of the teaching. Thank you to Albion-Andalus Books and especially to Netanel Miles-Yépez for his confidence in the Kedumah teachings, his friendship and support throughout the process, and for helping bring these teachings to the public. I am also grateful to Samantha Krezinski at Albion-Andalus Books for her patient and diligent work on typesetting and to Sari Wisenthal-Shore for her beautiful rendering of the cover-art. Thank you to the following members of our Kedumah community who transcribed the talks upon which this book is based: Daniel Halpern, Jenny Bertram, and Madi Lapidot. Thank you to Stella K. Bonnie, Emma Sartwell, and Audra Figgins for their skillful copyedits and to Daniel Battigalli-Ansell for crafting the diagram of the sefirot with its associated Kedumah terms, as well as his work on the bibliography and index. Kedumah is revealing itself through the sacred mandala of our growing community of students, and this book includes many of their insights and personal experiences. Thank you to our first cohort of students whose voices appear in this book, many of whom continue to participate in the ongoing revelation of Kedumah.

— Z.I-S.

Preface

THIS BOOK IS based on a series of talks I gave to a group of thirty students in the spring of 2014 in Boulder, Colorado. We met for eleven nighttime meetings in an old stone house in the Goss/Grove neighborhood, just a few blocks from Naropa University where I teach. Since this book is essentially edited transcripts of these talks, it maintains the original style and mannerisms of the oral presentation.

These talks were the first time I formally introduced Kedumah. As such, they present key principles of the teaching and provide an experiential overview of the path. For this reason I am making these first formulations of Kedumah available in book form—both for members of our Kedumah community as well as for the broader public.

Kedumah is an expression of my personal journey of spiritual awakening, which began with several periods of intense energetic and psychic upheaval in my early twenties. These experiences, which arose in the context of an Orthodox Jewish practice of prayer, study, and ritual, resulted in a cataclysmic shift in my relationship to God, Torah, the lineage, and all of reality.

In light of this context, I primarily use terms and concepts from the Jewish mystical tradition, as it is the system I am most familiar with and in which I was immersed when I had my early experiences. As such, Kedumah reflects my personal understanding and interpretation of the Jewish mystical tradition and it also offers a new approach to the practice of this tradition for the emerging age.

However, I also use concepts from other traditions in order to illustrate certain facets of my experience and of the teaching. Some of these traditions include: Buddhism, Hinduism, Sufism, Taoism, Christian mysticism, the Rolfing tradition and other somatic therapies, Western psychology, and the Diamond Approach. To be sure, all the teachings in this book are based upon my own understanding of these traditions in light of my personal experiences.

Throughout these talks I reference many traditional texts and teachings. I have therefore added notes at the back of the book with sources and further discussions, for those interested in studying more deeply.

Zvi Ish-Shalom
Boulder, Colorado

Each chapter begins with a meditation practice followed by a discussion with students and a talk. In the original presentation, following the talk there was often an interpersonal or group exercise to integrate the material, followed by more discussion with students. Please note that the instructions for the interpersonal and group exercises are not included in this book, only the conversations that took place directly after the exercises. I am not including the exercise instructions because they are best engaged in an intimate group setting under the guidance of a teacher. In Kedumah, spiritual awakening and insight occur in the context of human relationship. Therefore, I have decided to include my interactions with students that followed these exercises. Whenever the discussion followed an experiential exercise, I have indicated it with a heading. If no heading is present, this indicates that the discussion directly followed the talk. These conversations offer the reader a taste of some of the ways that we explore the essential nature of our experience on the Kedumah path.

1

The Primordial Torah

PRACTICE

WE WILL BEGIN with the ancient *Shema* chant. We will unpack the meaning of this prayer in more detail later, for now I invite you to chant it with me. We will chant it slowly and repeatedly for several minutes, extending the vowel sounds and allowing ourselves to be absorbed in the vibration of the sounds and in the silence that is present in between the enunciation of the words. There is also a *mudra* (hand gesture) that is traditionally associated with this prayer which is to cover the eyes with the right hand. I invite you to do that if you feel inspired to, otherwise you can just chant along or just listen and take in the ancient words.

Shema Yisrael Adonai Eloheinu Adonai Echad . . .

ZVI: What do you notice and experience in the field, in the space, right now?

STUDENT: Vibration.

ZVI: What kind of vibration?

STUDENT: It's a vibration, an energy.

1

ZVI: How do you experience it in your body or in the space?

STUDENT: It feels wide.

ZVI: Okay. So it feels wide. What do you notice if you just allow the wideness and spaciousness to be?

STUDENT: The sound of silence is a bit more noticeable in my experience.

ZVI: When you say "sound of silence," I have the sense that you are describing a palpable kind of silence, like it's a silence that is somehow full and present.

STUDENT: Indeed. Also, I notice that I'm not as focused on the words and thoughts that are usually flying through my head. I'm more aware of the space in between the words and sensations.

ZVI: Yes. What happens when you allow yourself to just be in the in between space?

STUDENT: Silence, stillness, peace, with some kind of subtle vibration or sense of fullness. It's weird because there is nothing really here to talk about. It's more like there is just an absence of everything, yet everything is in its right place and I feel fulfilled.

ZVI: Yes, thank you. Do other people sense the presence here? There is a dynamism, an aliveness, and at the same time there is stillness and a silence that has a palpability to it, a density.

STUDENT: I feel it more up here, like higher up, like heart and up.

ZVI: What does it feel like?

STUDENT: It is dense. Yeah, dense and alive, actually. Open. Awaiting and eager, an eagerness.

ZVI: So there's some kind of a potentiality?

STUDENT: Yes, the space is full, dense, and full of potential. There is a weightiness, and also a kind of expansiveness.

ZVI: You mentioned density and expansion. Those are things that, conventionally speaking, are usually mutually exclusive. However, in the immediate experience of this presence, you see that it's possible to be both concentrated and dense, and at the same time, spacious. This is one of the mysterious and paradoxical properties of presence.

STUDENT: I had the experience that you just talked about. There was a cohesive sense of awareness that then went out into expansion with each syllable. So it was a sense of being present, and at the same time consciousness expanding. Or the awareness of being that consciousness that is expanding.

ZVI: What do you experience right now, as you're speaking?

STUDENT: You know, speaking in front of people is always a little disconcerting to me but, you know, what the heck. I feel very big, like I am taking up the whole space of the room, but in a light way.

ZVI: How is that for you, to take up the entire space of the room?

STUDENT: Amazing. Free.

ZVI: Yes. Thank you. Did anyone notice that as we got to the fourth *Shema*, the quality changed? There was more spaciousness in the sound. I noticed that the awareness was becoming more expanded in that last chant. And then the vowels began to extend themselves, the spaces and the vowels.

STUDENT: I also had the experience that there was a shift in the harmonic that happened, all of a sudden it dropped, to where I could hear sounds that were much deeper than I could hear at the very beginning.

STUDENT: That first *Shema* reminded me of when you have a harmonica and you blow into the same note into the note hole, then you get this funny buzz. And I felt that we were all kind of coming into the same hole together. And, making harmony with each other, I felt the room and the room felt it too. It felt very personal. There is something about the words. I had the experience of singing the *Shema* where I actually felt like a prayer that was entering the land of Israel, and it's like a prayer that kind of includes that country and that place in the earth. And I felt that wasn't there tonight, which I really appreciated, because it helped me to drop into this space here and I remembered something you once said about how Israel represents on the mystical level an inner reality. I felt like that was nice, that it kept me in the density of this room and in this inner land.

ZVI: I appreciate that. Yes, there is plenty of Israel right here in the room. We don't need to get on an airplane. We don't need to go anywhere to find ourself.

STUDENT: At some point, I think I realized I was maybe just spaced-out; I wasn't aware of being in this space. And then all of a sudden I came back, and it felt that I was in the chant somehow, and I felt that I was a castle, with a lot of different configurations and steeples. I suddenly felt like I was basically in a really big castle. Different sounds and different qualities were different kinds of places in the castle. And then, when I opened my eyes I noticed the room had a different quality of light than prior to the chant. But there was also a sense of people, a sense of other people's presence or life being here in the space, which now felt merged with the castle.

ZVI: How does this experience affect you? I see you have some tears. It seems like it touches you in some way.

STUDENT: There was a lot of room, but it wasn't just an open space. There were characters in it. I am touched by the presence of these other beings that are here.

ZVI: Yes, we are not alone. There is a gathering happening, and we are all learning together. What a blessing that you feel them.

STUDENT: Can anyone else hear the lights buzzing?

ZVI: You mean the lights in the ceiling? [Laughter.] It's the *Shema* that did that. [Laughter.]

TALK

In order to understand what the hell is going on here as human beings in the world, it is useful to have a view of the situation. Every teaching has a view. In Hebrew there is an ancient term that we use to point to the view—*hashkafah*. It refers to how we look at things. It is helpful to understand the view of the teaching so that we can settle into it, trust it, and locate ourselves on the path.

Kedumah is a Hebrew word found in ancient mystical texts, and it means "primordial" or "ancient." Usually when we use the words "primordial" or "ancient," we think of them in terms of time and history. Something that is "ancient" is thought to have happened a long time ago. However, when I use the word "Kedumah" I do not mean it in this way.

There are ancient Hebrew texts that speak of a *Torah Kedumah*, a "primordial teaching."[1] The word "Torah" is the Hebrew word for "teaching." This term is used in the ancient Hebrew tradition in a similar way that Dharma is used in the Buddhist tradition: it points not to a particular text or to a particular body of literature but rather to the path, the teaching, and the truth in its totality. It does not merely refer to the Scriptures—what is known as the Bible or the Written Torah—which is just one expression of Torah. There is also the Oral Torah, living a life of Torah, and the living Master as embodiment of Torah. There are many such levels of Torah that are not often known.

The truth is that much of the Torah tradition, the ancient Hebrew wisdom path, is not known or understood even to people within that tradition. This is probably the case in many traditions; the institution-alization of religion and cultural inertia tend to obscure, limit, and even obviate the fresh revelation of the primordial truth. The same is true with regard to Torah.

The ancient Hebrew texts talk about a Primordial Torah that existed before the creation of the world. These texts state that all the teach-ings of the world are expressions of this primordial teaching. In fact, all of creation is an expression of this primordial teaching.

Now, when these texts talk about the *Torah Kedumah*, clearly they are not talking about the religion we know of as Judaism; they are not talking about any religion whatsoever. They are also not talking about the Torah as it is known in conventional terms. They are talking about something far more mysterious; something preexistent and pre-creation. The dimensions of time and space are expressions of the created realm, so the *Torah Kedumah* is prior to time and space, and therefore not bound by time and space.

As I have stated, Kedumah does not mean ancient or primordial in relation to time. Though I have cited ancient texts, this teaching does not come from some ancient time, and is not based on any historical texts. It is prior to the creation of the world, or perhaps more accu-rately, more primordial than the creation of the world. In a sense, even "the world" is itself just a concept. Some traditions and philosophies go so far as to explicitly declare that the world is nothing but the projection of our minds. What we call "the world" can thus be seen as merely a conceptual overlay.[2]

The Primordial Torah that existed "prior to the creation of the world" is the reality that exists prior to the creation of the world *of our concepts*. It is the most basic reality and truth that is eternally abiding as *what is* before our mind reifies our experience into conceptual categories and labels. That is to say, if we can somehow return to our primordial nature, our preconceptual, precreated, premanifest nature, then we are in direct contact with the Kedumah truth which is prior to, and independent of, time and space.

Kedumah is thus the primordial source that is present in the here and now. It is not something that existed long ago and that we must somehow recapture. We simply—and it is of course not so simple—have to learn how to wake up to what is right here and right now. This means that we have to learn how to include in our experience more and more of what we actually are, of what reality actually is, and to begin to discern directly this primordial ground of Being.

When we orient from this primordial ground, all of a sudden the true wisdom teachings of the world begin to make sense. They make sense not in the way that they are known conventionally, but they make sense because you can then taste and feel and see exactly what the vibrations of those teachings are carrying.

So we see that Kedumah is more fundamental than any particular religion or historical tradition. Although it draws from the Hebrew wisdom tradition (and from other related traditions), it is an intrinsically trans-religious approach to the spiritual journey, one that does not have any religious, institutional, ethnic, or tribal allegiances.

In Kedumah, we utilize some theoretical models and frameworks to talk about the spiritual journey, which entails shifting from a more conventional, conditioned way of experiencing ourselves and reality, toward a more inclusive, expanded and total way of knowing ourselves and reality. One of these models is what we call the teaching of the five journeys.

The five journeys are both linear and nonlinear at the same time. They outline a trajectory of the path that is progressive and developmental, but they may not—and often do not—unfold in a linear fashion. This is similar to the way the *yanas* (vehicles) are understood in the Buddhist tradition, whereby the three *yanas* can be engaged either sequentially or concurrently.[3]

In this teaching, the primary five journeys are called: contraction, expansion, wholeness, vastness, and freedom. Technically speaking, none of the five journeys is really a journey at all, because we never go anywhere. Nonetheless it feels like a journey, because a lot is happening; there is a great deal of transformation and opening, and new things revealing themselves.

Therefore, you can say that the spiritual path as a whole is perceptual rather than actual. A fancy philosophical way of saying this is that the journey is more epistemological than it is ontological. That is, reality is reality even before we "arrive" at it and come to perceive its true nature. It always was, is, and will be exactly what it is. But on this path, the way we perceive reality undergoes a transformation.

Ultimately, all of our practices in this teaching orient our consciousness to the possibility of freedom, which is the fifth journey. Freedom is a very difficult thing to understand with the conventional mind, which is why we spend a lot of time with the first four journeys. In a sense, with the first four journeys we are harmonizing, conditioning, and orienting our consciousness to the potential for freedom, which is the natural yearning of the human heart.

Freedom is not what the conventional mind thinks it is. It is not freedom from something or freedom to do something. Even to say that practice leads to freedom is not really true from the perspective of freedom itself, since the conventional categories of cause and effect do not apply to it. Although freedom is difficult to describe, it is nonetheless clearly recognizable as such when experienced directly.

To understand this principle more, let's turn to the Primordial Torah. As I mentioned earlier, by Primordial Torah I do not mean the Torah of time and space, which includes the Bible and the oral traditions of Judaism; this is the Torah that most of the world is at least somewhat familiar with. By Primordial Torah, I mean the Kedumah principle—the *Torah Kedumah*—which exists prior to creation and is fundamentally nonconceptual.

If we go back to the ancient source, the ancient teaching before the creation of the world, we are really going back to the primordial ground that is prior to and more fundamental than the conceptual, conventional processes that typically define our experience and our perception of reality. Since this wisdom is nonconceptual and prior to creation, it can reveal to us what this phenomenon of creation is all about.

Ķedumah is thus not just interested in articulating how creation occurred or why creation happened—which are ancient questions that the world's philosophical and religious traditions have attempted to answer—but is more concerned with charting the contours of our human condition, the conventional life that we ordinarily experience. It is interested in this because if we can chart the course of our human development, we can also retrace it back to our primordial roots.

What then is the process whereby the primordial ground that is fundamentally and radically nonconceptual and nondetermined manifests itself into the forms that we take to be who and what we are? These forms ultimately shape our body, our mind, our heart, our relations, and our actions in the world. The usual situation is that we take these forms to be our fundamental nature and we forget our true ground, our primordial nature.

However, before we get to the matter of creation it will be helpful for me to illustrate more about what I mean by the five journeys. One of the models we use in Ķedumah likens the human being to a Torah scroll: a roll of parchment upon which the Hebrew text of the Bible is traditionally written in a special kind of calligraphy. The embodiment of the Torah—the Teaching—is when we actually become a living Torah, a living Teaching. It is when our body, our consciousness, and our mind become a living expression of the Torah.[4]

To illustrate this, let's take a look at a Torah scroll. You've all seen scrolls, even if they were from another tradition. My office at Naropa University used to house a collection of ancient Buddhist texts which were written on scrolls with beautiful calligraphy. It is black ink on white parchment.

In the Kedumah teachings we use this image of a Torah scroll as a metaphor to help us better understand the five journeys. However, before I spell out the relationship between the Torah scroll and the five journeys, it will be helpful to first explain how we understand the different levels of a teaching, how they each correlate with a particular dimension of the human being, and how these dimensions, in turn, are reflected in the image of a Torah scroll.[5]

In Kedumah we talk about four levels of understanding a teaching. We call the first level the narrative level, which is the level of myth. This level houses the conceptual view of a teaching. Every teaching, every path, and every religion has its conceptual view. This includes the story of our origins and teachings on how we return to those origins.

The second level is the level of the practices. What do we do with ourselves in response to this narrative? The second level addresses this question by prescribing the rituals and practices—the action-directives of the path.

The third level is the essential level, which can also be described as the mystical or esoteric level. In many traditions, only the exoteric dimension—the expressed narratives and practices—are known to the public. But there is also the essential, mystical dimension—the third level—which is rarely familiar to the common practitioner of a path.

These are the three main levels. There is also a fourth level. We call it the primordial level. The primordial level is even more fundamental than the mystical level because the mystical level still uses the language of the accepted narrative and practices. Usually, if you go into any tradition and learn the mystical teachings of that tradition, you will not have any idea what they are talking about unless you know the narrative and the practices.

This is true with many traditions, including Judaism. If you were to open up a Kabbalistic text, it would likely make no sense unless you knew the narratives and practices of Judaism. The entire mystical teaching is framed by those traditional narratives and practices. However, the primordial level is not bound to any of the three basic levels. With proper training, it is possible to experience the truth of the fourth level without any recourse to the first three levels.

Another way of looking at these four levels is related to the nature of the human being. First, let us consider our garments, which in this metaphor relate to the narrative level of a teaching. The narrative is the clothing of a teaching. On the next level we have the practices, which involve our bodies. At this level, we move toward a more embodied experience of the teaching, in alignment with the view or narrative. The mystical level relates to the inner essence of the human being. The primordial level, in turn, relates the essence of the essence—it is the most basic ground of one's being.

Thus far we have discussed this model as it pertains to a teaching and to a person. Now let us consider this from the perspective of the scroll. On a scroll there are words. Words are a collection of letters, configured in a particular way. These words form narratives and stories that tell us something that we can wrap our conventional minds around and orient from. The words are the narrative level, the level of the garments.

Each of these words that can be configured to form stories are in turn comprised of letters. The letters are more fundamental than the words. They are the building blocks of the narrative. The letters correspond to the level of the body. Each body is a particular letter, an individual.

What is more fundamental than the letters? The ink is the very substance that constitutes the letters. This corresponds to the essential or mystical level. On the level of the person, it is the level of one's inner essence, correlating with the ink that animates our individual letter.[6] This same ink is also the basic material of all the letters. You could say it is the essential substance that is shared by all the letters. The same ink is used to write all the letters of the scroll. But the way the ink is configured and shaped determines the unique characteristics of each and every letter. And the way each of the letters constellate among a community of other letters forms the narratives that shape that particular letter's life.

Now we come to the essence of the essence. What we call the primordial level, with respect to the teaching, is the essence of the essence level when we speak of the person. Let's look at it on the scroll. While the ink (the essential level) is written on white parchment, the essence of the essence is the parchment itself, the primordial ground upon which all letters and words are written. The white parchment of the scroll contains all letters, all shapes, and infinite possibilities.

Now let's consider all of this in terms of the five journeys. Our usual experience is that we are identified with and very committed to our narratives, the stories that we hold about who we are, and what reality is. These stories are often constructed in relation to the words that we share with other human beings, that is to say, the words that are formed by the letters of our family, our tradition, and our community of colleagues, coworkers, friends, and neighbors. We construct a collective narrative in which we situate ourselves. In a sense, we define who and what we are and what reality is based on our location in that narrative.

However, this is a limited understanding of who and what we are. It is a perspective that is in need of ongoing support, what we call dependency. That is, we depend on our story remaining more or less intact and familiar in order for our identity to feel stable. We need to keep our experiences within a certain range. There is therefore a limited range of flexibility, beyond which our letters begin to fragment, to break down, or conversely to get overly rigid. Can you relate to this? This is our usual way of life. Any kind of disruption in our environment and in our story impacts us deeply and we scramble to reconfigure that story so that it forms some kind of cohesive narrative.

There is nothing wrong with this, of course. We need a narrative. It is part of our human experience and completely necessary as we develop. But, if we are overly identified with it, thinking it is who and what we are, then we are only seeing the narrative level of the teaching, and reading a very limited range of meaning into the scroll. This is what we call the Journey of Contraction. It is a contracted, or limited way of reading reality.

Kedumah offers skills and tools, and we learn very immediate, accessible methods of working with contraction. We learn how to work with a more limited range of experience, and we move through and with that in order to free ourselves from a certain kind of imprisoned view—an imprisoned outlook of who and what we are, and of what reality is. Through understanding our contractions and their associated narratives, a powerful impulse to separate from these narratives can arise. By recognizing the false and committing ourselves to the true, a sense of spaciousness can arise. This moves us into a broader perspective, which is the level of the true body. This true body—what we call the *Presence Body*—is marked by a sense of spaciousness and expansion beyond the usual confines of the self-narrative and its limited viewpoint.[7]

We refer to this experience as the Journey of Expansion. This is not meant metaphorically. The physical body literally feels more expanded, as if there is more space to breathe and move. This experience corresponds with the individual letter in the metaphor of the scroll, and represents the first stages of the awakening of the true human body—unconfined by the historical self-stories of the mind.

This brings us to the third journey, which correlates with the mystical or essential dimension on the level of the teaching, the inner essence of the person, and the ink on the level of the scroll. If we know our true individual letter, while it is one measure of freedom, our perception is still limited. The limitation is that while we may experience ourselves as an expanded and spacious individual letter in our own right, not dependent on the other letters, we may not recognize that the substance of our letter is the same substance that constitutes all letters. We may not recognize that, on a deeper level, the ink that beautifully crafts the particular shapes and contours of our individuality is the same substance that is expressing itself through every individual on the planet.

This is a further development that we call the Journey of Wholeness, and it provides the essential resolution for how we can simultaneously be both an individual and inseparable from the whole. In this process we learn to embody our nature as simultaneously having dual and nondual expressions, as being spacious and intimately connected to the whole while also being autonomous and distinct as an individual. Knowing our ink as the essential Presence that constitutes all form and manifestation brings a sense of profound fulfillment, richness, and depth to our human experience.

The Journey of Wholeness, which correlates with the individual essence and the recognition of the ink, does not mean that we dissolve into a puddle of ink. The letter and the words remain, but we have more freedom to craft the letters and the words in a way that actually makes sense, that is constructive and useful for us in life, and that makes sense given the reality of our situation. We do not have to force ourselves into something that is not authentic.

Finally, we have the fourth level, the primordial level when we speak in terms of teaching, and the essence of the essence level when we speak in terms of the person. If we recognize ourselves as the ink of the letters—which is the particular realization of the Journey of Wholeness—but we still do not recognize that there is a parchment on which this letter is being written, then our perspective is limited. If we do not see that this ink is manifesting as this particular letter on this ineffable, mysterious ground—the parchment—then we are not seeing the whole picture. Our view and our experience of reality and of ourselves is therefore limited. In time, the Journey of Wholeness will naturally lead to the recognition of the primordial ground of being—this white parchment that we call the Kedumah dimension.

In the five journeys, we talk about this as the Journey of Vastness. What exactly is meant by "vastness" requires an elaborate explanation. To illustrate it in a simple way, let us again invoke the image of the scroll. Usually when we look at a scroll our eyes will automatically focus on the black letters and the black words on the scroll; this is our habit. But how often do we open a scroll and read the white spaces, the white script that shapes itself around the black letters? What would it be like to open up a book and read the white script instead of the black letters? What would it be like to recognize the white parchment as having its own expression, its own quality of transmission?[8]

This is an analogy, of course. The white parchment is always here under the surface of things. Our lives are inscribed on this white parchment. The parchment itself is just vast open space. Our lives, our bodies, our minds, and our individuality are all inscriptions on this primordial parchment. Often though, we don't recognize this in our life. We have "kitchen blindness," which is something I definitely suffer from [Laughter.]. It's when there's something in the kitchen and you can't find it, but it's right in front of your face. It's right there on the counter, but you are looking everywhere and you can't find it.

In a sense we are blind. The primordial ground is right in front of us, but we are looking everywhere and cannot find it. The Journey of Vastness also opens the doorway to the perception of a certain kind of emptiness. This emptiness is difficult to recognize because it is completely featureless and radically devoid of anything recognizable to habitual perception. It is tricky to talk about because it cannot be described accurately, only pointed to.

To write a scroll, you need the parchment. Every new teaching, or any expression of an ancient, primordial teaching, needs a parchment.

That is where we start. If we are not in touch with the level of the parchment—the primordial ground—then all efforts to renew traditions are just reconfiguring the same letters into different words. For new letters to be written, for brand new words to be constructed, words that are fresh and immediate revelations from the primordial ground itself, we need to abide in that ground. We need to be vehicles for its mysterious revelations.

The awakened life is a life lived in openness to, permeability to, and transparency to this mysterious primordial ground. Then in every moment the letters are being written anew. The words are fresh. Our relationships are fresh. Life is fresh. Everything is completely unknown; what is going to happen next is a mystery. This is what I mean by being awake and alive. It means to be living expressions of reality. Living means you never know what is going to happen. Life has its own intelligent nature that is not prepackaged or predetermined, and is never familiar.

On the level of the teaching, every authentic teaching is a revelation from that ground, which means that any kind of inflexibility or calcification of a tradition is already one step removed from its ground, from its source of revelation. Living teachings are responsive and spontaneous. They have a quality of wonder and of mystery. The teaching is ultimately our life. We are the teaching and we live the teaching. Our lives are expressions of the teaching. As living beings we are that wonder, that mystery, that unknown, and that freshness of seeing things anew in each moment.

For most people it helps to have the support of a teaching that articulates a view and offers a path to follow and specific practices to engage. A teaching that has an understanding of the things that come up along the way and shares a community of letters; a *sangha*, a sacred society, a *kehillah*, a *minyan*, is the formation of an intentional narrative. It is the formation of an intentional collection of letters that forms a particular kind of vehicle. A particular presence is then able to reveal itself to this living being of a community, this communal body of letters. So it helps to have the support of such a living communal text.

The fifth journey—the Journey of Freedom—is more difficult to talk about explicitly. In the Kabbalistic system, it relates to what we call *Adam Kadmon* (Primordial Human) and points to *Ein Sof*, which means "no-end." Kabbalists did not talk very much about *Ein Sof*. The Journey of Freedom is the recognition that the parchment, the ink, the letters, and all the words constitute a singular and all-possible totality. There is no end to the revelation of truth. It is the totality itself.[9]

The implications of this are profound. Firstly, it means that all of our experience, the pain and the suffering, along with all the spiritual states, are included and welcomed without value preference. From this perspective, the perspective of freedom, everything is included because reality literally *is* everything. It is not that we are including it or that we are choosing to include it. It is simply the way things are when reality is recognized for what it is. With the truth of totality we see that literally we are all in it together. This is a radical kind of freedom because it is the unobstructed recognition of the freedom of reality to unfold itself according to its design.

In this path, the whole teaching and all of the practices we do orient toward this view of freedom from the very beginning. We do not make it explicit because you cannot help a person find the thing in the kitchen if it is not actually there, and we are indeed talking about something that is not there. More accurately, it is not there, nor is it not not-there. Neither is it not there nor there, see. You can see the radical kind of inclusivity, the radical kind of freedom that comes with simply recognizing that everything is included and nothing is alienated. This brings a whole other level and degree of freedom.[*]

Now I want to return to the question of creation. As I mentioned earlier, the blank parchment—which represents the Kedumah reality— is infinite in its potential. It is completely wide open. Anything can

---

* For a table of the five journeys and their corollary terms in Kedumah and in Classical Kabbalah, see page 293.

happen. Anything can be written. Any form can take shape. Any manifestation can arise. However, can you imagine the infinite primordial nature without any words? Without any manifestation? Without the form? Without life? Without the flesh and blood of its ink? It's hard to imagine. The basic assumption of Kedumah is that the primordial nature is indeed absolute in its infinite possibilities.

The only thing that can define it is that it cannot be limited in any way. Its nature is limitless, endless. This means that it is endless in its possibility; its nature is unrestricted. Notice how nothing can be said about it directly, rather, it can only be explained according to what it is not. It is not finite. It is not limited. What makes it infinite is that it has no end, so nothing positive can be said about it because that would limit it. We have to say what it is not in order to understand what it is. That is a way of preserving its true, limitless nature.

What I am presenting right now is the narrative level of Kedumah. This is the conceptual view. Every teaching needs a view and a narrative. The narrative of Kedumah is that the infinite, in order for it to be truly endless, must include all possibilities. Therefore, it is presented as a magnificent paradox; it must by its very nature also be able to be limited and finite. In other words, an infinite that cannot manifest as finite is really not infinite. The infinite must at least have some expression of finitude in order to complete its infinite possibilities.[10]

If you are thinking ahead, you may already know where this narrative is going. The creation of a finite world, of finite experience—what we call in some teachings the dualistic realm of apparent limitation, of separateness—presents the opportunity for the infinite, for *Ein Sof*, to know itself, complete itself, and fulfill itself through the experience of being limited and finite.

This presents another paradox, which is that from the Kedumah perspective it is impossible for there to be a finitude that is truly separate from the infinite, that is some kind of independent reality. This is where things get interesting. The infinite, as part of this narrative, therefore must have some way to experience things as finite or limited in order to facilitate the completion of its nature, even though this is an ontological impossibility.

That is to say, ontologically—having to do with how things are—it is impossible for there to be a true dissociation or split in reality. However, epistemologically—having to do with how we perceive—it is possible. The infinite must have a mechanism through which it can experience duality and finitude, even if ontologically it is an impossibility.

The mechanism through which the infinite completes its possibilities and through which it experiences finitude is the human being. The human being presents the fulfillment of the infinite's possibilities precisely because we experience ourselves as finite, dualistic, limited, and split off from ultimate truth, split off from our nature. If we did not experience ourselves as alienated and disconnected from the absolute ground, then the infinite would be limited in its possibilities, which must include the experience of being alienated and split off from this ground. So, unwittingly, our suffering constitutes the fulfillment of the infinite's potential. This should come as a great relief, because at the very least we can stop beating ourselves up for being dualistic, finite, and imperfect.

In this narrative, our suffering is meaningful; it is not a mistake that needs to be fixed. However, this is only one step of the process because what manifests is not just the dissociation, but also the recognition of it: waking up to our ontological nature, which is inseparable and in a state of absolute unity with the infinite reality. You could see that the view here entails a passage whereby we go through an epistemological transformation in order to recognize what was, is, and always will be our nature. This process is represented in the journey from contraction to expansion, from wholeness to vastness, and ultimately to freedom.

The principle of contraction is very nuanced and there are many teachings associated with it. By contraction, usually we think of it as something closed in on itself, but contraction can also manifest as concentration. It can be the concentration of energy, presence, or awareness. Collecting, gathering, focusing, and concentrating into a singular point is also a certain kind of contraction. These teachings on contraction also present a paradox: the more we concentrate our presence and awareness, the more spaciousness and expansiveness arises.

The Kabbalists refer to this principle of contraction with the term *tzimtzum*. *Tzimtzum* is a word that literally means "contraction," but it also means "withdrawal."[11] It presents the paradox of how consciousness works. Consciousness is the material of reality, of our human nature, and even of our bodies. In the Kedumah reading of the Garden of Eden story, this is expressed in the teachings on the body of light. In this narrative, the epistemological shift occurs in the shifting of our perception of our body as constituted by essential light, boundless and inseparable from totality, to a body of skin that is encapsulated by a body boundary.[12]

In the Hebrew, the word for light is *ohr* (אור), spelled with the letter *aleph* (א). However, *ohr* (עור) spelled with the letter *ayin* (ע), which is pronounced identically to *ohr* spelled with an *aleph*, means "skin." It is the same word, only the letter shifts. If you shift the first letter to the *aleph*, it is light. If you shift the first letter to an *ayin*, it is skin.

In the narrative of the Garden of Eden in the book of Genesis, one consequence of eating of the Tree of Knowledge of Good and Evil is that there is an epistemological shift whereby we cease perceiving our bodies as constituted by light and instead perceive our bodies as encapsulated by skin. That is, we shift from a nondual perception to a dualistic view of separateness.

The process of creation entails a series of contractions and expansions, very much like the birthing process.[13] With the birth of a baby there are repeated contractions and expansions. The contractions bring more space, more opening. The birth of our cosmos, the birth of our nature, requires the living pulsation that occurs in each and every moment. In each and every moment creation is happening anew.

This is reflected in the traditional Jewish morning prayer that states, *Ha-michadesh Be-tuvo Bechol Yom Tamid Ma-aseh Be-resheit,* "Who renews, in His goodness, every day, always, the act of creation." From that line, which is recited every morning by Jews across the world, it is clear that even in the traditional view, creation is not something that happened in time and space, not something that happened long ago. Rather, creation is happening in each and every moment.

The dynamism and essential pulsation that we were feeling earlier after chanting the *Shema* together can be a doorway to the recognition of the energy of creation itself, which is a palpable dynamism, a living truth that is eternally present right in this very moment.

This process of contraction and expansion has many levels to it. It proceeds from contraction as limitation to contraction as the possibility of opening and expansion. Contraction also represents the movement of the infinite light, the light of *Ein Sof*, into the manifestation of form, until its eventual presentation as the dualistic human experience of separation.

When we understand this process we can trace it back, we can follow the experience of embodied form as a portal to its primordial ground. We can follow it back through all the dimensions of light; this process of repeated contraction and expansion birthed into being, from the most coarse and material into the most subtle and ethereal. All the realms of reality can then be known experientially.

In this view, our personal individual life is ripe with meaning. Each one of us represents one letter, one of the irreplaceable bodies of reality.[14] There is a tradition that in order for a Torah scroll to be kosher and fit for use in the synagogue, not one letter can be missing. Every single letter is needed for the infinite to know itself in its completeness. We can interpret this as meaning that every individual life, with all of our suffering and all of our contractions, is the potential of the infinite expressing itself.

Based on this view, the practices that we will learn on this path will make more sense. Our practices are oriented from the understanding that exactly where we are, right here and right now, in our embodied experience, is the infinite expressing itself in this form as the infinite in its totality. We may not see it, we may not understand it, and we may not know it, but as we experiment with it, embrace it and include it more in our physical human experience, the paradox of the contraction and space, concentration and expansion, can begin to open. What is finite and limited can begin to open into expansion, which is the second principle. Contraction leads to expansion.

Here we have laid the groundwork of the view, but ultimately this must be learned experientially. It is not so important to ruminate on the view as an intellectual exercise. That said, it is important to articulate enough to satisfy the conventional mind so that we can engage the practices and be open to their impact.

[The following discussion takes place after an experiential exercise.]

STUDENT: In the exercise I realized that it's all perception, that everything is perception in the moment.

ZVI: What's it like when you see that? What's your immediate experience like when you recognize that?

STUDENT: It's a witness process.

ZVI: You experience yourself as a witness?

STUDENT: Yeah.

ZVI: What's it like to witness your experience?

STUDENT: Infinite and finite.

ZVI: And what's it like when you allow both infinite and finite at the same time?

STUDENT: Real.

ZVI: There's more of a sense of realness?

STUDENT: Yeah, it's authentic.

ZVI: There's something very solid about realness. Solid but not rigid. It's open, expansive, and right here.

STUDENT: Feels like the white on the paper. The witness piece.

ZVI: Yes. And allowing both the finite and infinite at the same time also includes the letters. There's something very whole and authentic about that. There's wholeness and there's realness.

STUDENT: Yeah. Amen. Thank you.

STUDENT: I definitely felt something shift during your talk. But it's weird because I feel both kind of stuck and spacious at the same time.

ZVI: So there is a mixture of things going on. And what's it like to see that and just allow yourself to fully be here with both the stuckness and the spaciousness?

STUDENT: Ah, like really, really pleasant, but also intense at moments.

ZVI: Does it feel intense right now?

STUDENT: Ah, yeah. But just not, not threatening, but intense.

ZVI: Can you describe the intensity?

STUDENT: Like a charge, my body's kind of charged.

ZVI: You feel charge in your body.

STUDENT: Yes, it's hard to describe.

ZVI: Is it okay to allow the intensity to do what it wants in your body?

STUDENT: Yeah, I think so. I mean, you know I could try to, like even resisting it is kind of part of the intensity. So, I guess if I recognize that it's just intensity, then it's just okay.

ZVI: Yes, very good observation. So there's a resistance, and then there's some kind of a charge. And the two of them, in this kind of relationship, are creating a certain kind of intensity. So what happens when you see there's this dialectic happening between them, and allow both of them to be there? And sense it? What happens to your body?

STUDENT: It kind of feels like when you're charged but you're also resisting the charge. It almost feels like your body's being uncontrollable in some way. Like it's doing things you might not want to do. Like you're trying to control your body. So it kind of feels like it's doing whatever it wants to do and there's not much else to do about it. It feels alright.

ZVI: So it's "alright," it's just doing what it's doing. I'm curious about the "it's alright." What is that quality?

STUDENT: Normally I feel laid back or more apathetic. It doesn't feel like that; it's intense, but not apathetic or disconnected right now.

ZVI: That's a really good discernment. There is an expression of "it's alright" that's more apathetic, which is more of a resistant kind of expression, and then there is an expression of "alright" that is more objective and real. This objective expression of "it's okay" realizes that there's nothing to do about anything, that whatever is happening is just fine. There's an implicit sense that reality will take care of things. Reality will reveal what needs to be revealed, in due course. Or not. And that's fine too. Does this resonate, what I'm saying?

STUDENT: Yes. What's weird is that, if this dawns on you or you arrive at this place of understanding from a place of not having had that perspective, then not having had that perspective again was just part of reality unfolding itself. What's so weird is that you can recognize that the entire time it's been that way, but you just didn't recognize that.

ZVI: Pretty trippy, yes? Reality is always this way, which is what's so wacky about it. You can see now what I'm pointing to in terms of freedom. Freedom in this teaching is not feeling good, necessarily. There can be contraction in our nervous system, in our psyche, in our lives. We can have all kinds of difficulties. When I talk about freedom, I'm talking about a radical kind of posture that doesn't have a value judgment about those experiences, because it recognizes that they too are part of the whole. It's freedom from our need to be free from contraction. It's freedom from our need to hold on to some ideal of enlightenment. It's freedom to be exactly where we are at any moment, no holds barred. That's a radical kind of freedom. This means that we don't have to have any particular kind of experience to be free.

From this perspective, any experience of expansion or nonduality or enlightenment that subtly holds the position that it's better to be here than it is to be wound up about something is still not completely free. There's a subtle kind of suffering in that. The freedom that I am getting at is a resolution of this subtle preferential holding.

One of the most ancient Kabbalistic texts states, "the end is embedded in the beginning, and the beginning is embedded in the end." *Na-utz sofan be-techilatan ve-tichilatan bisofan.*[15] Kedumah has this perspective. So the "end," which is what we call the Journey of

Freedom, is not really an end. It's embedded in the "beginning." It was always there. It is what is. So we're hoping to open that up.

This is all just a taste of some of the methods we use on the path. You may have a sense of the group field, just from being together for a few hours; it already has its own kind of life, its own presence, its own nature in a way that's beginning to form. The words on the parchment are beginning to come together.

2
Intimate Knowing

Practice

FIND A SITTING posture that feels in alignment with gravity, in alignment with the environment. A posture in which you feel the weight of
your body centered and rooted. And you feel the reach of your head
into the heavens. In this optimal posture, the spine has a sense of verticality but is also relaxed, so it's a posture that is naturally connected
to the heavens and to the earth. You may want to find the sweet spot
by shifting your weight, slightly and subtlty, forward and back, side to
side, until you find that spot where it just clicks. Where you feel that
sense of earthy support for you to reach above.

This practice cultivates the inner capacity for touch. We have external and internal expressions of all of our sense perceptions. We have
external sight and we have inner sight. We have external hearing and
we have the inner capacity for hearing. And so with all the senses—
smell, taste, and touch. This practice will invite our inner capacity for
touch to express itself more explicitly and more fully.

We'll begin by allowing our consciousness to sense itself in our feet.
Our living consciousness can touch our bodies from the inside out,
using its inner fingers. What's it like to sense into our toes, each one
individually, and then all ten of them? Allowing our inner consciousness, our inner sense of touch, to sense into our toes, can we discrim-

inate the bones? If we add now our whole feet, the soles of the feet, tops of the feet. Really feeling into them. Touching into them. What's the volume of our feet like? What is its three-dimensionality like?

Every time we notice our mind distracted with thoughts or our heart distracted with feeling, we just return to the raw sensation of this sensing consciousness, feeling, sensing, the dimensions of the feet, bones, muscles, all the tissues.

We add, now, the ankles. What's the dimensionality, the three-dimensionality of each of our ankles like? Now adding our lower legs, our calves. The trick is to allow our living consciousness to sense itself in our body, rather than pushing or forcing anything. We're just inviting its natural, organic sensitivity to express itself through sensing. What's the volume of each of our lower legs like? Sense the bones there, the two main bones, the tibia and the fibula. And sense the space in between those two bones, right at the core. The muscles, and the flesh, all the way into the surface of the skin.

And now still sensing our feet, and our toes, and the bottom of our feet, the ankles and the lower legs, now just add sensing into the knees. Again sensing the dimensionality of these. Just getting a direct and raw sense of the anatomical parts in the knees.

Now adding the upper legs, the thighs. With the massive and ancient bone, the femur. Sense into its ancient nature. The three-dimensionality of the legs. The thighs. The robustness of those muscles that carry us, carry our walking day to day.

Now adding the pelvis. Feeling our sitz bones on the chair or the cushion, but sensing the whole three dimensional bowl of the pelvis. Including the hips. All the organs. With their exquisite sensitivity and vitality. The genitals. Perineum.

Now allowing consciousness to sense both legs, from the bottoms of the feet, up to and including the pelvis.

Now adding sensing into the fingertips. And the fingers themselves. With all their bones and connective tissues. The palms of the hands.

The dimensionality of the hand. From the back of the hand to the palms. All of the bones. Musculature. Cartilage.

While still sensing the whole, both legs and the hands, we now add sensing into the wrists. And the forearms. See if you can discriminate the two bones in the forearms. The ulna and the radius, and sense the space, the interosseous membrane, the space between them.

Adding the elbows and the upper arms. Sensing the three-dimensionality, the volume, of the upper arm.

And adding the shoulders.

Now sensing both arms, from the tips of the fingers, up to and including the shoulders, and both legs, from the bottoms of the feet, up through the hips and pelvis. Consciousness sensing, touching.

Gently, including now, the belly. With a light touch, including the diaphragm, chest, and heart.

Sensing the neck. The face. Jaw. Cranium. With a light touch, just sensing the dimensionality of the cranium and the space at its core. And the top of the head.

Now the space above the head.

Now coming back centrally to the arms and the legs, and the living, sensing consciousness in the arms and the legs. Notice the sounds in the room. Listen, listening, from the sensing consciousness. So it's the sensing consciousness—the arms and the legs and the belly, that's hearing.

And then slowly open the eyes and add seeing. It's the sensing consciousness that's seeing.

I'm going to ring the bell to mark the end of the formal practice, but the practice continues. We can continue to play with orienting from the palpable sensing presence whose locus of activity is the body.

Zvi: So what do you notice right now in your experience with this practice?

STUDENT: I feel really heavy. And literally, someone's like pulling me down. It feels really hard even to lift my hands off of my legs.

ZVI: How does it affect you?

STUDENT: In some sense I feel more focused and more grounded than I did when we started. It was almost a little alarming. I feel like I just ingested something outside of myself, if that makes sense.

ZVI: It feels that you ingested something?

STUDENT: Yeah. It was just such an immediate reaction, I guess something about it is surprising.

ZVI: Yes, it is a powerful practice. What about others?

STUDENT: I feel lighter. And more empty, or spacious. But it kind of has a grounding quality to it at the same time, which is weird.

ZVI: So it's a spaciousness and a lightness, but it also feels grounded.

STUDENT: Yes. I had a sense of consciousness as actually a material, like as a liquid, almost like as a viscous, sort of bluish gel that came, that I could sort of guide through my body as we were filling up, and guided it where we were bringing our focus. And then when you directed us to move the senses out, I had the sense that all of that material was available for sensory input.

ZVI: So this material of consciousness is somehow impacted by sensory phenomenon?

STUDENT: Yeah. That it's like bringing your consciousness, your awareness to it. In a certain way it's very malleable like I have the sense that it will do anything you ask it to. Like if you ask it to see, there's a way that it can see. If you ask it to hear, then there's a way that all that material in your body can learn to hear, or can process data as sound.

ZVI: So the material of consciousness is malleable, and it's also impressionable. And there's an intelligence that it's responsive to. Those are good observations. How is it to feel that and see that, the truth of that?

STUDENT: It's powerful, and I feel like there's a lot of potential in that. If I could have that sense with me in my normal world, there's a lot of availability for intuition and for knowing in channels other than our normal cognitive process.

ZVI: Yes. There is potentiality too. Thank you.

STUDENT: I could really visualize and feel my bones, maybe because I've taken anatomy. They felt like they were vibrating, maybe something akin to what you're describing, but I felt like my bones were full and I felt like they could hear. It seemed like they could hear and I felt like they radiated, like I don't know if I look like a ball of light, but I feel like a ball of light.

ZVI: So the bones have a radiance, they are alive, and they have their own perceptive capacity. They can perceive.

STUDENT: Yes. Like they could perceive and receive what was in the room.

ZVI: How is it to experience this in such a direct way?

STUDENT: Great. It took a lot of concentration, a lot of like inner listening, but now it feels clear and spacious.

ZVI: Yes. Thank you.

STUDENT: I also had a sensation of heaviness like you're talking about. And it felt like my mind was dropping down in a way and there was a sensation at the bottom of my feet, like a sense of the ground, and it had a certain sense of heaviness to it. Also, my experience was that I found it to be a relief because it helped to pull me out of my head. And I also had the experience of pliability. I would call it a pliability of consciousness, where it could go to wherever I was asking it to go to. And I also had a sensation of feeling the skin as a boundary for the body, and feeling how that is one distinction of where consciousness goes, but that consciousness can also go beyond the boundaries of what the body is.

ZVI: Yes. What is it like to allow your consciousness to expand beyond the body-boundary?

STUDENT: It feels very open and spacious, yet grounded at the same time. Like I am not out of my body, but more fully in my body.

ZVI: Yes. Thank you.

STUDENT: I was aware of two things seemingly happening. One was the sensing, which I couldn't really say much about. And then there was my image or thought about the sensing. So, to actually look at a place or try to see the bones, it felt like an image. It was not like I was actually just in that sensing, but there was some sort of thing coming up or being projected onto that place. And yet there was definitely movement and things happening, but it was really fascinating to go back and forth between the thought about it and the direct experience of it.

ZVI: What's the qualitative difference between those two modes of experience?

STUDENT: Well certainly with the thought there can be a sense of pushing. It's very subtle but, for me at least, it manifested in the sense of trying to figure something out. And just being in the sensing—there's nothing else left. There's not really anything else happening but that.

ZVI: So when you are just sensing, it's more in touch with the immediacy of the experience.

STUDENT: Currently, it's much more. It's hard to talk about 'cause it's just there.

ZVI: So even talking about it is one step removed from what it actually is.

STUDENT: Yes, it's like a layer. I feel that there's a depth to just the experience, and it's not that the thought or the talking is outside of it, but somehow there's a shift in the perception of it.

ZVI: What's it like to just abide in the experience of the immediacy of the sensing?

STUDENT: It's actually very, very, immediate. [Laughter.]

ZVI: Can you express it with a sound?

STUDENT: Ha! You know me well. [Laughter.] Sure… *buuuUUOOOUUUuuum*. Kind of like a pulsing that I felt.

ZVI: Thank you. [Laughter.] That was the sounds of the bones, I think, too.

Good. So with this practice, the method is to keep coming back to the immediate sensing, the raw sensation. Various kinds of visualizations may arise, which is fine. But the practice is to continuously come back to just sensing, allowing the inner touching to be more of the foreground of your experience.

TALK

In the last talk we presented a skeleton outline of the view of the Kedumah Teachings through the lens of two conceptual categories, the finite and the infinite, and contemplated the relationship between the two and how the human being is situated in this narrative. There is actually a lot more subtlety and nuance in terms of what we mean by infinite and what we mean by finite.

The Kabbalistic tradition, although it is an expression of the primordial teaching, is necessarily intertwined with and an expression of the particular practices and narratives of the tradition from which it arose. Though mystical teachings of every tradition point to that which is beyond categories like finite and infinite, human and Divine, we still must rely on these words, which are conditioned by the conventional concepts of a particular path and therefore subject to misinterpretation and confusion.

This happens in every mystical teaching. Concepts that are attempting to point out that which is beyond concepts are inadvertently reified. This relates directly to what was presented in the last talk. For instance, when I was talking about the infinite, I meant it only as a transitional term. The term "infinite" is really pointing to that which is beyond the categories of infinite and finite.

This is the meaning of the term *Ein Sof* found in the Kabbalistic tradition, which literally means "no-end." We can translate that as infinite, but there is more subtlety involved to understand the view fully. This is because *Ein Sof* is not a thing. We say "infinite" and we think of a "thing" that is the infinite. By necessity, when we categorize something as "infinite" we are positing some kind of an existence. Its existence is relative to the finite, so the two always go hand in hand, conceptually speaking. Everything that has an opposite necessarily is one side of a dialectic and its very existence is dependent on the existence of its opposite.

If we say there is a finite we are implying there is an infinite, and when we say there is an infinite we are implying there is a finite. Otherwise we wouldn't call it infinite, we would have to call it something else, something that is not the opposite of finite. Or we would have to not call it anything at all, which is the preference of the Kabbalists, at least in spirit. They came up with the term *Ein Sof*, which they thought wasn't calling it something, although, of course, it *was* calling it something.

Some Kabbalistic texts actually lose touch with the implication of *Ein Sof* and write things like *Ein Sof Baruch Hu*, which means "*Ein Sof*, Blessed be He," which is an appellation reserved for the Divine. So you see there is an instinctual tendency to put God and the male pronoun into *Ein Sof*, when no such God, and no such male, are there.[1]

At the same time, however, I am also using the term "infinite" to invoke a very important principle which recognizes that there is a dialectical relationship between the infinite and the finite. That is to say that there is an experience of reality, of existence, and of ourselves that is not finite, nor is it limited by concept, boundary, identity, self-perception, self-image, or even a sense of having a body at all.

All of these concepts play into the dialectic between the finite and the infinite as they appear phenomenologically in our experience. Many traditions use the terms "dual" and "nondual" to point to this dynamic; experiencing oneself as a separate entity is dual, whereas the experience of being one with the totality, with God, and with the infinite, is a nondual experience. These are phenomena that are known and recognizable to many people from many traditions.

When we talk about creation of the world as we did the last time we met, it gets very tricky and subtle because we can approach it from two different vantage points. It can be viewed from the dialectical matrix of the finite and the infinite, dual and nondual experience, and it can also be viewed from the perspective of *Ein Sof*, which is not limited or conditioned by that dialectical relationship at all. However, it is difficult or maybe impossible to talk about the perspective of *Ein Sof* without sounding like a complete *meshugenah* (crazy person). For this reason we devise narratives and we use conceptual categories to communicate. It is what all mystical traditions do.[2]

These are all disclaimers to acknowledge that the reification of these concepts is unavoidable, because that is what the ordinary mind does. Nevertheless, it serves a purpose for the path, which is to use the ordinary mind as a bridge to that which is not limited by the ordinary mind. If we can orient the mind with a certain view, then the mind can become a bridge from the finite to the infinite—and even to that which is beyond the finite-infinite dialectic—rather than the mind acting as a hindrance, a confused congested passage.

The point is to condition the mind so that it is more in alignment with ultimate truth. This is the purpose of having a view: to bring the mind into alignment with what reality is, so that the truth can have more free passage through our consciousness.

When I talk about these principles, they are all situated within this understanding. Ultimately our direct experience is the teaching, the path, and the revelation, which will inform our consciousness one way or the other. And yet, the words, concepts, and narrative all serve a purpose.

One of the most ancient Kabbalistic texts, the *Sefer Yetzirah*, states: *Na-utz Sofan Be-tchilatan Ve-techilatan Bi-sofan*, which is translated as "The end is embedded in the beginning and the beginning is embedded in the end."[3] The infinite which has "no-end" is at one end of the spectrum and on the other end of the spectrum we have a "dead-end." This refers to the journey from the infinite in its most subtle through a series of contractions and expansions until we have the most finite material that we know of: physical matter.

Did you ever accidentally bump into a wall? That is the experience of dead-end. Our physical bodies are expressions of this finite material. Our bodies will die, their animation will cease. This is the dead-end. But it is important to keep in mind that the beginning is embedded in the end and the end is embedded in the beginning. So what does this mean?

Every Friday night in the traditional Jewish prayer service, at the entry of the Sabbath, traditional Jews sing the words: *Sof Maaseh Be-machshava Techila*, which means, "The end of the deed is the first in mind."[4] That is to say, the most material and finite expression of creation was the whole intention from the get-go. The first thought in the creation of the cosmos, reality, and ultimately the human condition is seen in this view as the completion of the infinite play. It is the completion because it is the mechanism through which the infinite knows itself as finite. This is what it means by "the end of deed is the first in mind."

The usual view is that physicality with its limitation, finitude, and materiality is a barrier to spirituality. Many religions see these things as barriers, and practices are therefore designed to transcend them. From the Kedumah point of view, in contrast, the whole purpose of creation is to be embodied and to experience finitude. The whole point is for the infinite to experience itself as finite, which is the original intention and fulfillment of the act of creation.[5]

Instead of transcending into the infinite, we have to learn how to become more finite. Or we should say, to experience the material of finitude completely and thoroughly, through and through. Our teaching holds that if we know how to do that, then the truth of infinity becomes apparent. Ultimately, even the truth of that which is beyond the categories of infinite and finite can reveal itself to us as well.

Earlier we talked about how the infinite must possess the ability to manifest as finite, for if the infinite were not capable of manifesting itself as finite, then that would mean the infinite is limited in how it can manifest, which would be a non sequitur. But what we didn't talk about yet, because this is a little trickier conceptually, is that to experience itself as finite, it necessarily must also experience itself as infinite and nondual.

As I've explained, the ultimate purpose of creation is to experience oneself as finite, and there is an epistemological twist that happens so that our perceptual faculties are contracted such that we don't recognize our ontological nature as infinite. Therefore, we engage in spiritual practices to undermine that contracted hold on our perception and then we are free to experience that which is known as nondual or infinite reality.

Many people report that when they experience a nondual state it is more like remembering something they experienced a long time ago but have forgotten. The Sufis use the term "self-remembering" to point to this. Experientially you may be familiar with something like this and there are different theories about why this is. Some psychodynamic theories hold that we experience infinite and nondual states as babies, and when we experience this as adults there is a sense of having known this in some way even though it is indefinable or vague.[6]

The point is that the completion of the self-knowledge of the infinite must include both infinite and finite experiences, dual and nondual, because they are two sides of the same thing. In other words, you can't have one without the other. Why not? Because ultimately the finite *is* infinite and vice versa; they are inseparable.

The usual situation is that we experience ourselves as limited and contracted. Many traditions have different practices to address the experience of contraction. Usually we are freed from contraction by various methods and then we experience ourselves in an expanded state, no longer contracted or in a state of aberration—we have nondual perception.

This is usually what is considered spiritual enlightenment: the recognition that we *are* this nondual nature. The term "self-realization" points to this; it is the "realization" that the true "self" is this infinite boundless nature.

Therefore, *Ein Sof* finds its completion in these two stages: in the experience of the finite and in the experience of the infinite, which as we've discovered is also finite relative to the radical nonconceptual reality of *Ein Sof*. All this to say that the nondual is as conditioned as the dual, from the perspective of *Ein Sof*, which is beyond the categories of both dual and nondual.

The normative view of enlightenment—which is the realization of the nondual—is thus still a subtle state of limitation from the view of *Ein Sof*, because it is beyond both categories of the infinite and the finite; indeed, even enlightenment is a limitation from this point of view.

That is why both the dual and the nondual are equally fulfillment, or equally self-realization from the perspective of *Ein Sof*, and the human being has the capacity to experience both. This is what makes the human being unique in terms of our potential; we can experience both the finite and infinite as contraction and expansion. This is the human condition. This is the nature of our perception. We have the capacity for both.

In this path we talk about contraction and expansion as the first two principles or stages. Most spiritual teachings deal with these first steps. Most teachings are concerned with what to do about our state of suffering, which is synonymous with what I am calling contraction. Suffering, or contraction, is simply the mistaken perception that we are a separate entity, defined by our self-concept. It is the implicit sense that we are self-encapsulated, separated and alienated from the whole.

If you think about it, it is usually not our physical pain that causes our most profound suffering; it is our emotional and psychological contractions in their various forms. That is what constitutes the core of our suffering as human beings. This implicit and deeper suffering is what we refer to as contraction. The wisdom of the perspective that I articulated in the last talk—that the tendency to turn away from suffering and contraction in order to try to bypass it and experience something more free and boundless—is a tendency that is moving in the wrong direction and ultimately will not free us from suffering.

If we come to experience and know nonduality it might take some pressure off things, but then it becomes very complicated trying to stay in that state all the time. Some people turn to substances and some to meditation—they become God-addicts. To stay in a certain state of nondual perception usually requires the development of very sophisticated means of avoidance of life and of the body in order to stay in the sanctuary of what feels like freedom. On this path, that is not the point, although it may be useful and even necessary to do at times. Ultimately, however, this approach of bypass won't lead to the third journey, that of wholeness.

Wholeness is necessary for the fulfillment of the human journey. It is not fulfillment in the ordinary, conventional sense. The trick is to be able to turn toward that which we most want to avoid. It is somewhat counterintuitive and counterinstinctual. We want to turn towards the dead-end because we recognize that there is no other way to freedom, and more importantly, because it is simply the truth of things. The way to freedom is *through* our suffering, not *around* it.[7] Freedom is found through the dead-end. The end is embedded in the beginning and the beginning is embedded in the end.

We are talking about the possibility of transforming our very faculties of perception through and through. To do this we have to go into what we usually refer to as the dark places, places that are not illuminated, painful places, the places of very deep and painful contractions.

In this teaching, the physical body represents the dead-end. Because we have a physical body we have an incredible gift. Because all of our contractions at whatever level they manifest—whether they are physical or psychodynamic or energetic, on whichever dimension of Being they manifest—they all constellate in physicality, in our body, which is the living expression of our inner essence.

Last time I discussed how the process of creation happens through a series of progressive contractions and expansions of what the Kabbalists refer to as *Ohr Ein Sof*, the "light of *Ein Sof*." *Ein Sof* itself is not really a light. It is not anything at all. It is not nothing, but it is also not something. Nothing or something are irrelevant to its incomprehensible nature. But all of creation, all of existence, all of manifestation, is an expression of this incomprehensible nature—what the Kabbalists call the "light of *Ein Sof*." And this light goes through various stages of manifestation.[8]

The most primordial condition of the light is the light of complete nothingness. The Kabbalists refer to this as *ayin*, which literally means "nothingness."[9] They also call it the dimension of *Adam Kadmon*, the Primordial Human, because it is the primordial blueprint of what is at the dead-end; the physical body is an expression of the subtle template of its primordial source.

From this primordial nothingness, the "non-light" manifests as the body of reality, or what is typically termed "God." There are many teachings about each progressive dimension and the various processes that unfurl its depths. What we mean by "God" is not the conventional meaning of "God." What do we mean by "God"? Why don't we just say "Reality" or "Universe"?

The word "God" typically refers to one or more of the ancient Hebrew Divine names from the Hebrew Bible, or Torah. That is where the word originally comes from, at least in the West. But there are actually many Hebrew Divine names in the Torah, and each of these names expresses a different pure quality of this primordial light. There are many kinds of light: light of creation, of knowledge, of love, of compassion, of strength, of will, of understanding, and so on.[10]

So we see that the English term "God" is very imprecise when it comes to the variety of colors and flavors that reveal themselves through the prism of reality. However, in the Hebrew Torah, there are two central Hebrew terms that point both to the heart of God, to its very being, as well as to its body, to its manifested expression as creation.

The first term is the four-lettered Divine name, known formally as the tetragrammaton, the *YHVH* (יהוה). This name is not traditionally pronounced because of the intensity of its power, so we refer to it by reciting the names of each of the letters, like this: *Yud Hey Vav Hey.* It is best translated as "Is-Was-Will Be" or just "Being" for short, because *Yud Hey Vav Hey* is a verbal construct constituted by the past, present, and future tenses of the verb "to be."[11] Is (הוה), Was (היה), and Will Be (יהיה), when combined together, yields the name *YHVH* when transposed into English. This name encompasses all of reality—the generalities and the particulars[12]—and as a verbal construct, it also expresses the dynamism and aliveness that is intrinsic to the nature of Being.[13]

YHVH is thus the total, living beingness of creation.[14] This is because reality as a manifest body is alive; it is a living being. What makes it a being is simply that it has the capacity for self-recognition and for self-awareness. *YHVH,* or what we simply refer to as "Being" in Kedumah, is thus the living spirit of God's body; it is its very nature. That is what we mean when we use the term "Being." We know the inner Divine nature any time we experience a sense of "Being." This is the experience of God.

When we experience the self-knowing property of Being, when we know ourselves as what we are—as the living universe—that is what I refer to as God. It is not that God is in us, rather it is that we are in God. We are part of the living expression, the living Being of God. We are part of the body of God. Each of us is an expression of its whole body.[15]

The Torah alludes to this when it states (Gen. 1:27) that the human being is created in the image of God: *B'tzelem Elohim Barah Oto*: "In the image of God He created him." Here the Hebrew Divine name is *Elohim*, the second of the two central names for God in the Torah. This Divine name refers more to the manifest expression of reality, to creation itself, what we call the body of God.[16] The human being is thus simply a microcosm of the body of God, the body of Being, the Divine body, which is the totality of the whole universe, the living universe.[17]

In this teaching, God is not the creator but rather God is what is created.[18] That is one of the subversive teachings of this path. We subvert the notion of God the creator. God is actually creation itself. It is what is created and we are part of that creation. I mentioned earlier that what makes God a being is its capacity for self-awareness and self-recognition. This is one of the chief properties of Being itself; namely, the capacity of creation—of God—to know itself.

The Hebrew term *da'at*, which literally means "knowledge," is the technical term used by the Kabbalists to refer to this particular property of Being. It is the capacity for Being to know itself through its very Being, not through some secondary process. Here, knowing and Being are inseparable.[19] Since we humans are expressions of Being, both in spirit and in body, then *da'at* also expresses itself through us as the capacity to know ourselves as expressions of Being. Ultimately, this property of Being—the capacity for true knowledge—is what is contracted and hidden from ordinary conventional perception.

Ontologically speaking, we are an expression of Being, which ultimately is an expression of that which is beyond the categories of infinite and finite. But we don't know this in conventional experience, because *da'at*—the light of knowledge—is coiled deep in our bodies, deep in our organism. When this property of light is contracted in our human experience, knowledge of who and what we are escapes us.[20]

True knowledge, or *da'at*, is the specific property of Being that is contracted. It is a property of consciousness that is necessary to be alive. In other words, we would not be alive if we were not conscious. That is what animates us; it is what makes us living. We are by definition alive and conscious, but there is a certain property of our consciousness that is hidden in the conventional experience. That is the property that has to do with self-knowledge and awareness of what we are as an expression of Being.

All the lights are on, but in a state of relative latency. Nevertheless, they have to express themselves to some degree for us to function as human beings, including the light of knowledge. How many essential lights are there? There could be an infinite number. In the Kabbalistic teachings they have a number: there are ten primary ones with subsets encircling each one, which go on infinitely. Other teachings have different maps of these qualities, of these lights. The light of knowledge is simply the capacity to become intimate with and to know directly the lights for what they are. Knowing itself as what it is frees more of its potential to express itself.

The first time the term *da'at* appears in the Hebrew Bible is in the verse from Genesis (4:1), *V'ha-Adam Yada Et Chava Ishto*: "... and Adam knew Eve, his wife." *Yada* is the verb "to know," which comes from the same root as *da'at*. The Kabbalists understand the word for "to know" as a mystical term. In conventional terms, knowledge is a commodity; we can store knowledge in our brain and apply it. Mystical knowledge on the other hand is direct immediate knowledge of how things are and of our nature. It is actually much more than just knowledge of our nature, it is God's knowledge of itself. We are allowing Divine knowledge to express itself through this portal, through this window of the human particularity.[21]

As you can see from this verse from Torah, Adam did not conceptually know Eve. *Da'at* is a Biblical term that refers to sexual intimacy and physical union. The text also states (Gen. 2:24), *Vehayu Le-basar Echa'd*: "and they become one flesh." When we use the term "knowledge," at least in this tradition, there is a deep association with the awakening of the capacity for physical touch and physical intimacy.[22]

Once I saw an exercise at my son's preschool in which they blindfolded the kids, gave them an object, and asked the children to figure out what the object was by touching it. Sensorial capacities are developed and refined in an exercise like this; it develops the external sense of touch. The internal sense of touch is the capacity to actually touch into our experience, to feel it with our inner sensing. There is something about sensing things using inner touch that is intimately related to *da'at* (mystical knowledge), which is the capacity of the Divine to know itself as a finite human entity.

If the whole purpose is for the infinite to experience itself through the human, finite, physical form, then the primary mechanism through which that knowledge is evoked is through exercising the sense of inner touch. This also demonstrates the importance of physical touch in general. Ultimately, Kedumah is tantric in its view of physicality in that it embraces the opportunities of physicality in all its manifestations as the ideal conditions for Divine awakening.[23] The objective is the awakening of the Divine body of which we are all physical expressions.

Inner touch is a practice whereby we sense into our body using the knowledge of our inner sensing. It has many functions on the path and offers many blessings. One function is that it gives us the capacity to bypass the conventional sense of knowing and awaken a much deeper, primordial, and immediate sense of knowing. We are then able to cultivate a sense of embodied presence, which is a palpable manifestation of the body of God incarnate, indwelling in our individual experience.

Presence can be experienced in an infinite number of ways. It can have a palpable sense of being and of fullness. There are an infinite number of ways of experiencing the body and of experiencing embodied presence: it can be dense, light, material, liquid, solid, or gas. It can have an infinite variety of textures and colors, but it is inherently a living consciousness—a presence that we feel with our organ of sensorial perception.

Using inner sensing opens up this kind of intimate, immediate knowledge and bypasses the monopoly on knowledge that conventional methods of data acquisition and storage typically enjoy. It is the primary and most accessible doorway that we have to what we refer to as the Lights of Being. The Lights of Being are the specific qualities of light that I mentioned. Activating *da'at* through inner sensing allows the organism to imbibe and integrate each of these qualities.

If you've studied Kabbalah then you know these lights as the *sefirot*, the Divine qualities of Being.[24] The more we embody the sense of palpable presence in our bodies, the more accustomed we are to perceiving—seeing and hearing—from this living palpability of Being. Furthermore, there is then more potential for the inner organism to perceive itself and the world through the lens of the Divine Presence. Ultimately it is the Divine Presence that is perceiving itself in others, hearing itself in others, and perceiving everything as an expression of itself.

When this is accomplished, the recognition of the epistemological transformation—which is the transformation of our sense perception—happens more from the bottom up than from the top down. In other words, because everything is in our body, it will push everything that is stored in our body up to the surface. All of the contractions and dark places in our unconscious will be pushed to the surface because our somatic sensing is going to illuminate whatever is there. The other benefit is that it provides a ground for the organism to land fully in the here and now, experience wakefulness with regard to what arises, and be more readily able to integrate it.

As you can see, there is a lot underneath the surface but this is essentially the relationship between the practice and the view. The further stages of expansion, wholeness, vastness, and freedom all traverse various phases of integration and represent the mysterious possibilities of the dance between the finite and the infinite.

STUDENT: Can you say more about what it looks like for different kinds of people to orient to their experience in the manner you are suggesting?

ZVI: There are different systems that attempt to map out the different character structures. Some character typologies are more avoidant, and others are more prone to act things out overtly. So each character type uses different strategies to navigate around that which is most uncomfortable for them.

I spent most of my life avoiding what was uncomfortable. I remember years ago when I was an Orthodox Hasid and I was engaged in prayer—which was the main practice I was doing at that time—and I was feeling all twisted up inside in so many ways. I couldn't even count the ways that I was twisted up inside. I was very contracted. Twists and knots in all kinds of places. For a long time I was using prayer and meditation to actually avoid those things. I would propel myself into some transcendent state, into some boundless condition in order to avoid feeling those painful places.

Then at some point, I had some experiences in prayer where I surrendered to what was twisted and painful in a visceral felt-sense way, without the concepts and the words—just the raw sensing of it. I realized that somehow the more I went into the pain—and it was very, very painful—it was almost like feeling that it hurt so good. You can come to a place on the path where you're just so grateful that something's being uncovered, like there's some pain to feel—because it feels so good. It's painful but it's real. It's been hidden and to feel it really frees up so much.

This is the gist of it. We come to appreciate the things that hurt. We come to realize that a great deal of the hurt and the suffering is around what we think about it rather than just feeling it and going through it. We have all these ideas about what it is and what it means and what it's going to mean and what it's going to do. But if we just feel it completely in the body as much as possible, then it's like magic.

Notice the quality of the presence in the room now, and how it's different from when we began this evening. Do you have a sense that there is more of a quality of expansion in the space? Do you have a sense of that? Sense it viscerally, with your body. The space is more open, more expanded, more free.

There's room for all the different contractions, but the qualitative way in which we're with the material that's in the space is very different. And yet, it's also concentrated at the same time. It's not an expansion that's diluted or dispersed. It's expanded, open, fresh. It's lighter. But there's also a hereness and a nowness in the presence. It's awake.

Working with this kind of a practice—and we're going to do more specific practices that hone this even more—develops a precise skill to perceive in this way. This is really an incredible gift to the living body of God to give God the opportunity to experience itself through us, in all these different ways. To reveal its possibilities, its expression.

So I invite you to continue to practice this until the next time we meet, to do the body sensing practice. Start with the feet and go up to the shoulders. Practice sensing into the arms and legs and the belly. That's the purification of the limbs practice. *Taharat ha-avarim* is the name of the practice in Hebrew. This practice is alluded to in the thirteenth-century Kabbalistic treatise called *Sha'arei Orah* written by Joseph Gikatilla.[25]

The wisdom is that the limbs, which are the arms and the legs, are in a deep way connected with the core of our being. Chinese medicine knows about this. You can access all the meridian systems through the arms and the legs. Actually, even through just the hands and feet. There is a lot of depth to this understanding, and it is the under-girdle, the underpinning, of this practice. It's not haphazard.

To sense the arms and legs shifts the center of our perception in a way that grounds and opens up the possibility of direct knowledge, of *da'at*, that is a knowing and perceiving directly through inner touch. That's where we're beginning. And as we go, we'll articulate more of the view and hone our practice to fill in a lot of details. This is good to get us started.

3
Erotic Awakening

So AGAIN WE are invoking our inner sense of touch, which is the capacity of our consciousness to sense itself as a form. In this case, we're sensing the form of our body, our physical body. And today, I'd like to introduce another dimension to this practice that we didn't make explicit last time, which is the orientation of the heart. We are sensing into the body. We are allowing consciousness to sense itself, to sense the form of our body. But when we really do it from a place of heart, like we really want to sense our body, then we really want to know what it feels like in every nook and cranny. That wanting to know intimately, to intimately touch our experience, is the dimension of the heart in this practice. So we gently invoke that as we sense, and just see and notice what happens when we bring that dimension more explicitly into the practice.

Okay, so we begin with the feet, sensing into the soles of the feet, the toes, each individual toe, as well as the whole foot. Sensing the top of the foot, the bottom, front and the back, and the dimensionality of each of the feet. Bringing in the orientation of really wanting to know every nook and cranny intimately. Notice how the sensing intensifies with that wanting. Now we add the ankles. The dimensionality, the volume of each of the ankles, the various bones, ligaments, tissue, connective tissue, muscles, and skin. And now adding the lower legs, sensing each of the bones in the lower legs, the two major bones, the tibia and the fibula. Notice what happens to the totality of your consciousness when you sense the bone itself. Notice the quality of bone. Now sensing the muscle, notice the quality of muscle in your consciousness. And what is the quality of that space between the bones?

Now adding the knees. All of it is intricate biology. Sensing the thighs and the femur. When you sense the femur, the big bone in your thigh, what's the quality like in your consciousness? Sensing the volume and the three-dimensionality of the legs. Now adding the hips and the pelvis. Sensing into the pelvic bowl and to the volume of the pelvis. Sensing the genitals, the perineum. What's it like to bring the heart orientation, really wanting to know, intimately, to our genitals? What's the quality of the consciousness when we allow ourselves that gift?

Now adding the fingers, the surface of the hands, tops of the hands, all the bones and the muscles, the connective tissue that forms these amazing instruments, our hands. What's it like to really know the inner life of these hands, that do so much for us every day? Without losing the sensing of the legs and the feet, we're now adding the hands and the wrists, and the lower arms, the forearms. Again, sensing the bones in the forearm, the radius and the ulna, and the space between them. Adding the elbows. The upper arms. Sensing into the humerus bone. Sensing its solidity, its porous solidity. Can you sense the life of the bone, and all of its ancient mystery? What's the quality of your consciousness like when you sense the bone? Sensing the volume of the arm, muscles. Now, adding the shoulders. Now just sensing both arms and both legs, from the bottoms of the feet up to the shoulders.

And with a light touch, sort of sensing across the chest, brushing over the heart, becoming gently aware of the belly, sense into the neck. Gently into the jaw, the mouth, the face and the occiput, and the cranium. Sensing into the space of the head, the dimensionality of it, gently. Top of the head. Gently, with an almost imperceptible touch, above the head.

Now returning to the arms and legs. We add listening. Presence is hearing the sounds. And then slowly open the eyes and add looking, the presence that is sensing the arms and legs is what is looking, and it's what is listening. [Bell rings.]

ZVI: What do you notice right now in your experience, doing this practice?

STUDENT: I had a sensation of a lot of clear light tonight. And it had the quality of being like a very subtle sparkler. And there was violet, a lot of violet energy, a lot of violet light, and also dark blue.

ZVI: How does it impact you? What do you notice?

STUDENT: A sense of *aaah.* Relief.

STUDENT: I feel that I have better access to my heart after being in my body.

ZVI: Better access to your heart through sensing the body?

STUDENT: Yeah. I'm such a heady person that these last two weeks, and also now, I have better access to just the presence in my heart.

STUDENT: I experience something similar. I would not have intuitively thought that feeling my hands and feet would actually give me more access to my heart. So ordinary.

STUDENT: Yeah, for me too, I was finding that when I was tuning into my heart to see if I could initiate the wanting. There was definitely some parts of my body that were more genuinely wanting to touch into, and those I found were more profoundly felt. I could kind of change the wanting a little bit for other parts of my body, but the best results were when it kind of flowed naturally.

ZVI: So in some parts of your body there was more of a natural sense of that wanting?

STUDENT: Yeah there was kind of more, you know, juicy areas.

ZVI: I see. What about for others, in terms of adding the heart element to it? Did you notice if and how that changed the practice for you?

STUDENT: One of the things I noticed was after about a third of the time, I started to become very aware of my heartbeat as part of my sensation. So that's kind of a literal heart. But what I noticed was that there was more sensation during the pump of my heart, and then there would be kind of like a lack of sensation. And so it would be this kind of dynamic, whereby I would feel the heartbeat, and I would notice all the parts of whatever I was focusing on. And then during the lag time, it was harder to perceive. But it was like this sensation-giving ability whenever the heart was beating that I felt through my entire body, by the end of it. And I still feel it right now.

ZVI: Yes. Do other people feel the pulsation? There's also the group organism presence which has its own beat too. Just feel it in the room.

STUDENT: I had this experience early in the meditation of becoming aware on a cellular level, like a cellular presence. Except there was a vastness to it. Like each cell was more space, had sort of a galactic quality to it. And when we went into the heart, it was more immediately here. It was a more physical experience than the earlier part of the meditation was for me. So the shift went from this broad, vast spaciousness into this very present humanness.

ZVI: So bringing in the heart brought in a sense of being even more physical, more human.

STUDENT: Yes. It made me start rocking too.

Zvɪ: Rocking? A little *shokeling*? [Laughter: *shokeling* is the Yiddish word referring to the swaying, rocking movement of Orthodox Jews in prayer.]

Student: Exactly.

Zvɪ: So how is that for you? I notice you are holding your heart.

Student: There is a sense of completeness in being able to be in the body with its heaviness along with the vastness and the space of the body, both at the same time. It's not that I felt incomplete before, but now the completeness is more visceral.

Zvɪ: Yes, there is some visceral sense of more completeness. So a little foreshadowing for when we get to the Journey of Wholeness. There can be a visceral sense of wholeness that's very human and yet not disconnected from the galactic. That's the miracle of wholeness.

Student: I was wondering if I had an easier time feeling my bones because I have awareness of the image of my skeleton, and how much of my brain was seeing this, projecting this sort of cartoon of my bones, and how much of it was, you know, sensation?

Zvɪ: That's a very good question. Many traditions use the imaginary realm as an important part of their practice. So I think it's recognized that it can serve a contemplative function.

Student: It feels less embodied though, sort of like you could go off forever into your imagination.

Zvɪ: That makes sense. One thing we can do is play with the visualization to see if it's helpful to bring us into a more embodied state, and if it feels like a distraction, then we can just note that and then see what it's like to just sense the rawness, the raw touching, without relying on the visualization. You can play with it.

Okay one more.

STUDENT: During the meditation, I just kept hearing again and again to feel the life in your bones, and the ancientness, the life, and the breath, like a brush over your heart. I think that kind of took me more into a sensation than projecting an image.

ZVI: So for you, it sounds like that "languaging" helped you get more in touch with the direct sensation. How was it to feel the life of the ancient bones for you?

STUDENT: I felt surprised that I felt life. It was a new experience.

ZVI: Pretty interesting, yes? We don't usually think of bones as being alive. We usually don't sense our bones, unless they are sore. But they're a pretty big part of our living experience.

The point of bringing the heart in is that it fuels our curiosity about our experience in a way that can help us engage our sensing more completely. The heart brings a kind of engagement, an interest, curiosity, and appreciation for what our experience is without it having to be any particular way. That's the beauty of the heart.

This is a good segue to say a few things about the heart and how it relates to the thread that we've been following in this teaching.

TALK

The last talk introduced the principle of *da'at*, which is a term Kabbalists use to refer to a particular property of Being that expresses the capacity to know. This property of Being is typically hidden in our conventional experience, and its obscuration is what accounts for the conventional experience of spiritual ignorance which is the opposite of knowledge. In Advaita Vedanta, the Sanskrit term *"avidya"* refers to this kind of ignorance.[1] In fact, many traditions describe the state of being occluded and asleep—of being alienated from truth and reality—as a state of ignorance.

In the Kabbalistic tradition there is a similar paradigm of understanding. On the spiritual journey, awakening refers to awakening to true knowledge. This is to say that awakening is the experience of knowing truly, assuredly, absolutely, beyond a shadow of a doubt what we are and what reality is. The opposite of this kind of knowing is what we call ignorance, which is an absence of this true knowledge.[2]

However, it gets more interesting because the capacity for knowledge, as we mentioned last time, is intimately tied to the physical body and to the flesh. Obviously, when we talk about knowledge and the truth of reality or Being, we don't mean ordinary knowledge. We are not talking about the discursive mind accumulating information; we are talking about a different kind of knowing altogether.

We saw this in the beginning of the book of Genesis (4:1), where the text states: *V'ha-Adam Yadah Et Chavah Ishto*: "And Adam knew his wife Eve." The Hebrew word *yadah*, "he knew," is the verb form of the word *da'at*, meaning "knowledge." This clearly demonstrates that knowledge in this tradition is something different than the conventional understanding of knowledge. It is pointing to an intimacy, a union; a total, direct and immediate knowing.

In the case of Adam and Eve, it was also a knowledge that includes the physical. That is why the text also states (Gen. 2:24), *Vehayu Lebasar Echad*: "and they became one flesh." In this case, knowledge is pointing to the union of flesh with flesh as an intimate knowing. That is to say, to know means to know in the flesh, to know in the body.[3]

However, the mystical and esoteric dimensions of this teaching can only be appreciated if we understand what we mean by "the body" in this tradition. What we mean by "body" is not the conventional sense of the body; it includes the conventional sense of the body but it is not limited by it. The physical body is a reflection of the Divine body, which we also call the body of Being, the body of creation, the body of God, or just simply "the cosmos."[4]

To help us understand and appreciate this more, let's look at the classic way of imaging the Divine body in the Kabbalah. I am referring to the famous diagram that has been borrowed by many traditions, especially in the New Age, known as the Tree of Life. This geometrical diagram presents an array of what are traditionally called the *sefirot*. I call them the "Lights of Being," which is one way of translating the Hebrew word *sefirot*,[5] but in the end there is no one good English translation for this term.[†]

The Lights of Being are the qualities of the Infinite Light, the light of *Ein Sof*. This is the light that emanates from a source that is beyond the conceptual categories of infinite and finite. Thus, *Ein Sof* is not "somewhere" beyond infinite and finite. "Somewhere" and "nowhere" are both conceptual categories and therefore do not apply to *Ein Sof*. It is beyond the categories of infinite and finite, of place and no-place, of something and nothing; it is beyond all the conceptual categories we use to delineate our experience.[6]

Ein Sof represents a reality that cannot be conceived or known by the mind. But, as we saw in the first talk, the primordial, original light shines forth from that which is beyond the categories of somewhere and nowhere. From this light, manifestation mysteriously arises in a series of contractions and expansions that ultimately produce the finite realm, with all of its gradations of emanation, with varying degrees of subtlety. All of these gradations and dimensions are expressed by the Kabbalistic tradition in the diagram of the Tree of Life, which is basically a map of the created realm.

---

† For a diagram of the *sefirot* and their corresponding Kedumah terms, see page 294.

In the Kabbalistic tradition, this is what is referred to as the Divine, as God. That is to say, God is not what created the cosmos; God *is* the cosmos.[7] This means that we, as embodied reflections of this cosmic body, are expressions of the Divine body, details of God, abiding inside God, as God. More precisely, we are functional, perceptive cells inside God's body. We are God's details.[8] When the Torah says that the human being is created in the image of God it is saying that even the gross physical body is created in the image of the Divine body. There are many implications to this, but one obvious one is that these various lights, represented in the Tree of Life with the symbolic number of ten, ultimately constitute the very nature of the physical human body.[9]

Let us explore this a bit more. If you shine the light of *Ein Sof*—which is neither existent nor nonexistent—through a prism, it refracts into the colors of the rainbow. These lights make up the spectrum of colors that form all of creation. This is a good way to understand the lights of creation, which are the ten *sefirot.* These *sefirot* are the specific colors that are refracted when the light of *Ein Sof* comes into its creative expression.

Each of these lights has a particular color, quality, and pure, essential light of this most primordial nature. The differentiation of this primordial light into the specific colors and qualities is what accounts for the variability and multifaceted appearances in the world of form, the human realm, including all expressions and experiences. One implication of this is that everything we experience—indeed, everything that exists—is an expression of these lights, because if you mix different colors together you can produce an infinite variety of colors.

Therefore, the number "ten" is not to be taken literally, because as I said, the lights are not static "things." This is one reason I am cautious of using diagrams; they tend to reify the *sefirot.* They are not static, contained things. They are living constellations of purity that have infinite potential of expression.

There are Hebrew terms associated with each of the *sefirot* and there are Divine names from the Hebrew Bible that are associated with each of them as well. There are the ten lights, represented by the ten Divine names in the Hebrew Torah. In short, the inner nature of this cosmic body is in the center of the Tree of Life. It is the name *YHVH,* the four-lettered name of God, which is the central Hebrew name of God in the Torah. It is simply the past, present, and future tenses of the word "to be" expressed in a verbal construct; *HYH* means "was," *HVH* means "is," and *YHYH* means "*will be.*

So, *YHVH*—Being—is the inner nature of the Divine body.[10] It is the soul of God, and thus the soul of the cosmos. When the undifferentiated, colorless light of Being *(YHVH)* manifests into the differentiated lights of the manifested world, it expresses itself with many colors and many lights. These are the essential, Divine lights, or qualities, that constitute the created realm.

What makes *YHVH* a being is that it is alive; it is a living being. That is why the name is in verbal form. *YHVH* is also the totality of all that ever is, was, and will be.[11] The totality of Being is alive, is living.[12] This is where the whole misunderstanding comes with the terms theism and nontheism. Usually people think if there is a God, it is a creator God that is distant and removed from creation. However, this teaching is not theistic in this sense, rather, it presents a kind of monistic theism, which means that all of reality is God, or is the Divine Being, including us.[13]

This Being is a living being, the living *dynamism* of Being. The capacity of Being that allows itself to know itself as Being is what we call *da'at*, meaning Knowledge. *Da'at* is actually the invisible eleventh light; on many diagrams of the Tree of Life, you can see it in the upper-middle area where there is a space. Often, it is delineated by dotted lines, because technically it's not included in the counting of the ten *sefirot*. Some charts just leave it out altogether. However, this principle of *da'at* is fundamental to the understanding of the cosmic body, and thus, our body.[14]

"As above, so below" is a common refrain found in the ancient Kabbalistic texts.[15] In order to understand our nature, we need to understand the Divine nature. In order to understand the Divine nature, we need to understand our body. In the Kedumah teachings, we start with our body, because it is the most accessible; we all have a body, whether we like it or not.

But it is much more profound than just, "Oh well, it's near us so let's use it." Actually, this is the body's primary function; it is the optimal vehicle for us to discover the whole, or the totality, as what we are and what we are expressions of. That is what makes this path tantric; we move through our embodied experience, not away from it. Our bodies serve as our vehicles to experience the totality of Being, the totality of the Tree of Life.[16]

Kabbalists describe *da'at* as a fundamental ingredient of all the Lights; it is the essential element that unifies and maintains them.[17] This makes sense, given our understanding that knowledge in the mystical sense means intimacy and union of flesh. It is the very element that unifies the body; in fact, it not only unifies the physical body but also the Divine body and all of creation. *Knowing* in this sense is the portal, the mechanism through which we are able to undergo a process of transformation that moves from contraction to expansion, and successively to wholeness, vastness, and, ultimately, to freedom.[18]

If taken to heart, we will also appreciate that *da'at* cannot be an isolated experience of knowing, but is necessarily interconnected with every other dimension of creation. The diagram of the Tree of Life can also be superimposed on the anatomical structure of the physical body. The *sefirot* and the channels that connect them thus intersect and interpenetrate every dimension of Being.

The Tree of Life is thus a map of the cosmos, of our human consciousness, and a map of our physical structure. Ultimately it is both the map and the territory of the one and only "place"—the singular location of existence. One of the classical Hebrew names for God in the Rabbinic tradition is *Ha-Makom*, which means "the place." The Tree of Life is a map of the only place where existence takes place. It is *Ha-Makom*.[19]

The Kedumah understanding of this Divine name reveals that all of existence is a singularity operating in a singular location. There is only one place—*Makom*—where reality manifests; everything that transpires in existence occurs within this singular *Makom*. Since there is only one place, this means that there is actually no distance between any two points in existence. Since we are all located in the same singular location, every single point contains every single other point in creation. This is the meaning of the statement in the Talmud that "one who saves a single life saves the entire universe."[20] This is a more precise formulation of what I was pointing to earlier when I said that everything in creation exists inside God.

Let us return to the Tree of Life. There are three important triads in the Tree of Life that I call the "triadic centers." For those of you who have studied Kashmir Shaivism or Hindu Tantra, you will appreciate all these triads.[21] Instead of the triadic heart of Shiva, we have here the triadic heart of Being, *YHVH*. The upper triangle is the head-center and is composed of the Lights of *Keter, Chochmah,* and *Binah*. The middle triangle is the heart-center and is composed of *Chesed, Gevurah,* and *Tiferet*. The lower triangle is the belly-center and is composed of *Netzach, Hod*, and *Yesod*. These are the three triadic centers. The lower center extends into the genitals, which is represented by *Yesod* and the channel that extends from it into *Malchut*. *Malchut*, or *Shechinah*, is the Divine Presence, which is the experience of presence in the body; she contains all of the lights within her. Classically, *Shechinah* is known as the feminine presence of the embodied soul.

These three triadic centers—the head, heart, and belly—are the three primary centers that help us conceptually organize the body and its relationship to the cosmos. Through these centers and their inner capacities of perception, we are able to know ourselves as expressions of the totality of creation. We can become more intimate with these centers by opening up their capacities for knowing, sensing, and perceiving. In this way, we become more and more of a vehicle for the Divine body to experience itself as a human being.

This, as was introduced in the first chapter, is born out of a ripple of desire that courses through the Divine mind prior to its expression and manifestation. It is the desire to know and experience itself in the domain of apparent finitude. This desire is reflected in the human experience of the heart with its longings. For this reason, when we talk about knowledge or knowing, we must include the engagement of the heart's natural inclination to want to know the truth without any preconditions. Our heart wants to know because it simply wants to, rather than based on a desire to get anything out of it or to win a prize or to avoid some experience of pain. The heart just wants to know.

Think of the desires of a child. They want cookies, presents, and any number of things. There is so much wanting that it is bursting out of them. Their hearts are bursting with wanting. They don't just want things; they also want to know how things work. They want to know why the sky is blue. They don't just want goodies, they want to know the goody in their body; they want to feel it. Then, once they get whatever thing they have been wanting, they forget about it a moment later and begin wanting something else. The wanting of the heart is a natural thing.

Children have a different quality of wanting than adolescents and adults. I call this the Three Stages of Sacred Wanting and they are represented by the three stages of life: childhood, adolescence, and adulthood. The Jewish mystical texts allude to this; they explain that the capacity for *da'at,* for knowing, which is intimately tied up with the human soul, and the embodiment of the human soul, matures in the human organism in distinct stages.[22]

First, the child is like a mirror for the Divine lights. That is to say, the purity of these qualities shines more unobstructedly through children; the lights include love (*Chesed*), strength (*Gevurah*), and beauty (*Tiferet*). Children appreciate beautiful things. For instance, if a child sees a butterfly, they are mesmerized. The lights of *Netzach, Hod,* and *Yesod* bring the pure impeccability of different kinds of steadfastness and support. *Yesod* is pillar-like support; *Netzach* is the capacity for steadfastness; *Hod* embodies the wisdom of objective restraint.

All the Divine lights shine through the child, but what they are missing is the property of *da'at,* which is an essential ingredient of all these lights. To borrow a term from Freud, it is in its latency and therefore not actualized. Therefore, children experience the lights in their purity, but they do not yet have the capacity to know what they are; they don't know that they themselves are the cosmic body. Though they experience it directly, they don't have the capacity to recognize that they themselves are expressions of Being, of the totality.

The property of *da'at* is then activated in the human organism at the age of twelve for a girl and thirteen for a boy, when they have a *bar* or *bat mitzvah* in traditional Judaism. In the mystical understanding, this is the age in which the sexual impulse is activated, and the awakening of the sexual impulse is the awakening of the potential for *da'at.* Perhaps now you are beginning to see how all of these things thread together. The sexual energy, which moves out of latency and begins the process of activation and actualization at this age, is completely intertwined with and inseparable from the energy of *da'at.*

This is why when the text states that "Adam knew (*da'at*) his wife Eve," it is clearly talking about sexual union. However, it is not just the genitals and the reproductive system that are activated in isolation. That is not what we mean in the mystical tradition by "sexual." We mean genital union, as well as a union of the heart and mind.

At the age of bar and bat mitzvah the heart also goes through a transformation. As a child, our heart is interested in getting presents and treats. At the age of sexual actualization we are interested in new things. The heart and mind are engaged and impacted by the energy of this maturation. It is a full-body process; the head-center, the heart-center, and the belly-center are all impacted by the activation of *da'at* at this age.

Later in life, at the age of twenty, there is a further development. It is realized when the impulse of wanting, which is infused with the energy of *da'at*, is directed towards the discovery of what is real and true. This drive to know the truth about ourselves and reality thus begins with the awakening of our sexual impulse and longing for union and intimacy.

This is all contrary to our cultural norms, because our tendency is to see sexuality as something that is a distraction from and distortion of the sacred. Not only do the Kedumah teachings not see it as a distortion or a distraction, they actually see sexuality as the optimal doorway *to* the sacred. In this third stage, wanting has the potential to integrate the totality of our soul into the drive for truth, which is what we mean by the sacred.

When I use the terminology of "sexual union," I am referring to a more holistic experience that integrates the heart, the head, and the belly-centers. The belly-center includes the genitals, so sexual union, because it aligns the belly-center with the head and heart-centers, has the potential for cosmic unification.

By the age of twenty, sexual energy has sufficiently matured and is refined enough that sexual experience can be recognized as a spiritual experience; there is potential to know all of the cosmos and go beyond the limited and individualistic experiences in earlier developmental phases. In the adolescent phase, the capacity for a deeper spiritual union is less accessible due to this increased individuation than it is after the age of twenty.

In the Zohar, these three stages correspond to the three levels of the soul.[23] The soul is a unified reflection of the entire cosmic body. We organize it conceptually into the head, heart, and belly triads. These centers of consciousness display different properties of a unified organism. We always need to keep this in mind when we utilize these sorts of conceptual models.

These three centers have parallels in the three levels of the soul, which in Hebrew are called *nefesh, ruach,* and *neshamah.* Each of these terms are variations of words meaning "breath" or "breathing." The breath is the life force; it is what animates life. *Nefesh* animates the lower center, the belly-center; *ruach* animates the heart-center; *neshamah* animates the head-center.

At first, children only have the *nefesh* level of soul. They are instinctual beings and all the instinctual energies are present, but the spiritual potentials of the head and heart centers are not yet activated. The potential of the heart-center is awakened once the *ruach* enters into the child at the age of thirteen. Then, at twenty, the third dimension of soul centered in the head, the *neshamah*, is activated.

As you can see, a lot of importance is placed on the sexual energy. These teachings were kept hidden for so long, out of fear that they would be misunderstood. Sensing practices are a way that we begin to channel this quality of *da'at*. It is latent in our daily experience, but we can begin to bring it to the surface of our embodied consciousness and into our felt sense in our body. By becoming more intimate with our body, we are actually beginning to open up to the inner potential of the cosmic body that we are reflections of.

The sensing practice is therefore a method that works with the whole organism. We bring the heart into the sensing practice in order to unify the heart with the belly. The sensing practice is primarily a belly-centered practice, but if we are just sensing through the belly-center, without the engagement of the heart, then the potential of knowledge, of union, and of realization will be limited. We bring in the engagement of the heart, which is the simplicity of the heart's innate desire to know the truth, and then we also bring in the subtlety of the head center which we will talk about in more detail in the next meeting.

STUDENT: Are there an additional two stages of evolution after the ones you were describing, for the fourth and fifth levels of soul?

ZVI: In the Kabbalistic teachings, there's a fourth and fifth level of soul, called *chayah* and *yechidah*. Those are not found in the Zoharic teachings, those are added by Isaac Luria in the sixteenth century. I don't include them as stages of evolution because they are subtle levels of soul that are not really subject to maturation and development.[24] That is, they are eternally abiding in their nature. *Chayah* means life; it's the cosmic life force, which correlates with the dynamism of creation, which is an expression of the light of creation.

When the first three levels, the belly, heart, and head are unified and matured, and in a state of realization, only then can we integrate the living energy of the totality, of all of creation. So you see that *chayah* itself is a trans-individual phenomenon. It's not an individual manifestation, although its wisdom can be integrated into the individual consciousness. It's a cosmic principle, which is why it's not included in the three stages of evolution. However, the *chayah* center does have an individual expression, and its the center located above the head. It's called the "life center" because *chayah* means "life" and the integration of this center into the individual soul has to do with the integration of one's realization into ordinary life.

And then the fifth level of soul is *yechidah*, which means "singular," and it correlates with the Kedumah dimension of reality, which is an absolute kind of nothingness, emptiness, and this dimension—which is really a non-dimension—brings in the recognition of the singularity of all of totality. From this perspective everything appears as a singular truth. This is a radical kind of realization of oneself as the body of totality itself, and not as an individual. This level of the soul seems to me to correlate with the *vajrakaya* in the Vajrayana teachings, when refracted through the lens of the *dharmakaya*.

So that's why I don't include these soul-levels in the stages of sacred wanting. There's no wanting in those levels. It's more of a state of Divine indifference. Which is challenging to our individuality because our individuality is defined by our wanting. That's why we save it for later teachings.

STUDENT: I'm still a little bit confused. I understand the sexual energy is the erotic sense of the whole being, not just sex, but is that a way to explain, besides hormones and stuff, adolescent craving for sexuality?

ZVI: Sure.

STUDENT: And then, is it also related to sexual union with another person as well?

ZVI: Yes, I don't mean in any way to discount the importance of sexual expression with another person, which is certainly the natural course of things. The awakening of the energy of *da'at* in the organism will naturally activate a very intense drive of wanting sexual expression with another.

And there is the possibility of it going through a process of refinement. At a certain point, it's not necessarily as fixated in the genitals. Some adults never actualize this. They stay fixated in less mature stages of sexual development. It's all about the charge and discharge of the nervous system, of the sexual energy as a charge and discharge. The point is that there is the potential for our sexual energy to be used as a vehicle for the awakening of all the centers, rather than just the lower centers.

STUDENT: When you say the sexual energy can be used to know in many other ways, is that like sublimation, like Freud talked about sublimation?

ZVI: When Freud talks about sublimation, he means using other activities to redirect and channel the sexual energy in more socially acceptable ways.[25] So no, that's not what I mean. I mean to actually engage the sexual energy head on.

To sublimate means to try to somehow mitigate the energy of the *id*. Freud's view is that the best we can do to manage the tripartite structure of the super-ego, ego, and id is to sublimate and channel the intense instinctual energies of the id into more socially acceptable behaviors, so our libido and our instinctual drives don't get the better of us and so that we don't create all kinds of problems. So, if I'm understanding Freud correctly, then what I am suggesting is different, in that our intention here is to awaken more and more of the possibility of experiencing and expressing our sexual energy more completely.

Now, the reason why there is a great fear of tantric practices—and again what I mean by tantra is not fancy lovemaking; I use the term "tantra" to refer to any practice that embraces all of our energies as fuel for transformation and for awakening and for realization—is because these energies can be destructive, can be dangerous, can cause us to act out in destructive ways, can be unwieldy, and can get the better of us. That's why sublimation is necessary in the conventional, traditional model.

In our approach we agree with Freud that the capacity for sublimation is useful, that a healthy ego structure is important, and that the child and adolescent stages of development require these structures. However, in adulthood—assuming that there has been a more or less healthy ego structure established (and that's not a simple thing to assume, because it's not the case for many people)—the work is to learn how to titrate, to open up that energetic channel. At first slowly, then more and more, in a way that our nervous system can hold more and more charge without acting out those energies, without repressing them on the one hand, nor acting them out on the other, but to simply sense them in their raw intensity. To feel them viscerally, to allow them to saturate the consciousness and the body, without repressing it on the one hand nor acting it out on the other.

This is the classic orientation of tantra. The classic traditions of tantra that I am referring to are Hindu and Buddhist tantra, which are almost identical in their approach. There are some differences here and there, but when it comes down to it they're very similar. Scholars have recently demonstrated a clear connection between them, showing how Buddhist tantra has its origin in the nondual Shaivite tantra (usually called Kashmir Shaivism). This makes sense, given that according to many scholars, Padmasambhava brought the tantric teachings from Kashmir to Tibet, so there is a direct line of influence.[26]

While there are subtle differences here and there in the view, the basic goal of practice is to be able to hold more and more energy. To do this is not a simple matter and it has its implications for the journey. Needless to say, this is not the religion of our parents and grandparents. That's why I say this is a post-religion teaching. Because Kedumah, which is a contemporary tantric path in the lineage of the Primordial Torah, is not concerned with beliefs and doctrines; it doesn't tell us to do this and to not do that. It's primarily concerned with how we—in our day and age—develop our capacity to tolerate more and more charge, which is the energy of *da'at*, which is the capacity of true knowledge, of the reality of truth itself, to awaken.

It's not that we as individuals become awakened, rather it's that we become more and more transparent vehicles for the awakened state of Being, which is the Divine Being, which is all of creation. We become more and more aligned and attuned and permeable and transparent to the life energy of creation, so that creation can live as a human Being through us, through the purity of its lights with all of their wisdom, intelligence, and beauty, in a way that is very human.

This is why the Journey of Wholeness is important. We'll talk about this more in later teachings. Ultimately there must be a human integration of our realization. To do this we need to transform from acting out in big ways to acting out in smaller ways, or acting out in ways that are more appropriate and constructive.

Acting out in and of itself is not a bad thing. It is typically necessary to act out to some extent in order to learn how to navigate these energies in more responsible, constructive ways. The best use of adolescence is to find out for ourselves—through experience—what kinds of behaviors work and which ones don't. But it is a long process that continues throughout adulthood. These are intense forces, and there are a lot of contractions in our system. When this intense life force rubs up against the contractions, then it gets expressed through the filter of those contractions. Either we have to discharge it because it's too intense for us or we repress it because it's too intense for us. But there is a third possibility, and that is to transmute the intense energy into fuel for waking up.

Getting angry is a good example. We need to remember that sexual energy is the life energy of the self. It's the eros of Being, of life. It's the juiciness of all of our experience. This means that anger is sexual. That is to say it's erotic. That is to say there's an intensity of life energy that's animating it.

If you read the *Vijñāna Bhairava Tantra*, one of the classic texts of Kashmir Shaivism, it's all about capturing those moments of intensity.[27] I don't mean "capturing" as in holding or locking them down, but capturing them as moments of awareness, as opportunities to feel them completely. The idea is to sense the raw energy of it, to sense what it feels like, what its color is, its texture. We want to be completely awake in the experience.

This is in contrast to the conventional way that we are taught to deal with things like anger and hatred, which is to either repress them or to discharge the intensity of the energy through acting it out. As a result, all the "negative" kinds of intense experiences that we have as children tend to get contracted into our body, structured into our soul, so that our soul becomes like a structured organism, and we experience ourself as a more rigid life-form.

STUDENT: Can you say that again?

ZVI: No, I don't think so. [Laughter.] The intense life energy gets structured through the contractions in our system. Our soul gets grooved, gets formed into certain structures that tend to predetermine and limit our range of experience.

Now there are contemporary paths of tantra that attempt to map out these associations between psychodynamics and the structures of the soul, like the Diamond Approach, for example.[28] There are all kinds of contemporary systems that are now integrating an understanding of psychology in the spiritual journey. We make use of some of these perspectives on this path because they can provide us with valuable knowledge that's part of our contemporary collective wisdom.

STUDENT: Can you repeat the word that you said was the Jewish version of tantra? Was it Kedumah?

ZVI: Yes, Kedumah. I did not say it is the Jewish version of tantra; I said that it is a tantric path in the lineage of the Primordial Torah. Kedumah is the name of this teaching; it is the path that I'm introducing in this series of teachings. This is the first time this teaching is being presented, so it is new even though it is also ancient; it is simultaneously new and ancient.

The Hebrew word *kedumah* means "primordial" or "ancient." But if you remember back to our first meeting, what I mean by Kedumah, by "ancient," is not the conventional sense of the term. I mean "ancient" in the sense that its origins are prior to the creation of the world of concepts. So it's an expression of a more primordial kind of wisdom.

However, you raise an interesting question, which is: What is the relationship between Kedumah and Judaism? One way to understand this relationship is to frame it in terms of what I call the Turnings of the Wheel of Torah, which is a model I am borrowing from the Buddhist teachings on the Turnings of the Wheel of Dharma.[29] In this model the first turning of the wheel of Torah is represented by the paradigms of Torah practiced by the ancient pre-Rabbinic Hebrews and Israelites and their prophets and prophetesses, kings, queens, and priests. The second turning of the wheel of Torah is Rabbinic Judaism, with their rabbis, scholars, and kabbalists. One expression of the third turning of the wheel of Torah is Kedumah, which reaches deep into the primordial wellspring of revelation and presents us with a

Torah—a Teaching—for our time, one that may be helpful for some people in the emerging age.

In my use of this model, I correlate each of these turnings with one of the three dimensions or axes of reality outlined in the *Sefer Yetzirah*, one of the oldest texts of the Kabbalah. These three dimensions are called *olam* (space), *shanah* (time) and *nefesh* (person).[30]

In ancient, biblical expressions of Torah, the emphasis is on the structures that inhabit *space*. If you go back and read the Torah, it is unbelievable how much narrative is dedicated to the description of the construction of different kinds of buildings, sanctuaries, and tabernacles, in the utmost detail. It is detailed to the point that much of the book of Exodus deals primarily with how to build a sanctuary, down to the literal nuts and bolts. In Hebrew, the term *olam*, which means "space," refers to this first turning of the wheel, and its distinguishing mode of practice is Temple worship and a general attention to sacred space.

In Rabbinic Judaism, which is the second turning of the wheel of Torah, the focus is on how we sanctify time. The concern here has to do with how we access the presence of Being through the dimension of time. The day, the week, and the month are all scrutinized, as well as the yearly cycles, in order to access and draw from its depth the light of Being. In Hebrew, this second turning of the wheel is called *shanah*, which means "time" or "year," and its central mode of practice is the Sabbath and the holidays.

The central practice of Inquiry—*drash*—is applied differently in each of these respective paradigms. The basis of the practice of Inquiry is wanting to know the truth for its own sake. This is the central orienting principle of the entire oral tradition of Torah. In the Talmud this principle is called *Torah Lishmah*, which means studying Torah and investigating it for its own sake.[31] "For its own sake" means that we do it not for hope of reward or for fear of punishment, but simply because we love it, because we want to know what the truth is.

In the Rabbinic paradigm, the truth is mostly accessed through inquiry into Torah texts: the Bible, the Talmud, other Rabbinic texts such as the Midrashim, and the texts of the Kabbalah. The entire focus of the Talmud, the Midrashim, and of many Kabbalah texts (such as the Zohar), is to discover the truth for its own sake through an open-ended investigation into the Torah and the creative interpretation thereof in order to unpack it, undress it, and reveal its innermost secrets.

However, in the third turning of the wheel of Torah, which is the paradigm that is expressed in the Kedumah teachings, we apply this same methodology of inquiry into the *nefesh*—the person or the soul. We therefore need contemplative tools to investigate and inquire into our experience in a manner that will penetrate through the layers of our experience in order to reveal our innermost parts, which are the light of Being and the light of our soul.

We are learning some of those tools. We have learned about sensing into the body using our inner touch in order to become more intimate with our experience moment-to-moment, sensing into the very texture and lifeblood of our experience using faculties of perception that we ordinarily don't apply in this manner. This is a practice of learning how to apply sensing in service of Inquiry, *drash*, and in service of wanting to discover what is really true.

Even in the Talmud they recognized this and stated explicitly that the method is to inquire into the Torah to understand the truth of God through the Torah, the truth of Being. Someone who has embodied these principles and attained knowledge of God through inquiry into the Torah is thus considered to be a living embodiment of the Torah itself. In the traditional Jewish community, when a great Torah scholar or sage walks into the room everyone rises; they are honored the same way that a Torah scroll is honored in the synagogue when it is removed from the ark. This is because they are recognized as not just having realized the truth of Torah, which is the truth of Being itself, but to have embodied the Torah to the degree that they *are* the

Torah.[32] This of course means that they have become, through their embodiment of Torah, the embodiment of the Divine. The Torah and the Divine are one and the same, according to the Zohar.[3]

There are many traditional rituals that are performed around the recognition that the righteous person has become the embodiment of the Torah, the embodiment of the teaching, and the embodiment of truth. Even if we apply the practice of *drash* and the principle of Inquiry to the Rabbinic paradigm of the second turning of Torah, it is easy to see how smooth a transition it is to the perspective of the third turning. This is because even in the second turning, inquiring into the nature of Torah is already implying inquiring into the nature of the human being, because ultimately the human being *is* the Torah.

We *are* the teaching. We *are* the revelation, embodied. However, we need tools and techniques to decipher and understand our experience and our being; we need a method to discover who and what we truly are. We need a meditative exegesis to decode and deconstruct the texts of our bodies and our souls.

So that's why when we sense into our body, which is a very simple practice, we're beginning to learn the skills to work with and develop the three centers. We do this in order to apply this development toward the third turning application of *drash*, of inquiry into the truth of our human experience.

In time, the practices of the third turning of the wheel of Torah can also open up the recognition of what I call the fourth turning of the wheel of Torah, which correlates with the Journey of Freedom, the fifth journey in the Kedumah teachings. The fourth turning is based on our understanding of *Ein Sof,* which is beyond the categories of both infinite and finite, and thus holds a perspective that is beyond the categories of space, time, and person. It's this fourth turning view that informs Kedumah as a trans-religious teaching and path; it is what frees us to make use of methods and practices from any of the first three turnings or from other paths and traditions. This is possible because we recognize the radical space and freedom of the white parchment and the totality of the scroll—the nonconceptual primordial ground that includes everything and nothing at all.‡

---

‡ For more on the relationship between Kedumah and Judaism and the Turnings of the Wheel of Torah, see the appendix.

4
Free Speech

THERE IS A verse in the book of Proverbs (20:27) that serves as the foundation for this next practice, which is the esoteric application of this verse. A lot of what we're doing in this teaching and in this path is revealing the hidden meanings of ancient texts in a manner that hopefully is more applicable and accessible in our day. This verse in Hebrew is: *Ki Ner Hashem Nishmat Adam Chofes Kol Chedrei Vaten.* The translation, at least on the literal level, is: "The light of *YHVH* is the soul of the human, seeking out the innermost parts of the belly." As we discussed, *YHVH* means "Is-Was-Will Be" or "Being," so we are talking about the light of Being, which is the main signifier for the Divine Being. *Ki Ner Hashem Nishmat Adam.* "For the light of *YHVH* is the soul of the human being." *Chofes Kol Chedrei Vaten.* "Seeks out all of the innermost parts of the belly." *Chedrei* literally are "rooms," a *cheder* is a room, so "all the rooms of the belly;" all the spaces, the innermost spaces. "The light of God, the light of *YHVH*, the light of Being, is the soul of the human, seeks out the innermost parts of the belly."

So far we have been doing the "sensing the limbs" practice. The sensing the limbs or the purification of the limbs practice is one way of accessing this center through the extremities, and this new practice is sensing more directly into the *chedrei vaten*, the innermost parts of the belly. This is a way of beginning to open up this center of our being to its nature, to the light of Being, to the light of the cosmos itself. To the light of the Divine.

So it's very simple: The "innermost parts of the belly" is the innermost center of the belly. The center of the belly is a spaceless space, a placeless place, located in the center. In the Taoist tradition they recognize this center as the lower *tan tien*. Usually it's described as being two fingerbreadths below the navel.[1] I've also seen it in texts described as four fingerbreadths below the navel, so I guess it depends on how thick your fingers are. [Laughter.]

STUDENT: Four *tsun*. *Tsun* is the actual measurement…

ZVI: So that's probably more like four fingerbreadths. So can someone go around and make sure we're all sensing into the right spot? [Laughter.] You can approximate. And also inward towards the spine.

I just thought of a joke, so I have to tell it to you. Do you know what a *Yeche* is? It is a German Jew. We have jokes about the *Yeches* (who have a reputation for being exactingly precise). How many *Yeches* does it take to screw in a lightbulb? 1.0.

Here is another one. It's not a *Yeche* joke but it's about the *misnagdim*, those from the Rabbinic establishment who were anti-Hasidic.

What's the difference between a Misnagged and a Hasid? A Hasid doesn't *davven* (pray) on time. A Misnagged doesn't *davven*, on time.

Anyway, nothing like a few stereotypes to throw into a spiritual teaching to make it legit. All this to say that this is more of a Hasidic path [Laughter.] with a healthy dose of *Yeche*-ness.

I know some of you are practitioners of the Arica tradition. In the Arica tradition, they call this the *kath* point. The belly-center point. This has its roots in the Sufi tradition, and is one of the central practices in the Diamond Approach. Similar practices are also found in the Hindu tradition, where this center is called the *hara* point, and in the Buddhist tradition corollaries can also be found.

The practice is simply to sense this center, this belly-center, using our inner touch. It's a concentration practice, so that means we bring our attention, our concentration, and allow our consciousness to gather in this point, and we come back to it with whatever distractions come our way, whatever thoughts or feelings arise. Or with whatever jokes come into the field. [Laughter.] We come back to focusing our attention, our awareness and our sensing, our inner sensing; we are actually sensing into that point. I call this practice the *tzimtzum* practice, because it works with the dynamic of concentration and expansion, and this point in the center of the belly is the *tzimtzum* point, the location in the body where presence is concentrated and sourced.[2]

Now there is an art to it, because you can locate the point intuitively; you can feel it through sensing it. You can start by sensing into the general area of the lower *tan tien* in the belly and at some point you may feel a kind of subtle energetic click, like something clicks into place. And then when your consciousness gently clicks into itself in that area, you just concentrate on that point and keep coming back to it if you find yourself distracted. If you don't locate it, that's fine; you can just notice your breath going into the belly and note the sensation in the belly and use that as an anchor; continually keep coming back to the sensation in the lower *tan tien* area.

I'm using these terms from these other traditions to help us orient to this spot. The verse that I pointed to expresses the Kedumah tradition's knowledge of this zone and maybe we will have a chance to look at some of that. So I'll ring the bell and we'll just sit with this practice for a few minutes and then I'll ring the bell again at the end. Any questions about the practice?

STUDENT: Can you repeat the verse again?

ZVI: Yes. *Ki Ner Hashem Nishmat Adam Chofes Kol Chedrei Vaten.* "For the light of *YHVH*, the soul of the human being, penetrates the inner chambers of the belly." You can see that the verse is pointing us to open to the light of our soul, to the light of Being itself, through this center. This practice, if you actually practice it, over time it will begin to open up this center of the light of our soul. The soul as a lamp reflecting the light of Being.

TALK

In previous meetings I introduced the sensing practice and we learned about the function of the heart in the journey of contraction. We discussed how, without really wanting to know what is there— certainly with regard to the difficult places—then our investigation will fall flat at some point. We will have reached the end of the road in terms of what we can discover if we don't really want to know. That is where the heart comes in to the practice of *drash* in the third turning of the wheel of Torah. There are many Divine qualities of the heart and this is simply one of these qualities: a sincere, almost innocent desire to want to know the truth for its own sake.

In the last chapter we also opened up another dimension of the heart's desire to know the truth, which is the genital dimension. That is to say that the principle of *da'at*, of knowledge, is an intimate kind of embodied and erotic union with our experience. The heart's engagement with wanting to know and understand for its own sake is then fueled with the eros of Being itself, which is the intrinsic movement toward manifestation and revelation that is the nature of the erotic impulse. It is the impulse for creation, for manifestation, for birthing, and for becoming. All these principles point to an embodied union with our experience that includes the heart and also includes an engagement with the faculties of our body, the sensing faculties. These are not two separate things; this is one unified movement.

Although we did not explicitly discuss this yet, implied every step of the way is the orientation of the mind. Much of the conceptual view and narrative dimension of the teaching is to harmonize the mind so that it aligns with the process and can become more of a bridge to awakening rather than an obstacle. That is part of the function of the conceptual view.

It is interesting that many traditional societies do not discriminate so much between the mind and the heart when it comes to knowing and understanding.[3] The separation of the mind from the heart is a more recent innovation of the West.[4] For example, many phrases found in the ancient Hebrew tradition put heart and wisdom, heart and understanding, heart and knowledge in the same breath.[5] The discrimination and the compartmentalization of the mind from the heart is an artificial one that reflects the dissociation of the mind from the heart and body in our culture.

There is another element to the mind—to the involvement of the head-center—that I want to discuss, and this will be the third ingredient in the practice of *drash*. So far we have discussed the sensing practice and the orientation of the heart. We actually discussed several different qualities of the heart: the wanting to know, as well as the union of the heart with the erotic and dynamic impulse of creation. There are many other qualities of the heart, but hopefully we will get to them, if not in this series of lectures, in a future one.

The head-center embodies another dimension that I would like to bring forth. I am referring to the subversion of conventional knowledge with the principle of "not-knowing." Many of you are familiar with this because many traditions and practices have an understanding of this and apply it in various ways. It is therefore important that I explain what I mean by not-knowing in the Kedumah tradition.

To reiterate, when we use the word *da'at* we are not talking about conventional knowledge. We are talking about an immediate, intimate perception of experience or reality as it is in its rawness, not overlaid with conceptual biases or labels. In order for this kind of knowledge to reveal itself in its fullness, there needs to be a certain posture of the mind. We call this posture "not-knowing," which is of course paradoxical and ironic given that we are using the word knowledge to talk about true perception.

Thus, what we mean by "not-knowing" is adopting an inner attitude of not-knowing; we suspend our conventional orientation to knowledge as a commodity, as something that we possess. We also suspend our need to interpret our experience in ways that conveniently fit into our self-identity box. Another way of saying it is that to have an open mind—a mind that is truly not-knowing—means to be willing to be surprised and to have our ideals, beliefs, opinions, and biases challenged and overturned. It is not a simple thing.[6]

The degree to which our self-identity is invested in our concepts and in our way of thinking is impressive. We deeply identify with what we think we know. Therefore, having an open mind will really challenge the rigid boundaries of our self-identity box and in the process allow the possibility of more permeability, of more openness. When we sense into our experience, we want to know what is happening. The attitude of not-knowing here is crucial, because otherwise we are not really open to discovering something new, something that we did not already know. This attitude of the mind is what we mean by not-knowing, and it is the third ingredient in the practice of *drash*.

To review the three ingredients:

1. the capacity to sense into the immediacy of our experience and to stay with our experience as it unfolds even if it's painful;
2. really wanting to know the truth, the engagement of the heart's curiosity and its unification with the fuel of creation, the dynamic and erotic life-force;
3. an attitude of openness, of not-knowing, with the willingness to be surprised by what we discover.

If we can integrate these three orienting principles we have the foundational workings for the third turning practice of *drash*, which is the full-bodied inquiry into the person, into our personal experience.

There are many other aspects of our nature that actualize themselves in this practice, and that are needed for the *drash* practice to realize its full potential, but these three ingredients provide the working foundation; these are the conditions that will allow the movement of discovery to begin. They will allow us to begin to open beyond our more familiar and fixed way of navigating and identifying and knowing ourselves and our world.

You can see that we are laying the foundations for understanding this practice. We are laying the conceptual foundations but also the applied and experiential foundations. Now that we have articulated this practice more clearly, I want to go back and say a few more things about contraction and expansion from this perspective.

In the ancient Hebrew tradition, the process of contraction and expansion is symbolized and articulated most explicitly in the biblical story of the enslavement of the Children of Israel in Egypt. If you don't know the narrative, all you need to know is that according to this ancient legend the Children of Israel were enslaved in Egypt. This is the way it is talked about in English, but if you go back to the Hebrew it reveals something really quite fascinating.

In the Torah, the word for Egypt is *Mitzrayim*. The word *Mitzrayim* in Hebrew means "the contracted places."[7] *Metzar* in Hebrew means narrow, constricted, or contracted. The same word root is found in the book of Psalms (118:5), where we read the verse, *Min Hametzar Karati Yah, Anani Bamerchav Yah*. This verse, which is recited in the traditional prayer service, means, "From the places of contraction I cry out to you, God; answer me, God, from expansion." You can see here the clear movement from contraction to expansion.

In the biblical narrative the people of Israel are enslaved in *Mitzrayim*, in "contraction." The word "Israel" is a transliteration of the Hebrew word *Yisrael*, which means "one who wrestles with God." It is a combination of the word *yisra* (wrestle) and *el* (God). When the text says that the people of Israel are slaves in Egypt, on the mystical

81

level it translates as "those who wrestle with God are slaves to contraction."

This ancient myth reflects our universal human condition of being enslaved by our contractions. This means that it is not necessarily our contractions that are the problem, but instead the fact that we are enslaved to them and under their control. We have a slave mentality about them. In this sense, it is easier for a person to get out of *Mitzrayim* than it is for *Mitzrayim* to get out of the person. Thus, the tradition tends to understand the enslavement in Egypt to be more primarily a psycho-spiritual enslavement rather than a physical one.

Our enslavement to our contractions includes all the ways that we are stuck and trapped in the narrow, constricted places in our being. This includes psychological contraction as well as physical, emotional, and energetic constriction. The movement into expansion is reflected in the story of the exodus of the Israelites from slavery in *Mitzrayim. Min Hametzar Karati Yah Anani Bamerchav Yah*: "From the places of contraction I cry out to you, God; answer me, God, from expansion."

The movement out of contraction and into expansion can be experientially understood through this narrative and its secrets can be unlocked. There are many secret teachings in this narrative that relate to the spiritual journey and are applicable in the present day. For instance, we can see some of these teachings when we consider the ritual of the Passover *seder*.

The Passover *seder* is a central Jewish ritual, a traditional feast that marks the passage from contraction into expansion. On a deeper level, the *seder* can thus be seen as ritual of transformation, similar to the function of feast practice in the tantric lineages of Tibetan Buddhism. In normative cultural Judaism, we have preserved the ritualistic remnants of the *seder* practice but for the most part we have lost the contemplative and mystical import of it. So there's a lot of eating and drinking and talking, which are also, of course, very traditional Jewish practices. [Laughter.]

If you can believe it, I actually have a reason for including "talking" in this list that goes beyond just making jokes. Talking practice is actually an integral part of the mystical practice of what is known as Passover, which is an attempt to translate the Hebrew word *Pesach*. *Pesach* is the Hebrew word for this festival that marks the passage from contraction to expansion. In the Kedumah tradition, we read the Hebrew Bible as a map for the inner journey; we are not that interested in cultural and historical things. They are beautiful and rich and very powerful if a person is linked to that tradition culturally, but that cultural or tribal link is not a necessary ingredient for this path.

Our interest in the teaching is only relative to the inner journey. Talking is important because it is the main practice of the Passover *seder*, the ritual Passover feast. In the traditional Passover *seder*, the central practice is to read the Haggadah, which is a formal liturgical text. The Haggadah means "the telling" or "the talking." The telling or saying of what? It is the telling of the story of the movement from slavery to freedom, the journey from contraction to expansion.

Moreover, the central section of the Haggadah is a section known as *Maggid*, which means "one who talks" as in a narrator or storyteller. The Haggadah specifically emphasizes telling the tale of the exodus from *Mitzrayim*—contraction—to our children. Why? The mystical masters point out that the Hebrew word *vehigadeta* ("And you shall tell") that serves as the biblical source for the requirement to tell the Exodus story to our children (Exodus 13:8) can also mean "to draw down."[8] We are thus required to tell our children the story of the movement from contraction to expansion because in the telling we are "drawing down" to them—transmitting to them—the actual experiential knowledge of this potential for freedom.

This text is filled with references to the importance of telling the story of enslavement in *Mitzrayim*. The Hebrew word *Pesach*, which is the word used in the Torah to refer to this holiday, is read by the mystical sages as two words combined—*pe* and *sach*; *pe* means "mouth" and *sach* means "speaks."[9] The whole holiday has to do with the mouth that speaks.

There are many jokes made about Jews being talkative, and as you can see these jokes are made for good reason. I don't think it is an accident that at the beginning of this cosmological and historical third turning of the wheel of Torah, which emphasizes inquiry into the self and human experience, many Jews (including Freud and many of his students) were deeply involved in the whole psychoanalytic movement and with the development of techniques that use "talk therapy."

In other words, there was a recognition of the power of talking and its relationship to the healing process, and how it could be used as a tool for understanding and awakening. I think the spiritual roots of our contemporary Western tradition of psychodynamics and talk therapy come from this very ancient Hebrew understanding of the relationship between the inner journey and the faculty of speech and the power it can offer on the journey of transformation.[10]

There is a Rabbinic teaching in the Midrash that states, *Bizchut Ha-emunah Nigalu Avotainu Mi-Mitzrayim*: "Our ancestors were redeemed from contraction (*Mitzrayim*) through the merit of their trust."[11] Thus, freedom only came because they had trust. Therefore, the principle of trust was foundational in the possibility of moving from contraction to expansion. This *Midrash* continues: *U'bizchut Ha-emunah Atidim Lihiga'el*: "And it is through the merit of their trust that they will be redeemed in the future."

The mystical masters teach that when the Israelites were slaves in *Mitzrayim* they were actually at the forty-ninth level of *tumah*, "impurity," which points to a condition of extreme alienation from the Divine.[12] The forty-ninth level is the last level before the fiftieth, which represents complete hopelessness and desolation, the level of no turning back.

What is the significance of the number forty-nine? Of the ten *sefirot*, the seven lower ones—from *Chesed* to *Malchut*—are called the seven "days" of creation because they constitute the essential material of the manifested realms of form. The upper three *sefirot* are precreation and thus formless and unmanifest. The term "days" is a code word in the Kabbalistic tradition that refers to the essential lights, the *sefirot*.[13] When the Hebrew Bible relates that the world was created in seven days, it means that the world was created with the light of these seven *sefirot*. So these lower seven *sefirot* constitute the seven "lights" of the world of creation. Because each light also contains within it the light of the other seven *sefirot*, this means that there are a total of seven times seven, or forty-nine total elements of essential light in the world.

There are thus forty-nine levels of spiritual realization and an equal number of levels of potential disconnect from these Lights of Being. When the tradition relates that the Israelites had fallen to the forty-ninth level of *tumah* (impurity), it means that they were almost completely cut off from the essential Lights of Being, from the Divine body of light. The degree of their enslavement to contraction was such that they could not find in their experience the light of Being in any of its forms. There was just a little bit of a trickle of light left; that was the fiftieth, the last level. They were so lost and so contracted that all the light was nearly squeezed out of them.

Now, according to the ancient Kabbalists, the exile into *Mitzrayim* was an exile of *da'at*.[14] Exile of *da'at*! *Da'at* as we have seen is true knowledge, so this was an exile of true knowledge, of intimacy with the immediacy of our experience in the here and now. When we understand *da'at* correctly as an experiential truth, then it is easier to see how it is the underlying property of all the *sefirot*, and not a distinct *sefirah* (singular for *sefirot*) in its own right.

Since *da'at* is the underlying property of all of the Lights of Being—of all the qualities and colors of creation—then if it is in exile it makes sense that we would not have experiential access to any of the lights. The movement from contraction to expansion requires the actualization and the reintegration of *da'at* into our felt-sense awareness. This requires the intimate union of flesh and perception, accomplished through our practice of embodied sensing, aligned with the living dynamism and eros of the heart and the engaged wakefulness of the mind.

However, there is one very important underlying ingredient that we must integrate into our consciousness for such a transformation to occur. This ingredient is trust. There is a verse in Psalms (116:10), an amazing verse, that reads: *He-emanti Ki Adaber.* It means, "I trusted because I have spoken." We see here an intimate relationship between the faculty of speech and the development and revelation of the hidden dimension of trust that is within each of us. Trust is another one of the properties of Being; it is so intrinsic to our nature, to the nature of our soul, that it is difficult to pin down as a quality. However, it is clear that without it nothing can blossom, unfold, grow, reveal, or transform.

You can see now how we have revealed a constellation of concept terms: trust, *Mitzrayim*, contraction, expansion, the movement from contraction to expansion, freedom from slavery, Pesach, the mouth that talks, the relationship between speech and trust, the relationship between trust and the possibility of redemption. *Bizchut Ha-emunah Nigalu Avoteinu Mi-Mitzrayim*, "Through the merit of their trust our ancestors were freed from contraction." Do you see this whole constellation of interconnected principles? This brings us to the next ingredient in the practice of *drash*, which is the ingredient of talking, and the relationship between talking and trust.

In order for talking to make any sense there must be somebody listening, so we see implicit in talking is an interpersonal dynamic; there is an interaction with an "other." In the Kedumah path we speak with each other—through inquiry—as a spiritual practice. We do interpersonal exercises and dialogical meditations as a way of deepening that essential ingredient of trust in our souls. *He-emanti Ki Adaber*: "I trusted because I have spoken."

Speech itself is a practice. It is a way of unpacking and deepening our own process, our own being, which also brings blessings to others. Ultimately, when we move through the Journeys of Contraction, Expansion, Wholeness, Vastness and Freedom, it becomes clear why speech works the way it does. At some point we realize that it is not actually the case that two separate individuals are talking to each other. We recognize directly that we are all different cells of one cosmic body, of one living Being. How sweet it can be to say hello to another part of ourselves, to a different cell of our own cosmic body! When viewed from this perspective, speech is recognized as the dynamic expression of intercellular communication and the autoerotic activity of the one galactic Being. Sharing words of truth is very erotic and pleasurable.

Because we recognize that we are each an individual cell of one cosmic organism, when we converse with each other there are not two, nor is there really one, but rather, more accurately, there is both two and one—or both not-two and not-one. We can appreciate more fully how the interpersonal processes and dialogical exercises in which we engage have much more esoteric intelligence to them, which accounts for their powerful effect.

Practicing *drash* with a partner is different than sensing into our experience alone in our room. There is a different impact when we articulate the truth of our experience using speech. In the Aramaic, the word *maggid*—which is understood to be the principle of storytelling as it relates to the Exodus from *Mitzrayim*—also means "to transmit" or "to draw down." When we speak and tell our stories of contraction and expansion to one another, we are also transmitting to one another. Ultimately, we are one living organism in a process of self-recognition and self-evolution. We can gain an immediate understanding of this process just based on our own experiences engaging the practice.

This is why when we practice *drash* with a partner—called a *chavruta*—or with a group of people, we inquire into our experience and we speak it out-loud.[15] We describe the truth of what is happening in the immediacy of our experience. This embodies the principle of *emet* (truth) and *da'at*, and this deepens our trust, *emunah*. From this, naturally our experience will open up to deeper and deeper dimensions of truth and of reality. You can see how this is a practice that has a particular orientation and form; it is fueled by the love of truth for its own sake—*Torah Lishmah*—and includes the dynamic participation with other cells of the Divine body—our *drash* partners.

Speaking the truth in this way is itself the unfolding and the revelation, is itself the movement from contraction to expansion. According to the Zohar, the exile of *Mitzrayim* was not only an exile of *da'at* but also an exile of *dibur*—of speech—which means that freeing our speech is itself the way out of contraction.[16] Thus, speaking itself is the mechanism of transformation, which is why sitting at the Passover *seder* and telling the story of the Exodus from *Mitzrayim*, if done contemplatively and mystically and from this third turning perspective, is itself a movement from contraction to expansion.

And now it should be clear why in the third turning of the wheel of Torah, speaking our truth in any moment (not just on the night of *Pesach*) opens up the possibility of moving from contraction to expansion. What was confined to a particular sacred time in the second turning practice of Judaism is now recognized as a possibility in every moment in the Kedumah practice of the third turning of the wheel of Torah.

The Rabbinic sages of the second turning path of Judaism foresaw and perhaps intuited the wisdom of the third turning of Torah when they stated explicitly that we are not doing the rituals and performance of the *seder* because our ancestors were freed from Egypt in the past. Rather, they taught that we are doing it right now because we are slaves in Egypt *right now*; we are in contraction right now and we talk about it—the Haggadah and *Maggid*—as a way of moving into freedom.

We read in the Haggadah: *Chayav Adam Lirot Et Atzmo Ki-ilu Hu Yatzah Mi-Mitzrayim:* "Every person is required to see themself as if they themself have been liberated from *Mitzrayim.*" Even in normative Judaism this is actually the contemplative practice that is intended to be done on Passover, but because these contemplative methods of the third turning path have not been publicly explicated very much, few practitioners of Judaism know how to engage it in this manner.

STUDENT: Is Kedumah a Jewish teaching?

ZVI: I use the term Kedumah in two distinct ways. The first way I use the term is in reference to the Kedumah principle, which is the primordial nonconceptual ground and the source of all wisdom teachings. The second way I use the term is as a shorthand for this particular body of teachings that I am presenting in this series of talks, which is one expression of the Kedumah principle. Certainly this particular set of Kedumah teachings can be seen as an expression of the Judaic wisdom stream, since I am utilizing primarily Judaic concepts and language to articulate the teachings. However, because Kedumah does not hold any tribal allegiances, nor does it adhere to traditional Jewish law or rely on sacred texts as authoritative, it operates from a different paradigm than does Rabbinic Judaism, which is what I call the second turning of the wheel of Torah. The Kedumah teachings presented in this series describe a third turning practice of Torah but hold a fourth turning view of Torah. To say it another way, Torah is not limited to Rabbinic Judaism but Rabbinic Judaism is one authentic expression of Torah. Rabbinic Judaism is one of the *yanas* of Torah, just like Mahayana is one of the *yanas* of the Dharma. Since all of the turnings are expressions of Torah, even the first and second turnings can be enriched by the Kedumah teachings; in fact they may make a lot more sense for some people when viewed through the lens of these Kedumah teachings. These Kedumah teachings can therefore be seen as one new paradigm of Torah—a contemplative and universal version of Torah—for the emerging age.§

---

§ For more on the relationship between Kedumah and Judaism, see the appendix.

STUDENT: You mentioned trust in your talk, but can you say more about what you mean by it?

ZVI: Yes, I mentioned briefly the element of trust. Trust is a big issue for many of us. Do we trust that it's possible to be free? Do we trust that reality is inherently good and benevolent and will hold us as we move through the pain of our contractions? To have this kind of trust is not a small thing. The deeper in contraction we are, the more difficult it is to trust that it's okay to really sense into our contraction and embrace it and welcome it in the manner that we practiced in our first two meetings. What we found—and many of you reported this—was that just by orienting to contraction differently, by sensing the immediate rawness, the temperature and texture of our contracted experience, without labeling it or judging it, it tends to have its own way of revealing its inner nature to us. This takes a lot of trust, especially when it's a difficult contraction.

There are different ways of working with contraction in the body. In the Rolfing tradition we use different techniques of moving into the contraction as a way of releasing the energy that is bound up in the tissue. Sometimes if there's a contraction in the tissues we use movement to exaggerate the contraction, that is, we move the body deeper into the constricted pattern as a way of training the body to be more comfortable with the sensations of contraction. We have discovered that this is what allows the tissues to release, to reveal their potential for expansion. And of course trust also plays an important role in the Rolfing process; you really have to trust your Rolfer as they dig their elbows deep into your *kishkes*. [Laughter.]

So trust is not a small thing and I don't want to just brush over it, so we will have more teachings on it later on. Interpersonally, of course, the issues of trust become even more pronounced because it's not just abstract trusting but rather entails actually trusting another human being. All of us know what it feels like to be wounded in various ways by people in our lives. This is why our group here is a sacred gathering, a community where we have an opportunity to practice together and to challenge some of those conditioned ways of knowing and relating with reality and with each other.

When we do these interpersonal practices we are really exploring what comes up for us around trust. How does it feel to be vulnerable with another? Is it okay for me to talk about my experience with this person, or does it not feel okay? It's about learning to trust our presence, to trust the spontaneous wisdom of being in the moment, and also to respect ourselves enough to trust when it does not feel right to share. That has its own wisdom and vulnerability, to trust one's immediate sense unconditionally.

We put ourselves into vulnerable situations in this sacred context in order to learn about ourselves; to learn about trust and how we express it or not with others. To learn how to trust oneself and one's sense. To learn how to trust when it is constructive to do something ego dystonic—that is to say, something that's against the ordinary tendency of the ego—or to trust our sense if it feels like no, this is not the right space or time for this investigation. This learning happens through sensing into our body-soul and coming to know—and trust—its wisdom from within.

[The following discussion takes place after an experiential exercise.]

STUDENT: I noticed in the exercise, how when I started telling my story I was very consciously saying, "Okay, now I'm feeling some shaking, and checking in with my body." And once the story got rolling, it wasn't until after I finished telling the story that it was like, "Oh, I wonder how my body was during all of that?" And, I think there was some subtle recognition, but I realized that it didn't feel like I was bringing my body into it as much, just because I forgot, I got carried away in trying to tell the story and let it be conceptual and linear and make sense, compared to when I actually did voice how what I was feeling in my body and sensing as I did in the beginning, that the body actually felt like it was much more there as the story went on.

ZVI: So speaking to the immediate experience of the sensations in your body seemed to help ground your experience in the here and now.

STUDENT: Yeah. Because then when I was in the story, it was really like I was there again, in the past, and as it happened just reliving it, but only in my mind. Whereas when I said how I felt in my body, I knew that I was in this room and that that story was in the past. Linearly, I guess.

ZVI: You said that there was some subtle recognition in the telling of the story. What was the overall effect on your consciousness of recalling your experience and speaking to it in the here and now?

STUDENT: There's a strengthening of being present, of not getting carried away in it. Even though, when I was telling it I was pretty carried away in it. Now I'm feeling a sense of being able to go there in my mind as a story and to have some distance from it, and to be stronger in where I am right now.

ZVI: What do you experience in your heart right now, as you recognize that?

STUDENT: It feels able. There's a definite sense of daringness, and bravery, and also a sense of openness and willingness to go there and to go into the shit and trust in myself, and that I won't be carried away in it. I won't get lost in it; I won't get lost in the contraction.

ZVI: Yeah. That's good. Thanks for sharing.

STUDENT: I noticed that once I started defining what was happening as a contraction or an expansion, it became confusing what exactly was a contraction and what exactly was an expansion. And I noticed that with everyone, as they were talking, that it could actually go either way, and that I was defining it as a contraction means like, this bad-feeling place, and an expansion is like, *Oh!* But it could also go the other way, where contraction could be this good-feeling place, but it's actually contraction, and expansion could be really hard and feel really bad. That's something I noticed about, and then I got confused, about what to define as a contraction and an expansion.

ZVI: You say there's confusion. Do you feel confusion right now?

STUDENT: No. When I speak from a place of truth, it feels really good. I feel lighter.

ZVI: So when you say it feels "really good," you mean "lighter"?

STUDENT: Yeah, lighter. And like, high almost. Like, after any time, actually, if I have a good discussion with someone that goes to a deep level, and we touch upon things that feel true, I feel really good.

ZVI: It seems to me that what you are saying is that when you speak truth, it doesn't really matter if it's about contraction or expansion. It's not about the content. It's more the fact of its truth, and true speech produces some kind of a state of "high," what you're calling "really good" and "lighter."

STUDENT: I don't know any other words to describe it.

ZVI: Those are good words. Can you describe the sensation of it? I think people are picking it up in the group field, but how would you describe it?

STUDENT: Just light. Just lighter. A lightness of body. And it doesn't matter if I get lost in it either. Because I still feel the lightness of body. So, I wasn't actually really in tune with my body when I was talking, but I can tell if I'm speaking from that place because of how I feel afterwards. So, I feel like really good and light and high, and I know that truth was being spoken.

ZVI: Very good. It seems that when we speak the truth of our experience, that itself leads to a certain state. That state is what we call expansion. Everyone will experience it in their own way. What makes it expansion is that it's not dependent on the content of our experience. It is not bound by our ordinary self-identity and has an inherent sense of spaciousness and goodness. This is a good illustration of the effect on our consciousness of speaking truth.

STUDENT: I just wanted to share something that was connecting for me which I find really really poignant. I'm taking a class at Naropa talking about the Torah and our teacher always talks about the biblical heroes as "mistake heroes." As people who are sharing their story, which is not just a story of expansion, but is more so a story of contractions and a lot of mistakes. He describes it as kind of like putting a placemark on a dead end in a maze, to kind of help everybody out. And I think it points to the power found in sharing and speaking about our negative experiences. And I think it's really poignant. I just wanted to share that because I think it's really interesting.

ZVI: It's true, the greatest heroes of the Hebrew Bible have made pretty big "mistakes"; they are very human. If you remember the first talk, I discussed what it's like to hold both the finite and infinite perspectives simultaneously. That was an expression of the principle of "the end is embedded in the beginning and the beginning is embedded in the end." That is to say that in the very beginning we started with the principle of freedom, which is the recognition that contraction and expansion are not on a value spectrum. There's no valuation that expansion is good and contraction is bad, for instance, or that one is positive and the other negative. Freedom is simply freedom from those categories of judging our experience one way or the other.

STUDENT: I was just thinking about what you said about the role of talking in Judaism and the role of talking as a spiritual tool in general. In the exercise I noticed that I went places that I didn't know I was going to go to, and as I said things, I felt them, and felt whether they were true or not. So I was kind of surprised about that, and I felt a transforming experience. And I'm curious if there's something inherently Jewish about that. Because you were talking about "talking" as a part of it.

ZVI: In the Torah tradition, talking is an integral element throughout. In contemporary times it has become more of a central principle in our Western culture as a result of the influence of modern psychology. The applied tools of psychoanalysis are a huge influence on the way we orient in the West. *He-emanti Ki Adaber*: "I trust because I speak." This is from the Psalms. So the transformative power of speech, of talking, is rooted in the Torah tradition, and probably other traditions as well. But it's interesting that in Jewish culture it's become, you can say, a specialty. [Laughter.]

In the Rabbinic tradition, which is the second turning of the wheel of Torah, this is rooted in the understanding of the way creation took place. In the very beginning of the book of Genesis (1:3), when it describes the creation of the world, it states: *Vayomer Elohim Ye-hi Ohr Vayehi Ohr,* which means: "And God said, 'Let there be light,' and there was light." So creation happens through God's speech. Since the human being is formed in the "image of God," it makes sense that our human speech also holds that very power of creation. We have the potential to create and shape reality through the power of our speech. So it's a cosmic power; our speech has cosmic implications. So the roots of this understanding go all the way back to the creation narrative in the book of Genesis.

STUDENT: It's interesting because it also requires trust to speak something you're not sure of yet and to see how it feels.

Zvi: That's a good observation. Trust is a crucial ingredient for the process, to be able to speak what we don't know, which is also inherent in the process of creation. Creation is bringing something forward that's never existed before. It's a completely new manifestation. And so too, we also need a lot of trust to speak our truth; to just say what our truth is, to really be where we are without us knowing what will be created or what will manifest as a result of our speech.

For many reasons, many of which are psychodynamic, we do not trust that it's okay to speak our truth. Most of us were shunned, disregarded or simply unseen as children, especially when we spoke our truth. Children don't speak their truth in polished, refined ways. It often comes out with a shout or a cry or a movement with the body. How many adults know how to hear what the child is really saying? Probably very few.

So there are many psychodynamic obstacles oftentimes that originate in childhood that we have to work through in order to trust that we can be who we are and say what we need to say. To express ourselves in the world really freely for many people is a big issue. It requires a lot of trust. So we have to work through issues of trust, in order to be able to speak authentically. And the irony is that when we do speak our truth, it reinforces and strengthens our trust in our truth and in our being and in our capacity to be full expressions of our own unique humanity, of our own unique being that we are. So they reinforce each other. It's like a dialectic, the two. Trust and speech.

We often don't appreciate the power of speech in our day-to-day interactions, both its destructive and creative, or healing, potentials. Creation and destruction are also in a dialectical relationship. So commensurate with the power our speech has to create, it also has the power to destroy. In our group here we are creating a sacred environment—a sacred context—in which we can use speech in a way that amplifies the power of blessing and healing into the universe. This happens when we apply our speech in a way that celebrates and reinforces what is true, rather than what is false. This amplifies the light of divinity in the universe because the truth *is* the Divine, as we have discussed. Truth—*emet*—is actually one of the Hebrew names for God in the Jewish tradition.[17]

Another interesting thing that we've seen is that to speak the truth doesn't mean that the *content* of what we are saying necessarily feels good. Speaking the truth is simply saying what is, what's really happening. The content can be an experience of contraction, or it can be expansion. The content is, on a fundamental level, irrelevant. The truth is, as a famous rabbi once said, what sets you free. The truth sets you free. Do you know which famous rabbi said that? Jesus, who we will discuss in more detail in later teachings. "The truth will set you free" (John 8:32). In a nutshell this is what we're talking about—it's really the essence of what we're talking about.

So it's not about content but about the transformative potential of the practice of speaking from our truth-center. In this tradition we recognize the power of speech and its transformative, creative potential. So the power to speak the truth embodies a whole other kind of potential that we have in our human experience and we are here, in our Kedumah community, creating a sacred environment to support this possibility.

STUDENT: As we're speaking, I'm wondering about the fifth *chakra* which is in the throat. It must parallel what we're talking about right now, and I just keep thinking that maybe you have something to say about it.

ZVI: In this series of teachings, we're not working directly with the *chakras*. We have teachings about this energetic system in the Kedumah tradition which we will explore in advanced teachings. Many people do experience constriction and contraction in the throat *chakra* when they have issues around being able to speak their truth. The channel of the *chakras* deals with a particular manifestation of the energy of presence, and we have a whole teaching around how to work with it.

Working directly with the energetic channel of the *chakras* is the quickest path of awakening, but it can be the most difficult to work with, because it can be very intense and powerful, and thus can also be very disruptive. So, in the Kedumah path we usually work more directly with the channel of presence, rather than *Shakti*. *Shakti* is the Hindu term for the energy of creation that moves through the *chakras*. We're working here with a different level, a different kind of subtle channel system. Sensing the limbs and the belly actually opens up a different subtle channel. There is, of course, some correspondence with the *chakras*. But we organize it more around the three centers, the three triadic centers that we talked about last class, as well as the fourth and the fifth also that we mentioned last time. Later, more advanced teachings deal with those fourth and fifth centers.

Our practice is just to notice and sense into—feel as deeply and totally as we can—whatever happens in our experience. We apply the tools of this path—sensing, curiosity, erotic dynamism, and not-knowing—and things unfold on their own on the level of presence, rather than directly trying to stir up the energetic channel, which can lead to other complications that can be ungrounding for many people. So ours is a more sober approach.

5

Being True

I'D LIKE TO introduce a new practice that builds upon the previous two practices that we learned, the purification of the limbs and the *tzimt-zum* practice. This new practice—which I recommend only be done in the context of a contemplative group of ten or more people such as our own—is a chant that invokes the Divine Presence in a particular form, in a particular way. To do this we use an ancient Hebrew word that in the Kabbalistic tradition invokes a particular facet of the Divine Presence. This Hebrew word is actually one of the Divine names in the Hebrew Bible, the name *Adonai. Adonai* consists of the four Hebrew letters *ADNY* (אדני) and is also a moniker for *YHVH*, the ineffable name which is not pronounced by traditional Jews. As we discussed, *YHVH* points to Is—Was—Will Be or Being; so here we will chant *Adonai* as a way of manifesting in the dimensions of time and space that which is ineffable and beyond dimension.

There is a lot to say about it but for now I invite you to just sense into the immediate experience of it, and not overlay it with concepts. The practice is to chant the name *Adonai* one-hundred times. One hundred has a particular significance which we'll have a chance to talk about later. For now you're just going to have to trust me that there is a good reason why it's a hundred. Or don't trust me; that's fine too. You can do the practice whether you trust me or not. [Laughter.]

I'll keep count with my special one hundred-beaded *mala* here. You can just follow my lead. And I invite you to also make use of the previous two practices as a kind of introduction for yourselves. Sitting here right now, really sense your body using inner touch. Sense into the groundedness of presence in the body. Allowing your consciousness to settle, dropping into the innermost parts of the belly, as a grounding point. The anchor of the light of the Divine which is the soul, the light of our being. From this posture we chant *Adonai* one hundred times. I'll extend the last *Adonai* so you'll know when we are at the end, and then we'll just sit in silence, sensing the presence until I ring the bell. That'll be the end of the practice.

TALK

So far we have discussed three orienting postures, which correspond to the three triadic centers of consciousness: the belly-center, the heart-center, and the head-center. The orientation of the belly-center is one of embodied presence, experienced as a palpable gathering of essential substance in our body-soul. It can manifest as an immediate and heightened sense of grounded presence in our body, a full-bodied infusion of dense light in our enfleshed soul-organism. We work to develop this center through the practice of sensing the limbs and the direct sensing of the belly-center that were presented in the previous talks.

Those two practices develop an experiential knowledge of embodied presence. We also discussed another ingredient of embodied presence that is necessary for the journey: *emunah* in Hebrew, which means "trust." This arose in the last chapter in terms of the relationship between trust and the journey from contraction to expansion in the archetypal, prototypical story of the exodus from Egypt. We also saw the role of speech in the redemption process and the relationship between speech and trust on the journey.

The inner posture of the heart-center is one of really wanting to know the truth of our experience. We need to want the truth enough to fuel our journey into the contracted places, which are difficult and painful. It would not be possible to move into and through these painful contractions without the heart's love and desire for the truth for its own sake, without the heart's dynamic engagement.

The heart needs to be willing to give up everything to fulfill its desire. If we allow the heart to have its way, it would give up everything for what it wants. Therefore, the orientation of the heart and the posture of the heart is a willingness to give up all of our ideas, all of our attachments, all of our ingrained habitual ways of experiencing in order to truly know what the truth is. The orientation of the head-center is one of an open mind with an attitude of not-knowing. To have a true open mind requires that we adopt a posture of not-knowing.

These are the three orienting postures: staying with our embodied experience, engaging the heart's desire to know the truth for its own sake, and adopting a posture of non-knowing. The magical cocktail of these three orienting postures endows the consciousness with the potential to become an organ of perception that can begin to know in a true sense what we call *da'at*, which literally means "knowledge," but actually points to a nondual intimacy with the immediacy of our experience in the here and now. We use the orienting postures and the techniques of sensing to develop certain muscles—inner muscles—to begin to cultivate this intimacy with our experience in a way that is radically different than the conventional way of experiencing ourselves and the world.

As we discussed, whenever we experience contraction, what is actually contracted is the property of *da'at*; that is, we lose touch with our true knowing. The exile of Egypt, according to the Kabbalah tradition, is an exile of *da'at*; it is an exile of our immediate embodied intimacy with what is happening in the here and now. With *da'at* in exile, with this essential property of reality and our experience unavailable, we are left in an epistemologically narrow and limited place. Our perception is narrow, limited, and constricted. That is *Mitzrayim*. These orienting postures provide us with the optimal alignment of the three centers and the conditions of our consciousness that are necessary to free *da'at* from its exile. It provides us with the conditions necessary to begin to align our epistemology with our ontology—that is to say, to align our perception with the way things actually are.

The journey of harmonizing our perceptions with reality occurs not by bypassing or circumventing the difficulties, the challenges, and the constrictions, but actually by going through slavery in *Mitzrayim* and experiencing all our forty-nine levels of *tumah*—impurity or contraction. The wisdom here is that by sensing into our contractions and redeeming this property of *da'at* in our experience, we are granted the possibility of entry into a new way of experiencing altogether.

This new way of knowing ourselves is what I am calling "expansion." All of a sudden, even if there is the experience of pain, we no longer identify with it; our sense of who and what we are and what reality is can be freed from identification with this pain. We open to a more expanded view. It is like if you try to take a picture of the blue sky with grey clouds, but the picture is cropped so you only see the grey of the clouds. Someone looking at the picture may think that only clouds were present, but if we can zoom out we begin to see that there is actually open sky all around the clouds. This describes the feeling of expansion.

There are a few more things I want to say about these orienting postures because I think it is important for us to establish a solid understanding of them before we enter into the Journey of Wholeness. One point I would like to revisit is how this relates to the principles of trust and truth, both of which I have mentioned in the last few talks.

We discussed last time how speaking the truth invokes an immediate sense of authenticity, regardless of the content. That is to say that when we speak the truth, in the moment, the space opens up to an immediate sense of the real. The space feels real and the content of the speech somehow becomes secondary or background. The foreground is more the quality of space, which is infused with the sense that "this feels true" or "this feels real."

It is no accident that in the ancient Hebrew tradition the main practice commemorating this movement from contraction to expansion is invoked through speech, the ritualized speech of telling the story of the passage from slavery to freedom on *Pesach*, which as I mentioned earlier means the "mouth that speaks." This practice invokes the power of speech, and the power of truth. Truth is fundamentally grounded in the heart-center, because you could say it is the heart's deepest desire. This is why the word for "truth"—*emet* (אמת)—is a technical term that refers to the *sefirah* of *Tiferet*, which correlates anatomically with the heart-center.

But, what exactly is truth? We know it doesn't have to do with content. It is not about finding the "thing" that is true, the content that is true. It is more a quality of Being that is invoked whenever we speak truth, even if we can't say it right. Even if someone's words are broken and their speech is impeded, when their speech is being true you can feel it.

Emet is spelled with the three Hebrew letters: *aleph* (א), *mem* (מ), *tav* (ת). Before I say more about these letters, however, there is an interesting phrase that is recited at the very end of the traditional recitation of the *Shema* prayer. Traditionally the *Shema* prayer contains three paragraphs, all derived from the Hebrew Bible, or Torah. At the very end of the recitation of the third paragraph of the *Shema*, the phrase is chanted: *Adonai Elohaychem Emet*. This means: "YHVH, your God, is Truth."[1] As we discussed, *YHVH* is the ineffable name that is the name of Being.

The relationship between *YHVH* and *EMT* is actually an equation. *YHVH* = *EMT* (אמת=יהוה), is what the phrase is declaring. In the most central prayer of the tradition, the one that is recited every morning, evening, and as death approaches, we declare that *YHVH* is truth. The prophet Jeremiah declares this explicitly with the words, "*YHVH Elohim is Emet*" (Jer. 10:10). The Talmud also explicitly states: The seal

of *YHVH is emet*, truth.² And the *sefirah* associated with the word
emet is *Tiferet*, which is also the *sefirah* of the Divine name *YHVH*.³

When truth is invoked and expressed, we are invoking and expressing Being itself, the Divine itself. We are calling the soul of creation
with all of its light, purity, luminosity, and love into the immediacy
of our experience. Furthermore, when we more deeply examine the
Hebrew word, it reveals even more secrets.

We find the first secret in the unique construction of the word itself.
If you know the Hebrew language, you might notice something very
interesting about it. The first letter of the word—*alef*—is the very first
letter of the alphabet. The last letter—*tav*—is the very last letter of the
alphabet. The middle letter—*mem*—is the very middle letter of the
alphabet. If Is-Was-Will Be is *emet*, then we can begin to outline the
nature of this equation. *Alef* corresponds to "was," *mem* to "is" and
tav to "will be." Another way of mapping this follows the Rabbinic
teaching that *alef* is past, *mem* is present, and *tav* future.⁴

According to the most ancient Kabbalistic text, the *Sefer Yetzirah*,
which means the "Book of Creation," all of creation is an expression
of the Hebrew letters and numbers.⁵ *Alef, mem,* and *tav* thus sym-
bolize or point to the totality of the Hebrew alphabet, which is the
totality of creation. It is the totality of the cosmos, which, as we have
discussed, is the Divine itself. When we say "God" in this tradition,
we mean the very Being of creation in its totality, the one Being that
we are all part of. It is not only that God is in us; we are also in God.
Let's look at this more deeply.

If *alef* is past, *mem* is present, and *tav* is future, then this word holds
a deeper secret in terms of our orientation to the three centers. *Mem*,
the middle letter, which represents the present, is significant in the
ancient Hebrew tradition in several ways. Firstly, its numerical value
is forty. Every letter in the Hebrew alphabet is assigned a numerical
value. Much of the western tradition of sacred numerology comes
from this numeric system that we call *gematria*, the system of sacred

correspondences between the numbers and letters in the ancient Hebrew tradition.

The number forty appears many times in the Torah. Noah's flood lasted forty days. Moses spent forty days on the mountain waiting to receive the revelation. For forty years the Children of Israel wandered in the desert. The list goes on. The question is, why forty? The number forty, which is really just the letter *mem*, has to do with the potential for transformation that is present in every moment.[6] If we are able to immerse ourselves completely in the moment, or as I like to call it, the *mement*, then transformation is guaranteed.

For example, *mem*, or forty, is the required volume of water in a kosher *mikvah*.[7] A *mikvah* is an ancient ritual bath that was used as a means of purification of the body-soul. It's found in the ancient Hebrew texts, in the Torah. The *mikvah* is used to this day in traditional Jewish communities as a means of purification. There are very strict ancient laws that determine what constitutes a kosher *mikvah*. One of the requirements is that it contain forty *se'ah* of water, which is an ancient measure of volume. Forty is therefore not only transformative in the realm of time, but also in the realm of space. In this example, a body of living water constitutes the transformative space.

We can see a correlation here with the three Turnings of the Wheel of Torah: space, time, and in the third turning of the wheel of Torah—which is our current paradigm—person. Interestingly enough, the great medieval sage Maimonides, who was not a Kabbalist but posited an Aristotelian metaphysics, has a fascinating comment in his magnum opus, a code of law called the *Mishneh Torah*. In the section that discusses the laws of a *mikvah*, he states that if you do not have an actual *mikvah* available, that entering into what he calls *meimei ha-da'at*, the "waters of *da'at*," you can experience the same phenomenological process of purification and transformation of consciousness.[8]

It is quite amazing to hear Maimonides talking about the "waters of *da'at*" because it speaks directly to the Kedumah perspective. Kedumah declares that in our day and age we are called to embody the "waters of *da'at*"—the forty *se'ah* of the *mikvah*—in our being, immediately and directly. These are the waters of nondual intimacy with our experience in the here and now. The letter *mem*, the number forty, and the present moment are all the truth. The heart of the truth, the *mem*, which is at the center of *emet*, is the now. For us to enter into the waters of *da'at*, our heart needs to engage our experience in the now, as fully and completely as possible.

However, the heart of course is not an isolated organ, even though it can sound that way when we talk about it. The heart is intimately unified with all the other centers of our consciousness and with the body, the belly, and the head. In particular, there is an inner channel that threads the heart to two organs of our being: one is the tongue and the other is the genitals.[9] Erotically, this makes sense given the centrality of the mouth and the genitals in the expression of eros, which is fundamentally grounded in the heart's desire and engagement with the intimacy of the moment.

Eros can be expressed both with another person or on one's own in the form of intimacy with one's own life force. Both the tongue and the genitals perform the particular function of expressing our heart and sharing it with the world, with another. When the tongue speaks the truth, which is grounded in the center of the heart, then the mouth becomes an organ of creation. In the book of Genesis (1:3), it says *Vayomer Elohim Ye-hi Ohr, Va-yehi Ohr*: "And God said 'let there be light,' and there was light." The act of creation occurs through Divine speech. We see here the potential for us human beings to be God incarnate, to create light and blessing—as well as, God forbid, destruction and harm—through our speech, through the expression of the tongue, which is connected in this invisible channel with the heart. You can now see the deep relationship between speech, truth, contraction, expansion, and the power of creation.

This also applies to the genitals. The genitals, of course, are organs of creation. Both male and female genitals are organs of creation for they embody the generative potential of reality. Ideally, the generative expressions of the genitals and the tongue happen in tandem with an experience of immediacy with what is real. If we use the example of sex, which is a particular expression of the creative potential, we see the important role of the heart. Ideally, qualities of love and appreciation saturate our organs of communication as they express themselves sexually. That is to say, this is an experience in which the mouth and the genitals are not dissociated or split off from their source in the heart. The Zohar and other Kabbalah texts often use the metaphor of kissing to describe the mystical union that can occur both through the mouth and through the genitals.[10]

When we integrate the three orienting postures, and we include the expressive potential of the tongue and the genitals, then we have the workings of the *merkavah*. *Merkavah* is a Hebrew word that means "chariot" or "vehicle" and is described in the ancient texts as a particular kind of mystical wisdom vehicle.[11]

In the Kedumah tradition, the *merkavah* is the essential form our consciousness takes when it becomes an instrument for the spontaneous expression of *drash*. The practice of inquiry, *drash*, in its optimized form, is the immediate, open, engaged, grounded, and spontaneous inquiry into the here and now. But, this is only possible when the very substance of our body-soul—our living consciousness—manifests as the mystical vehicle of the *merkavah*. For this to happen, the three centers of the central channel of the Tree of Life (the head, heart, and belly) need to be integrated and activated along with the expressive potential of the genitals and the tongue. Ultimately the *merkavah* is one expression of the Presence Body that I mentioned in the first talk. We will explore this in more advanced teachings.

Contrary to conventional belief, when we simply allow our experience to be what it is and sense into the raw immediacy of it, on the sensation level, with an interest and openness to being surprised, then our experience unfolds in an organic manner, free from the usual storylines and narrow range of experience predetermined by our thinking, conditioned mind.

We discover that other realities are not only possible, but are brewing and bubbling under the surface, ready to reveal their riches to us. We open to the possibility of discovering what is beneath the surface by harnessing our capacities of consciousness in an intentional manner. This is where practice becomes important, because our practice develops these capacities. We harness and develop these capacities of our soul through our practices and the sincerity of our heart. Through our practice and through the power of grace (which we will discuss in more detail in a later session), our consciousness transforms into a vehicle that can go where no human has gone before. That is to say, we go beyond the slave mentality of being in contraction, and we open to the unknown vistas of expansion.

Now it should be clearer why it is important that we integrate some degree of trust. We are talking about going into experiences that can be scary and opening to them could even potentially expose hidden layers of trauma in the nervous system. Opening to these dimensions can challenge all of our internalized ideas of who we are and what reality is. This requires a great deal of trust—trust that somehow we are held by something real, by something true, by something loving. We trust that it is okay to venture beyond our limited range of familiar experience, beyond our *arba amot*, our four cubic feet of contraction.

The phrase "four cubic feet"—*arba amot*—comes from the Talmud, and it refers to the range that constitutes our personal space.[12] We all have our four cubic feet of conventional space, our conditioned optimal distance with our experience. We live within these four feet, and all of our experience we fit into those four feet. To venture beyond, we need to have trust that we won't splat, get crushed, be admonished, rebuked, shamed, or castrated.

In other words, we have all kinds of unconscious material that keeps us trapped in our four *amot*, that keeps us afraid of expanding into what is actually here beyond these four *amot*. Trust is the ingredient that is necessary to even begin to move beyond our conditioned sense of contracted space. That is why last session we talked about the phrase *Bizchut Ha-emunah Nigalu Avoteinu Mi-Mitzrayim.* It is through the merit of their *emunah*, their trust, that our ancestors were redeemed from *Mitzrayim*, from the constricted places. Only through the merit of trust is this possible.

Mishkan is a Hebrew word that means "dwelling place" or "sanctuary." In the Hebrew Bible, this word refers to the sanctuary that was built by the Children of Israel in the desert after they left Egypt. They constructed a traveling sanctuary that they could take down and put up, wherever they went. This is such a central principle that much of the book of Exodus deals with the exact details of the construction of this structure, down to the literal nuts and bolts. It might strike you as bizarre that the Hebrew Bible would devote so much time and energy to the construction of some portable structure. Why were these details so important to the ancient lineage holders?

In Kedumah, we do not read these things historically, but instead we read them mystically. *Mishkan* literally means "a dwelling place." It has the same root as the Hebrew word *Shechinah*, which is the Divine Presence. Thus the *mishkan* is a dwelling place, a structure that was designed to hold the light of *YHVH* to shine into the world—the light of Being, the light of creation. Somehow, a sacred structure was necessary for the light of Being to shine in the dimension of space.

In this teaching, we understand the function of the *mishkan* through the lens of the third turning of the wheel of Torah. That is, we do not relate to the structure of the *mishkan* through the dimension of space, but rather through the dimension of person. This is similar to how we related to the function of the *mikvah* ritual discussed earlier. In the third turning of the wheel of Torah, the *mishkan* resides within us, as well as without us. The *mishkan* is thus a structure of consciousness that holds the individual light of our soul, which is a reflection of the light of Being.[13]

In fact, as is often the case, this third-turning perspective is alluded to in the ancient texts. A verse in the book of Exodus (25:8) states, *Va-asu Li Mikdash Vishachanti Bitocham*: "Make for me a sanctuary that I may dwell within them." The Torah commentaries ask, "What does that mean?" "Make for me a sanctuary that I may dwell within them" contains a contradiction. It should say, "Make for me a sanctuary that I may dwell within *it*." Why does it say 'within *them*'?"

One of the most famous medieval biblical commentaries, Rashi, explains: When the text says, "that I may dwell within them," it means that God intends to dwell "within each and every one of them," that is, within each and every person. The physical sanctuary needed to be built so that the light could shine within each person. What does this mean? What kind of physical structure facilitates the Divine light shining through the individual soul?

The one hundred *Adonai* chant that we did at the beginning of this meeting is what I call the *mishkan* chant. Through it, we are constructing a dwelling place, a structure of consciousness, that holds us so our light can shine, our expansion can ripple through the cosmos unabated. This chant is one of the hidden practices that Kedumah is revealing in our day. This practice is not explicitly mentioned in any texts nor is it known to practitioners of the second turning of the wheel of Torah; that is, it is not part of the normative tradition of Judaism. However, it is alluded to in the classic Kabbalistic text, *Sha'arei Orah*, by Joseph Gikatilla.[14]

We chant the Divine name *Adonai* one hundred times because, when it describes the construction of the *mishkan* in the Bible (Ex. 38:27), it says that it was constructed with one hundred *adanim*. The term *adanim*, which is translated literally as "sockets," is the same word as the plural form of the Divine name *Adonai*. In the first turning reading of the text, these one hundred "sockets" refer to specific elements of the sacred architecture of the portable *mishkan* built in the desert by the Israelites. The text describes a series of beams going into one hundred sockets. The word that is used is *adanim*, which is the plural form of *Adonai*, one of the Divine names.

On the mystical level, the text is alluding to reciting *Adonai* one hundred times, which corresponds with the traditional Jewish custom of reciting one hundred blessings a day.[15] In the Kedumah teachings, this practice serves to help develop our own personal *mishkan*, which is the structure of presence that holds the essential inner vehicle—the *merkavah*—which corresponds with the innermost chamber, the Holy of Holies, of the *mishkan*. We need the sacred structure of the *mishkan* to support the development of the inner vehicle of the *merkavah*. It is the *merkavah* that we travel with into the hidden worlds. When we enact this chant, a very powerful presence is generated.

You can say that the sensing practice and the belly practice develop the inner vehicle of presence—the *merkavah*—and the one hundred *Adonai* practice develops the structural vessel of presence—the *mishkan*. That is how these practices work together. In the book of Exodus (38:27) it states that the one hundred *adanim*, or sockets, were made out of silver. That is why I have one hundred silver beads on this *mala* that I carry around. It represents the one hundred *adanim*, to invoke the one hundred silver sockets that hold the *mishkan* together.

How does all this relate to trust? We trust when we know we are held. If we don't think or believe that we are being held, we do not trust. We need to know and feel the supportive holding of the *mishkan* vehicle in order to settle and drop into our experience more deeply. Only then can the *merkavah* develop. We generate an intensification of the *mishkan* consciousness, so that we can settle and relax, so that we can be steady.

This is alluded to in the book of Exodus (17:12) where it states, *Vayehi Yadav Emunah*, which is usually translated as "And his hands were steady." This verse refers to when Moses' hands are held up while fighting the nation of *Amalek*, which represents the forces of evil and darkness. It states that "his hands were steady." The Hebrew word there is *emunah*, the same word that means "faith" or "trust."

This is to say that *emunah* is a particular kind of trust that has a sense of being held up, of being held steady, so that we do not fall. That is the kind of trust that *emunah* invokes. When it says that the Children of Israel were only redeemed because of their *emunah*, it means that they had trusted that they were held by the Divine Presence enough to move through *Mitzrayim*, to move through those constricted and contracted places. That is the kind of trust that we need.[16]

Trust is also intimately connected to *da'at*. There is a verse in the book of Hosea (2:20) that states, *Va-erastich Li Be-emunah Vi-ya-da'at Et Adonai*. God says, "And I will betroth you to me with *emunah*, with trust, and you will know *YHVH*." The Hebrew states "You will have *da'at* of *YHVH*." That is to say, if we betroth ourselves to the Divine Being through *emunah*, then *da'at* of *YHVH*, of Being, will open and become available.[17]

You see now how all these facets of the journey are essential ingredients, and how they are all interconnected. I am just explicating them as they appear to me in my consciousness. I can sense the intelligence of Being, how it reveals truth; it is very mysterious how it comes out of nowhere. It just arises out of complete emptiness. We need a great deal of trust to abide with what arises in our experience, and also with our speech, to trust what comes out of our mouths.

[The following discussion takes place after an experiential exercise.]

STUDENT: We observed that there was a palpable safety in our little group, a sense of trust. We also observed that when someone in our group said something that came across as very true and meaningful, my experience of space changed for me. Like I felt my body in a different way, in a new way. And it was good.

ZVI: How would you describe the experience of safety or trust? What did that feel like?

STUDENT: I felt that I could say what I was feeling and it would be okay.

ZVI: And what about your experience right now?

STUDENT: It feels very different than the usual experience. My body feels light and transparent. And there is a loving feeling to it.

ZVI: How is it for your heart to feel this loving light?

STUDENT: I am deeply touched.

ZVI: Thank you.

STUDENT: I found the more that I was in my body, the more I could trust. Because the feeling of okayness is something in my body.

ZVI: Are you aware of the feeling of "okayness" in your body right now?

STUDENT: Yes. Now I do.

ZVI: So just allow it to do what it wants in your body. What happens now?

STUDENT: It spreads, and it spreads beyond my body now, too. So, like, the feeling of trust was the same as feeling expanded.

ZVI: What's your heart like?

STUDENT: Inspired, and joyful. Connected.

ZVI: What about your head-center?

STUDENT: Light. I can't say any more on that part.

ZVI: You can't say any more? Why not?

STUDENT: Because that's it, up there. Just light.

ZVI: Just light. What kind of light? Can you describe it?

STUDENT: Like a pulsing or buzzing.

ZVI: What was it about the question that made you laugh, when I asked you about the head?

STUDENT: Because I knew that you were going to ask me and I knew that I couldn't find another word for it. Just "light."

ZVI: It sounds like there's a particular kind of light. There's a buzzing, a pulsation. What's its impact on you, when you just hold the totality of your experience right now?

STUDENT: The first thing that came to me was the *mem* word, or truth. A space of truth.

ZVI: Yes. Truth has a particular kind of presence to it. There is a dynamism and at the same time there is an unchanging and steady quality to the presence. It impacts the whole field.

STUDENT: I have a comment or question about the *Adonai* chant, and I wanted to bring it up because something sort of unusual happened to me. While I was doing it, I normally don't get olfactory hallucinations, that's only really happened to me a handful of times ever. But while I was doing the *Adonai* chant, in the beginning, I got this really strong smell of marijuana in my nose. I'm not a pot smoker at all. I like the smell, but marijuana isn't really part of my life, so I was surprised to have that come up, and then it stayed like that for a while, and then it evolved to just a very nice pleasant wood-burning smell. And I mentioned it to other students and one of them mentioned that back in the day there would have been a lot of incense burning in the temple. I'm just wondering if there's a scent connection with that. And it occurred to me that the smell that I wound up smelling smelled like a piñon incense that I have, so I don't know what to make of that. I just wanted to mention that and see if you have any ideas about the fact that I smelled marijuana while I was doing the chant.

ZVI: Thank you for sharing that. In general, the olfactory sense—the sense of smell—is significant when it opens up in meditation. In the Kedumah teachings—which in this series of talks is primarily drawing from the Jewish mystical tradition—the prototype for the understanding of the sense of smell is found in the story of the Garden of Eden in the book of Genesis. In this story there is a tree—the Tree of Knowledge of Good and Evil—that Adam and Eve are not supposed to eat from. In chapters two and three of the book of Genesis it discusses how alluring this tree was to the physical senses, and ultimately it describes how all the senses were engaged in the process of eating from the fruit of this forbidden tree.

The text specifically states how they "looked" at the tree, which was pleasing to the sight, and how they "touched" it. "Hearing" is also mentioned, and obviously "eating" is mentioned. The only sense that's not mentioned is the sense of smell. And for this reason some of the Kabbalists posit that the sense of smell, of all our senses, is the most pure in terms of its perceptive capacities. It is the only one of our human senses that did not participate in the act of eating from the Tree of Knowledge of Good and Evil.[18]

Also in the book of Genesis (2:7), where it describes the creation of the human being, it says that God "breathed into his nostrils the breath of life," *Va-yipach Be-apav Ruach Chayyim*. In this verse the Hebrew word for "breath/spirit" is *ruach*, which is the same word for "smell," *re'ach*. So we see the human spirit is intimately connected to the nostrils, to our breath and to our sense of smell. An alternate Hebrew word for breath, *neshimah*, is also the same word as that for soul, *neshamah*. Only the vowel sounds are different, but the letters are the same.

So when someone comes into more direct contact with their spirit or soul, they may notice a more subtle and ethereal sense of smell opening up. The fact that you are having a pronounced ethereal sense of smell opening up makes a lot of sense to me in terms of just the phenomenology of meditation in general and in terms of this practice in particular.

However, in terms of the ethereal smell of marijuana, I don't really know. It might have something to do with the fact that we are in Boulder, Colorado right now. [Laughter.] I've never researched the herbalogical origins and roots—so to speak—of marijuana, and I don't remember having a personal experience of the ethereal scent of marijuana, so I can't say what the inner significance is. I do remember reading something a while ago where someone claimed that there was evidence of cannabis in the Torah. But I don't know if that's true or not; I personally have not looked into it.

Now about the *bisamim*, the incense in the Temple, it's true what you say. The piñon smell, I wonder if that's related to one of the spices used in the incense in the Temple. There was a very special combination of specific spices that were used in the incense used in the Temple, and we actually know exactly which spices were used, but the tradition of the exact proportions is shrouded in mystery. Some people claim to have knowledge of that. So that would be interesting to get ahold of that formula and see if that indeed is what you're smelling.

STUDENT: Do you know what the spices were?

ZVI: Yes. There are eleven of them, and I can show you what they are if you are interested. They are listed in detail in the Talmud, the ancient Rabbinic collection of oral lore, and they are also mentioned in the traditional daily prayer liturgy.[19] One of them is *mar dror*, which is usually translated as "frankincense and myrrh," and a host of others. I can show you the text and maybe you can do some research for us about the marijuana and let us know if there is a relationship.

There is a Hebrew phrase that's used in the Hebrew texts when there is something being discussed that is not fully understood, or is complex and difficult to discuss or explain. The phrase is *tzarich iyyun*, which means, "It requires further inquiry." I think this is an area of experience and knowledge that warrants a *tzarich iyyun*.

It would be interesting to investigate which ethereal smells arise with the chanting of the different Divine names. The *Adonai* chant is a very particular practice that evokes a particular presence, and a very particular smell came up for you. Let us not forget that this group is a laboratory. We are in some sense reawakening an ancient mystical tradition here, even as it is simultaneously the revelation of something new. So all of these experiences are worth paying attention to, so we can gather our collective wisdom and learn what we can from them. *Tzarich iyyun*.

I've had a lot of different inner smells come up in meditation and many other kinds of strange experiences. And by the way they're not all pleasant smells. There can be the "ethereal dung" scent, for example. There can be all kinds of beastly and noxious inner substances that arise as we move through different parts of our unconscious. All this information comes through our senses, and if our senses are open on the subtle levels—and partly what we are doing here is developing our capacity to sense these subtleties more deeply—then we begin to experience all kinds of things that are fascinating and strange and delightful and confusing. This is all part of our inquiry.

Drash doesn't stop with the contraction. As we enter into various states of nonconventional experience, we continue to investigate those experiences to find out what their truth is. The discovery unfolds ad infinitum, into every nook and cranny of our experience. Ultimately our inquiry has the potential to become an organic expression of life; we become a living vehicle of discovery. This vehicle is what I call the *merkavah*, and the *merkavah* is in constant transformation. The *merkavah* can travel to different dimensions of nonduality, to radically different realities altogether. There's all kinds of interesting terrain that's not mapped out by science or by geography.

STUDENT: It's amazing.

ZVI: It is amazing. It's an amazing world that we live in. It's a blessing to be able to perceive it, actually, without the usual filters.

I also want to mention one more thing, and this has to do with trauma. We're doing practices here that tend to make the unconscious conscious. If there's trauma in our system, these practices may expose it in a way that may be difficult to integrate. If while practicing inquiry you notice yourself in a dissociated state or if there is any other sign of trauma being triggered, then just come back to the foundational practices. Just sense your arms and legs as deeply as you can. It's not really useful to inquire from a condition of shock or dissociation.

If you do notice those things come up, that's really good information to have. If it becomes problematic then you may want to get very targeted kind of trauma work. There's all kinds of modalities now that work with trauma in very precise ways. What we're doing here is not therapy. This is a spiritual path. This means that we are not oriented to working with severe trauma in a therapeutic way. One value in doing trauma therapy is that it will allow us to actually be more in our body as we go through those things, and then our practice, our inner inquiry, will be more effective and spiritually transformative. Then, in due course, we can bring the presence of inquiry to those traumatic imprints in constructive ways.

6
The Now

WE WILL START today with a few minutes of the *tzimtzum* practice, followed by the *mishkan* practice of chanting *Adonai* one hundred times, which generates the *mishkan*—the structure of presence—as described in our last session, followed by a period of silent meditation.

STUDENT: Is the chant supposed to be done with the whole body, with all of our centers? It's hard for me because I'm kind of in my head when I'm using words. And it's also new and I've never really been a chanter. I guess the question is: Are we meant to or supposed to be coming from a deeper place in our body, in our belly; is there a way to engage that with more of our body even though we're using words?

ZVI: Yes. We start with sensing the belly, which is the practice we did a few meetings ago. This helps to open up the belly-center of our consciousness, of our soul. Then, if we engage the chant after we settle more, after our presence gathers more in the belly, then we'll naturally be more embodied and whole in our body. The embodied presence of the soul can then be engaged and impacted more deeply by the sacred sound of the chant. We're invoking these sacred sounds because they invoke certain qualities of presence. There are also the

119

ideogrammatic shapes of the letters that impact us that we haven't talked about yet.

So it's more about being in an open, receptive, and embodied posture and invoking the sound and just allowing it to saturate the consciousness. And, like any practice, this is a practice. Meaning that if we have other things going on in our life and our mind is occupied, then we just keep coming back to the chant, allowing it to become more the foreground of our immediate experience. If we find ourselves getting distracted, then we just come back. In time, the practice will work its wisdom on us.

Last class we talked about the origins of this particular chant and its place in the teaching, its particular contemplative function in terms of developing consciousness. The impact of the practice is also cumulative and exponential. That is, the more people we have practicing it together, the greater the force of the impact.

This is the whole function of the tradition of having a *minyan*, having a quorum of people practicing together. This has to do with the amplification and the intensification of the presence that is invoked when we practice together in a group. In this tradition, which has its lineage roots in the Kabbalistic tradition, ten is the magical number. This has to do with the ten *sefirot* of the Tree of Life and the way in which these ten Divine qualities provide the architecture of the cosmos as it manifests in creation. So when we have a *minyan*, we have a minimum of ten people, which is what fills in Living Being, the living soul of the cosmic universe.

How do you experience the presence of the group right now? What's your sense? What's the field like?

STUDENT: I experience the presence inside of me being more heightened and that I have kind of my own scale, like I could kind of compare when I'm more or less present. So that's how I feel the presence of the group. And also I experience my presence taking up a wider space. It's like in the whole room. It's more delocalized.

Zvi: You can feel yourself in the whole room?

Student: Yeah.

Zvi: So you are recognizing an important property of Presence, that it is not bound to our conventional body boundaries or to space.

Student: What you said resonates for me, because it feels like the space is holding something already that seems to have accumulated. There seems to be a Presence in the space. And I find it doesn't have that much to do with the specific practices. In fact, I kind of did my own version in the beginning, and I kind of dropped down, like really down, into the feeling of gravity in the body. And then—and this part is a little far out because I have been connecting with the dead and I've been actually reading about some Hasidic masters and their work in that area—I instantly had an image come of a certain place where I have been and I felt connected to those souls. So that's what came. But that was more just a furthering of my own process, which I'm already in, and it was just opening that door a little wider. But in general the space just feels safe and the sense of presence is that it has a sense of texture that is warm and accepting in some way.

Zvi: What's the texture like? Use your inner sensing, your inner touching.

Student: Well it's kind of also like what you were saying, that you feel yourself, so there's a texture that is just the texture of "feelingness," rather than a particular feeling. And at the same time I feel it around myself, rather than just inside. And the surprising part is that in the space I feel a certain kind of warm, holding texture.

Zvi: Yes, thank you.

STUDENT: As you [and the other student] were talking, a verse from the Torah came to my mind and it just circled there, repeatedly, and I was trying to find explanations for what it means but it just circled there like a mantra, and it's not even a sentence that I recall often. There is this place when Jacob has this dream and he says, *Yesh Adonai Ba-Makom Hazeh Va-ani Lo Yadati*. So we chanted this Divine name and I was kind of fascinated to see what it means for me. And I'll keep exploring it.

ZVI: Yes. This verse, from Genesis 28:16, means: "*YHVH* is in this place, but I did not know it." And the verb for "I did not know" is the same word *da'at* that we've been exploring. Yaakov—Jacob— couldn't sense *YHVH*, which, as we have discussed, is best translated as "Being" or "Is-Was-Will Be." When we do the *Adonai* chant, we're not pronouncing the *YHVH* because traditionally we don't pronounce the ineffable name. Instead we say *Adonai*, which represents the embodied presence of Being in the Kabbalistic tradition.

So we're invoking more the sense of Presence, in the particular form of the structure of the *mishkan*, which is the essential structure that holds the light of Presence in every single person's being and in the environmental space. We talked about it in more detail last time, but many of you are speaking to the sense of the relationship between the inner and the outer when it comes to the experience of Presence and how our relationship to space shifts when we're more present.

STUDENT: During the practice I had this very powerful experience where I felt deeply held by the group and there was this care, not the fake kind of care where you feel like you have to be nice because you're supposed to be but genuine care that's connected to the heart. And so, like my experience of interconnectedness of everything, it felt powerful. Every time I tap into this Kedumah group, I can feel a very high vibration and it comes right away, so it's very powerful.

ZVI: What do you notice in the center of your head right now?

STUDENT: I feel like one of the Alex Grey paintings where there is a lightning rod going through my head and it's filled with light.

ZVI: I don't know the paintings, but I think I'm getting the gist of it. So if you sense the lightning rod and the light, what do you notice happens to your whole consciousness?

STUDENT: Well what happens is that there's a dropping that happens, and then I can feel into myself as part of everything.

ZVI: So you feel like you're not separate from everything. Is that what you mean?

STUDENT: Right. I mean, I know that I am, which is really good.

ZVI: You know that you are what?

STUDENT: Separate.

ZVI: Oh. You are?

STUDENT: Well. [Laughter.]

ZVI: It doesn't look that way from here.

STUDENT: Well. [Laughter.]

ZVI: What's happening right now?

STUDENT: I'm laughing. [More laughter.] It's just like, it's sort of interesting to try to describe, you know, like states and experience with words.

ZVI: Yeah. Don't try.

STUDENT: Now I just feel a tremendous amount of awe. I guess it could be associated with *yirah* [the Hebrew principle of awe], but it's really just not-knowing. Like, how everything can be so mysterious, or so beautiful, or, and I know sometimes so horrible, and just, sort of feeling like the whole spectrum of life.

ZVI: Yeah. Thank you. Good segue for the talk ...

TALK

In the last session we explored the Hebrew word *emet*—truth—and its mystical meaning. We discussed the relationship between truth and Being, between *emet* and *YHVH,* and how the inner essence of truth represented by the letter *mem*, the center of the word *emet*, represents the Now, the present moment, the *mement*. This means that the truth of Being is accessed in our immediate intimate experience through direct contact with what is happening in the moment.

That is why our *drash* practice, our practice of inquiry, is guided by the three orienting postures: the head-center, the heart-center, the belly-center: a posture of openness, of not-knowing, in the head; a posture of engagement and interest of the heart; a posture of the embodied experience of the present moment in the belly, extending to the whole body.

Each of these centers has many capacities and qualities that are activated and necessary for the full engagement of the throttle of the *merkavah*. We talked about the *merkavah* last time. The *merkavah* is the vehicle that we journey with and through. It is the vehicle of our consciousness as it is primed and fueled and launched into the present moment. The journey through this portal opens up our experience into unknown terrain, and the paradox to the ordinary conventional mind is that being in the unknown opens up the doorway to true knowing, *da'at*, which is an immediate, intimate union with our experience in the here and now. As we have discussed, *da'at* is rooted in the sense of intimate union.

I want to talk a little bit more about this dialectical relationship between contraction and expansion, and how it relates to wholeness. We talked about the constellation of speech, trust, *da'at*, knowing, being, and the moment. Now I want to look at how this constellation relates to the Journeys of Contraction and Expansion in each of these three centers and also to talk more experientially about what exactly we mean by expansion.

Many of the exercises I have introduced explore how, when we go into our contractions and fully embrace them, we move through *Mitzrayim*, we move through the constricted and contracted places with an orientation of trust, of *emunah*. We discovered in the last chapter how *emunah*—basic trust—works, but there is a lot more about expansion itself that is already in the field here, experientially.

In the head-center, contraction appears in many forms. Usually it manifests as a kind of psychological contraction. In other words, how we view or perceive reality is determined by historical or conceptual overlays, images, beliefs, and ideas. That is the normal way of development of the mind and the way of perception. Usually we do not think of those things as contractions, but from the purview of expansion we recognize that actually seeing reality through the lens of concepts is a kind of perceptual contraction.

Many teachings talk about this and have various mechanisms of working with these overlays. In Advaita Vedanta, for example, they talk about this process in terms of *adyaropa*, the Sanskrit term that means "superimposition." From their perspective, the way we see with our conventional view of reality is not true reality; what we are seeing is a superimposition, an overlay that occludes true reality. It is an overlay of concepts, ideas, and beliefs about the way reality is.[1]

In Advaita Vedanta, they employ certain methods of inquiry, called *apavada*, which attempt to discriminate what is false perception from what is real perception. Shankara uses the example of someone walking down the street and who sees what appears to be a snake in the road. It looks like a snake, but upon further investigation they find out in fact it is not a snake but a rope. This image is not just used by Shankara, but also more broadly in Indian philosophy, including in Buddhist texts.[2]

So you see, there is a superimposition of an image over what was actually there. And this represents the entire way we conventionally perceive reality. There are many kinds of contractions in the head-center, but this is the most ubiquitous. It actually affects the way we perceive and typifies a contracted view.

Another way contraction appears in the head-center is when we identify with our thoughts. Identifying with thoughts can happen in two main ways: rejecting them or believing them. They are both expressions of identifications. One is simply a rejecting identification and the other one is an internalizing identification. Penetrating and developing understanding of either of these contractions has the potential to open up into expansion. Expansion through the head-center is simply seeing reality as it is, without any superimposition or overlay. This is also an expression of *da'at*, true knowledge.

When we talk about expansion in the head-center, we talk about it in terms of its relationship to conventional knowledge. Conventional knowledge is the identification with a thought, with information as a kind of object, a commodity that we collect in our memory and utilize for some purpose. It could be some bit of information that we identify with ourselves, or that we correlate with another person or some other object in the universe. All conventional knowing entails a separation between the knower and the known. Somebody knows something or someone. There is always a duality of knower and known. That is the conventional experience of knowledge.

In the expanded experience of knowledge, which we are calling true *da'at*, there is a nondual kind of knowing. It does not make sense to the conventional mind, but in the experience of it, the knower and the known are one and the same. There is no separation between the two. That is to say, the one who knows and that which is known are the same thing. They are not separated; the knower and the known are one.[3]

Contraction in the heart-center also appears in many ways, although it is often recognized as a contraction in our emotional experience. Again, this most commonly happens through either blocking our emotional experiences, on the one hand, or identifying with them on the other. When we neither repress our emotions nor act on them but rather allow them to fully manifest, the heart-center can then open up into expansion.

Da'at on the heart level brings in more of the richness of intimacy, of union; it is the heart knowing the other through being one with the other. We usually recognize this as the experience of being intimate with another. When we say we know someone well, we do not mean intellectual knowing. It is true that if we are open in the head-center then we may be aware of that dimension of intimacy; there can be a knowing that is a meeting of the minds. Usually, however, the more familiar experience of intimacy is when the heart melts and you feel that you know the other through and through. This can develop to the point of union, where there is no longer any separation. "I am to my beloved and my beloved is to me." *Ani Lidodi Vidodi Li*, as it says in the Song of Songs (6:3). This is heartfelt union.

The heart is also the doorway into what are traditionally called in the Kabbalistic texts the "patriarchs of the *merkavah*"—*Avot Ha-Merkavah*—though personally I prefer the word "ancestors." Occasionally they are called "forefathers," but really we should call them the "three-fathers," after Abraham, Isaac, and Jacob and the "four-mothers" should really be in honor of Sarah, Rebecca, Rachel, and Leah.[4] [Laughter.]

The ancestors of the *merkavah* are Abraham, Isaac, and Jacob, but there are also Moses, Aaron, Joseph, and David as well as Sarah, Rebecca, Rachel, and Leah. According to the Kedumah view these are not historical figures. They are code words for the *sefirot*—the various Divine qualities—the qualities of Being that manifest in the existential realm of presence as the created world. These are the pure qualities, which are the differentiations of the nondual light of Being that manifest as creation.

Abraham is Love (*Chesed*), Isaac is Strength (*Gevurah*), Jacob is Truth or Beauty (*emet* or *Tiferet*), and so on.[5] Each ancestor represents a primary expression of this pure light of Being. Working with our emotions, with the contractions of our heart, is the necessary gateway to open up to the integration of our ancestors. Our ancestors in this view are literally the ancestors of our inner being; they are the *sefirot*—the primordial Lights of Being that have manifested who and what we are. These primordial lights are expressions of a realm that is not bound by time and space. Nevertheless, they manifest themselves into the many forms of manifested creation. These are our ancestors from the Kedumah perspective.

Thus, working through our emotions as well as the contractions of the heart- and belly-centers is a way of integrating our ancestors, and they become the ancestors of the *merkavah*. The *merkavah* is not just the vehicle that we use to journey; it is ultimately a nondual phenomenon because it is both the vehicle and the terrain. Through the integration of the ancestors, as what we are and as what we live, we become not just a vehicle of transformation, a *merkavah*, but we also embody the full expression of that vehicle. This is becoming a full human being, a full-bodied human expression of Living Being. We become the cosmic body of God, as we have discussed in past meetings.

This brings us to the Journey of Wholeness, which has to do with the integration of the ancestors and the embodiment of the Divine lights into our mundane human experience. But before wholeness is even possible, we need to be more firmly situated in a process which is referred to in the first chapter of Ezekiel as *ratzo vashov*, which means "running and returning" (1:14). The first chapter of Ezekiel describes what is traditionally termed the *ma'aseh merkavah*, the "workings of the chariot." Many of the secret teachings on the *merkavah* are found in that chapter.[6]

This points to a dynamic dialectic in our experience in the movement from contraction to expansion, and then from expansion to contraction; there is a back and forth. That is what we usually refer to when we talk about the "spiritual journey." The journey is the movement from contraction to expansion, from dual to nondual, back to dual, back to nondual, integration, expansion, integration, expansion, more contraction, expansion, and so on. The Hasidic masters sometimes refer to this process as *ratzo vashov*—"running and returning"—or *yaridah kitzorech aliyah*, which means "going down for the sake of going up."[7]

These are the traditional catchphrases, but what they are pointing to is that going down into Egypt is necessary in order for wholeness and expansion to be possible. We have to go down in order to go up; we have to go into contraction in order to move into expansion. So you see, ultimately, it is not like contraction is bad and expansion is good. They are both part of a reciprocal polarity. You cannot have one without the other. Expansion only exists relative to contraction. We are harkening back now to the first few talks when we presented the metaphysical view that contraction is not a mistake but is a necessary and integral component of the journey of Being, a journey from the infinite to the finite and back again.

We need to become more comfortable with both the dual and the nondual. So now let's talk a little bit about the nondual, because we have already talked a lot about contraction. But first, we have to discuss the belly. Contraction in the belly-center usually has to do with instinctual reactivity, reactions, and processes, where the actual organism can freeze or react in response to various stimuli. Oftentimes different kinds of traumas are stored and evoked in the contractions of the belly-center. The belly-center is really the physiological center of the whole body; the nervous system is deeply tied to the belly-center.

If the contractions in the belly and body can be effectively processed, then expansion of the belly-center is possible. Expansion of the belly-center reveals what we call the Presence Body, which is the direct and immediate experience of the body as a mysterious essential presence. The Presence Body can manifest as a clear and transparent body of light, or it can be dense and luminous, or it can manifest with a particular color or hue. It often has the paradoxical property of being both spacious and dense at the same time. We call it a body because it is functional and relational, it has a particular form, but it's not separate from its environment. It is both nondual and particular at the same time. There is an inherent sense that the body is part of the natural world, of the entire cosmos, and inseparable from the whole. There are many variations of the experience of expansion in the belly-center, in the body, but this gives you a sense of the possibilities.

Now trust, or *emunah*, is crucial for each of these three centers to open. We talked about this last time. The Slonimer Rebbe, a Hasidic master, explicitly talks about the three centers in terms of *emunah*. When trust is integrated in the head-center he calls it *emunat hamoach*, which means "trust of the mind," when it is integrated in the heart-center he calls it *emunat halev*, "trust of the heart," and *emunat ha-evarim*, "trust of the limbs," refers to trust integrated in the belly-center, and by extension the whole physical body.[8]

He uses the phrase "trust of the limbs" because the limbs are an extension of the belly-center. This understanding is also found in Chinese medicine, where the meridians that extend into the limbs originate in the lower *tan tien,* which is located in the belly. This is also found in the Rolfing tradition, where the origin of contralateral movement of the arms and legs in walking is found in the lower center of the belly, towards the anterior side of the lumbar spine, in the environment of the attachment sites for the psoas muscle. Gyrotonics calls this the "seed center." Many traditions know about this center and its relationship to the arms and legs.

We can see how the Slonimer Rebbe explicitly correlates each of these three kinds of *emunah* with the three centers of consciousness. We can also see how contraction and expansion can manifest in each of these three centers, and how *emunah* is a necessary ingredient for our consciousness to allow vulnerability and intimacy through these three loci of perception.

Intimacy requires trust because it entails a loss of self, regardless of which center we are moving through. Ultimately the centers are not separate from each other. We talk about them as if they are distinct as a heuristic device, a way of conceptualizing these phenomena to help us understand them better. Truly, the three centers are part of one unified organism: they are the eyes, the perceptual lenses, through which our soul is able to experience the world.

Trust is necessary for us to be vulnerable, and vulnerability is necessary for intimacy. Intimacy is necessary because it is the doorway into the nondual and the expanded state of ourselves. This requires a loss of self, which can feel like a death, and to die for the sake of truth requires a great deal of trust; trust that our soul, our being, our individuality, is an integral part of Being and is held in fundamental goodness and love.

The practices that we engage help generate these qualities. In group sessions, students speak of a sense of safety, and the feeling of an essential vessel that is generated in our group field. When we practice together we invoke the qualities of Being that are needed for us in the moment. The qualities themselves are the very nature of Being and are always present. It is like we invoke them to the foreground of our experience even while they are always there in the background.

I would now like to unpack this on the macro level. What do I mean by the terms "Presence" and "Being"? According to the Kabbalists, the central Hebrew Divine name is *YHVH. ADNY*, pronounced *Adonai*, is the feminine principle, which is the embodied principle that I call Presence.[9] Presence is the manifestation of existence, the world of creation as we know it and experience it through our physical senses; it is the embodied expression of Being. This is what we invoke with the Divine name *Adonai*. The Divine name *Elohim* also represents this embodied expression of Presence.[10]

YHVH is the central Divine name, best translated as "is-was-will be" or Being, which represents the inner nature of creation, of existence. It is the inner nature of all expressions of form, of embodied Presence.[11] Ultimately, everything that exists is the expression of Being as Presence. We use these Divine names to discriminate between the different forms that Presence takes. That is all that we are doing. Being and Presence are not separate things.

When we evoke the name *Adonai*, we are verbally saying *Adonai*, which is Presence, but in actuality we are visualizing and intending *YHVH,* which is the inner nature or essence of Presence.[12] When we say *Adonai* and intend *YHVH*, we are invoking the union of Being and Presence—the union of *YHVH* and *Adonai*—which declares that the inner nature of Being and its external expression as Presence are one reality, one inseparable truth. This is also the esoteric meaning of the *Shema* prayer, which declares that *YHVH* and *Elohim*—Being and Presence—are *echad*, which means one.

On a more subtle level, Presence is our speech and Being is our voice before it is articulated as speech. Our voice is therefore the essence of our speech.[13] Our voice is the *Beingness* of the discriminated sounds that articulate the words into speech. The primordial source of our voice is the Divine name *EHYH* (pronounced *Ehyeh*), which is associated with the *sefirah* of *ayin*, nothingness or emptiness, and is expressed as absolute silence.[14]

So there are three central realms or dimensions of our experience and of reality, represented by the three primary *sefirot* that constitute the central channel of the Tree of Life: Emptiness (*Ehyeh* or *ayin* or *Keter*), Being (*YHVH* or *Tiferet*), and Presence (*Adonai* or *Shechinah* or *Malchut*).

When Presence is experienced directly, it has a substantial quality to it. It has an ethereal kind of density, a thickness and a texture that you can touch and feel, because it is the essential substance that manifests the forms of creation; it is what manifests the material of our world. We can sense Presence in our bodies because our bodies have the capacity to perceive and directly touch into this kind of textured subtle substance. That is why we cultivate and develop our inner capacity for sensing on the Kedumah path; it is what endows us with the capacity to sense presence directly in our embodied experience.

Because Presence is the outer expression of the inner nature of reality, our bodies are the optimal organs—the most available doorway that we possess—to feel and know Presence. This is because our bodies *are* Presence.[15] However, the conventional experience of the body is more opaque and separate. The assumption is that we have separate bodies. Our individuality is determined by our separateness from others and from other objects. That is what we call the dual experience, or the contracted experience. Whatever our experience is—however limited, contracted or dualistic—it's still all Presence. There is nothing that exists that is not Presence. All forms, whether material or spiritual, are expressions of the inner nature of Being, which we call Presence.

Dual experience, contraction, is a perceptual distortion of Presence. Presence is not dual, not separate, and not bounded, even though that is usually the way we experience our bodies. Presence is simply the outer expression of Being, of the inner essence of existence. So the spiritual journey, you could say, is an epistemological one, not an ontological one. Our perception of materiality as separate from essence—in other words, of Presence as separate from Being, is what undergoes a process of transformation. Ontologically speaking, however, there is no actual journey. Presence always was, always is, and always will be one with and inseparable from Being. They are simply two sides of the same coin. What this means, of course, is that there is never any separation between physical and spiritual, between body and soul, and between human and God.

The spiritual journey entails freeing *da'at* from its exile in our experience. We are seeking to free the immediate, intimate property of *knowing* in our experience from its perceptual enslavement. When we contact and open to the immediate sense of *da'at* (knowing) in our experience, when we are vulnerable to the raw naked sensation of our experience, this experience can then reveal the truth of our physical bodies. It can reveal that our body is not a bounded, separate entity, but is a body of palpable light, a body of Presence—what we call in Kedumah the Presence Body.

When we recognize the body as Presence and we follow it all the way through to its inner core, to its essence, then the inner nature of Presence can reveal itself to our perception. This brings us to the nondual, the more vast and boundless dimensions of reality. These are the dimensions of Being that are beyond time and space. Gaining perceptual access to the boundless dimensions of Being is often referred to as a state of enlightenment or spiritual realization. The practice of sensing the physical body can lead us all the way to enlightenment. In the Kedumah teachings, we refer to this experience with the term "expansion."

The experience of expansion can happen through any of the three centers. When we experience it through the belly-center, we sense the body as a boundless form, as a nondual expression of Being. The body can be luminous and transparent, or it can feel like a substantial presence; it can take a variety of ethereal forms. When we experience expansion through the heart-center, we can experience the richness and the sensitivity of the texture of presence as the manifestation of everything, of all of life. Through the head-center, we can experience it as an intimate knowing of reality, as the recognition that the knower, the knowing, and that which is known; these are all one.

Going deeply into the three centers, or into any experience of expansion, can bring us to direct perception of *YHVH* itself. The direct experience of *YHVH* entails a radical shift in our perception. With the perception of *YHVH,* or pure Being, we no longer perceive ourselves as an individual bound in time and space. *YHVH* is experienced as boundless, formless, expanded space, which is the nondual inner nature of *Adonai*, of Presence. While we can still experience ourselves as an individual, we recognize that we are boundless and inseparable from the expanded space of Being.

At this level of experience, we can perceive ourselves and reality from two different vantage points: from the perspective of the individual or from the perspective of *YHVH*. Since *YHVH* is the boundless, formless space itself, if we perceive reality from the perspective of *YHVH* then there is no individual self, only the purity and clarity of nondual Being. However, from the perspective of the individual, there is an individual located within the vast space of Being. Either way it is a radical shift from the conventional perspective.

We use a technique in this teaching as a bridge to the immediate experience of *YHVH*. I call it the *ayd* practice. *Ayd* is a Hebrew word that means "witness." In the *Shema* prayer, which is found in the book of Deuteronomy (6:4), it says *Shema Yisrael Adonai Eloheinu Adonai Echad*. If you look inside the ancient Torah scroll, you will see that there are two Hebrew letters in this prayer that are bigger than all the others. There is a big *ayin* in the word *Shema* (שמע), and there is a big letter *dalet* at the end of the word *echad* (אחד). They actually write these letters really big on the scroll. These two letters spell *ayd* (עד), which means "witness."[16]

So we see that in the primary unitive prayer in the ancient Hebrew tradition it highlights with big letters this word *ayd*, or "witness." Some of you may be familiar with the contemplative practice of "witnessing," which is an awareness practice where you witness all phenomena, thoughts, emotions, and sensations; in this practice, we assume an inner posture of bearing witness to whatever is arising. We are gazing from our inner eye, free from the identifications that typically cloud our external vision.

By highlighting the Hebrew word *ayd* in the *Shema*, the Torah is alluding to how this secret method—the witness practice—can be a bridge to the nondual experience, to the realization of the union of *YHVH* and *Elohim* that is proclaimed in the *Shema*. The witness practice itself is still an expression of duality, because there is somebody looking at something; it is a more subtle form of duality, but a duality nonetheless. At a certain point though it can transform. The one who is witnessing can disappear, and then there is no differentiation between the one who is perceiving and that which is perceived. This is the nondual *echad*—the ultimate One—that is the promise of the *Shema*.[17]

Earlier I discussed the principle of speech (in talk 4) followed by the principle of truth (in talk 5), and I spoke about how these two principles come together in our Kedumah practice of speaking the truth. This foundational orientation is necessary before we can fully establish the *ayd* practice. This progression is reflected in the verse from Proverbs 12:19: *Sefat Emet Tikon Le-ad*, which is usually translated as "The lips of truth will be established forever." However, this verse can also be translated: "True speech will establish the witness." This is because the last word *Le-ad*, meaning "forever," can also be read *Le-ayd*, meaning "witness."[18] This is why we begin this path with first establishing the practice of speaking the truth (talks 4-5), which then establishes the possibility for the *ayd* practice to bear its fruits.

Now, *YHVH* can also be accessed through the dimensions of space or time. Space itself, when stripped of all content and free from perceptual limitations, is pure openness. It can feel like fresh, crisp, open space. In the dimension of time, *YHVH* is accessed in the immediacy of the Now. That is how *YHVH* is accessed experientially. The more we can be completely present in the Now, the more we will ultimately be Being itself.

When we are abiding in Being, there is no time or space in the conventional sense: no time to pass, and nowhere to go, because there is infinite time and space for things to happen. You can say that it is timeless and spaceless. There is a sense that there is nowhere to go, nowhere else to be but right here, right now. We can feel that we are simply sitting and being, and all phenomena just pass by.

What I mean by "timelessness" is that in this state we may realize that there is no time that actually passes. From this perspective, we realize that the passage of time is really the movement of phenomena through our experience and perception. In nondual perception, time does not expire, nor does it transpire; it is completely nonexistent. Time does not pass. When we experience the Now, that is all there is.

One of the hallmark characteristics of *YHVH*, or pure Being, is that it is not subject to change. *Ani YHVH Lo Shaniti*, as it says in the Prophets: "I, *YHVH*, do not change" (Mal. 3:6). It is the changeless ground from which all phenomena manifest and unfold. This is why the *ayd* practice is effective as a contemplative bridge into the dimension of *YHVH*. The *ayd* practice basically orients the consciousness to perceive phenomena from the nondual changeless ground of Being.

However, the *ayd* practice itself is still dualistic since there is still someone perceiving something. In other words, there is an implicit distinction between subject and object. That is why the practice is only a bridge into a deeper nondual reality. This happens when the one who is witnessing dissolves into the formless, timeless nondual reality. Then there is no separation between subject and object. They are one. All is *echad*.

Thus, in my experience, time and space are both manifestations within the changeless, formless, ground of Being. They are differentiations and particulars within the uniform and unitive space of *YHVH*. *YHVH* is the experience of pure Being, before it differentiates into particular forms. Therefore, when we are abiding as *YHVH*, there is not a sense of time or space in the same way. Space is open and vast, without differentiated forms. Time is suspended in the eternal moment, in the Now. There is no sense of one's self as a separate individual.

You can see how we have to be willing to die, in a sense, in order to open to this way of being; we must be willing to allow our conventional sense of self to die, dissolve, and disappear so that the truth of Being can shine through. On a more subtle level, expansion into Being entails an expansion beyond our ordinary sense of self.

The movement between contraction and expansion ultimately is what develops our human potential. The constructive friction in the human soul that is generated in this organic movement between contraction and expansion cultivates the potential for wholeness in the human consciousness. Wholeness is the embodiment and integration of both the unitive ground of Being and the differentiated forms of Presence into our human life. The integration of the pure nondual Lights of Being into our lived experience afford us the possibility of becoming fully human—a human form that is transparent to Being.

One more thing I wanted to mention about the difference experientially between *YHVH* and *Adonai*—between the formless inner nature of Presence as Being and the manifest expression of Presence in the created world of form—is that the experience of embodied Presence, or form as the expression of Presence, is that it is subject to change, and the experience of *YHVH*, or pure Being, is that it does not change.

There is a changeless quality to the experience of *YHVH*. That's what I mean when I say that it feels like time stands still. Space also stands still. That is, there is a pristine stillness in the vastness of space. Everything is suspended in the constant, changeless, timeless, mystery of Being.

[The following discussion takes place after an experiential exercise.]

ZVI: Okay, any questions about the exercise you just did exploring the Now?

STUDENT: I notice that I kind of got out of my head and into the experience of being here, and just engaging myself, and getting into my own experience, and it made the teaching a little more present and relevant. It kind of became alive a little bit, when I started doing the exercise.

ZVI: So what do you experience right now?

STUDENT: I feel alive, I experience myself as alive.

ZVI: You feel aliveness.

STUDENT: It's more like I'm engaged, and I am more in my body. I'm not just listening to you talk and thinking about what you're saying and sorting it out and writing it down, like I usually do. I'm more here, with more me, and it feels good. You know, if you keep yourself all bottled up for a while, something wants to come out, so I kind of feel like that. I feel like a breath of fresh air to start talking and engaging.

ZVI: Yes. Speaking truth brings more of us into the Now. Thank you.

STUDENT: When you were talking about knowing and not-knowing, I actually woke up. I woke up this morning and looked at my notes, and three weeks ago I had written this down: "You want to know, and know that you know, but you can't, because what you want to know is when knower and known merge." But, from what you were saying, that seems not right. And experientially reading it this morning, it also didn't resonate as true. That it's actually the opposite. Well that is what you want to know when knower and known merge, but you can know it. I said you can't know it, but, paradoxically, you can. I guess I just wanted to bring that to the floor and kind of explore that. Does that make sense?

ZVI: No.

STUDENT: Ha ha! Good.

ZVI: Yes, good. I see you got it. What are you experiencing, right now?

STUDENT: It's like my brain is trying to grasp, but there's nothing anywhere for it to grasp, and it's kind of like giggling, like my consciousness is giggling at its own impossible task of trying to grasp.

ZVI: Yes. Exactly. What happens if you accept that there is nothing to grasp and really let yourself go into that space?

STUDENT: It's like a really smooth expansion that's not stopping. It's kind of gentle, but persistent. It's kind of like the softest thing overcomes the hardest thing. It's unstoppable but it's not really forceful, because there's nothing for it to contend with.

ZVI: Right.

STUDENT: It's really peaceful, and as soon as I just said that, I kind of just dropped into my heart and it had an almost melancholic kind of feel. Not melancholic as in sad but like, returning home, but not in a victorious way, like in a kind of tender way.

ZVI: Yes. What's the size of your body right now? How big is it?

STUDENT: When you first asked, it felt really, really big. But then right when I sensed how big it was, it immediately contracted into the exact size of my physical body.

ZVI: So was there some kind of a contraction that happened when you realized how big you actually are?

STUDENT: No. It didn't feel like a contraction as opposed to expansion, but more like concentration, like Goldilocks, like "just right," like I fit perfectly in my body. Body is perfect.

ZVI: Got it. So you feel actually more yourself, in your body.

STUDENT: Yeah, like really. It feels like it fits. And it's like yeah, it feels like it fits.

ZVI: It seems like your body now is more in harmony with what you were experiencing in your heart.

STUDENT: Yeah, because the feeling in my heart was kind of separate; that tenderness felt almost separate, and now that feeling has gone away, and I can feel the words in my throat, and the presence of my vocal chords ringing, like the basic physical experience of talking, and of sitting, of everything.

ZVI: When you were talking about the melancholy in your heart and the tenderness in your heart, and then I asked you about the size of your body, it seems that you brought more awareness to the contours of your body-soul and then your body reconfigured and the sadness in your heart went away.

STUDENT: Yeah, because it was wanting, it was longing to be, it was longing to know that, and to be in my body.

ZVI: Very good. It is important to understand what the longing in the heart was. It was more to really feel your body in its natural condition, for you, as an individual soul. Then your voice is able to express itself more completely, coming from your heart and your body in alignment with each other. Does this make sense?

STUDENT: Yeah, totally. I'm smiling really, really big right now.

ZVI: Right. It doesn't make sense to the conventional mind, but I'm not speaking from that place, so you're hearing it, because it makes sense in some mysterious way.

STUDENT: Yeah, my heart is like "AAAAAAAAAH!"

ZVI: Right. Very mysterious, yes. Sounds good.

STUDENT: Yeah, it was good, thank you.

ZVI: Alright. Anybody else? What do you notice in the space right now? What's it like? What's the Now like now?

STUDENT: Well, earlier it felt more like there was a texture in the space, and in retrospect it felt kind of fuzzy, like cotton candy-ish, like clouds. But now it doesn't feel like that for me, it feels more like there's a stillness but it has a less tangible texture and so it feels more like a tunnel or a triangle or something.

ZVI: What about the space around you? Is that what you're talking about?

STUDENT: Yeah.

ZVI: It feels like a tunnel or triangle?

STUDENT: It's not so much that it's a tunnel or a triangle, it just doesn't have the chewy quality of texture. It's more like the contrast from all the activity of engaging in talking has a more vacuous quality, which is maybe just contrast.

ZVI: So it feels more vacuous.

STUDENT: Yeah.

ZVI: So, vacuous implies empty. So there's a sense of emptiness?

STUDENT: Yes.

ZVI: What's it like to allow the emptiness to be completely empty?

STUDENT: Well, kind of a relief.

ZVI: So it brings relief.

STUDENT: Yes. It feels a little restful, and a little bit like rejuvenating also. A little bit of that feeling of a shift in the nervous system where the nervous system can come back and receive a little bit.

ZVI: So the nervous system is able to settle, it seems. To settle and to have more ease of regulation.

STUDENT: Yes.

ZVI: It seems that the emptiness allows the body to be more at ease in its natural environment.

STUDENT: Yeah, but also, as you started to talk, I realized there's still a sense of breathing with the environment, so it almost feels like the movement of a tide. But it's something that is subtle, like my body has to slow down into that tide. But I know the tide is here. There's a tide.

ZVI: Yeah. There's a way that emptiness breathes through you—as you. The tide implies a natural rhythm. There is a sense that you're in alignment with the environment. And it's part of the living organism, of the environment. So your system can settle and it seems that there's trust also here to allow your organism to be regulated by this mystery, as part of it. Sounds really nice.

Do you notice that there is something very ordinary about it?

STUDENT: Oh yeah, very much. Extremely ordinary.

ZVI: Yeah.

STUDENT: It actually doesn't make sense to say extremely ordinary, because it's not extreme.

ZVI: Right. It's extremely ordinary. And yet, it's awakened. Like there's a wakefulness in the space.

STUDENT: Yeah. Which is why it's funny.

ZVI: Yeah. It brings a lightness of being, actually. It frees the organism to be more itself, a more free and natural state.

Yeah. That's very good.

So we got a little taste of emptiness. We weren't going to get there for a few weeks, but we don't control the way reality unfolds. Emptiness leads to freedom. Freedom is not what the mind thinks. Do you want to speak to that?

STUDENT: No, it's just funny. You were telling a joke right? [Laughter.]

ZVI: [Laughing.] I wasn't telling a joke! I was being very serious! Sometimes we miss the best things because they're so ordinary.

7
Waking Down

TALK

THUS FAR, WE have been talking about the journey of waking up; we have not yet talked about "Waking Down." Waking up is seeing things as they are, without anything filtering our perception. Waking Down involves living our realization in the world. It is one thing to wake up, but it is a whole other thing to Wake Down.

In some sense, waking up is the easy part. Waking Down is usually very messy. Perhaps you can relate to the experience of going on retreat and struggling to integrate newfound expansiveness upon returning to ordinary life, especially in an intimate relationship. I call this the "bungee cord effect." I used to call it the "boomerang effect," but the boomerang moves far too smoothly to really do justice to the intensity of the snap-back that typically follows expanded states.

As we discussed in the last session, there is usually a back and forth movement between the Journeys of Contraction and Expansion. Now we see that the degree of our expansion tends to have an equally intense contraction in its wake, though they do not often tell you about that before the retreat. Once you have returned home, you realize that you are left to figure out what the hell is going on. If you were not warned about this dynamic beforehand, you may be dismayed and confused to find that the feeling of freedom, light, and expansion is gone and you are overcome with a feeling of irritation and reactivity.

If people only knew how challenging the spiritual journey actually is, they probably would not undertake it to begin with. Romanticizing the journey may be helpful to get people motivated in the first place, but it is not so helpful when we realize what we have gotten ourselves into. On the Kedumah path, we speak openly about the challenges from the get-go. There is no romance brewing in these teachings. The journey is painful and freedom is unremarkable. It is true that the experience of expansion is at first very alluring and pleasurable, but that is only because it is still in a dialectical relationship to contraction. Freedom, as we will discuss down the road, is freedom from identifying with both contraction and expansion. Ultimately, we cultivate freedom because it is natural and it is our birthright; freedom is just what happens when things are left to be as they are.

On the journey of waking up we see a lot of things that are difficult to experience. We do not only wake up to the pleasant things; we also wake up to very painful, hidden, and buried wounds in ourselves and in others. Living our expansions and our contractions from an awakened condition requires a different kind of development, a different kind of maturation of our consciousness. It has its own kind of waking up, but not in the way that it is discussed in many traditions.

Many traditions focus on spiritual realization, which is the waking up of our perception. To wake up means to perceive reality in a more direct, immediate way, but that is only one side of the coin. The other side of the coin is actually relating and acting as a human being in alignment with that realization in a way that expresses the truth of what we are. This is what I mean by "Waking Down." You can see that a different kind of development is needed to be able to integrate the journey in a way that is not just real but also authentic to who we are as individual souls, as personal expressions of Being.

How each person lives a true life of wakefulness is completely unique. It is totally one's own and not to be duplicated by anyone else. It is completely precious in its uniqueness. To directly perceive reality as is and to express yourself completely and thoroughly—both relationally and functionally—means to Wake Down into who and what you are as an individual and personal expression of Being.

To Wake Down means to integrate what we perceive and know to be true into our life, as a living expression of the totality of Being itself. In the five journeys that we have been using in this teaching, this is the Journey of Wholeness. The Journeys of Contraction and Expansion are ongoing; we are always working with the process of *ratzo vashov* that we discussed in our last meeting: the dialectical process of "running and returning" that is the movement between contraction and expansion that is the ongoing rhythm of life.

It is not just the rhythm of our personal lives; it is the rhythm of the cosmos. The in-breath and out-breath of contraction and expansion enliven and infuse the entire cosmic reality with life and existence. If everything were always expanded, there would be no form, no embodiment, no manifestation of particulars; everything would dissolve into the boundless, unchanging reality. The unchanging nature of the nondual condition is balanced by the constant flux and flow of life, by the endlessly changing forms of manifestation.

We see that the dynamic movement of contraction and expansion is the natural rhythm of life. When we invest all kinds of psychic energy and historical narratives into this organic rhythm of contraction and expansion then we invite the experience of suffering. The suffering that results from identifying with our experience of contraction is probably very familiar to all of us. However, even if we invest psychic energy, historical identity, and self-images into expansion, there is also suffering. A person can experience a state of expansion and nonduality, a state of perceiving beyond the limitations of the conventional dualistic perspective, but still be investing some content or sense of self into the experience.

Underneath the expansion there may be a voice lurking down there, commenting on our experience. There may be a self-identity appropriating our experience of nonduality for itself. Perhaps it is patting us on the back for experiencing the nonduality, or it may be contemplating all the good fortune that is now going to come to us with such perception. In other words, while it is true that the state of expansion does alleviate a certain kind of suffering—namely, the suffering of identifying with our contractions—it does not, in and of itself, bring freedom from a more subtle and fundamental kind of suffering.

This more nuanced experience of suffering has to do with a deep and persistent attachment to our self-identity and our internalized concept of having a separate self. There are many levels and degrees of self-identity, and many variations of the experience of freedom from their grip on our perception. We will unpack these subtleties in more advanced teachings, and make finer distinctions between the layers of self-identity and self-entity.

The Journey of Wholeness is a journey of integration, where the dual and the nondual meet in the human consciousness. When I say "meet," I do not mean to imply that these are two separate things. Even though that is how we tend to talk about it, it is really the embodied integration in the human soul of the universal and the particular as one and the same thing.

On the spiritual journey there is usually a subtle split between the dual and the nondual, the particular and the universal, the individual and the cosmic, the human, and the Divine. We tend to self-perpetuate this dialectical suffering of contraction and expansion by subtly going along with this split, with the belief that duality sucks, and that nonduality is great. The goal of most spiritual paths is to somehow move into an expanded state. Some people even go to extreme lengths to have an experience of expansion, engaging in severe forms of austerities and prolonged meditation retreats. There is nothing wrong with this and we hold no judgment about it, it's just illustrative of the dynamic I am speaking to.

If we have a living aspiration for truth then that is what calls us to embark on the journey and that is what carries us home. It is actually rare to have an aspiration for the truth, and therefore it is a blessing to know that within yourself. Usually we only apply ourselves in a practice if we believe there is something else—something better—waiting on the other side. Something other than what we already have. It is not always this way but it is the usual thing.

In other words, on the spiritual journey there is usually the motivation to experience something other than what we are already experiencing now. As you can see, this is not exactly an aspiration for the truth, but rather it is an aspiration to feel better and to heal. There is nothing wrong with this; it is natural and normal. In fact, it is what first moved me to explore meditation and spirituality.

Often spiritual teachings will engage practices to help create conditions whereby we are more attuned to perceive things in a different way, from a different vantage point that tends to bring more space and freedom from our suffering. These practices do impact us and they can change our lives. There actually *is* more space and all those things are true, and yet, unless we move into the Journey of Wholeness, we can spend our entire lives still holding onto this subtle split between dual and nondual. By holding onto this split, we ensure that we are still enslaved by the suffering that is inherent to an attachment to nonduality and expansion.

As it turns out, it is very difficult to organize our lives in a way that would allow us to stay high all the time. We can become a "God addict." It gets tedious and cumbersome to have to structure our lives around God all the time, to have to meditate *x* number of hours a day, and so on. Life is pretty complex these days for most people. Many people have to work a lot to get by, and if you add family and community to the mix, even on a practical level it is hard to stay in a state of expansion.

The realization of wholeness turns this dualistic split on its head. Because it reveals that there is a resolution to the split. This resolution, however, is not a resolution of the mind; it cannot be understood with the ordinary mind. It is a resolution of presence. It can only be known directly and experientially in the human consciousness.

In the Kedumah tradition, we refer to this expression of Being as the Pearl. The term "Pearl" comes from the ancient Hebrew tradition. First, I will offer a bit of context, then I will speak directly about the experience of it.

The Pearl has to do with the Lights of Being, the Divine qualities that we discussed. Let us use the cycle of the Hebrew calendar and the cycle of the Hebrew holidays as a model to map these things out.

Earlier we discussed the movement from contraction to expansion as reflected in the holiday of *Pesach* (Passover), which recalls the exodus from *Mitzrayim* (Egypt). This movement into expansion is the journey out of our enslavement to the narrow perspectives of our perception (*Mitzrayim*) into a more expanded state of realization. We can build on this lesson through exploring how it goes beyond contraction and expansion, and relates to wholeness.

Right after the movement out of *Mitzrayim* there is a fifty-day period highlighted in the Torah between *Pesach* and the festival of *Shavuot*. Traditionally observant Jews mark this fifty-day period between *Pesach* and *Shavuot* by counting down each day in a practice called *Sefirat Ha-Omer,* or counting of the *Omer*. On each day of the *Omer*, there is a specific blessing and a ritualized counting in Hebrew in which the person recites: "Today is the first day of the *Omer*" and so on, until the fiftieth day is reached.[1]

The fiftieth day is the festival of *Shavuot*, which is known and recognized in Christianity by the Ancient Greek term *Pentecost*. *Pentecost* literally means "fiftieth," and it refers to the fiftieth day counted from *Pesach* on the Hebrew calendar, which among other things celebrates the receiving of the Torah—the Revelation—at Sinai.

The Rabbinic tradition understands the experience of revelation on Sinai as a marriage ceremony between the ancient Israelites and God.[2] In the Talmud it states that the mountain was "suspended over their heads like a ceiling," which the Rabbis interpret to mean that the mountain served as a *chuppah* (the traditional canopy under which a bride and groom are wed) that was held over their heads as they were betrothed to God.[3] In this metaphor, the Torah serves as the *ketubah*, the marriage document, which stipulates the agreements of their union.[4]

The Kabbalists understood these fifty days between *Pesach* and *Shavuot* to be the most auspicious time to integrate all of the *sefirot*, the Lights of Being, into one's consciousness, which is achieved by consciously working through the obscurations and distortions of these qualities in our lives.[5] In the reality map of the Tree of Life, the "lower" seven *sefirot* are called the "seven days of creation" by the Kabbalists, since they are the Lights of Being that manifest in the world of creation. "Days" is a classic codeword for the *sefirot*, used extensively in the Zohar.[6] The "upper" three *sefirot* of *Keter*, *Chochmah*, and *Binah* are pre-creation and pre-existence. They are more primordial. I put lower and upper in quotes because I do not mean them hierarchically; these terms denote their degree of subtlety and the density of their essential substance relative to *Ein Sof*.

The seven lower *sefirot*, from *Chesed* down to *Malchut*, are expressed in the world of creation and manifestation. Each of these seven are included in each of the other seven. For example, that is how we correlate the forty-nine days with the *sefirot*: they are seven *sefirot* times seven *sefirot*. The contemplative practice during this time is to work on the subtle variations of the obscurations of each of these forty-nine levels of the *sefirot* as they manifest in our lives, so that the fullness of each of the Lights of Being can shine through our individual window of consciousness without obstruction.[7]

The first day that is counted is *Chesed She-bichesed*, which means "*Chesed* that is in *Chesed*," the second day is *Chesed She-bigevurah*, "*Chesed* that is in *Gevurah*," then *Chesed* that is in *Tiferet*, and so on and so forth until you complete all forty-nine days. The idea is that at the end of these forty-nine days you enter into the fiftieth day—*Shavuot*—in a state of wholeness. In this state all of the issues obfuscating and distorting these Divine qualities have been worked through and the purity of the Lights has been integrated into our consciousness. Only then are we ready for union with God at Sinai and receiving of the revelation and transmission of the life-teaching (the Torah), which on the mystical level is the union of the dual and nondual in our human experience and life.

These fifty days of integration between Passover and *Shavuot* are understood by the Kabbalists to be the most auspicious time for Waking Down. The Aramaic phrase that is used to refer to this process is *Itaruta De-litata*, which literally means "awakening of below" or more poetically, "waking down."[8] The period of the year associated with "waking up" is Passover, which represents the movement from contraction to expansion, as we discussed in earlier talks.

Waking Down has to do with the reentry and integration, the digestion and metabolism of our experience of expansion achieved on Passover into the world of human relationship and activity, culminating with wholeness—the union of contraction and expansion achieved on *Shavuot*.

So we see that even in the ancient Hebrew narrative of the Torah the movement from contraction to expansion is only the first step on the path to freedom. The journey from *Mitzrayim* (contraction) into the *merkhav* (expansion) opens up the opportunity for a more conscious engagement with our personal issues and conflicts; it gives us the opportunity to integrate into our individual consciousness all the pure Lights—the pure qualities of Being—that are needed to live an authentic human life.

In conventional experience these essential qualities of Being are only recognized through their distorted expressions in our life. We usually only get a very watered-down or twisted version of these qualities. Every experience we have is an expression of one of these essential colors, or mixture of colors. There are an infinite number of possible variations of colors that constitute the manifested human life. They are the phenomenological contours of human existence.

However, if we are identified with the distortion of the quality, then we miss its essential beauty and purity.

We have to apply our practice of *drash* (inquiry) and sense into the raw, palpable, embodied texture of the experience itself, without going along with the conceptual overlays and the stories and the psychic investments that we have in our experience. If we become vulnerable enough to be in intimate union (*da'at*) with our experience in an immediate and direct way, engaging the heart, head, and belly, inquiring into what is happening in the moment, going deeper and deeper into it, then, because it is a natural law, we *will* encounter the essential light of Being. This light is then able to permeate our consciousness and express itself in our life.

When I first realized how this works, I was in graduate school and as a young Orthodox rabbi, I was also working part-time as a *mashgiach*—someone who oversees an establishment in the food industry to certify if it is kosher or not. My job at the time was to ensure that a particular Chinese restaurant was indeed kosher. I would check all their deliveries and inspect their inventories to make sure everything was properly certified. While I was overseeing this restaurant, they hired a new manager who was uncooperative. There are many very strict rules for a restaurant to be certified kosher, and for some reason she kept trying to push the boundaries and break the rules. For example, she was bringing in food from outside of the establishment for her own personal use. That was a no-no. You cannot bring in McDonald's to a kosher restaurant. My job entailed not only overseeing but revoking certification if necessary.

I noticed, as I was engaging with this woman around this issue, that it was really upsetting me in a way that did not fit the situation. It was much more disturbing to me for some reason, to the extent that it was keeping me up at night. I was perseverating over it and strategizing how to best deal with her and with the chief rabbis at the certifying agency. I felt tormented. At a certain point I began to ask myself, "What the hell is going on here? Why am I so upset by this?" When I thought about it, it seemed like a very straightforward situation, yet I realized that I was totally engulfed in this story in a way that did not make sense.

Finally, I decided to pray about it. At that time I had a daily prayer practice, so the next morning when I was *davening*—praying—I asked God for help to understand what was happening. It was a very sincere prayer. I really wanted to know what was going on. I really wanted to know the truth. I suddenly realized that my sincerity was enough. In a way, the felt-sense of wanting to know the truth became more foreground and the details of the situation fell to the background. I no longer even cared about how to fix the situation. I was more interested in the question, "What is happening here for me?" I really just wanted to know.

I remember that, as I surrendered more deeply to the truth of really wanting to know, something spontaneously opened up in me. First, I saw the Divine name *Elohim*. Because I was immersed in the Kabbalistic teachings at the time, I knew that the Divine name of *Elohim* has to do with the Divine quality of justice, of *din*. In the system of the Tree of Life justice is represented by the *sefirah* of *Gevurah*, translated as "strength."[9] I was not at all thinking about it intellectually at that time, but when the name *Elohim* came up I immediately knew that I was dealing with an issue around *Gevurah*.

Then, as I stayed with the experience, I started to have memories come up from when I was a kid, experiencing people who were my caretakers and teachers of mine and who used their authority in abusive ways or in ways that were not pure. As I remembered these things I could feel the impact of those experiences somatically and viscerally, in my body-soul. As I stayed with the painful sensations in my body-soul, I understood in that moment how experiencing those behaviors as violations, as attacks, made me distrust this quality of *Gevurah*, this true light of strength, when I was a child.

I understood in the Now of this experience how when I was a boy, I equated all expressions of strength with some kind of a violation or abuse. I could feel the pain of that and then there arose the sensation of loss, a feeling of deficient emptiness. When I allowed the raw embodied sensation of the emptiness to be there without judgment or manipulation, something very interesting happened. My entire consciousness became instantaneously absorbed in a pure, clear, spacious, red light. I felt this magical light shine through my heart as a discriminating clear red light. It was as if my entire body-soul had become more heartfelt and heart-centered with this particular quality saturating my experience.

Embodying this light, I could now see the situation for exactly what it was. With my consciousness absorbed in this light, and with this light expanding through me, I could see clearly how this pure light of *Gevurah* was blocked in me, and how as a result I was relating to the situation in the restaurant with the feeling of inner conflict and turmoil. From this perspective the situation was absolutely straightforward and simple. The rule is you cannot bring McDonald's into the restaurant. If the rule is violated, there are consequences: you are fired or I take away the certification. It became clear that I was having difficulty acting decisively, because I was feeling the stuckness and ambivalence that comes when the red light is blocked.

I noticed that when the purity of *Gevurah* was shining through my consciousness unobstructed, I had no hesitation and no inner conflict. I remember being in awe at its magnificence, at how magical it felt. I then remembered having experiences like that before, but it was clear to me that until that time I did not recognize it for what it was. I did not feel it through my heart-soul with such vivid richness. I realized that I had not appreciated it as the embodiment of the Divine red light of *Gevurah*.[10]

So, the next day I went back to the restaurant and felt an amazing freedom as a result of not having any inner hesitation, resistance, or conflict. No self-consciousness. It was very straightforward and matter of fact. I walked in and I said my piece; I spoke my truth. I noticed that when it comes from that pure place, there is no psychic investment and no other content to it. I also noticed that it burns absolutely clean. It is not blaming or attacking, nor is it cowering or mincing words and trying to say things in a polite way. It is utterly straightforward and simple.

What I realized in that encounter is that when we actually live these pure lights in our life, their authenticity is so powerful that people respect it. They can agree or disagree, but this is my truth. I come as I am. People feel it. It is palpable. It was all very simple; I expressed myself, I stated the consequences, and she got it. It was not a problem after that.

As I reflected on this experience, I realized that there were certain ingredients that went into the process that allowed this to happen, which I had never recognized in that systematic way before. This experience was the beginning of my exploration into the integration of the lights and into what I am calling the Journey of Wholeness.

I soon realized something similar about the Divine light of *Tiferet*, the aspect of compassion. I realized that there was a way in which I would get uncomfortable around other people's pain. I would avoid it or not be able to be fully present with it. I would distract myself interiorly or try to fix it for them. Inquiring into it I discovered how I was avoiding the discomfort of feeling my own pain and suffering. As I stayed with my own deep pain, the pure quality of *Tiferet* opened up; it was pure, crisp, delicate compassion.

When you experience one of the Divine Lights, you absolutely know that it is not a conventional experience. For example, when you experience the Divine quality of compassion, you know implicitly that it is not an emotional state of compassion. There is a direct and self-evident knowing that this is the pure, clear light of Being shining through. There is no impulse to pull away or to manipulate the experience. It can just abide as is. There is the unmistakable simplicity of Being.

With compassion, there is the most exquisitely refined sensitivity, tenderness, and acceptance in the heart of whatever pain and suffering is there. The pristine light of *Tiferet* with its subtle green hue abides without a ripple.[11] There is a spacious openness and acceptance that is palpably felt. Other people in its presence can also feel it; in its presence, we can all relax and feel whatever painful feelings are there.

All of the Divine qualities, the Lights of Being, are real. They are the underlying matrix of all our experience. To live our life as a clear expression of these Divine Lights brings a sense of wholeness to our lived, embodied experience.

Interestingly, each one of the Lights feels whole unto itself. That is to say, each one is complete. It is not even nondual or dual. There is no other thought. It is what it is, completely. The Lights themselves are pure, unchanging realities. The quality of strength which I described was this pure, unchanging, red, expansive, clarity, with its decisiveness of action. A lot of people are addicted to this red quality. They try to conjure it up by doing extreme sports or extreme activities that will push them to some limit or place them in some kind of physical danger. In response to such a crisis, an adrenaline rush can course through one's system, mimicking the intensity of the red quality.

Sometimes in certain crisis situations the real red quality can also shine through in its purity. An example of this is the popular anecdote in which a mother miraculously has the strength to lift a car if her child is in danger. When a person is in a life-or-death situation the red can burst through. Where does that strength come from? This gives a sense of the capacity of the red *Gevurah* quality that can do anything whatsoever that is needed. Absolutely whatever is needed is done. Period.

This is true with all the *sefirot*. Each quality has its own flavor, its own color, and its own particular manifestation. Each of the holidays in the yearly cycle also embody a different one of these ten lights. Therefore, if we were to do a series of retreats we could do an entire year following the Hebrew calendar, with the holidays serving to invoke, embody, and integrate the full spectrum of these Divine Lights into our experience and our lives.

Now let us return to the pearl. The Hebrew word for "pearl" is *penina*, which is a popular name in Israel to this day. The name appears only once in the Hebrew Bible; in the book of Samuel there is a guy named Elkanah and one of his wives is named Penina.[12] He actually has two wives. One is named Channah (the popular English name Hannah is the transliteration of this name), who was barren, and his other wife, Penina, bore him children.

The "Pearl" bears children. This makes sense, because the pearl is a Divine quality that is experienced in the body-soul as a palpable fullness; it can feel like you are pregnant with the presence of potentiality. Let us now unpack this word more fully. The Hebrew word *penina* is very interesting, because it is very similar—indeed, almost identical—to another Hebrew word, *penima*. The word *penima* is almost the same as the word *penina*; the only difference is one letter; *peniNa* has a *nun* ("n" sound) and *peniMa* has the letter *mem* ("m" sound). Not only that, the difference also happens to be literally the difference of one letter, since in the Hebrew alphabet the letter *mem* is immediately followed by the letter *nun*. (This is similar in English, where the letter "n" follows "m.")

Penima is a word that means "the innerness" or "the inside." This word is found many times in Torah, in various forms. What is interesting is that the word *penima* comes from the same root as the word that means "face" (*panim*). So "inside" and "face" are two expressions of the same root word in Hebrew. As an illustration of this, in one of the sections of the Torah, Moses talks to God and says "I want to see your face," and God responds to Moses that "No one can see my face and live": *Lo Tuchal Lirot Et Panai Ki Lo Yirani Ha-Adam V'chai* (Ex. 33:20). But based on our discussion above, another way to understand it would be, "No one can see my inner nature and live."[13] You can see that this way of reading it actually makes more sense, but you will never find it translated that way in an English Bible.

In another example, on Friday nights traditional Jews sing the Kabbalistic prayer *Lecha Dodi* to welcome in the Sabbath. The translated words are, "Come my beloved, let us greet the bride, let us receive the face of *Shabbat*." *P'nei Shabbat nekabelah* is the Hebrew phrase that is translated as "Let us receive the face of *Shabbat*." The word *p'nei* is a shortened form of the word *penima*. It means "face," but like the example above it is a double entendre; it also means "innerness." Understood this way, on Friday eve we are declaring with this prayer that we are ready to receive the inner essence of the Sabbath.

The double-meaning of this word is not an accident. The point is that our face, our countenance, is an expression of our inner nature. People who are good at reading the Pearl, the *penima*, can read people's faces; they can see their facial expressions and can determine by their face the condition of their soul. It is actually an ancient metaphysical art. The fancy word for reading the face is physiognomy; metoposcopy is the reading of the forehead, which was the particular gift of Isaac Luria, the famous sixteenth-century Kabbalist.[14]

Now there is another verse in the book of Psalms (45:14), and this is going to bring us to the zinger. The verse reads, *K'voda Bat Melech Penima*: "The glory of the princess is *penima*." *Penima*, as we discussed, is both the inside, the innerness, as well as the face, the countenance, the outside appearance. The glory of the princess is *penima*; it is the inside/outside. The word for "glory," *kavod*, is found many times in Torah, and it is often used explicitly to refer to the Divine Presence. *Kavod* is the word that is used to refer to the presence that fills the sanctuary, the *mishkan*; therefore, the *kavod* is the indwelling presence.[15]

So is the presence (*kavod*) of the princess (*bat melech*) on the inside (*penima*) or is it on the outside (*penima*)? Is it the inner or the outer? Is it what is internal or what is external? You see, it is a paradox. Really the word *penima* is pointing to the paradoxical unity of the inside and the outside. The beauty of the princess, the presence of the princess, the "glory" of the princess, is the condition in which the inside and the outside have become one and the same. This is the correct mystical reading of it.

So this is the princess part, but what about the Pearl? If you remember, *penina* and *penima* are almost identical except for this one letter. We talked about the letter *mem* in an earlier talk. *Mem* represents the inner essence of truth. It is the middle letter of the word "truth" (*emet*), which represents the present moment, the Now, which is also the innerness of Being, of *YHVH.*

As the middle letter of *emet*, *mem* represents the unchanging essence of *YHVH. Ani Adonay Lo Shaniti*: "I am *YHVH*, I do not change" (Mal. 3:6). The unchanging ground of Being is the essential *YHVH*; it is the eternal Now, the *mem*. All transformation and renewal happens in the eternal Now of the *mem*. The letter *mem* has the numerical value of forty, and the difference between *mem* and the letter *nun* is ten, because the letter *nun* has the numerical value of fifty.

As we discussed, there are fifty days between Passover and *Shavuot*. The number fifty—the letter *nun*—represents wholeness, the integration and the maturation of the individual consciousness when it integrates the purity of all the Lights.[16] So the movement from *penima*, the nondual inner/outer Princess Presence, to *penina*, the Pearl, is a movement or a development of consciousness from the state of the eternal Now, from the unchanging ground of Being, the nondual state, into the manifested, completed, full expression of our human nature as the fifty, as the *penina* with a *nun*, as a Pearl.

In the Kedumah teachings, the technical term Pearl refers to the integration and the unification in the matured individual consciousness of the Princess Presence.[17] The Princess Presence itself is the precious, innocent, intimate beauty of openness and receptivity. It is the inner vulnerability and the outer permeability as one; however, it is immature and not yet fully developed for optimal human functionality. You can say it is the Pearl in its unripe condition.

The Pearl represents the embodiment into mature human life of the two sides of the one reality whose essence is expressed by the Princess Presence. It is the embodiment of the unity of the inner and the outer, the transcendent and the immanent, the unchanging and the transient, the nondual and the dual, the universal and the particular. The Pearl reveals the possibility of living a truly integrated personal-nondual life, whereby the personal and the nondual live as one whole and unified being.

Now let us turn to the mystical dimension of this teaching which is completely experiential; it is not abstract. The Pearl is oftentimes experienced as a precious fullness, ripe with potentiality. When you embody the Pearl you feel more round and full, more filled in, more whole. Your countenance glows in an earthy and embodied way.

You can see this in pregnant women. Their faces look different, their entire body-souls are shining in a particular way. That is the relationship between the face and the inner essence of the Pearl, the full development of the Princess Presence. The integration and embodiment of the Pearl has that kind of light. It is the light that is the fullness and collection of all the Divine lights as a living organism of presence, a developing human body-soul. If you remember, *penina*, the Pearl, bears children.

The first time I recognized the Princess Presence and its development into the Pearl was after engaging a prayer practice of talking to God.[18] This is a powerful practice of personal prayer. I would talk to God about mundane, everyday things, and I would also share whatever was in my heart, mind, and soul. The practice was to talk spontaneously and without hesitation and censure. I started to notice after a short while that something very real was growing in me. It felt like there was some precious intimacy with myself that was developing as I became more and more vulnerable in my relationship with God.

I became accustomed to saying everything to God, and things started coming out of me that I did not even know were there. I started crying a lot and processing all kinds of unconscious conflicts, pains and wounds. I realized that a really important part of the practice for me was to engage my body and to feel into the somatic dimension of the unconscious material that was arising in this practice.

At this time, I would go out into nature and put my hands and feet into the earth; I would feel my body pulse with the life force of the earth. I found myself rolling on the ground, screaming and crying and beating the earth and yelling at God. I found myself telling God to go fuck himself and telling God to make love to me; I asked for guidance, begged for forgiveness, and ordered God to heal my loved ones. Basically, I was out-and-out completely *meshugah* (crazy) with God. It is a powerful practice to get real with God.

In this practice God becomes your lover, your parent, your friend, your teacher, and your child. All of the relational dynamics and all the psychodynamics that we transfer onto our relationships in their myriad expressions get worked on in this practice. After a while I realized that all of the relational transferences that I was projecting externally were somehow getting integrated and digested inside me as I engaged God relationally. More and more I realized that I was not seeking so much to get things from outside of myself.

As my intimacy with God deepened, I began to feel a deepening intimacy with myself. I realized that something was growing inside me; there was a living presence inside my body, in my consciousness. It had this sweet preciousness to it, like a treasure that I wanted to protect. I did not want to expose it to the world, like a precious jewel I did not want people to know about. It felt like my own hidden treasure. It felt like the Divine life pulsating in me.

What else could I want? It felt like I had found the most beautiful, precious, and satisfying substance in existence. I would look forward to the time that I had set aside in the evening when I could seclude myself and bask in the grace of this magical substance. It became my whole life; I did not care about anything else. I could feel the glow and the fullness of it all through the day, and I would long to be alone with it, to be intimate with it, at night.

This presence changed over time. It had its own journey and development that deepened in various ways. At some point I realized that this living presence was integrating the Divine Lights and expressing them in the world. What is magical about it is that it is whole. It is whole because it does not hold a split between the dual and the non-dual. It is both fully human and fully Divine.

Embodying the Pearl, there is not a sense of something outside of myself that will bring fulfillment. There is nothing else that is desired; all fulfillment is already living inside me as this magical presence. It therefore heals the relational transferences that are projected onto others by realizing those beautiful qualities inside me, as me. As such, it resolves the tendency to see inside and outside as mutually exclusive, to see self and other as separate.

One interesting paradox arises with the Pearl. One might think that with the elimination of needing anyone or anything outside of oneself for fulfillment you would cease to be a relational human being, but the result is quite the opposite. The Pearl enhances one's engagement with the world. You begin to see the potential for that Pearly presence in everybody. It becomes a noble and magical world. The experience of the Pearl has a sense of nobility and royalty to it. The princess, and its development into the Pearl, has a precious royal quality.

When the Pearl integrates the Divine qualities, it lives without self-consciousness. There is a clear sense of "this is who I am" or "this is what I feel." You can feel angry or hurt, Divine, or like a child. The content ceases to define the condition of this presence. You can feel contracted or expanded, it makes no difference. The Pearl remains in its living evolving life, whether it feels contracted or expanded, whether it feels like this or that. So you see how it integrates and resolves the split of the spiritual and the material, the split between the human and the Divine.

All of the relational energy of talking to God somehow became integrated with—and digested into—the Pearl, all the while without giving up the relational capacity. This resolves the paradox of having simultaneously a dualistic practice with a nondual view. How can you pray and talk to God if you are holding a nondual view of reality? It does not make sense to the mind.

While this cannot be understood with the ordinary mind, from the *penina* perspective—which is the integration of the inner and the outer, the face and the inside, the integration of the *mem* into the *nun*—it can be understood experientially. It can be known and palpably felt. It is possible to talk to God, to relate to other, without it violating the nondual truth. In fact, it feels like a natural and organic expression of that truth; the most natural and organic expression of living a human life.

[The following discussion takes place after an experiential exercise.]

STUDENT: I remember one time in another class you said a relationship with God can feel more intimate than any other relationship you have. So, exploring this practice of talking to God together in the group, I really felt that. I didn't feel comfortable watching someone else. I felt like I was looking at something too private, too intimate. I feel a bubbling in my belly.

ZVI: Your face looks pretty bright.

STUDENT: It wasn't a bad uncomfortable, it was a tender uncomfortable. Like a little girl trying on a dress and wanting to show it to a friend.

ZVI: Sounds like you got it.

STUDENT: Yes, I can feel it now.

ZVI: Yes. When we feel that embarrassment, or that shyness, that's a great opportunity to notice the quality that's coming up and allow that to shine. A certain kind of presence can arise. A lot of aliveness in that. It has that kind of innocence in it. There is that impulse to protect it.

STUDENT: I noticed that I started off as myself and I was really anxious and self-conscious and then I moved into the God-seat and explored what it felt like to relate to myself from God's perspective. I was both supportive and supported. And then I supported myself, and when I moved back to myself, I felt more comfortable. Like it kind of showed me something that happens a lot but that I never directly see. When I'm alone I don't feel judged and I can be myself, and somewhere along the line when I go into the world I lose that. So, just saying that out loud pointed that out to me, where normally I don't notice. It feels good to share with other people.

ZVI: You look pretty clear right now. Yes, it is very easy to forget who we are.

STUDENT: Here's one thing that I wanted to address that happened during the exercise, but it was kind of a tangent. I was sitting in God's seat, and someone brushed up against me and said, "Sorry Mike," and I thought to say, "I'm God now." I related to what you said earlier about the unapologetic quality of speaking what is.

ZVI: Do you have a sense of what inhibited the expression?

STUDENT: A sense of staying appropriate, keeping the space sacred, not making a joke. I can experience both what happened and what didn't happen as both being okay. No blame, just a supportive sense of strength. I feel clarity through my throat. Sturdy legs. My abdomen and belly area feel very connected. A sense of clarity, connectedness about me. Integration and a space that allows for things that I might want to say to be said.

ZVI: Yes, so there is a spaciousness and a capacity to be who you are, directly and really, without any modifications. How is it to experience that right now?

STUDENT: Pretty powerful.

ZVI: Yes, it is powerful to know ourselves and to express it fearlessly.

STUDENT: I had a powerful experience being God, because I didn't really think about it, I just let myself go into it. Then I had this experience that the words were just coming and I was surprised at what was coming out. The idea of God on the outside and nondual. At school where I'm studying, there is no space or permission to have a nondual experience so it's quite profound.

ZVI: What do you sense right now in your belly?

STUDENT: It's really grounding. I feel energetically connected.

ZVI: Seems that you need this grounding presence to be in school right now, to do what you need to do in life, in a way that is authentic to you.

STUDENT: It's very easy to forget my own experience and to slip out into everybody else's space. I have to keep grounding to stay centered.

ZVI: You could practice coming back to sensing the presence in your belly, all the time, until it becomes second nature.

STUDENT: I feel deep gratitude for this teaching and for this space that is being supported here. It is so rare in the world.

ZVI: It's true, there is a very powerful presence that's being cultivated here. It's not just an ordinary course of study that we're doing. We're building an organism of Presence here and it's a resource for all of us. So, from one meeting to the next, we could draw from the group field of all of our practice. We are all impacting each other. That's actually the function of a *minyan*, the traditional quorum of ten for prayer. It is to create the supports that we need for the path. So, even if you forget, you're sitting in class and you remember, the Now is always here; it doesn't go anywhere. Any moment we remember truth is a moment of eternity that is accessible to us.

In a word, what is the quality of presence in the space right now?

STUDENTS: Settled. Blended. Thick, density of Presence. Creative. Love. Sweet. Gift. Compassion.

ZVI: Yes. Do you notice all of these things? There is also a very sober kind of quality. This is what I mean by "Waking Down." There's a sobriety and an earthy, human, practical quality. There's an ordinariness to it even though it's magical and mysterious.

There is also a sense of Being. There is the sense that we could sit here forever; it has the quality of eternity to it.

See you all in a few weeks. Notice what happens in your dreams and in your life. We're moving into interesting territory now.

8
The Chamber of Sorrows

Practice

LET'S BEGIN WITH the *Shema* prayer, the chant that we did in our very
first meeting. The *Shema* chant/prayer is from the ancient Hebrew
tradition, and it is the prayer of oneness. It calls us to realize in a direct experiential manner that the formless and the formed are one and
the same. The dual and the nondual, the changeless and that which
changes, the *Yud Hey Vav Hey* and *Elohim*, are all one unified reality.
The Hebrew carries the hidden transmission of the experiential truth,
so just let the vibration, the sacred sound, saturate your consciousness
as we chant. And notice what happens experientially. We will chant it
numerous times and then we'll sit in silence afterwards until I ring the
bell. And that will be the end of the meditation.

Talk

In the last chapter we discussed the princess and the Pearl, the *penima* and the *penina*, as well as the transformation and movement from
the inside to the outside and from the outside to the inside, the unification of the two, manifesting as an organism of presence. *Penina* in
Hebrew means "pearl." The Pearl is the resolution of the fundamental

perception of being alienated from God through the embodiment of our Divine nature as our human nature. You can say it is the resolution of all splits, even the most fundamental split of all, which is the split between the human and the Divine, the nondual and the dual, the finite and the infinite.

The Pearl does not offer a resolution of the mind; rather, it is a resolution that is known experientially, in the body-soul. It entails actually becoming and embodying this Pearl, this matured Princess Presence with its vulnerability, innocence, preciousness, fullness, life, and being. The Pearl comes with the innate sense of being a child of God, a child that is one in essence with God. The experience of the Pearl is a paradox to the ordinary mind. It is experienced as relational with other and with God and yet—at the same time—not separate from other and God. It is simultaneously dual and nondual, as a full and embodied expression of human presence.

The Pearl is also the resolution of the conceptual conflict between a devotional path and a transcendent or nondual path. The Pearl has no conflict with both of these being simultaneously present. "Devotional" for the Pearl does not mean devotion to something that is separate from itself. It is the essence of devotion itself, the heartfelt sense of yearning, of vulnerability to other and to all life. It is the appreciation for all forms of creation.

Even as it experiences itself as a full and particular expression of creation, it recognizes that it is inseparable from all of creation. There are no fragmented parts in the experience of the Pearl. It is all one creation of which we are a particular and precious offspring. We are enwombed in the very bosom of creation and we are its expression in life. The practice we explored last time of talking to God—talking to the benevolent consciousness that permeates all of reality—can open up the possibility for this kind of experience.

The Pearl is the mature individual Princess Presence that relates in life with other. It relates in a contactful, appreciative, and respectful manner. Not from a place of being a separate other, but with a pure sensitivity for other as another manifestation of oneself. It does this all the while without diminishing one's experience of being an individual, a particular expression of Being. This is a paradox the mind cannot wrap itself around.

I first came upon the experience of the Pearl through the practice of talking to God. It was an accident. I was not looking for it and I did not know what it was at the time, but it was certainly palpable. I felt my whole body and consciousness transforming into a whole different kind of organism. I could feel a union with God that was so intimate that the discrimination between me and God was blurred and yet, at the same time, I was an individual relating to God.

There is such a sweetness and fullness that comes with this. The whole world looks different. The birds are singing, the sun is shining, and people are beautiful. Even people that I hated started to look beautiful. It is a remarkable thing. It felt like meeting God again and again in another form.

I will share with you more in the coming talks about what happened after this. I did not fully appreciate what it was at the time. I did not have a framework to situate it exactly. As things unfolded, I came upon what I now call the Journey of Vastness, which is the next stage in the five journeys of the Kedumah path. When I began to experience vastness, I thought that this experience of the Princess Pearl—this experience of the fullness and beauty of the union of human and Divine—was somehow not real or true. In my experience, the Pearl felt displaced by a radical spaciousness and emptiness that at the time seemed to be somehow more fundamental.

In a way, I rejected the Pearl as something of the ego, and somehow less real or less significant. It took me a long time to realize what I had forsaken. Not only is it real, but it is also necessary to live a human life that is an expression of truth and of our human potential. In a way, the Journey of Wholeness—the integration of the many aspects of Presence into one's individual consciousness—is really the core of the path. It is the centerpiece of the path because it is the integration into life of the Journeys of Contraction and Expansion; it is the mechanism through which all experience, all enlightenment, all the vast possibilities of freedom are able to live freely as a human being.

In the very beginning, we discussed how the whole purpose of creation is the embodied human experience, the experience of the infinite becoming finite, of living in and as form. Without this very human integrative possibility, then the whole project of creation loses its wholeness, fullness, and potential. We could do a whole year of teachings just on all the intricacies of this Journey of Wholeness, but in this series I will just speak to one or two aspects of it.

I mentioned in the last chapter the movement from the *mem* to the *nun*, from *penima* to *penina*. As you may recall, we talked about the difference between the number forty, which is *mem,* and the movement to fifty, which is *nun*. Forty represents transformation and there are many forties in the Hebrew Bible: forty days of the flood, forty years traveling in the desert before the people of Israel entered into the promised land, forty days on the mountain before Moses received the revelation, and so on.

I also mentioned that forty is the required volume of the *mikvah,* the ritual bath, which is used to mark the process of transformation and rebirth.[1] The number forty and the letter *mem* also represent the womb, which is a transitory stage.[2] But if forty is good, then fifty is even better. This is because fifty is a further development of forty and is the fruition of the transitory stage of forty. The Jubilee is the fiftieth year. Have you heard of that word? It is a transliteration of the Hebrew word *yovel* which comes from the Hebrew Bible and means "the fiftieth year." According to the ancient custom, in the Jubilee year all property would return back to its original owner, including slaves, who were freed in the fiftieth year. It is the year of freedom and of return to origins.[3]

It is also no accident that there are ten digits between forty and fifty. The number ten in Kabbalah represents the ten lights, the ten Divine qualities on the Tree of Life, the ten *sefirot*. The movement from contraction to expansion is celebrated in the exodus from *Mitzrayim* (Egypt) on *Pesach*. Then there are seven weeks between *Pesach* and *Shavuot*. Incidentally, *Pesach* was last week, so now we are free in case you did not know. [Laughter.] It is a joke because really there is no history; it is all happening right now. That is why Pesach and the exodus from contraction are not events that occurred at a particular moment in history. This is the Kedumah perspective, at any rate. In reality, the exodus from contraction to expansion can happen in every moment.

There are seven weeks between *Pesach* and *Shavuot*, which as you will remember is Pentecost, also known as the Festival of Weeks. It celebrates the revelation and receiving of the Torah at Sinai. As we discussed in the last chapter, these seven weeks are counted day by day for forty-nine days until we reach the fiftieth day, *Shavuot*. The number fifty represents the next stage after the movement from contraction to expansion into wholeness.

This movement from expansion to wholeness is represented by the number fifty, which is why the movement from the *penima*, or the inner essence, to the *penina*, the Pearl, is a movement from the letter *mem* (forty) to the *nun* (fifty). The movement into wholeness is the integration of the dialectical process of expansion and contraction and the ten Divine lights (the difference between forty and fifty) into an individual living organism of Being, a human being. Thus, the mature, authentic human being is the living Pearl that is formed through the constructive friction generated in the back and forth movement of contraction and expansion, just as a natural pearl is formed from the many years of friction generated by the salt and sea meeting inside the crucible of the clam or oyster.

The true human being, the mature human being, shines like a pearl. He or she shines with an aged, ripened nobility. This magical presence of personal royalty is shaped and cultivated in the struggles and frictions of human life. This can feel like a paradox. On the one hand, we may feel contracted, stuck in patterns of experience or behavior.

And yet, on the other hand, we know that we can perceive who we are and what reality is in an expanded way, not bound by those identities and self images; even energetic confinements and physical limitations cease to be issues in expanded states.

When we experience expansion we don't feel confined by the physical body in the same way that we did before. While we still have a body and it has its limitations, the body image is freed so we know that we are not limited to our body. We know that who and what we are is not bound by the limitations of the physical form. This is one of the hallmarks of the experience of expansion. This kind of dialectic between contraction and expansion—*ratzo vashov*, "back and forth"—is the refining mechanism in the development of this Pearl.

Friction is necessary to form an authentic and mature human soul. A real human being is born out of this process of refinement, out of this struggle. To be a human being is difficult. We have many conflicts, many struggles and much suffering; we feel bound by a body and we struggle with issues and conflicts that are emotional, physical, and psychological. All of this contributes to the suffering of life. It is quite radical to propose that there is a reality or an experience of ourselves that is free from these sufferings.

The Pearl, the Jubilee of our human experience, is the resolution of human suffering as it manifests in both contracted and expanded states. The suffering of contraction is most obvious in our human experience. We all know that very well. But as we discussed last class, there is also a suffering that happens in the expanded state. It is a more subtle and preferable kind of suffering than that of contraction, but it is a suffering nonetheless.

It is true that the suffering of the expanded state gives us more space and freedom from our bounded identities, but because we are still orienting towards expansion relative to contraction, then that too is a certain kind of suffering. It is the suffering born of a split, however subtle, between contraction and expansion that we are holding deep in our unconscious. To be free from suffering we must actually go beyond a nondual state, because even nonduality has its own suffering.

In some ways it is a much trickier kind of suffering because it is less recognizable to the mind. It is easier to recognize this more subtle kind of suffering when we are struggling to integrate an experience of expansion into our ordinary life. We may find ourselves swinging back and forth between contraction and expansion. We may discover that we can feel very expanded when we are alone, but for some reason when we are with others—especially the people we love most—we cannot be expanded or it is much more difficult. We may find that we are irritated, anxious, or disturbed when we cannot seem to hold onto the nondual state.

Wholeness is the essential resolution to this split, because it is the integration of the two sides of this dynamic spectrum of experience. They are no longer split into two. The Jubilee state—the *nun*, the fifty, the *penina*, the Pearl—is one in which the experiences of contraction and expansion are no longer seen as two separate events but rather are known and appreciated as different manifestations of one unified reality. Having this orientation radically alters the way we relate to contraction; from this new perspective the goal is no longer to get out of contraction and into expansion, which is the usual way we approach the spiritual journey.

In the usual perspective we dislike contraction because it feels unholy and godless, and it hurts. But in this new view of wholeness, we accept the experience of contraction and the human experience of struggle with more appreciation for its Divine nature. With this appreciation comes a greater curiosity about its significance, its meaning, and its purpose for us personally. There is an appreciation that there is something waiting, wanting to reveal itself to us. Rather than seeing contraction and its suffering as a problem to get rid of, it is seen as an opportunity and a handout from God, as a gift to unwrap. It is through understanding our contractions that we unwrap these gifts.

The number fifty is associated in the Kabbalistic tradition with the *sefirah* of *Binah*.[4] In the Tree of Life, the upper triadic center consists of *Keter*, *Chochmah*, and *Binah*, whose three Lights are the most primordial in that they existed prior to creation. The lower seven Lights, from *Chesed* to *Malchut*, are known by the Kabbalists as the Lights of Creation. Those are the Lights that manifest in the world of creation, in form. *Binah* is the feminine primordial Light. She is known as the Celestial Womb, the Celestial Mother. She is also known by the code terms Jubilee and Living Waters.[5] These are all technical terms used in the Kabbalistic tradition to refer to this Divine quality. She is also the number fifty.

The Hebrew word *Binah*, the most common name given to this *sefirah*, literally means "understanding." There is an intimate relationship between the whole constellation of terms that we have been using to describe the Pearl: the letter *nun*, the number fifty, the maturation of the human consciousness, and understanding. The way I see it, understanding our contraction—our pain and suffering, its genesis, its origins, and how it manifests for us personally—is the gateway for the development of this quality. Furthermore, it is the gateway to real transformation on a cellular level.

Think back to the story I told of when I was the *mashgiach* and I discovered that the quality of *Gevurah*, the Divine quality of strength, was blocked. It was not until an inquiry into my experience unfolded that there was a transformation. In particular, it was not until I understood the origins of this particular contraction that my experience was able to open to the pure red light of Being. The process of understanding is thus a central fulcrum in the journey of awakening.

When I use the term "understanding," I do not mean it in the conventional sense. Understanding, on the level of the Divine Light of *Binah*, is an essential quality of Being, a true and pure expression of fundamental reality. This dimension of understanding can only reveal itself to us if we orient our consciousness in a certain way. In the *mashgiach* story, there was already a sense of Presence in my experience; I really wanted to know the truth and I was willing to be in a state of not-knowing. Because there was enough alignment in my consciousness of these three orienting postures, it opened the possibility of true understanding.

Only once there was understanding, was the contraction able to open into expansion and integrate in my soul. You can feel it in the body, you can feel it on the cellular level, and you can feel it saturate the body and the consciousness. This is the kind of nourishment that feeds the growing Pearl in our consciousness. The Pearl grows like an embryo in the womb of our soul. Every time we understand another layer of our experience this embryo grows another layer of derma, until this organism that is growing can make you feel like you are pregnant. It can feel like your spiritual womb is growing. You can feel full and glowing and present. There is a living being, an organism that is growing and maturing in one's consciousness and as oneself.

Understanding is one aspect of this process. *Binah*, which is understanding, which is the Celestial Mother, the Celestial Womb, the Celestial Waters, is also associated with the ritual of immersing in the *mikvah*, a ritual body of water.[6] The practice of immersing in a *mikvah* is an ancient tradition that existed thousands of years ago and continues to be used in some circles to this day. For a *mikvah* to be kosher according to Jewish law, it must contain living waters; that is to say, the water must come from a natural source that has not been manipulated in any way by artificial processes.[7]

For example, a living spring, a river, or rainwater that gathers in a receptacle would all serve as a kosher *mikvah*. Earthen channels are ideally used to transport the waters because they maintain the connection with the earth; the waters cannot be solely transported using metal pipes. The reason for this is that *Binah*, which is the *sefirah* associated with the mystical process of transformation that occurs in a *mikvah*, is also called the Upper Earth. She is the Celestial Earth, the supernal counterpart of the Terrestrial Earth, a code term for *Shechinah* or Presence. She is also the Living Waters that fill the Terrestrial

Earth, which is why an actual physical connection has to be maintained with the earth for the waters to maintain their power for celestial transformation.

The practice is to fully immerse oneself in these Living Waters. By doing so a person's consciousness returns to its primordial condition in the Celestial Womb of *Binah* and is then reborn. The Christian tradition of baptism comes from this ancient tradition of *mikvah*. In the Hebrew tradition, the *mikvah* is also equated with *YHVH*. There is a verse in the book of Jeremiah (17:13) that states: *Mikvah le-Yisrael YHVH*, which means, "The *mikvah* of Israel is *YHVH*." It is an immersion into Being, into *YHVH*, and it is specifically associated with the quality of *Binah*.[8]

Another term the Kabbalists associate with *Binah* is *teshuva*.[9] *Teshuva* is a Hebrew word that literally means "returning." Often it is mistranslated as "repentance," but not only is this an inaccurate translation, the word has a bad connotation. Nobody likes to "repent," but everyone wants to "return." On the mystical level it refers to the process of "returning" to our primordial condition. That is why *mikvah* is associated with this process of *teshuvah*, of returning.

The concept of returning is a whole teaching in the Kabbalistic tradition. There is an entire world of revelation around its significance. It is explicitly related to the *sefirah* of *Binah,* known as the *Imma Ha-Elyon*, or the Celestial Mother. This primordial Light is explicitly referred to as the *Olam Ha-Teshuvah*, the "world of returning."[10] That is why the Jubilee year, which is *Binah,* is the year that has to do with returning to origins.

In traditional Kabbalistic circles, there is a period of forty days during the year, between the first day of the month of *Elul (Rosh Chodesh Elul)* all the way until the holiday of Yom Kippur, usually known as the Day of Atonement. Those forty days are known as the *Yamei Ha-Teshuvah*, or the "days of return."

In many traditional circles, pious people who are devoted to this process immerse in the *mikvah* every day as part of this ritual of returning. They use the practice as a ritual of transformation, as a "returning" to the Jubilee state, the Celestial Mother, and the wholeness of the number fifty. Ultimately this process entails the integration of the fifty into our human experience as the Pearl. It is the return of the "lost princess," for those of you who are familiar with Rebbe Nachman of Bratzlav's famous story by this name. This is what he is talking about. He is talking about the Princess Presence that has been lost and we long to find her and return to a state of union with the Divine, to be in a state of knowing ourselves as Divine.

This opens up an inevitable discussion that is very important around the Pearl and around the principle of return, which is encountered on the Journey of Wholeness. Wholeness has to do with behavior. It has to do with how we live our life. It has two axes: The vertical axis, which has to do with our behavior being in alignment with Divine truth, and the horizontal axis, which has to do with our behavior being in alignment with relational truth. The integration of the vertical and horizontal axes is the essence of wholeness.

How we live our life is thus the domain of the *penina*, the Pearl. These two axes are reflected in the Talmudic teachings on commandments that are "between us and God" (*Bein Adam L'Makom*) and those that are between "us and our fellow humans" (*Bein Adam L'chaveiro*).[11]

We can be completely realized on the vertical axis, but our relational behavior may not be aligned with it. The way we relate may not be reflective of what we know to be true, because that muscle, that cellular living material of consciousness, is not necessarily developed on the horizontal plane. This organ of wholeness is the Pearl. As you see, it has to do with behavior and with relationship. It has to do with how we act and how we are in the world.

This means that inevitably, in working with the Journey of Wholeness, we must contend and deal with the way that we are in the world. We will inevitably come upon what I call the Chamber of Sorrows. The Chamber of Sorrows is a chamber in the heart that holds all of our buried regrets, remorse, and sadness related to our actions in the world: how we've treated others, how we've done or not done one thing or another. We have to come to terms with our character limitations, with these oftentimes buried feelings of remorse.

Of course, this path is hard work; it is painful and because it digs deeply, it leaves you incredibly vulnerable. In a sense it is really about getting to know our brokenness as human beings—or what feels like brokenness—and really feeling the sorrow that we have around that. On the Journey to Wholeness you can see, even just logically, how it would be impossible to know and experience wholeness without knowing and experiencing brokenness, because they are two sides of the same thing. Wholeness is a concept. As a concept it can only exist relative to brokenness. We only know ourselves as "whole" relative to feeling "unwhole."

As long as the Chamber of Sorrows is buried, there is really no possibility for wholeness. It has to be integrated. This is a challenging dimension of the spiritual path, and it is oftentimes not dealt with on the spiritual journey, because usually the emphasis on the path is on becoming nondual. Instead, on the Kedumah path, we emphasize wholeness, which is a journey of maturation and of becoming a more complete human being; this means there is no dual and nondual split, and nothing can be hidden. It is the state also referred to in the Talmud as *tocho ke'varo*, which in Aramaic means, "the inside is like the outside."[12] A true human being has no split between inner and outer, which means there is no Chamber of Secrets lurking beneath the surface. What you see is what you get. That is what we are talking about here.

So, what this means of course is that we are totally screwed! [Laughter.] It means there is no way out and there is nowhere to hide, and moreover nothing to hide. This is what is referred to as the *teshuvah* process, the process of returning. In normative Judaism they translate this term as "repentance," but this is a limited way of talking about this process. Confessing and repenting for misdeeds is important, but this is a limited way of understanding *teshuvah*. Kedumah, as a mystical path, understands that confessing sins is not necessarily transformational in and of itself.

On this path, when we recognize that our behavior is not in alignment with truth, we may experience a heartfelt aspiration for transformation. Such a sincere wish is then held in the womb of the Celestial Mother, which offers a true "return" and a true wiping away of all misdeeds. According to the Kabbalists, in order to engage the process of *teshuvah*, we must take an accounting of our behavior and feel our remorse. We must feel the sorrow that comes with recognizing the impact of our behavior, recognizing its distortion and how it has hurt others and ourselves.

We have to enter into the Chamber of Sorrows with a kind of radical acceptance and compassion. What is called for is not ordinary compassion; it is radical, because it is a compassion that is born of love. Remorse will naturally lead to a commitment, a vow not to engage in this kind of an action again. That is the natural consequence of truly feeling the remorse.

However, if we engage the process of *teshuvah* out of fear of punishment, desire for reward, or to please someone else, it will lack the cellular transformation on the level of the Pearl. In this process there is not hope for something and it is not conditioned. We need to penetrate the Chamber of Sorrows deeply enough that our remorse is sincere and we want to change because we see the truth. It needs to be undertaken because of our love of truth, ourselves, our loved ones, and love of Divine Being. It is a spontaneous feeling that "I will change my life for the sake of what I am feeling, even if it means I lose everything and even if it means I die." That is the depth of the feeling and the felt sense of it. This is when you can feel the body-soul begin to integrate the understanding and the wisdom. The actual lived consciousness begins to change into a different kind of organism, one that is able to express what it knows and what it perceives in a more authentic and whole way.

I mention all of this because I do not know if there is any way around it. An integral part of the horizontal path of becoming fully human is coming to terms with how we are in our lives, including how we relate and how we act. According to the rabbinic tradition, when we do *teshuvah* out of love, all of our past sins are "transformed into merits." This is a quote from the Talmud. When we do *teshuvah* out of love—in other words, for its own sake and not to get anything in return—all of our past sins are transformed into merits.[13]

Can you imagine that? It is not just saying that our sins are erased or disqualified. Of course, when I use the word "sin" I mean it according to its original meaning in the Hebrew. It is a translation of the word *chet*, which means "to miss the mark."[14] From the Kedumah perspective, "sin" refers to when we act in a way that is not in alignment. When we enter into the *teshuvah* dimension—also known as the Jubilee, the fifty, the Living Waters, and the Celestial Womb— which requires moving through the Chamber of Sorrows, it is not just that all of our misdeeds are erased, disqualified, or forgiven. It is far more radical than that. In the mysterious celestial realms, all those misdeeds are mysteriously and alchemically transformed into merits on our behalf.

This does not make sense to the conventional mind. However, this can be appreciated based on the lived experience of the growth of this Pearl, which is borne out of the friction of our suffering and our sorrow. From this view, it is in fact our misdeeds that give us the possibility and the hope of becoming truly human. Without them we could never be the Pearl. Without them we could never become living embodiments of the Divine Being in human form.

Whereas the realm of time and space is ephemeral, the realm or world of *teshuvah* is primordial. It predates the creation of the material world and its Divine quality is pre-creation. This is why entering into the realm of *teshuvah* is able to transform reality, transform the past, in a magical, mysterious way. This is a very mysterious and profound realization that really turns on its head how we orient to sins and shame because it reveals the place that misdeeds have in the developmental process, if we can learn and appreciate the gift that they provide us. They give us a gift, an opportunity to become the human possibility that we can be. They allow us to see through a new lens all of our character "defects" and all of the mistakes we have made. We can see them as opportunities to really feel the remorse, the brokenness and the natural movement of our heart from that space. We can move toward the rebirthing of a new dawn, of a new life. Our intention has the power to transform all of these blockages into nourishment and material for the birth of an altogether new kind of human being.[15]

STUDENT: During your talk I thought about the story of Adam and Eve. It seems that original sin was actually a good thing. Like, Adam and Eve eating from the fruit of the tree is what allows them to become fully human. I was wondering about that.

ZVI: I think you just said it. Don't forget the serpent says (Gen 3:4-5), "If you eat of this tree, you will become like God." Yet they become human. So are they human or are they God? See, the wisdom of the Pearl is that we are both; they are both true. And yes, there is the sin which allows the possibility of integration of good and evil.

STUDENT: I guess my point is that it seems like God rigged it. The story goes that God said they weren't supposed to eat the fruit, and they ate the fruit and they messed up. But eating the fruit has to be a sin for them to become fully human, so God rigged it.

ZVI: Yes, God rigged itself. Good insight. What are you experiencing right now?

STUDENT: There's nowhere to hide. It feels like even if this primordial sin is all a part of the perfect Divine plan, it's like I can't mess up, I'm surrounded, I can't not be enacting the Divine plan perfectly. It's kind of nice: it's a relief, I can let go, I can just be myself—it's not like the universe is in my hands and I can mess it all up. But it's weird, it's paradoxical, because I can. All my actions reverberate infinitely in the cosmos, but none of them are my actions, anyway. I'm kind of baffled actually, but it's kind of nice. Like my brain can't, so it gives up.

ZVI: What does your brain giving up feel like?

STUDENT: Nice.

ZVI: What does "nice" feel like?

STUDENT: Like an effervescence, like a bubbling, very active. Like free to act. Unafraid to act. Like I'm not going to mess everything up. Whatever I do, I'm going to learn and it's going to be okay.

ZVI: What happens when you look at me right now?

STUDENT: It's like speaking integrates it. It's almost as if the floor is floating above my head, and it's become my own wisdom. It doesn't feel like I'm re-saying what you said. I get it because I can say it. And it feels, like, *in me*, very intimate.

ZVI: Intimate, integrated, and an authentic expression of you as an individual. You're integrating. So, it is a paradox. On the one hand, there is nothing we can do that would be out of the perfection and the perfect design of creation. On the other hand, part of that perfection is that it doesn't mean we have license to do wrong. We don't have the license to act in unethical ways, even though it's true that there's nothing we can do that is out of the Divine perfection. It is a paradox.

What's interesting is that we can't use this teaching as license for a nihilistic way of living. I mean, of course we can choose nihilism if we want, but the paradox is that seeing things from this perspective, in an integrated manner, typically leads us to choose modes of life that produce less suffering.

That's why it's so important to move through the Chamber of Sorrows and the process of remorse. We can't disrupt the perfection, but we can create more suffering through our actions. So, it's a paradox. And the more sincere we are, the more likely that we won't perpetuate more suffering, even if it's true objectively that nothing that we do is out of the perfection. It's not something the conventional mind can comprehend. This is one of the reasons why some of the nondual teachings were concerned that the people could misunderstand and misuse the teachings. They feared that people would take license based on these principles, that they would just do whatever they desired. And that's the paradox. There's nothing we can do that would disrupt the design, yet we can't shirk our responsibilities to ourselves and to each other.

STUDENT: I just wanted to share that it's interesting, because it's almost like realizing that we can't mess up invigorates me with a desire to be that much more meticulous in my uprightness and my behavior. It's weird though. It's both.

ZVI: Right, that's the amazing thing about the Pearl. It's fearless in terms of being itself and expressing itself and doing what is true and authentic, and yet it becomes naturally more impeccable about the integrity of that behavior in the world. It comes from within, it doesn't come from without. It doesn't come from moral standards, laws of society, or from religion. It comes from the inner wisdom of knowing oneself as a living expression of the Divine Being. It is the natural thing to want to be clear and precise and impeccable; to provide beneficence and blessing rather than suffering. That's what we mean by the integration; the wisdom and the intelligence comes from within. So, that's good. Thank you.

STUDENT: I realized a little bit into the talk and also in the exercise that I don't relate so well to the word "remorse," but I do relate to the Chamber of Sorrows. But in my feeling, my experience, it's bigger than remorse. It's not that remorse isn't a piece or a part of it, but somehow it doesn't feel like remorse is the guilt, repentance kind of principle. And my feeling is that there is something even more fundamental about the sorrow than remorse. Or maybe because it's not just tied to things we've done or that we know we've done, but it's things actually we can't even name yet, but that we feel. Like we could be feeling other people's remorse, or something like that. But again, the word "remorse" feels too tight for me. To me that experience has always felt like a very huge kind of doorway that cleanses and opens the way for something. But I just have to say that I don't like that word "remorse."

ZVI: I appreciate that there is a more fundamental sorrow than remorse. Remorse is one of the antechambers, and there are many others. It's an antechamber that pertains more to a certain kind of regret. It's a sorrow that is associated more with our behavior. But it's just one layer, one antechamber in the Chamber of Sorrows, which is a much bigger reservoir.

STUDENT: Yeah, it's almost like feeling bad about something you did is like slipping on the ice, and then you fall into something much bigger, which is really this desire for goodness or this desire for wholeness. It's this feeling that I missed or overlooked something. It is a kind of remorse, but "remorse" is not the exact word.

ZVI: Yes, I appreciate that. Remorse is a very specific part of the whole picture. If we have the opportunity to unpack it more, we will see that there are many teachings and tools we use to excavate the Chamber of Sorrows. We can move through all the antechambers.

STUDENT: Can we talk about that sometime?

ZVI: Well, you will have to do the whole series of the Chamber of Sorrows retreats. I'll have to get permission from Dumbledore before we open it up. My inner Dumbledore has to give me permission. [Laughter.]

STUDENT: I just wanted to add that with this "remorse" word, I feel the same way. I think it's like a basic badness, this feeling of alienation from God. And when we were talking about the last question, "What is it like to feel remorse?" at first it feels like I'm this bad person, it feels horrible and alienating. And then I can't help but see all these things I've done to hurt people, yet I was innocent the whole time. I never intended to hurt anyone. This underlying goodness that was always there in its purity and innocence just confirms that.

ZVI: What's it like to sense the innocence and the goodness? To allow that to really be in the foreground right now?

STUDENT: I don't know.

ZVI: What do you experience in your heart?

STUDENT: Tenderness and love. And kind of a vulnerable feeling.

ZVI: So, there's vulnerability and tenderness and love.

STUDENT: And a desire to expand it. And I feel a desire to be impeccable in my life.

ZVI: It's interesting, because when you describe it and talk about the impeccability, it seems that your consciousness shifts. What do you experience right now, when you speak to the impeccability?

STUDENT: Are you trying to suggest something?

ZVI: No, this is just what Jews do. We ask a lot of questions. [Laughter.] Usually we have a sense of our consciousness in the shape of our conventional body, but what does your body feel like now?

STUDENT: I don't know.

ZVI: Something to explore, maybe. Often when we talk about vulnerability and tenderness, sometimes there's a delicacy that comes with that. But you look right now to me like there's more precision and clarity.

STUDENT: I was going to say that I feel kind of strong and very clear. And also like melted butter.

ZVI: So there's a sense of melting, a desire to be impeccable, and there's also a strength. There's some kind of capacity that is expressing itself through that. Oftentimes the Pearly quality is like that because it's an integration of the softness, the vulnerability, the tenderness, and the openness, with a sense of "I can be vulnerable in the world, and express myself in my authenticity, and have that clarity of will to do that at the same time."

I'm just pointing these things out so you get the experiential contours of this possibility. It's something to look at when you experience these things. These are questions you may wish to ask yourself. "What is the tone and texture of the presence as I'm feeling this? How do I experience it in my three centers or in the total sense of my body-soul?" It can be in the physical body or in the subtle sense of the body.

We are learning the practice of *drash*. We hold the orientation of inquiry not just to the contraction, but also vis-a-vis the states that are part of the development of the organism of consciousness, the Pearl principle. The essence of understanding, which is *Binah*, which is *teshuvah*, which is the Jubilee, which is the Pearly presence—all these terms point to the celestial instantiation of the Pearly presence. All of these subtle facets constitute the basic orientation of this path which uses understanding as a primary path of the method.

This is why we do these exercises. The exercises are rooted in a methodology that has certain metaphysical assumptions. Firstly, that we are not all separate individuals. We're Being unpacking itself through these different locations. So when it exposes vulnerability and all the issues that come up, we're creating opportunities to expose those things. So we can bring them into the light and work with them, so Being can work on them, and work on itself, and know itself. We ask questions to understand, because understanding is the gateway to the integration. So, I'm just giving you a sense of where the methodology is coming from. This is actually very much a Jubilee teaching. This teaching is based on the Jubilee principle and all of its constellations.

Sorry for keeping you guys overtime tonight. I feel very remorseful. [Laughter.]

9
One-Love and Pleasure

PRACTICE

OKAY, LET'S BEGIN with a new practice. This may be similar to practices that you have done in other contexts. First, find a comfortable sitting posture and allow the weight of your body to really just drop into the ground, into the earth. Allow the body to settle, to drop down. Allow a natural verticality that's not held in a rigid way but is naturally positioned with ease as it's situated and settled above the base of our spine and its support in the earth.

From this posture, choose a word, any word that rises up from the ground of your being. It could be a word that is connected to your relationship with Being or the Divine. It could be "love" or "trust" or something like that, whatever word manifests for you. We will sit with a posture of just allowing. Allowing our presence to drop into the center of our being, and any time we find ourselves distracted, pulled one way or another from this center, we come back to our chosen word, allowing the word to gently land on our consciousness, on our soul. Keep allowing it to land, like a feather settling on a cotton ball.[1] A soft landing of the sacred word. We can keep coming back to the word, allowing the word to center us. And then if we find that the word disappears and we're just abiding in the center of our being, then we just be that. Be that center. That silence. That stillness.

THE KEDUMAH EXPERIENCE

We'll just sit with this practice for a few minutes and then I'll ring the bell, and that will be the end of the practice.

TALK

When we open up the Chamber of Sorrows, we never know what we are going to find inside. But if we take the time to explore the Chamber of Sorrows and all of its antechambers, we may discover that it can be a portal to a new kind of life—to the life of a different kind of human being. This human being who is reborn feels whole and integrated; all of the hidden parts are metabolized to the degree that the inner and the outer are no longer split. In the Talmud, the completely matured human being is described with the Aramaic term *tocho k'varo*, which means someone whose "inside is like their outside." This is the ancient Hebrew vision of the awakened, embodied, and complete human being.

We talked last time about one of the antechambers, that of regret or remorse, and the process of *teshuvah* or transformation, also called the journey of returning, which happens as a result of coming to terms with our life as it is. The raw sweetness of brutal honesty bares many wondrous fruits when we trust enough that the truth indeed sets us free, regardless of how painful it may feel or seem to be through the conventional perspective.

We saw how *Binah* and the Living Waters of the Celestial Mother allow for a kind of cleansing, a kind of clarification of the soul, such that we can actually experience ourselves as reborn, emerging anew out of the womb of the Divine Mother. There are many facets and ingredients to this that we do not have space to explore in detail in this introductory series. However there is one vital ingredient for this process of *teshuvah* to even happen at all. It is a particular dimension of reality, of Being. This dimension of Being is always here, always in the here and now, even though we may not always perceive it or

192

appreciate its presence, and even though we may not even recognize it at all. It is the major factor that allows the Journey of Wholeness to take hold, and for the Pearl to manifest.

I did not recognize this aspect of Being until I was already experiencing this sense of wholeness in my soul. It could be that going through the pain of the *teshuvah* process and coming to a more immediate embodied sense of wholeness, of the Pearl, facilitated the necessary transition to perceive this dimension more directly. It is not as if it is not here and then it appears; it is always right here, but we may not perceive it directly. Although, I do think it is possible to feel it without necessarily knowing and understanding what it is.

Just stop for a moment and sense into the space in the room right now. What do you notice in your experience? What is the field of presence like in the room right now? Notice how it is impacting you. It is a very subtle kind of presence. In the Kabbalistic tradition, it is referred to with the term *Olam Ha-Ahavah*, which is best translated as the dimension of love.[2] The word *olam* means "space," "world," or "dimension," and *ahavah* is the Hebrew word for "love." They are referring to a particular dimension of Being that has the quality and texture of Divine Love.

This is a particular kind of love that has a particular effect on the soul when we perceive it, recognize it, and experience it. The key characteristic of this sublime love is that it is radically unconditional. That is, it is clear in the experience of it that there is nothing that we need to do to deserve this love. It is not dependent on anything we do or do not do. It is an inherent quality of Being, of reality. The sense of it is that all is accepted and all is forgiven. There is nothing that we can do to somehow make us worthy or unworthy of this love. In English, the word "grace" captures the essence of this kind of love. There is nothing that we can do to get it. It is freely offered and it is ours if we know how to receive it.

This is difficult for the ordinary mind to understand. One might ask: "What do you mean? I can murder somebody and God will still love me? That is obviously not true, right?" That is the conventional mind saying it cannot be. It cannot conceive of a love that is absolutely unconditional, that is absolute in its bountiful generosity. But that is precisely the remarkable thing about it. The verse states (Prov. 10:12): *Al Kol Pesha'im Tichaseh Ahavah*, which means: "Love covers 'all' transgressions." Yes, the word all means that even murderers are embraced in this love.[3] They may not be aware of it, nor will the loved ones of their victims tend to be.

Our distorted actions may contribute to the occlusion of our perception and our capacity to receive this love, which means more suffering for others and ourselves, but the realization of this love is that it is indeed radically unconditional. It is present in the hearts and minds of all beings; it is the very substance of which our bodies and souls are constituted. Its presence permeates all of reality.

Furthermore, there is a clarity and an objectivity to this love. You see, it is not a mushy kind of love; it is not sloppy or gushy. It is very clear and very subtle.[4] And, it has an interesting effect on the consciousness. In my experience, this love brings the soul into a more full, integrated, and whole expression of itself. This is where it gets a little bit mysterious.

When we chant the *Shema* prayer, which invokes the experience of wholeness, we chant the ancient words, *Shema Yisrael Adonai Eloheinu Adonai Echad*. This, however, is only the very beginning of the full traditional prayer that is recited every day by many pious practitioners of the ancient Hebrew path. The traditional version of the prayer continues with several paragraphs that are taken from the Hebrew Bible, from the Torah. This first line of the *Shema* declares the union of dual and nondual, form and formless, finite and infinite, *YHVH* and *Elohim*. It proclaims the union of the feminine and masculine principles, which is the state of the soul that is both Divine and human simultaneously. At the end of the sacred formula we declare the word *echad*, which means "one." The form and the formless, the human and the Divine, the dual and the nondual are all *echad*—one truth and one reality.[5]

Traditionally, this prayer is recited three times a day and at the moment of death. After the word *echad*, there is a short prayer recited in an undertone and then the next paragraph begins with the words from the Hebrew Bible (Deut. 6:5): *Ve-ahavta Et Adonai Elohecha.* This means, "And you shall love *YHVH* your *Elohim.*" *Ve-ahavta* comes from the Hebrew word *ahavah*, which is the Hebrew word for "love." Right after we declare the principle of unity, of wholeness—of *echad*—we invoke the dimension of Love. This is also how it appears in the Torah, where the word *ve-ahavta* (Deut. 6:5), appears immediately following the word *echad* (Deut. 6:4). The principle of *ahavah* (love) thus comes right after *echad*, "one," almost in the same breath; this makes it *echad-ahavah*, which means "one-love." This must be the source for Bob Marley's famous song. [Laughter.]

When we experience the mystical state of wholeness in a particular way, it opens up the dimension of Divine Love. There are many different ways that the presence of wholeness can manifest in our experience—probably an infinite number of ways—but there are specific ways that are perhaps more central. For instance, there is a particular expression of wholeness that tends to open up the dimension of Divine Love.

The characteristic feature of this kind of love is the realization of oneness. That is why there is a direct relationship between "love" and "one," between *ahavah* and *echad*. There are many ways to experience love as union or as oneness, but this kind of oneness is a particular kind that opens up the floodgates of what I call the Realms of Oneness. In conventional experience—and even sometimes in mystical or spiritual experience—we experience love as the union of self and other. That is one kind of love. When we experience this kind of love it can be intoxicating because we can feel ourselves merged with another. It does not even have to be a person. It could be a pet, or God, or even our Xbox. I am raising a teenager, so I am practicing union with the Xbox. It is not so simple with *Grand Theft Auto*, but you would be surprised what is possible! [Laughter.]

When I use the term "oneness," and the phrase "Realms of Oneness," I do not mean the kind of oneness that I just described, which is the experience of being an individual merged with something else; rather I mean it in the more fundamental sense of perceiving that everything is permeated by one of several Divine qualities, in this case, Divine Love. It is not only inside you and me, but it is everywhere and in everything. The field is love; everything is colored with this love.

The unconditional nature of this love comes from the fact that there is nothing that we can do as individuals to disconnect us from the whole. If everything is Divine Love then we too are an expression of that love; we are each an integral part of it. The Realms of Oneness represent subtly different perceptions of reality as a unified whole. Each of these realms or dimensions—called *olamot* in the Hebrew— is colored in a different way; in this case, it is colored with the quality of Divine Love.

You can see that this condition of oneness is different than the state of union with God that we have been talking about with the experience of the Pearl. Union with God is an experience of being merged with the Divine Being, Divine Life, and Divine Spirit. Oneness is the realization that everything is saturated with a subtle, loving light. It is a more holistic integration of ourselves with the totality in the sense that we recognize ourselves as part of a whole. We recognize that we are an expression of that whole.

Without integrating this realm of Divine Love into one's experience, it will be very difficult to experience the other, more subtle Realms of Oneness. If these other dimensions are dissociated from the Divine Love, they can feel quite terrifying and they will be difficult to integrate into our life in a balanced way. These more subtle Realms of Oneness, such as the dimension of emptiness, are very challenging to our conventional perceptions.

Without the integration of this realm of love, even the experience of Pure Awareness—a state of being where there is no self and just a naked awareness of everything—can be difficult. Without knowing the loving truth of Being, it is difficult to experience Pure Awareness because it is so bare naked, so stark in its perception of reality. Without true knowledge of the Divine Love, there can be a split.

In my experience, the loving dimension is directly related to our experience of wholeness as a human being. It is very mysterious, but, when we experience this love, there seems to be an immediate impact on the soul that allows the Realms of Oneness to integrate more completely into our human life. Without love, I do not know if true integration is possible. I imagine it would look somewhat imbalanced and not whole. For example, someone may have the realization of emptiness, but lack the ability to relate in a sensitive manner with the conventional world. There can be perception of the truth of emptiness without the embodied appreciation of, and compassion for, the suffering of others.

The words *echad* and *ahavah*, "one" and "love," both incidentally have the same numerical value: thirteen. If you add up the letters in Hebrew they both equal thirteen. This further points to the intimacy of the relationship between these two principles. Love is the doorway to oneness and is its defining feature. Another term that is used to describe this state is the word "grace." Some traditions emphasize the principle of Divine Grace. Usually the defining feature of Grace in these traditions is that God's love is unconditional; that is, there is nothing we can do to get it. It is a bounty of love that is freely given with nothing received in return. That is what we mean by Grace.

The Hebrew word for "grace" is *chayn*. The realm of Divine Love is the realm of grace, the realm of *chayn*.[6] The Hebrew word "*chayn*" consists of two letters, *chet* and *nun*. If you reverse the letters and spell it backwards, you get *nun* and *chet*, which spells "*nach*," which can also be pronounced as the Hebrew word "*noach*."[7] The popular name

Noah is a transliteration of this Hebrew word. The words "*nach*" and "*noach*" both mean "rest."

When we experience the Divine Love dimension, the soul is profoundly impacted with the sense that it can finally rest. We feel that we can finally settle deeply. We know with absolute certainty that we are indeed held in love, that we are intrinsically and inherently worthy of love. Not only are we worthy of it, but it is here for us; we are swimming in it and it is available to us personally. The transformative moment occurs when we feel it and know it on some level. Even if we are not completely conscious of it, our soul has in some sense tapped into it and recognized it. In that presence, the soul can finally let go, rest, and abide in its center.

In that moment, the soul can drop into its center and abide without conflict and without disturbance. So much of our inability to rest and to abide in the center is because we are not feeling this unconditional love. We are not feeling held and we do not know that love is an ontological fact. We do not know that there is nothing we need to do to have that love and to be loved by God.

This love allows us to drop into a deep state of rest—*noach* or *nach*, the noun form of which is *menuchah*. Instead of "rest," I like the English translation of *nach* or *menuchah* as "repose." The soul can abide in a state of repose. I call it the "armchair state." Life can be hard work. We have spent many years working hard trying to get this or that, trying to get love from here and from there. With Divine Love and Grace, we can finally drop into the depths, into the center.

With the experience of this state, my prayer practice shifted. I mentioned the practice of talking to God as a way of cultivating the presence of wholeness. As the realm of love opened I noticed that my prayer changed. The Divine Presence revealed to me a different kind of prayer that was more relevant and aligned with the emerging condition of my soul. I noticed that when I would try to talk to God in the old style something felt forced. The words felt like too much noise, too distracting.

My soul just wanted to be still and silent, so my prayer transformed into a prayer practice of repose. Intuitively, I began to sit and simply allow my consciousness to drop into the center of my being. I felt held in this sublime love and so it was easy to let go into it. I would drop in, drop down, and completely let myself be in a state of repose in the still, quiet, and dimensionless ground of Being.

Then, the journey shifted again. This prayer practice became a journey into deeper and deeper states of silence and stillness. This center point felt like it was the center of my individual consciousness and also the center of God. That is what I mean by dimensionless. As I dropped into deeper and deeper degrees of silence and stillness, the more a sense of where I ended and where God began became less and less demarcated and clear. I had the sense that I was no longer practicing or praying but that I was just abiding in the silence of Being.

I say all of this because, in hindsight, I now recognize how talking to God and the cultivation of the state of union and intimacy with God opened up the possibility of dropping into something far more mysterious.

So I want to talk about another impact of Divine Love on the consciousness that I think is very important, especially in our day and age. It is also an integral part of the Kedumah teachings and path. Coming more into wholeness is not possible, in my experience at least, without going through the Chamber of Sorrows to some degree. This means working out those nooks and crannies hidden in the recesses of our being. The realization of wholeness is the realization of the unconditional nature of Divine Love. When I recognized all of this, the meaning and function of sensual pleasure was revealed to me.

The Hebrew word for pleasure is *oneg*. When we integrate the dimension of love, our relationship with physicality changes; we may notice that pleasure itself becomes a vital nutrient for the soul. Sensual pleasure in particular becomes nourishment for the soul because the Divine Love dimension exposes that the physical body and the soul are not separate things. The physical body, it turns out, is an expression of the soul, and both are expressions of Divine Love.

The experience of pleasure usually is generated either by the buildup or discharge of energy in the body. The conventional appreciation of pleasure is typically relegated to the sensations of intensity in the nervous system. There is a certain kind of pleasure that comes with allowing energy or charge to build in the nervous system, and there is a different kind of pleasure that is experienced when this build-up of charge is released. Both types of pleasure have to do with a certain kind of intensity and the pleasurable sensations it produces in our physical body.

These kinds of pleasures that are generated in our nervous system are important in satisfying our instinctual drives. There is not anything wrong with this; the pleasure of eating, drinking, and having sex are all a part of life. But if our soul is in a fragmented state and not in a state of wholeness, then the pleasurable sensual energy will tend to feed only one fragment or another of our being. The influx of sensual energy, erotic energy, and pleasure—and by these terms I do not just mean sex but any kind of sensual pleasure, such as eating, drinking, and all the pleasures of our senses—will tend to nourish only those fragments of our soul that we are open to experiencing. In such a case there will not be a sense of wholesomeness in our experience of pleasure. It may feel like the pleasure-energy is not nourishing the totality of our body and soul, or it may feel disrupted or fragmented or split off.

But with the integration of the Journey of Wholeness, sensual pleasure becomes like food for the soul. This is the best kind of visceral description I can offer. The soul eats it up, like some kind of essential nutrient. The soul then actually grows from sensual pleasure. The soul gets richer and more robust and more complete. It becomes a living organism of spirit.

This is not usually what is taught in Sunday school, so it should be a very lovely surprise. The visceral experience of it is like eating a very nourishing meal, a very healthy and satisfying meal. There is a physical sensation of satisfaction that is inseparable from spiritual fulfillment. The spirit is nourished through sensual pleasure, enjoyment in its subtlety and its depth, grounded in the rich manifestation of biology. This kind of satisfaction allows the body-soul to rest deeply.

In the Kabbalistic tradition, the principle of deep body-soul rest is the central organizing principle of the Sabbath, or *Shabbat* in Hebrew (the Ashkenazic pronunciation is *Shabbos*). It states explicitly in the Torah that *Shabbos* is the day of "rest," the seventh "day" of creation on which the forces of manifestation rested. I put the word "day" in quotes because it is a code-word in the Kabbalistic tradition for the Lights of Being, for the *sefirot*. The seventh "day," *Shabbos*, is thus a hidden reference to the seventh *sefirah* (of the seven lower *sefirot* of creation), which is *Shechinah*, or Presence.

However, technically speaking, *Shabbos* represents the union of *Shechinah* or *Malchut (ADNY* or Presence) with *Tiferet (YHVH* or Being).[8] In the human realm, this union is performed through sexual intercourse on *Shabbos* eve between two spiritually-bonded lovers. The deep rest on *Shabbos* is thus induced through the charge and discharge cycle of sexual union, interpenetrating both the celestial and human realms with erotic fluids.[9]

According to traditional Jewish law, on *Shabbos* a person is required to experience *oneg* (pleasure), sensual pleasure in particular. One is encouraged to eat good food, drink wine, and have sex. There is even a sensitivity to the aesthetic sensuality of ambience; you light candles, you drink some wine, eat delicious food, and gather with your loved ones. There is a sensuality to being with others, a pleasure in sharing a sacred space which nourishes the body and soul. According to Jewish tradition, sex is also particularly encouraged, which for many people is the climax of the evening, no pun intended.[10]

The traditional phrase pointing to the contemplative requirement for rest on *Shabbos* is *Shabbat Menucha*, which means "Sabbath of rest." This language comes directly from the Torah (Ex. 20:11): *Vayanach*

Bayom Ha-Shevi'i, which means, "And [God] rested on the seventh day." The root of both of these words for "rest" is *nach* or *noach*, which you will remember is the reverse of the word *chayn*, grace.[11]

Therefore, on *Shabbos* it is customary to take a nap, to rest, and to literally enjoy the delights of sleep. Sleep can be very sensuous. Have you ever had a really sensuous sleep? Have you ever woken up from a nap and felt very heavy, as if you are saturated with sleep? It can feel like sleep itself is a substance that is oozing out of the pores of your body.

We may not even recognize or appreciate these subtleties in the hustle and bustle of the work week. We may not appreciate the sensuality of the simple things, of having a physical body. And yet, in very traditional Jewish practice, an entire day of the week is carved out to enjoy these pleasures. It is important for our body-soul to take the time to appreciate the blessings of sensual pleasure. This is what *Shabbos* is supposed to be. It is meant to be a day for the spiritual practice of the unity of body and soul, and sensual pleasure is the optimal vehicle for the realization and experience of this unity.[12] For many people, sex is the closest experience they have to God, so why not make sex an intentional practice, a ritual prayer?

Many religions are still afraid of sex. In Kedumah, which is not a religion, we appreciate sex and sensual pleasure in general as essential nutrition for the body and soul. However, we also recognize that because of the intensity of sexual energy, it takes a certain stability of presence in our soul to stay in touch with our experience enough during sex to tap into its nourishing potential.

That is why we do our various meditation practices. The function of some of our practices is to develop more of a sense of embodied presence, more capacity to stay present through the intensity of the charge and discharge cycles of our experience. The purification of the limbs and the *tzimtzum* practices both work to develop our experiential capacity for more expanded states of spiritual intensity. Other practices that we do serve to invoke particular states of consciousness, particular Lights of Being or Realms of Oneness.

The practice we did earlier, some of you may recognize it as very similar in form to the Centering Prayer practice as taught by Father Thomas Keating.[13] A similar practice also appears in the Hasidic tradition.[14] My experience of experimenting with this particular practice over the years is that—when engaged in the context of Kedumah—it invokes the dimension of Divine Love. This makes sense, given that the Divine Love dimension is the realm of essential grace. Grace or *chayn* opens up the state of repose in the center of one's being, which is represented by the Hebrew word *nach* (the reverse letters of *chayn*) meaning "repose," abiding in the still and silent center.

We do this practice using a sacred word as a bridge into just being, abiding in the still, silent center of Being. There are deep, rich, metaphysical teachings on why the word is a bridge. It has to do with everything we have learned before about the power and importance of the word, of speech, and the mystical function of it. It is not just an arbitrary thing. The word is a powerful tool that has its mystical roots in the creation of the world. And it is a bridge to a deeper kind of contemplative prayer that is not a "doing" at all, but rather a complete letting go and dropping into the depth of silence, into the still center of one's being.

Interestingly, the dimension of Divine Love, the state of mystical repose, and the experience of sensual pleasure as spiritual nourishment all coalesce and constellate around the mystical principle of *Shabbos*. All three of these corners of the triangle appear as the central teachings of the contemplative practice of *Shabbos*. The mystical texts state explicitly that *Shabbos* is the day of Divine Love as well as the day of union, of oneness.[15] The Zohar states in Aramaic, *Raza De-Shabbos ... Raza De-echad*: "The secret of the Sabbath ... is the secret of Oneness."[16] So love, oneness, rest and pleasure all constellate as the defining features of this traditional practice of wholeness.

The Talmud teaches that on *Shabbos* the soul is endowed with a *neshemah yeteirah*, which means an "additional soul."[17] This explains why people eat so much on *Shabbos*. [Laughter.] One can actually experience this "additional soul," and I do not mean just on *Shabbos*. We must not forget that while the Sabbath is carved out as a formal practice one day of the week, we are training for the "day that is always *Shabbos*." This is a traditional reference to the "messianic age," which is the epoch when human consciousness will permanently abide in the *Shabbos* state of being.[18] So the potential is for *Shabbos*—love, peace, rest, stillness, pleasure, oneness of body and soul—to be present all the time, in every day of the week.

In this sense, Kedumah is a messianic teaching. It is messianic in the sense that we are cultivating the capacity to experience Divine Love, unity, and oneness in the body. That is why we start with the body. We start with the understanding that the end is embedded in the beginning and the beginning in the end. In this path we start with the messianic perspective instead of ending with it. This is why the Kedumah path opens up the possibility for us to experience and know *Shabbos* directly and intimately as the everyday condition and nature of our very being, not dependent on any formal ritual or religious doctrine. This is why Kedumah is a teaching for the emerging messianic age. I will discuss more about what I mean by "messianic" in the next talk.

The fruit of this realization is the experience of sensual pleasure, which is the vehicle for the realization of the unity of body and soul. It deconstructs all splits: between human and Divine, between pleasure and pain, between body and soul. When I use the term "soul" I am including the body; the soul is not something other than the body—the body is an expression of the soul.

The *neshamah yeteirah*, the "additional soul," is the sensual body-soul that can only display itself when we know that we are inherently and intrinsically loved. If we do not appreciate our lovability deeply in our body then there is always going to be a maintenance of that split between love and self, between body and soul, between God and human. In other words, the soul will unconsciously or consciously be seeking love in some way from outside of itself, from some source that is external to itself. Only when we know we have love no matter what, that it is the very nature of the water we are swimming in, and that we are an intrinsic expression of it, only then can sensuality be an expression of this kind of one-love.

This is also true of love in general, which is an intimate part of a sensual experience. You cannot experience true sensuality without love. Sex without love is not sensual, at least not in the way that I am using the word. It is a fragmented experience if it is split off from love. I am not making a judgment or suggesting that there is some-thing wrong with having sex without love. I am only suggesting that there is a different kind of potential, a different possibility that is more whole and integral. This is true of any sensual experience, not just sex. We need to have already integrated some degree of Divine Love in order to be able to appreciate the spiritual nature of a flower or to soak in the exquisite presence of sleep. A soulful experience is any experience that includes the wholeness of our being.

This is what I mean when I say that you cannot have sensuality without love. Explore it in your own experience. See if it is ever the case that you experience real sensuality, where it feels like it is feed-ing and nourishing and saturating your whole being, and there is not an implicit sense of love and appreciation that is already there.

This is what I mean when I say that these things are all connected. All these different facets of reality open up and are integrated, and different possibilities emerge as a result of that integration. In Kedu-mah, we are interested in the manifestation of Being, the realization of the potential of our human experience in form, which is the pur-pose of creation, the purpose of life. It is not enough to just experience oneness as an abstract, nondual perception. It is not enough because that is not the whole story. It is a fragment. The nondual experience can also be a fragment if it is not embodied in life. All the Lights of Being and all the Realms of Oneness have the potential for human integration and embodiment. In such a condition of human whole-ness, there are no longer dual and nondual categories; instead it is just Living Being manifesting itself through this window of a human soul—dual and nondual integrated as one.

One obstacle to appreciating sensual pleasure as a Divine gift is the unconscious belief that is often held that pleasure is somehow im-pure or unholy. This is most likely a cultural influence, but there may also be more primitive roots to this as well. Many people experience a great deal of conflict around pleasure, especially sensual pleasure. How much is enough? How much is too much? How much is okay? Often there are different kinds of unconscious positions and reactions about it, including a lot of guilt.

Of course, if someone has a history of abuse, sexual abuse in partic-ular, that could make things more challenging or complicated around certain kinds of sensual pleasures. For instance it could bring up trau-ma. There are many factors that can contribute to our relationships to pleasure and rest.

STUDENT: So when you say "sensual," you are not focusing on sexual pleasure?

ZVI: What I mean by "sensual pleasure" is not necessarily sexual. For some people that may be what comes up, but I mean any kind of sen-sual pleasure, of any or of all the senses. Some people are very sen-suous and erotic, they have a lot of erotic and sensual sensitivity, but it may not be genital-focused. That may not be their primary way of expressing their eros. Everyone is different in this way. In Kedumah we have a very holistic view of sensual pleasure, because in the ex-perience of wholeness, even sexual pleasure feels more whole. That is to say it's like the whole consciousness is experiencing it. It's not split off into any particular body part. This is the hallmark of the expe-rience of wholeness; the whole consciousness is experiencing every-thing as a unified expression of the totality. And then beyond that you can feel that actually the whole field is experiencing the sensuality. You can come to a point where you feel the whole universe is engaged in pleasure, is experiencing pleasure through our engagement with sensuality. It's like bringing pleasure to the cosmos. There are many levels of experiencing this.

We've never done an exercise where everyone is so reluctant to come back to the group; you all just want to keep talking about pleasure! [Laughter.] That's good. So what came up, what do you notice, questions or comments about your experience?

[The following discussion takes place after an experiential exercise.]

STUDENT: One thing came up for me, which we talked about in the group and I was also wondering while you were talking about experiencing divinity and sensual pleasure, is: what about addiction and distraction, which can take you off of your path of awareness and be an escape? And also what about the downside, what about the swing of the pendulum, in pursuing sensual pleasure that then results in going into the darkness, or depression afterward.

ZVI: One way of understanding addiction, is through the example I gave earlier of using indulgence of a certain kind of sensual experience as a way of actually not experiencing more of the heartfelt vulnerability to the love that is permeating the sensual pleasure. This is because the indulgence numbs and dulls our consciousness. Have you ever seen the Zen folks doing their walking meditation? It's very slow. Every micro-movement is engaged with awareness. Why don't they just run? [Laughter.] Running can work, but you may have to run a hundred miles before it kicks in.

And some teachings would say that addiction can work in that way too, eventually. Some crazy-wisdom type schools of teaching use extreme tactics to provoke people to wake up. Some people have told me interesting stories of teachers who gave them practices to do that involved an over-indulgence into a particular pleasure. This is not the same thing as addiction, of course, because it is being used to wake-up and not to dull. So you see it is not so much the particular behavior or the amount that we engage it, but rather it is the function that it is serving in our consciousness.

Ultrarunning is another example. Some people—here in Boulder it is more than just some—literally run a hundred miles barefoot in the mountains. There are even some people sitting in this room who do that. At a certain point something transforms, something opens up, and there is nobody running anymore. Running is just happening and the consciousness is free. That's why some people get addicted to that kind of a thing. I mean, is it really healthy or balanced to run a hundred miles barefoot in the mountains? Maybe it is, I don't really know. The Tarahumara tribe in the Copper Canyon region of Mexico have been doing this for centuries.

So some spiritual teachings or teachers that subscribe to certain methods will actually go to extremes in terms of exhausting our energies in a certain direction to wake up. And then other teachings will go the opposite direction; they'll slow everything down to its micro-motion as a way of heightening our sensitivity to each and every nook and cranny of our sensation.

I don't mean to equate these examples with addiction. They are not the same things exactly. Someone who's suffering from addiction, the problem isn't that they're necessarily doing something too much, it's more that their behavior is being used to numb and dull their consciousness, usually to cope with some difficult pain. The addiction then can cause more suffering and can thwart a certain kind of awakening. So it can be used as a defense from really allowing and feeling into a wound. Does this make sense?

The point I am making is that indulgence of any kind, whether it can be identified as an addiction or not, can dull a person's sensitivity to the sensual experience of that substance. This, in turn, will limit the person's capacity for spiritual awakening in the dimension of wholeness.

STUDENT: Does it have to do with attachment and nonattachment, both pleasure and pain?

ZVI: It depends on how you are using those terms. Pleasure and pain are part of a physiological process. Our nervous system regulates itself in a cycle of charge and discharge. Our experience of sensual pleasure is regulated and determined by our nervous system. If our nervous system is in a charged state, then it will naturally seek to discharge because that brings regulation to the nervous system. There is a certain kind of pleasure that comes with discharge. So too, when we're in a state of quiet and stillness and our parasympathetic nervous system has exhausted its range, there'll be a natural tendency to bring charge into the system. To bring stimulation and intensity into the nervous system is then also experienced as a certain kind of pleasure.

In the Kedumah path we work to expand the range of our experience by extending our capacity for tolerating more intense charge on the one hand, and more intense discharge on the other. Tolerating more and more charge brings more and more sensual pleasure, which then expands the dimensionality of our direct recognition of embodied reality, which is what I mean by the Divine Presence. On the other hand our path also expands and extends our capacity to tolerate more extreme states of discharge. We train ourselves to be able to go into deeper and deeper states of silence, stillness, and emptiness. Silence and stillness can open up extreme dimensions of emptiness and nothingness, which are also very difficult to tolerate without training and practice. These states of discharge also bring a certain kind of pleasure, a particular kind of bliss.

So we work with both sides of the cycle. We need to learn to tolerate a lack of charge in our system, which brings silence, stillness, and emptiness, as well as charge, which brings fullness, richness, and presence. We emphasize sensual pleasure because it's such an available experience to our body and to our nervous system, and it's a powerful energy that can be used for the transmutation and awakening of our consciousness. The more pleasure-charge we are able to hold in our nervous system—without repressing it on the one hand, nor discharging it on the other—the more our consciousness will be free to be itself without accommodation. Ultimately we discover that the state of freedom is one in which the intensity of presence and the intensity of emptiness are both completely co-emergent and simultaneously abiding in every moment.

Now, this also explains why we tend to experience a downer after an upper, and an upper after a downer. This also has to do with the way our nervous system is conditioned. When we expand into a state of charge and have really pushed up against the threshold of our tolerance level then we will tend to swing to the opposite side of the spectrum. The more pressure placed on one side of the spectrum, the more intense the swing will be back in the opposite direction, to try to somehow balance and regulate the system.

For example, you might have the experience of being in a state of deep stillness and at a certain point—when you have rubbed up against your threshold of tolerance—you may find yourself itching to do something. The silence and stillness may start to feel intolerable and you have the impulse to generate some kind of charge to assuage the frustration of nothingness. You may have noticed this kind of a thing while being on retreat; as soon as it's over you want to go party or something like that. Same thing is true in the other direction.

So we're seeing that there is sensual pleasure on both sides of this spectrum. It's present on the whole spectrum. There's sensual pleasure in silence and there's sensual pleasure in stimulation. We're attempting to appreciate the nuances and the possibilities of sensuality in the full range of human experience. No matter what we're experiencing, even if it's pain or suffering, we can appreciate it as a doorway to a more fundamental truth. That's my short answer to a long question. [Laughter.]

STUDENT: I wanted to say something specifically about addiction and pleasure, and addiction is something that I've worked with professionally for a long time and specifically in my private practice, I do a lot of work with food addiction and sugar addiction. It's important to remember that addiction is actually not about pleasure. Addiction is using a substance or an activity to numbout or medicate or get high because of feelings we can't tolerate. But for example, like to use the example of sugar, because I work with sugar a lot, and drugs and alcohol function this way too, it's not that when we take in sugar we get pleasure, and that's it. Even in the body, what's happening physiologically is actually there's a toxic reaction. The body goes haywire. It is a pain reaction. But the result of that is that neurotransmitters get secreted. Those are the feel-good chemicals that kind of get us high. So, I just want to sort out that it's not that addiction is about getting too much pleasure from something or using something too much for pleasure, it's that the thing that is being used has this very addictive sticky kind of pleasure-pain twist, which is why it works so well, for a while.

ZVI: Yes, thank you.

And this may explain further the experience of *oneg*. I'm using the term "sensual pleasure" as a translation of this principle of *oneg*, and it may be a little problematic in the English because the Hebrew word "*oneg*" points to a particular kind of pleasure that we don't have an exact English word for. For example, the way the term *oneg* appears in the whole constellation of teachings around the meaning of *oneg Shabbat*, the "pleasure of the Sabbath," presents *oneg* as integral to the wholeness of our being one with the Divine—in body and soul. This implies a kind of pleasure that includes all of our experience, including our most painful experiences. So, it's the kind of pleasure that's really the wholeness of our being participating in the natural world as a living being, as a sensuous being, inseparable from its environment.

STUDENT: Thinking about it in this way, I wouldn't even now use the word "pleasure" at all with addiction. I know I just did, but to differentiate it from the pleasure you're talking about, it's more about getting high, which is very ungrounded. But true pleasure is very grounded.

ZVI: Yes. Makes sense. What do you notice in the space right now? In your experience?

STUDENT: I feel like there's a certain buzz in the room.

ZVI: So there's a certain kind of buzz. And there is also something else.

STUDENT: It's kind of quiet in here and also kind of still, almost too still. I mean, not too still like stillness is bad, but there's a little tension because we're talking about something that we're not sure where we're at. Like we are stirring the pot.

ZVI: Yes, there is tension.

STUDENT: Well I was actually going to say exactly what was already said, which is that from my experience, there's no pleasure in addictive behavior. I'm slightly addicted to Coconut Bliss. [Laughter.]

ZVI: Only slightly? That's pretty good. [Laughter.]

STUDENT: I'll admit various times in the past few months I have eaten an entire pint of Cocount Bliss in a single sitting.

ZVI: What flavor? [Laughter.]

STUDENT: Most flavors. But no, seriously, after one of these times, not only did I eat the whole pint, I ate the whole pint in huge bites, extremely rapidly. There's no pleasure in that. I didn't enjoy it really. It was just manic. Addiction is not about pleasure; it's not pleasurable. It destroys all the pleasure, and that's when it becomes psychosis, because it's like you are chasing something that actually doesn't feel good.

That's what I was going to say, but if I can also add something else: when we were talking, I was wondering if there are any experiences that are not sensual? And my answer was no, because even the mind is sensual. I mean, there's no experience without the senses. Is there an experience that's not sensual?

ZVI: It's true, all perception and experience happen through our senses. So in that sense everything is sensual. But the richness, the depth, the wholeness of the experience, oftentimes in conventional experience escapes our awareness. So, I guess what I mean when I use the word "*oneg*" is a more conscious appreciation of the subtlety, depth, richness, and Divine nature of our sensual experience, which is all experience.

Ultimately, *Hayom She-kulo Shabbat*, this messianic vision of the "day that is all the Sabbath," is the day in which all experience is recognized as an experience of the Divine sense-body. Don't forget that I talk about things in a certain way so that we can work with things from the conventional perspective. But the view that we are ultimately holding in this teaching is that all of our bodies are organs of one Divine Being. So ultimately that's the potential of awakening. When we talk about the awakening of the planet, the awakening of humanity, it's not like there are all these individuals separate from each other. We're talking about the awakening of the Divine Being—the cosmic organism—as the Divine body of which we ourselves are a part. So yes, ultimately we're priming our individual organs to be fully awakened perceptive sense-organs of the total Divine body, the Divine Being. That is what we're pointing to.

STUDENT: This conversation is helping me realize that I've been confusing a certain kind of attachment with pleasure. And that pleasure actually has very distinct qualities that are opposite of manically eating Coconut Bliss. I've been experiencing it as very soft and very passive, like it's okay that things come into my sense faculties and they can be very pleasurable, and I can feel a kind of union of the outer world with my sense faculties, and then the objects go and there's no residue. And that's what I feel in the space, a kind of softness.

ZVI: Can you describe the softness?

STUDENT: Yeah, like I can sense it now with my eye faculties. Like we were talking one day about having the diamond vision of seeing things very clearly and seeing the boundaries very clearly, and this is more like a soft vision, and I can see the periphery more, and I feel it also tactilely, like feeling myself on the floor, feeling my hands on my body, like there's a softness.

ZVI: So everyone sense the soft presence in the room. It's very subtle but see if you can allow it to rub up against your skin. If you hold a receptive, allowing posture, what's it like to allow the softness of presence to just mold itself around us, rub up against us and touch us? When we allow ourselves to be receptive to this presence, how does it impact our consciousness? What do you notice happens in your soul?

STUDENT: I like that you're using the word "wholeness," because there's a completeness to it. I'm not trying to pull something extra into the experience.

ZVI: Yes. Exactly.

STUDENT: And the sense of time, it feels different.

ZVI: How is it different?

STUDENT: I think it's slower.

ZVI: Yes. Isn't that interesting? You can actually sense each tick. There's a lot more "time" between each second. Which demonstrates that the way we usually orient to time is a conceptual overlay.

What about other people? What do you notice right now?

STUDENT: When I was tuning into the feeling of the pleasure on my skin, and I was talking about this a bit in the group before, but I really felt it more palpably. It was a sense of being loved, and I keep having this image of me enjoying a piece of chocolate or something, like a chocolate chip, but eating it extremely slowly, like on *Shabbos*. For whatever reason that's the image that keeps popping up, and it's this feeling of being loved; it reminds me of when I was a child and my mom would bring me and my brother dessert or something, and it was just like being held in love in this physical pleasure. So that's what I felt and I think it's the connection you were talking about before.

ZVI: Yes, that's it, you got it. The only way to recognize presence is to sense it. It's not an intellectual thing. It can be perceived through the head-center, but it can only be embodied through sensation. When we let it actually touch us and hold us, in our body, then we feel the visceral sense of being held in something that is the presence of being loved. Now, the impact that it has on my consciousness—and I notice that it's also in the room—is that the soul just relaxes. It's able to rest in this holding presence. This loving, holding softness that has a particular kind of sensual, sensational, and sensorial dimension to it—almost like being swaddled.

STUDENT: Exhaling when you sigh.

ZVI: Exhaling when you sigh. Is that how it feels?

STUDENT: Yes.

215

ZVI: Like a big exhale?

STUDENT: Yes, like everything's okay. Like it's all okay no matter what.

ZVI: Exactly. Everything is okay. Which then allows us to actually be what we are. Do you feel the space now, how it's different? Now that people are speaking to it? The softness of the presence, it's kind of implicit, it's a subtle but earthy, light love; it's becoming more palpable in the space. There's a sense that it's becoming more concentrated and holding each of us.

Sleep is an important part of this. I mentioned sleep for a reason. There is something about actually allowing ourselves to just be that allows this presence to saturate through the body, in the body. You might feel the sensation of the weight of sleep, of a deep *Shabbos* nap. Have you ever had an afternoon nap, maybe on *Shabbos* day? When I use the word *Shabbos* I mean any day that you're more or less held in a structure conducive to repose. Next time you wake up from an afternoon nap on a relaxing day and you feel like your body is very heavy, then stop and sense the presence.

You can actually feel the texture of the heaviness of the presence, the density of the weight of the presence in your physicality. Take advantage of the opportunity to sense this presence after a deep sleep. It's a concentrated form of this presence. It concentrates itself when we sleep. We're held in this presence in a very concentrated way when we sleep. That's why babies and children, when they sleep, they're actually heavier. You ever notice that? Did you ever try to pick up a sleeping baby or a sleeping child? They're heavier than they are when they're awake. Their presence is heavier. There is a density of presence in their bodies.

There is a mystical relationship here between the state of sleep and the effect of this presence on the body because really if you think about it, when we're asleep, we're in a state of deep surrender. We're just totally in the arms of Being. So then the presence concentrates itself to hold us. Usually we're not aware of this throughout the day. You might be able to feel the density of the softness now. It contours itself in a way that allows us to drop in, to just surrender into it. It can sometimes feel like we're getting a subtle massage. You can feel it from the inside out. You can feel the presence in the bones, in the muscles; you can feel it giving you a massage from the inside out. It can feel like the presence is saturating your body with a kind of sensual, essential presence that is deeply pleasurable.

These are all possibilities, but this presence can also provoke a lot of issues. It can push up to the surface a lot of conflicts that we have around love, and around being held like this. Issues around the unconditional nature of love. So that's something to also pay attention to and be gentle with yourselves about. If you notice things surface, material that feels reactive to this, then invite self-compassion, utilize the tools that we've learned here to work with the material and to help it digest in this presence.

10
Starlight

PRACTICE

LET'S BEGIN WITH a meditation practice. Just allow yourself to drop into your seat, both literally and figuratively. We want to drop down into our seats and just be here, without doing anything. We're just being, without doing anything to be. Be like a star, with its light shining. A star doesn't make its light shine; its light simply shines. So just sit, and be that light, without doing anything to be it. We'll sit with that for a few minutes and then I'll ring the bell.

TALK

In the last chapter, we talked about the dimension of Divine Love and its relationship to wholeness—to unity, oneness, and essential pleasure. You can see how absolutely necessary it is to be in contact with this pure, unconditional loving truth for us to be able to be vulnerable, for us to allow our hearts to be permeable enough that we can begin to perceive reality through a different sense organ, in a different way that is not cultivated and supported so much in conventional life.

As children we are not usually supported to be steadfast in our tenderness, our vulnerability, and our openness. It is a rare thing for that to be held unconditionally. We learn the hard way that it is not safe to be open and permeable—not just to others—but really to ourselves, to our own suffering, and to our own essential expansiveness. Usually we learn how to harden ourselves into a certain shape to minimize our hurt and suffering. Of course, in the process, we forget the gifts of grace that come when we allow ourselves to be in that tender place. That vulnerability gets exposed in the journey through the Chamber of Sorrows.

That is why I do not think there is any way around the Chamber of Sorrows. In my experience it is a necessary tenderizing capsule, a refining crucible. It tenderizes the heart and the soul when we allow ourselves to be broken, to feel the locked up feelings of sadness, sorrow, and remorse. I do not mean the harsh attacks of the inner-critic or the shame of guilt. That is not what I am talking about when I talk about remorse and the Chamber of Sorrows.

I am talking about the genuine heartfelt sense of recognizing what has been out of alignment with the truth, as well as the recognition that there is usually not much that we could have done differently. Usually we make the best choices that we can, given what we know and understand at the time. We are only capable of doing things differently once we appreciate and accept how narrow the range is of what we can actually control, what we can ever choose or decide in life. There are so many factors that go into every instant that, when you really contemplate it thoroughly, it is impossible to assume that we are solely responsible for anything at all.

That said, it is natural to feel regret or remorse for our actions that have brought pain and suffering to others and for the choices we have made that were consciously motivated by greed, hatred, or anger, for this is the narrow range that we can actually influence. When we allow these difficult feelings, the heart opens to the sweetness of surrender and acceptance of how things are. With that acceptance comes the realization of the unconditional loving presence that reality bestows to those who relinquish their authority and control to the will of its loving embrace.

This brings great relief, rest, and relaxation to the soul. The soul recognizes that there is nothing that we ever could have done to alienate ourselves from this presence, that we are its offspring. We are the offspring of this loving presence, born in love. The direct perception of this truth then allows the soul to really give up its fantasy of having some kind of an independent authority to determine the circumstances of our lives. You can see how this relinquishing of control would bring great relief to the soul. It can give up a little bit of its incessant need to control things.

With this settling and restfulness there begins a new journey, what I call the Journey of Silence, whereby the soul drops deeply into its center and can now trust Being to take care of things. It is able to trust because it now recognizes without a shadow of a doubt the truth of the holding, the unconditional love of reality's presence. It can then let go and drop into whatever mystery is hidden deep beneath the layers of our perception. In this state, reality begins to reveal different dimensions of silence and stillness that are inconceivable to ordinary perception. There are realms of silence and stillness that are absolute, meaning that they are not defined by the presence or absence of noise but are instead radically silent.

The interesting thing is that there is another aspect to wholeness that reveals itself when the Journey of Wholeness interpenetrates with the Journey of Silence. Wholeness, as we discussed, is the realization and embodiment of the light of *Binah,* which is the Jubilee state, a condition of fulfillment and completion. It is the Celestial Womb, the dimension of *teshuvah* or returning, and a whole constellation of other terms that the Kabbalists use to point to the possibility of fullness and wholeness that is the cosmic Divine Mother.

Of course, it is not the Divine Mother in the sense that it is somewhere outside of ourselves. This is the spiritual reality that presents itself when we move through the Chamber of Sorrows. At this time, the

Celestial Mother reveals to us the dimension of Divine Love and the Journey of Silence opens up. Along with the interpenetration of the Journey of Silence and the Jubilee state yet another aspect of reality presents itself to us. I will say a bit about my own experience of it, and then I will say something about how it is framed in the metaphysical map of Kedumah.

When I first experientially entered this territory, I was not able to articulate and map these things out in a very precise way. I did not have a very precise teaching or cosmic map at the time so I have only been able to see in retrospect how it follows this trajectory. At the time, I was immersed in traditional Jewish practice. Though I studied Kabbalah and Hasidism, I did not have any teachers who had a precise understanding of the inner dynamics of mystical experience. I knew the texts were describing my experience, but it was also clear to me that a person had to have the experience directly in order to understand what the texts were describing. It seemed to me that all the living teachers of Kabbalah were understanding these texts only mentally, because they could not seem to relate to anything I was experiencing.

When I first started experiencing what I call the Pearl, the *penina*, I thought that this was it. What else could I want? I figured that this was what all the mystics and the sages were talking about. I was feeling at one with God with a sense of fullness and completeness. I felt saturated by intimacy with the Divine Presence. There was a sweetness that was so satisfying and fulfilling. There was a period of time in my early twenties when I was engaged in the practice of talking to God; I would stay up all night in my bed, communing with God. It was odd because I was talking to God, but I was feeling it all inside. It felt like a paradox.

Everything that was happening inside me was also happening outside of me at the same time. There was something so nourishing about that. We know through the mirror of intimate relationships how sweet it is to be in that kind of communion with another. This was kind of like that, but much more intense. It was as if I was intimate with all of reality, which I should say can also happen in union with another person. In this case, however, there was no "other." That was what was so interesting about it. There was no actual other. God was not even an "other," even though I was acting as if it was.

I thought that was it. I would have been happy to just stay with that. But, as I mentioned in the last session, I noticed that I naturally started to move into more and more contemplation and silence. I felt a deep longing, a craving to drop in and surrender into the depths. And so my prayer started to change. It became more a prayer of silence, of peaceful abiding, and that is when I noticed the Journey of Silence opening.

I did not discern the dimension of Divine Love until many years later. I recognized that it was there, but it was implicit in my experience; it was not something that I was able to label. It had to have been there though; otherwise, I could not have trusted the process of dropping deeply into the silence. As you go into silence, it begins to challenge very deep psychological structures, deeply held conceptual attitudes about who we are and what reality is. I noticed that as I went more and more into the silence, my notions of self and other—who and what I was and who and what other people were—were exposed as constructs of the mind. This is very difficult terrain to travel through because it conjures up all the instinctual energies of survival. You feel like your very life is being challenged by this exposure. This is because the deep silence is really a movement into the death space.

Along with this confrontational exposure of my self-identity, all kinds of other primitive structures emerged, which were very challenging to stay with. Regardless, I stayed with the practice without repressing this energy or acting on it, and I delved into the intense difficulty of this terrain and metabolized this material. At a certain point, there was a very distinct moment in which I had to choose between life and death. It was very clear: I knew that if I continued to go deeper into the silence, I would die. I realized at that moment that I also had the choice to stop. I could just emerge from the silence and go back to being a regular person.

When this happened I was in an altered state of some kind, deep in meditation. The meditation was ongoing even when I was not formally meditating. Then, I was faced with this choice of life or death. I wonder if this is a universal phenomenon. I wonder if at some point in the Journey of Silence everybody encounters this crossroads of life and death.

STUDENT: Do you mean the death of your body, or the death of your ego, or the death of your senses? What does that mean?

ZVI: Well, at that time, it meant the death of everything. I felt that my body too would die. I wasn't framing it in terms of ego, at the time. The feeling of it is life or death. I knew that if I chose death, I would have to be prepared for physical death. That was my understanding of it at the time.

I am not really sure what happens in such a situation if someone chooses life, but I imagine that conventional life would come back. I do not know because at that time I chose death.[1] My attitude was, "I really want to know what the truth is, and if that means death, so be it." In that instant I was willing to die in order to know the truth of reality. I was not going to turn back, and so be it if I die. It was a conscious choice; it was as if I was saying to God, "I want truth, I want you, so do what you will with me."

At the time, I figured that would be it. I figured that I chose death and that I would actually die. And, in a sense, I did die. There was a lot that happened in that instant that I am not going to go into detail about here. Basically, there was a very intense black fire that consumed my entire body-soul and burned me away. There was literally nobody and nothing left at all. I know this does not make any sense, but I am not trying to make sense. I am simply reporting to you the nature of the experience.

What is important for this teaching, is that what emerged from this experience was the realization that nothing actually exists in the way we usually think it does. All the forms that we take to be solid and real in the conventional mode of perception were revealed to be empty of existence and substance. Even my physical body felt utterly transparent and empty, as if it didn't exist. In this state, there was the distinct absence of all of the usual human concerns about body, life, death, and so on. With this sense of vastness those concerns were erased, because it was evident to me that I am not bound or defined by any of those things. In other words, nothing was ever born and nothing will ever die. Reality is not bound by the concepts of time and space.

There is a lot to this, of course. For a long time I could not find any sense of self whatsoever. I was not prepared at the time for that kind of absence. I was twenty-two at the time and I did not have any teachings or a path that explained that this was something that can happen. I had lived my entire life until that point in the strictly Orthodox Jewish world, and I had never encountered or read other traditions and their teachings. I had no spiritual teachers either; I was completely alone with it. The few rabbis that I discussed this with at the time had no clue what I was talking about.

At the beginning I thought that maybe something had gone terribly wrong because there was no longer any sense of "I" or "self." Yet, everything carried on as usual around me. I was still doing things and communicating with people in a normal way. But my body felt very different, my senses were different, and everything looked different. My perception had utterly changed. You know Van Gogh's painting "Field of Poppies"? Everything kind of looked like that. The colors were very bright, vibrant, and vivid, and everything was very sharp and distinct, yet at the same time, transparent. I felt super alive. Life unfolded in a spontaneous way. There was intense aliveness but there was not anybody there that was alive.

Needless to say, there was a long process of adjusting to this new reality. For a while I thought, "Well, maybe I actually did die, and this is what happens after you die." I could not tell exactly what had happened. It certainly was not the way life was before; it was totally different. While it was an incredible relief to realize that I was free from time and space, not bound by a body, and that I will never die, at the same time it was like, "Well, something is not quite right here. This can't be. How am I living? It doesn't make any sense. What is it that's left here? Who is it that is actually doing things?" Everything was happening on its own, even though there was not anyone there doing anything. This cannot be described very well with words; it can only be known through one's own direct experience.

What I realized was that while there was no self in any conventional sense there was still a location from which perception was occurring. There was also a reflective mechanism that was operating. That is, there was something that was able to reflect on the experience of not having a self.

As I explored this phenomenon of no-self and explored this mode of perceiving I realized that it was possible to discern a very subtle presence of a being-self at the very center of things. I say "being-self" to distinguish it from the ordinary sense of self that is a product of the mind. This sense of self is not at all a conceptual phenomenon; it is a clear manifestation of Being, with its properties of timelessness and dimensionlessness. Specifically, it appears as a scintillating point of light, like a spark of light suspended in vast space. This is why I say that it was at the center of all things. This is a tricky thing to try to describe, but this is how it is experienced and I don't know how else to describe it.

This spark of light was the first sense of any kind of existence of my individual soul. It felt like its most primordial origin. Sometimes it would display itself with precision and exquisite grandeur, like a star shining brightly in black space. Sometimes it was more the sense of vastness itself, without a distinct point of light. So there were two ways this was revealing itself: as the bright Star, with its distinct sense of a timeless, dimensionless being-self, and as the pure Starlight, without any distinct sense of self whatsoever, just vast nondual transparent light. These two modes of experiencing seemed to be two sides of the same reality.

It was clear to me that this realization of the Star and the Starlight was not the Pearl and it was not Divine Love, so I figured it must be what comes after these realizations. This is what I was thinking at the time. I mentioned this a few talks back when I explained that at some point I rejected the Pearl. I was referring to this juncture of my experience, because it felt radically different than the Pearl. It felt like there was no Pearl. Not only was there no Pearl, there was nothing that I could call a "self" whatsoever, at least not in the conventional sense of self.

When the Pearl disappeared, that sense of intimacy—that relational dynamic—also disappeared. There was no "I"; there was just a sense of everything appearing and disappearing in the same instant. There was not a boundary between me and anything else. At the time I felt that the Pearl must have been just a stage to get to this vast nondual light, which was more real and fundamental than the Pearl. At least, that was how I understood it at the time.

Now I see it differently. I see that the experience of the Pearl was really the integration of *Binah* into the Presence Body along with all the *sefirot* in potentia within her.[2] She is the light of wholeness, the Celestial Womb. There is a seed that is planted in her womb. That seed is the point of light. In fact, this is exactly how the Kabbalists describe it. The light of *Chochmah* is, if you remember the chart of the Tree of Life, the masculine counterpart to the feminine *Binah*. It is the right side of the upper triadic center. *Chochmah* literally means "wisdom," and the Kabbalists, in the Zohar and elsewhere, describe it as a point of light. In the ancient texts they call it the *nekudah*, which literally means "the point."[3]

Chochmah is prior to time and space. The upper triad is a primordial triad, existing prior to the world of creation. The world of creation— in Kabbalistic terminology the "seven days of creation"—are the seven *sefirot* from *Chesed* on down. *Chochmah* can be experienced as a formless, dimensionless, timeless Point of Light. In Kabbalistic code, it is also called the "beginning," because it is the beginning of creation, and the origin point of the individual soul.[4] It is the beginning of manifestation and it is called the Seed. This Point of Light is planted and impregnates *Binah*.[5]

Of course, in the ancient Kabbalistic tradition, they use very explicit language of masculine and feminine when they talk about this. *Chochmah* is the masculine seed, the Point of Light. That is the Beginning of creation, the beginning of form that is planted and enters into *Binah*, the Celestial Womb, the feminine Divine Mother. She receives this Point of Light, and then nourishes it, gestates it, and brings it into fruition as the world of creation. This seed is birthed into the world of manifestation, which are the lower seven *sefirot*.[6]

Chochmah in a sense represents the very beginning of the experience of being an individual consciousness. It is the most primordial experience of being an individual soul. But it is only by *Chochmah* entering into the loving womb of *Binah* that the soul itself is born, and this how the Kabbalists describe it. The souls are born and created in *Binah*.[7] You could say that *Chochmah* is the primordial light of the soul before it manifests as a living, embodied consciousness. That only happens through the process of being nurtured and enwombed in *Binah*.

It is possible to experience *Chochmah* directly, which is this dimensionless Point of Light as well as the vast primordial Starlight itself. It is also possible to experience it in a way that is dissociated from the lived life of the Pearl, which is the life of the embodied human soul. In Lurianic Kabbalah, this aspect of the primordial nature of the soul is called the "spark of light." The Point of Light can also be experienced as a spark of shining light.

It is interesting that the Kabbalists also use the Hebrew term *Yesh* to refer to *Chochmah*.[8] *Yesh* means "something" or "existence." *Chochmah* is thus the first expression of reality that can be called "existence"[9] and it emerges out of what the Kabbalists call *ayin*, which means "nothing" or "nothingness."[10] *Ayin* is one of the code terms for the *sefirah* of *Keter*, the "crown," which is located at the very top of the Tree of Life. It is the most subtle, primordial dimension. *Chochmah* is thus the first light that emerges out of nothingness or emptiness. This is the esoteric meaning of the verse (Job 28:12): *Chochmah Me-ayin Timatzei*, which is translated by the Kabbalists as: "*Chochmah* comes from *ayin*."[11]

In my experience, I first entered into a state of no-self or nothingness before the Point of Light revealed itself. That is to say that after I was self-extinguished through the raging black fire there was nobody and nothing left. This is a condition of bare naked reality, with nothing at all to hold onto. Thus for me, experiential contact with the *ayin* or *Keter* space—the dimension of nothingness—preceded the realization of *Chochmah*, the Point of Light.[12]

One Hasidic text—*Netivot Shalom* by the Slonimer Rebbe—describes this process in a way that fits my own experience quite well.[13] The author explains that when we plant a seed in the earth, in order for it to grow it first must completely dissolve into nothing. Then, from that nothingness, life sprouts forth. He calls it in Aramaic the *Kusta de-Chiyuta*—the "remnant of life." The seed of life sprouts out of complete nothingness. The "seed" is a reference to *Chochmah*, the Point of Light, and the nothingness is *ayin*, the *sefirah* of *Keter*. Experientially we must completely dissolve into nothingness—a condition of no-self—in order for the first light of our being to shine forth.

In Kedumah we call this dimension the "Starlight dimension" and it correlates with the Journey of Vastness, the fourth journey in our teaching. It has to do with the Hebrew word for "star," *kochav*, and its mystical significance.[14] We do not have time right now to get into this aspect of the teaching, but—as I often say—we could do a whole retreat on the Starlight dimension. The nature of this light is very particular and very specific. You can sense it in the room right now. Starlight is the first light, it is the original primordial light of creation. It has that nondual quality to it—formless, dimensionless, timeless.

And yet, when the primordial point, the Star, displays itself more distinctly, it carries an implicit sense of "I." There is a sense that "I am this light" because it is the first light of the individual soul. It is the seed of the soul, the soul spark.

If we are in touch with our nature on this dimension of our being, then we have the possibility of freedom from the cycle of life and death. Our spark of light, in and of itself, is free from life and death. It is what we are when we transcend the concepts of life and death. When I was faced with the choice of life and death, I thought it was literal. While on some level perhaps it is, what actually died, however, was the concept of life and death. The person who died was the one who was holding a dichotomy, who was viewing reality from a certain vantage point.

In reality, of course, nothing and nobody died because what disappeared in that event never existed to begin with. What disappeared were nonexistent concepts. What was left after the "burnout" was simply what I am in truth without any conceptual overlays—my primordial nature, which is not bound by life and death. There is tremendous freedom with getting in touch with this light.

The interesting thing is that there is nothing that we can *do* in order to *be* what we are. We just are. The star of light always is, always was, and always will be. We are always what we were, always what we are, and always what we will be. Whether we like it or not, that is what we are, and there is nothing we can do to be that or not be that. That is the mind-boggling realization of it. So you see, there is no practice that we can do to become this Point of Light. We already are that. The Journey of Vastness thus has to do with integrating the wisdom of just being—it is the journey of being.

Some practices may help us recognize what we already are. Sometimes, however, practices can obscure what we already are. Our very nature is always-already just being. Our star is already shining, no matter what is happening; no matter if we are suffering or we are dying or we are dead, or whether we have a body or we do not have a body, or whether we take another body or whether we take another form altogether, on this planet or a different one. Our star is always-already shining.

There are many interesting phenomena that open up in this mode of perception, and while I can't speak to all of them now, I want to mention one more thing because it relates to this teaching. There is a certain kind of direct wisdom that is available in this state of realization that is not conceptual and does not require any mental processes. For instance, one can open up the Hebrew Torah or any sacred text, and the hidden living transmission will reveal itself to them directly, without having to go through any conceptual understanding or interpretation.

There is a verse from the Psalms (119:18) that speaks to this phenomenon: *Gal Einai Ve-abita Nifla'ot Mitoratecha*: "Open my eyes that I may behold wonders of your Torah." When I first came upon this realm of Vastness, it literally felt as if my eyes were opened and I was able to perceive the hidden layers of the text and teaching that were opaque to ordinary perception. This opened up a whole new relationship with the Torah and the lineage that has continued to this day. It also affords someone with this capacity the ability to recognize the hidden transmission in any wisdom teaching; it is not confined to a particular tradition.

The Journey of Vastness, which correlates with this realization of the opened eyes of perception, the Star and the Starlight, is the primordial ground of Being itself, the realm of the Primordial Torah—of Kedumah. It is the source and origin not only of the individual soul but also of all wisdom and teachings. It is the blank parchment of the scroll, upon which all manifestations appears. This teaching is called Kedumah because it comes from this mode of perception, this primordial dimension of reality, this nonconceptual source.

The Journey of Vastness and the Point of Light are also associated with the Messiah. The English word "messiah" is a transliteration of the Hebrew word *Mashiach*. This word is found in the Hebrew Bible and it means "anointed one." Therefore, in the Bible, someone who is a *Mashiach*, a "messiah," is usually someone who is anointed with oil as part of a sacred ceremony, such as a king or a priest.[15]

I am not going to go through the whole history of the term "*Mashiach*" and its various expressions in different traditions, but we all know that "messiah" has been a big buzzword in the West for the last 2,000 years. It is kind of a big deal. It defines, actually, much of our culture. So, this is an important thing that we must come to terms with, at least culturally speaking. This messiah business is still very relevant for our day.

According to the Kabbalists, the Messiah, the anointed one, represents the realization of *Chochmah* consciousness, the Point of Light.[16] This is because, when we enter this dimension of light, it can open up the channel of Divine oils. It is possible to actually experience an ethereal oil descending from the top of the head down the whole body. The celestial oil saturates the consciousness, like you are being anointed. This can be an actual sensory experience that is felt in the body. The first time I experienced this, I was amazed how the subtle sensation is felt so distinctly flowing down the head, face, and over the entire body.[17]

The channel of oils can only open once the dimension of *Chochmah* is accessed.[18] This is because the oil descends from this particular primordial sphere of the cosmos and our consciousness. This seems similar to the teachings on *amrita* in the Vajrayana tradition. Some texts describe this deathless ambrosia in similar ways, flowing down the body from the crown of the head. It is an interesting correlation.[19]

One who is a *Mashiach*, a messiah, is one who experiences this state of being anointed with oil. That is to say someone who has realized their true nature—their most essential nature, which is timeless, dimensionless nature that is beyond life and death—can then bring forth the anointing of the celestial oil. That is the esoteric understanding of what we mean by "messiah." This has interesting implications, not the least of which is that we are all the Messiah in drag. That is to say, contrary to popular belief, there is no one single Messiah. Rather, the Messiah is our very nature; it is the origin of our individual soul—our individual star. We all have the potential to recognize our messianic nature, to be a messiah.

It says in the Hebrew Bible (Num. 24:17): *Darach Kochav Mi-Ya'akov*, which means: "and a star shall go forth out of Jacob." The ancient commentaries understood this verse to be an allusion to the Messiah.[20] Who is this star that will go forth out of Jacob? The commentaries—in line with the Oral Tradition—explain that it is the Messiah. We can see that the Messiah is associated with the *Star*, the Point of Light.

Next I will share with you some other things in the spirit of esoteric wisdom. I will just allude to some things, and as they say, *hamaivin yavin*—"those who understand will understand."[21]

If you read the second chapter in the Gospel of Matthew (Matt. 2:1-2), it mentions the "magi from the East" (Μάγοι ἀπὸ ἀνατολῶν) who see a star, and based on this vision, they proclaim the birth of Jesus. Of course, it should make more sense now what they saw, and why it was significant in terms of the recognition of him as a messiah. The Gospels, especially the book of Matthew, are expressions of the ancient Hebrew wisdom tradition. It is impossible to understand the mystical allusions in the Gospels without an experiential and traditional understanding of the Hebrew transmission.

In the text, these "magi," an ancient Greek word which is often translated in English Bibles as "wise men," see the star of Bethlehem and declare: "Where is the king of the Jews?" This begs the question: why do they use the word "king"? Because that is what the Hebrew word "*Mashiach*" refers to in the Bible. The king is the one "anointed with oil," so the star and the king are both allusions to the Messiah, or the messianic state of consciousness.[22]

Furthermore, the phrase "magi from the East" from the Gospel is an allusion to those who have realized the *sefirah* of *Chochmah*, which literally means "wisdom." Although "wise men" is a problematic translation of the ancient Greek word, "Μάγοι," it is still commonly used in English versions of the Gospel. These "wise men" are thus "men (and I would add, women) of wisdom, of *Chochmah*," alluding to those who have realized this dimension of consciousness. Moreover, the word "East" in Hebrew, *Kedem*, has the same root as the word *Kedumah*, which is also a technical reference to the *sefirah* of *Chochmah* in the Kabbalah.[23] The Greek phrase "from the East" thus alludes in multiple ways to the realization of the light of *Chochmah*, the messianic Point of Light.[24]

Moreover, the word *Kedem* can mean "primordial" as well as "East." In fact, the Bible (Gen. 2:8) refers to the Garden of Eden with the phrase *Eden Mi-Kedem*, which means "Eden in the East." John Steinbeck got the name for his novel, *East of Eden*, from that biblical verse. Most English Bibles translate this phrase as "Eden in the East"; however, *Kedem*, like *Kedumah*, also means "primordial." The biblical phrase "Eden in the East" is thus pointing to the "primordial Eden," which would be an appropriate translation of the phrase *Eden Mi-Kedem*.[25]

The problem is that people will read that the Garden of Eden is in the "East" and they will think it is a physical coordinate. Translating the Hebrew Bible into English is problematic because it does not capture the esoteric dimension of the words. The phrase "magi from the East" in the Gospel of Matthew is an esoteric allusion to people who have realized this dimension of primordial wisdom, the *sefirah* of *Chochmah*, the messianic Point of Light. That is to say, these *magi* had the capacity to recognize the Messiah because they had realized and embodied this light in themselves. Otherwise, how would they be able to recognize it in someone else, in this case, Jesus?

There are many dimensions to the teachings about Jesus that you can say have been lost in translation from the Hebrew to the Greek and then to the English. Right now, most people are reading the Gospels in English, which are translated from the Greek, but there is a lot in the Greek which is actually derived directly from the Hebrew, and that is lost both in translation and transliteration. Another example of this is the traditional epithet "Jesus of Nazareth" that is found in the Gospels. When understood properly through knowledge of the Hebrew and Greek, it is obvious that this does not refer to a place-name, but rather to a mystical messianic title that was known to first-century Jews.[26] I can show you more about this another time. The esoteric and mystical significance of the teachings of Jesus are nearly lost, and the Kedumah teachings can offer insight into these primordial revelations.

To understand what is being alluded to requires not just knowing the Hebrew (and in some cases the ancient Greek), but it also requires recognizing the experiential states that are being invoked. The teachings of Jesus are actually part of the Kedumah tradition, or more accurately, part of the Kedumah revelation. Those who recognized Jesus, the "magi from the East," were, according to the Gospel of Matthew, holders of the Kedumah lineage. They were, literally, the "masters of Kedumah," which is another way to translate this Greek phrase (Μάγοι ἀπὸ ἀνατολῶν) from the Gospel of Matthew.

The Kedumah lineage is an inner lineage. It is an esoteric lineage that transcends and traverses traditions. That is why I made it very clear in the beginning of this series that Kedumah is not a religion, and that it holds no allegiance to any particular tradition. It is the lineage of the experiential wisdom that is able to discern and recognize truth in any tradition, and in any person. That is why the Kedumah teachings also express revelations that are relevant to other traditions; Christianity would be one example, with the teachings of Jesus. Kedumah is part of that lineage as it comes through the ancient Hebrew prophets and kings, and it traverses time and space, with the capacity to express itself through the framework of other lineages and traditions as well.

Kedumah is mysterious, and it will not make complete sense to the conventional mind. I am saying some things about Kedumah in order to make it more palatable to the conceptual mind, but as you can probably tell, it is actually something far more mysterious. Who knows what impact it will have, or what its destiny will be, but, for whatever reason, we have congregated here, mysteriously, this group, this *minyan* has come together to participate in this teaching, which in my experience is a revelation that is coming directly from the dynamic intelligence of the primordial vastness of Being.

Alright. So, anybody have any comments or questions? Anything you want to share about what you've seen or about what your experience is?

STUDENT: Gratitude. Gratitude and looking forward to more.

STUDENT: I'm noticing, largely because of how scattered and how much I had going on over the past five months, that one of the things I would love is to have the individual practices that are associated with each of the energetic movements that we've gone through, parsed out, so that I can sit and practice them, until I can fill in…

STUDENT: I'm also feeling this desire to take this home and work with it more, and feeling like I'm not totally clear how to do that.

ZVI: Makes sense. We haven't had the time or the space to work with some of the material that's come up for some of you, in terms of really applying the transmutational capacities of the *drash* practice, for example. It's a whole art of how to work with things in that way. So yes, I appreciate that.

The best way to continue to work with these teachings at home is to regularly set aside time to practice the purification of the limbs and the *tzimtzum* meditations. Then, see if you can practice staying with your experience in an embodied way as much as you can without repressing your experience on the one hand nor acting it out on the other hand. If you can be curious about the embodied felt-sense of your experience, and explore it on the sensation level then that is also good to work with. It will help to stay connected to our group as well, and I will see if there is a way to set up an interim group to support us all on the journey.

STUDENT: Just wanted to say thanks for sharing all of these teachings. My experience has been that so many of the teachings have felt so true, and just so precisely laid out in a way that just feels so right on to me. And then, the experiences we have all had here, just profound experiences of being held and loved, and then to have the Hebrew rootedness emerging together with that, and just the learning aspect of that has been really amazing too. So, my whole experience has just been really profound, and thank you.

ZVI: Yes, you are welcome. I'm wondering about the "wise ones from the East." What happens in your experience when I talk a little bit about the origins of this teaching?

STUDENT: I've always felt a similar kind of experience, some kind of intuitive sense of these wise men or women from the East, but actually particularly related to the Messiah and to Christianity, and something powerful that emerged, and is emerging, related to that and somehow is at the root of every single tradition. I don't know, I've always had those kinds of thoughts and feelings and just intuitions since early on, and so the description of light that goes along with that feels right on to me.

ZVI: Yes. Thank you.

STUDENT: Maybe this is just in myself, and maybe it's in the room, but I noticed a sense of excitement and also intrigue that this lineage—which is in a sense primordial—continues to operate in the world. The idea that maybe in every time there is a way that this primordial teaching takes form and that there are people who are able to recognize it and that those people may be able to connect through time in a certain way. This seems like a beautiful and exciting idea to me, that there is something that is passed through lineage that isn't specific to any religion per se, but across religions and can be recognized in a broader sense. When you said that it felt like a wider thing opened, like the possibility of placing all of these traditions in a broader perspective, in a broader point of view, for me seemed really amazing.

ZVI: Yes, it is amazing.

STUDENT: I just realized that the experience for me is a lot like getting an intense download and then needing to just let go and sit and let it all process and churn and just make sense of it. All this information—it's like pure information from a fire hose. And I appreciated it and it's been percolating. I feel it continuing.

ZVI: Thank you.

STUDENT: Well, I've always felt like the things that come through the teachings each time I'm here are so relevant to what's going on in my life and things I recently learned and things I'm already feeling in myself changing, so it's always been amazing. I don't know, there's a lot that I've seen and experienced. I wish it wasn't over.

ZVI: It's not over; it's only just begun.

STUDENT: My experience is multifaceted. I think in terms of concrete spiritual practices, it's been really a gift to be given instructions on body-mindfulness practices, as particularly expressed in this tradition. And then the practice of talking to God was actually extremely powerful for me and it's something that I've continued since the day you gave it. And then in terms of the kind of aspects that brush up against normative Judaism, it just completely changes my relationship to the Jewish tradition. For instance, to hear the teachings about the wise men and the revolutionary potential that this has is very powerful. I'm just very excited and I want to thank you for sharing your teachings, and I hope it continues.

ZVI: You're welcome. Yes, it's not easy to explain what Kedumah is because it's not an existing tradition in the normative sense. It is a trans-religious expression of the Kedumah principle—the nonconceptual primordial source. It is part of the emerging paradigm and teaching. It is a revelation responding to the particular needs of our time. And it has a particular force to it. That's why I'm asking about the stream of the teaching, to see how you experience it. The teaching has its own stream, has its own force. It can be sensed. That's what I'm curious about with this exercise; I want to know your perception and experience of the stream of this teaching. It's still very young; it's first emerging from the womb. So it's subtle.

STUDENT: Tonight I have a very distinct feeling. I wouldn't describe it exactly as a star, but rather like a point, like a line that is so deep and sharp, or, it's not quite the word, but it has a great space and loneliness to it, and yet it's so distinct. So it's not loneliness in the usual sense of loneliness; it's just this large space with a point in the center. That's the best way I can describe it. And there's a strong feeling about it. And there's a lot of longing connected with it also. And also because my training has been mainly Buddhist, I'm very interested in crossovers, and I find it very interesting and powerful to have that wider perspective.

STUDENT: I have experienced the teachings as a tenderization of the heart, a Journey of Wholeness through the Chamber of Sorrows. There's a relief to me to be able to enter wholeness through the tenderness of the heart, the exquisite vulnerability of the heart. To go through the Chamber of Sorrows is necessary and it was almost comforting in a way. For me, the contemplative practices, the meditations, and specifically the meditations with the body, were breakthroughs for me. To hear with my bones, for instance. That was a new kind of meditation for me. And the trans-traditional part of it for me was also very powerful, because of my relationship with Jewish mysticism and the Hebrew letters, so it helped me release my identity with all those things and I experienced great freedom in these contemplative practices that I had not experienced before. And so, I have a lot of gratitude. I also have this feeling that this is all just a taste, but it seems like the right kind of taste, of a sweetness that resonates with my own spiritual experience of how I experience relationship to the Divine, and relationship to many aspects of our Divine unity. I really appreciate the way in which you're able to teach and orchestrate it, so thank you.

STUDENT: I feel that the force of your teaching, it feels like mystery, like this alive unknownness. And even though you're giving us information, it feels like it just opens up that mystery of the universe, and makes me feel like I haven't really gotten anywhere and I have a lot left to go. Or I guess I don't, because I'm already shining, but I haven't really realized that. It's humbling.

ZVI: You don't realize that you are shining?

STUDENT: No, I don't think so. Otherwise, what am I looking for still? I mean, after every class, I feel so inspired to keep exploring. I guess I kind of in a way don't really want it to end, because that's the fun part. But, that's the force that I feel. It's like this mystery.

ZVI: That's a good way to put it.

STUDENT: So I wanted to say that one word that expresses how these teachings have felt for me is just "honest." I was thinking of the Chamber of Sorrows, having this very tender vulnerability, and realizing that I can project a lot of things onto what tenderness might be, and associate it with weakness. And there's also the ability to address conflict, and the strength of that, so it's not just weak and tender, it's tender and vulnerable and strong. And I realize that it kind of dismantles my projections onto what these concepts are, and instead I'm left with just an honest, heartfelt care, or an honest, heartfelt "no," or whatever is needed. So it's just being honest with whatever I'm feeling, whether that's being vulnerable or putting up some barriers, without judgments on it. It's just very poignant authenticity.

ZVI: Yeah. Thanks. My intention with this exercise is to expose more of the exploration of what it is that's moving this phenomenon, this teaching. To expose its nature. And it is very mysterious, multifaceted, authentic, honest, etc. I say all of this because even though the external form is manifesting in a particular way, and I'm sitting up here teaching, I know that I am not the source of the teaching. Kedumah can be expressed in many ways, through different people and times and places. I'm curious about its possibility for our time. I'm curious to see how the teaching will express itself through each of you.

11
EMPTINESS AND FREEDOM

PRACTICE

OKAY, LET'S START with a practice. In the first ten talks we explored the five journeys: Contraction, Expansion, Wholeness, Vastness, and Freedom. Each of these journeys has its associated practices. Tonight we are going to talk a little bit about emptiness from the Kedumah perspective, since emptiness is a transitional realization between the Journeys of Vastness and Freedom. So I want to introduce a practice that relates to a particular facet of the experience of this kind of emptiness. This is a practice that appeared in my own process, and it was related to this phase of the journey.

This practice builds upon the other practices we have learned. So take a few minutes to feel the groundedness of your presence in your body, your belly; see if you can sense the light of the belly-center. Those are good ongoing practices to do regularly, to really establish and develop the sense of presence in your being and your location in time and space. They develop the concentration of presence in one's location. This new practice in a sense takes a lot of that development for granted. It builds on it.

This practice will not make any sense on the conceptual level. Well, it can make sense on the conceptual level, but it will be a paradox. I will recite a phrase and we will use it as an invocation to being—to just being, to just sitting. But the invocation has a particular effect. That's why I'm introducing it in this manner, to invite us to just hold the phrase lightly, as a light orientation. Allow the phrase to abide in your field, your energetic or presence-field, as you just sit. It's not used like a mantra; you're not repeating it over and over again. It's more similar to when we did the sacred word practice. Do you remember that? We are just allowing it to gently orient us, while we just abide in our presence, in our being. We are just being. We're not doing anything in particular and we're just aware of what's happening with a sense of being here, with this orientation, letting this orientation guide our mind. Does this make sense so far?

The phrase is: "Thinking more and more about less and less." That's it, believe it or not. This is the magical formula. "Thinking more and more about less and less." So let's just sit, with a sense of presence, open, thinking more and more about less and less. You may find that your mind will begin to think more and more about less and less. Just let your mind work that phrase. And notice what happens in your consciousness. Does this make sense?

STUDENT: No.

ZVI: Haha, good, you got it.

So I'll ring the bell and then we'll just sit, and I'll ring it again to end the practice.

TALK

The Journey of Vastness, the fourth journey in this teaching, opens up the possibility of experiencing the truth of emptiness. Emptiness can arise in the Journey of Vastness, and it serves as an important and necessary stage in the path to the fifth journey, the Journey of Freedom. "Emptiness" is a popular word in some traditions, so I want to say a few things about emptiness in general, and about how we use this word on the Kedumah path.

There are three primary types of emptiness: The first kind of emptiness is what I call "deficient emptiness," the second type is called "beneficent emptiness" and the third type is called "radical emptiness." First I will discuss the first category, that of "deficient emptiness."

Deficient emptiness is the experience of a certain kind of emptiness in one's consciousness. It can be experienced somatically, emotionally, or in an energetic body. Usually it is experienced along with a constellation of sensations and feelings, and it is a kind of emptiness that is very familiar to us as human beings. It is called "deficient emptiness" because it is marked by a painful sense of a lack, a feeling that something is missing. This kind of emptiness manifests in the human experience in an infinite variety of ways. Any feeling of inadequacy or that we lack something is what I mean by "deficiency." When we feel a sense of deficiency, we feel we are lacking in one way or another.

Within this first general category of deficient emptiness, there are two subcategories. The first subcategory is what I call "Tree-Holes" and the second I call "Tree-Hollow." I use the word "tree" as an allusion to the Tree of Life, which we have been discussing and unpacking in each of the ten previous talks.

In the Kabbalistic system, there is an eleventh *sefirah* that is hidden and invisible[1] and is not usually included in the ten *sefirot* of the Tree of Life.[2] This eleventh *sefirah* is *Da'at*, which is the principle of direct, intimate, nondual knowing that we have discussed at length in earlier talks. According to Lurianic Kabbalah, in the most primordial dimension (the realm of *tohu*, of "chaos"), the Tree of Life includes all eleven *sefirot* as a singular unit and serves as the ultimate rectification of all distortion and evil in the world.[3] These eleven *sefirot* also parallel the secret blend of eleven spices that were used in the ancient Temple and that we discussed in an earlier talk.[4] As such, this eleventh teaching completes the *mandala* of the Tree of Life that has been building in the first ten talks; it represents the hidden eleventh *sefirah*, the magical eleventh "spice," and the completion of the Tree of Life in the most subtle and primordial dimensions of reality.

The Tree of Life, the *Etz ha-Chayyim*, is one of the primary models that we have used to talk about the Divine Lights and their expressions in our consciousness. These Lights are the essential qualities or aspects of Being as they express themselves in our experience, through our consciousness and in the world. The Tree of Life, which maps out the ten primary Lights, is thus both a representation of the cosmos as well as a representation of our human soul, which itself is a reflection of the Divine, or cosmic, body. In essence, we are each a microcosm of the Tree of Life. This is alluded to in a verse in the book of Deuteronomy (20:19) that states, *Ve-ha-Adam Etz Ha-Sadeh*, which means, "The human being is a tree of the field." Equating the human being with a tree is thus an ancient principle.

We have an entire teaching in the Kedumah path on the relationship between the Tree and human consciousness. It is a fascinating dimension of the path that has to do with the awakening of what is known in the East as the *kundalini*. We do not work directly with this channel in the entry-levels of the Kedumah path because doing so can cause a lot of problems if the nervous system is not properly conditioned. So we have a deep understanding of the tree as a symbol of consciousness and the awakening of the human potential.

It is within this context that I use the term "Tree-Hole," which refers to the experience of what feels like a hole in our body-soul. I am speaking of any time that one of the lights of the tree is blocked from our awareness, blocked from manifesting in our experience. In that particular area, we will experience what feels like a hole in the tree. We will experience this hole as a lack of that quality.[5]

I will use the quality of *Gevurah* (strength) as an example since we are already familiar with it. If our essential strength is unavailable to us for whatever reason, then we will experience a deficient emptiness in place of the full expression of that real true quality of Being. Such an obstruction could occur because our awareness is cut off from a particular quality, which can happen if there is trauma around this quality or maybe a lack of development of it, or perhaps we have simply not exercised it enough or practiced expressing it.

This deficient emptiness might manifest as a lack of capacity to set boundaries, for example. That would be one expression of the Tree-Hole of *Gevurah*, this quality of strength. We might not be clear around our boundaries, or we might not express our needs clearly and assertively. If we feel that we cannot express our needs, then implicitly there is a sense of deficiency. We may be cut off from the immediate feeling of deficiency, but if we inquire into it—or any issue that we have in our life that relates to a hole around one of the qualities—it seems to be a universal phenomenon that we will encounter a sense of lack. We will find a hole in the tree and emptiness of that quality.

I am using the word "emptiness" here in a particular way. We are speaking of the deficient emptiness of that quality, meaning there is something that feels lacking or missing. This same principle can apply to any of the qualities; it could be a feeling of deficient emptiness around our erotic energy, for instance, which is something many people feel cut off from. People may experience conflict around expressing that energy or feeling it deeply or being it. If a person sincerely investigates they will likely encounter that underneath the defenses of feeling the deficiency is a raw feeling of pure void and emptiness, a deficient emptiness.

All along, from the very beginning of these teachings, we have been talking about deficient emptiness even though I have not named it explicitly. We talked about sensing into contraction and working with contraction. At the heart of every contraction there is usually some kind of deficient emptiness. Any contraction in our system is an attempt to fill in a hole with an overcompensation of congested energy. In place of the free, spontaneous, expressive qualities of Being, we place a contracted approximation of the real thing.

When our essential presence is cut off from our consciousness, from our Being and from our life, then we unconsciously maneuver to fill in that empty hole with something we can hold onto. We create all kinds of psychic material to fill the hole, usually some kind of self-image or identity. For example, if we feel a lack of the quality of strength, we may fill that hole with a grandiose sense of strength, like a kind of false machismo or a neurotic masculinized sense of strength to compensate for our feelings of deficiency. On the other hand, we may identify with the weak victim, the empty and deficient one. Believing in that self-identity, which is really an identification with the deficient emptiness, then becomes another way of avoiding staying present with what is a very difficult feeling.

All of the Divine qualities—the Lights of the Tree or the fruits of the tree—have their associated Tree-Holes. The Journey of Wholeness, as we have discussed, is the process of cultivating the real fruits of our essential nature so that they can ripen as the real, authentic tree that we are, which is a Tree of Life, an *Etz ha-Chayyim*.

In order for this process to mature, we have to learn how to Wake Down. It is all about Waking Down into the earth. That is what the tree has to do. The roots have to go really deep in order to Wake Down; it must do this in order to have the strength, the will, the fortitude, the steadfastness, and the capacity to really be a strong tree, even with the holes. If the tree does not have deep roots, then usually what happens is that when it develops holes, the tree gets destabilized and weakened. In this metaphor, we identify with the hole or we become something that we are not—or more accurately we pretend to be something that we are not—in order to not feel the depth of our pain of lack. You can see how growing our wakefulness deeply into the earth—Waking Down—is necessary in order to develop the resilience and steadfastness to endure the destabilizing impact of our holes.

Have you seen these tree holes? Do you know what I am talking about? The sporadic holes you see in the trunks of the tree? There is a sense that despite these holes the tree is whole and solid. A tree is grounded and situated deep in itself. The hole does not take away from its realness, from its rootedness, from its authenticity. That is the kind of capacity that we need in order to endure the pain of our Tree-Holes. We find that when we really sense the raw sensation of the hole itself and all the feelings that come with it, then the Tree-Hole is no longer a deficient hole. Rather the real quality of our being then spontaneously manifests in its fullness and is then able to express itself through that portal. This is why when we look at a tree, and there happens to be a hole, we do not see it as a problem. We do not judge the tree by its hole. We see the hole as an integral part of the tree. It is not a lack.

In the tree of our consciousness—what I call our Tree-Soul—there is no actual hole. It feels like a deficient hole when we identify with our usual self and all its self-images and beliefs, but if we investigate the Tree-Hole itself—and we saw this when we worked with contraction and expansion—we will discover that it can be a portal to something very real and expansive. We must inquire deeply into the feeling of a hole, using the three orienting postures that we learned about in earlier talks. Most important here is to develop a sense of grounded presence in the body. That is why we work so much with the body, which has to do with "Waking Down" the roots of the tree. The tree, stabilized by its roots and trunk, is like, "Here I am, come what may."

It states in the very first chapter of the Book of Psalms (1:3): *Ve-ha-ya Ke-etz Shatul Al Palgei Mayim Asher Piryo Yiten Bi-ito Va-aleyhu Lo Yibol Ve-Chol Asher Ya'seh Yatzliach.* This means, "And he shall be like a tree planted by streams of water, that brings forth its fruit in its season, and whose leaf does not wither; and in whatsoever he does he shall prosper." That is the image of what is possible in our human potential. This verse is pointing to the capacity of our human consciousness to be rooted, even if there are streams of water coursing by. There can be wind blowing, termites eating through our trunk leaving holes in their wake; whatever comes our way, we remain stable in our ground.

This capacity to stay rooted in our being is the first of the three orienting postures that we work with. This capacity is cultivated with the practice of sensing into the limbs as well as the *tzimtzum* practice. They develop the capacity for this kind of grounded presence. The curiosity of the heart—the awakening of the life-force, the *eros* of the heart-genital-tongue connection—is the second orienting posture that we discussed. And the third is the orienting posture of the mind, being in a state of not-knowing. If we are engaging our practice of *drash* with these attitudinal postures, if we are really sensing into our experience in the here and now, we might find that however difficult or painful our experience is, if we stay with it, it will tend to open into more spaciousness. Have you ever had an experience like that?

If we simply relate to our experience on the embodied sensorial level and suspend all of our ideas, projections and biases about it, it will tend to open up. It is like clockwork. It is actually an amazingly inviolable spiritual law of reality. Our experience opens up and transforms when we apply these principles. If we are really awake and paying attention to the phenomenology of this process, we may notice that as we go deeply into a Tree-Hole and stay with it, the sense of deficient emptiness will transform into an experience of open space.

Sometimes we are not even aware that we feel contracted until it releases and we feel the space open up. Then we might reflect, "Wow, I cannot believe I was seeing things in such a limited way." Whatever story we were holding on to or whatever self-image we were identifying with had become so second nature that to conceive of another possibility was unlikely. When the space opens, all of a sudden even the sense of the body-boundary is bigger. There is a sense that the boundaries are more dissolved and there is more permeability. There is more of a sense of space in oneself and in the room. This is what we mean by the term "expansion;" this is the Journey of Expansion.

However, when I discussed the Journey of Expansion in earlier talks, I did not make this dimension of the process explicit. There is a nuance in this process that we are not often aware of because we jump over it or move through it very quickly. When we move through the deficient emptiness, we typically encounter all kinds of unconscious material that is difficult and painful. There may be memories, psychic and energetic imprints of what feel like wounds, somatic contractions, and so on. But it is this very psychic content that fills the hole that is actually so painful. When we are able to stay with the sensations and this content dissolves, then all that is left is the phenomenological imprint of whatever this hole is. That hole turns out to be space—pure space, without content. This space is simply the nature of our being. When we move through our contraction and the feeling of deficient emptiness, then pure spaciousness opens up.

To review, there are three categories of emptiness and two subcategories of deficient emptiness. So far we have only discussed the first category of emptiness and the first of its two subcategories, which is the deficient emptiness that I am calling the "Tree-Hole." This is the experience of deficient emptiness that is related to a specific quality of the Tree of Life.

There are many Tree-Holes. Sometimes on this path you can feel like a pockmarked tree, with holes everywhere: hole of strength, hole of love, hole of compassion, hole of will, and so forth. When we start to sense into our experience more deeply, it exposes what is there beneath the surface; it exposes the unconscious. Once the unconscious is exposed and the holes are gradually uncovered, we might wonder, "Oh my god, what have I done!"

This is why I wanted this series of talks to be a prerequisite for more advanced teachings. I want everyone to understand what kind of process we are talking about. Kedumah is not a romanticized version of spirituality. The path can, at times, be quite uncomfortable. It is difficult to be with our contractions and to develop the capacities to work with them effectively and constructively. We have to love the truth enough to stay with and work through our discomfort.

I think it is worth it, but everyone should know that this is not a bypass methodology. We can easily do practices that will quickly invoke the Divine qualities, or that will open our experience to all kinds of dimensions of nonduality and oneness. While there is a place for those things on the path, it is not an approach that cultivates a solid and unwavering tree. Have you seen those zip lines that connect one tree to another, and you can fly on these ropes from one tree to another? I saw these huge zip line parks when I was in Costa Rica with my son. At the end of the day you come back down and you go to your hut, and then you get knocked over in a hurricane! The trees usually do not get knocked over, so what we want is to be the trees and not just swing from the trees for fun.

Really we are talking about developing the capacity to be real in the world, regardless of our circumstances, so that we do not need to organize our life around having pleasant spiritual feelings all the time. We need to develop the qualities of consciousness that are necessary to live a fully human life in the world. Life is difficult and we have to deal with painful truths. We need to cultivate the capacity to live fearlessly and fully, come what may.

Ultimately, the process of working through our Tree-Holes brings us to the state of being that I call the "Tree-Whole;" this is the fully embodied and actualized Tree-Soul in the form of a human being. This model is another way of explaining how the journeys of contraction, expansion and wholeness all lead into one another. "Contraction" is the term that describes the phenomenon of filling in the Tree-Hole with psychic material and content, as an attempt to defend ourselves from feeling the deficient emptiness and pain of loss associated with the absence of a particular Divine quality in our soul. Expansion is what opens up when we move into and through a Tree-Hole and digest the difficult material that is held there in contraction. Moving through our experience in this way—rather than around it—reveals that the experience of the Tree-Hole as deficient and lacking only occurs when viewed through the lens of the stories and identities stored in the hole. When this content is assimilated, what remains is pure open space, revealing our nature as unbounded and free. Each of the qualities on the Tree of Life expresses a different hue and flavor of this boundless spaciousness. This is what we mean by "expansion."

Once we have worked through all the Tree-Holes associated with the ten primary qualities in the Tree of Life, and we integrate the real, expansive nature of each of these Lights of Being, then we are engaging the Journey of Wholeness. This is alluded to in one of the most ancient Kabbalistic texts called *Sefer ha-Bahir*, which means "Book of Clarity." This text describes the cosmic tree with the Hebrew term *kol*, which means "all." It is called the "tree that is all," because it is the tree that has realized and actualized all of the Lights of Being, all of its Divine potentialities.[6]

The real esoteric zinger here is that the *Bahir* echoes the Talmudic tradition that Abraham had a daughter whom he named *Kol*.[7] We know that Abraham never had a daughter according to the Hebrew Bible. So what is the Talmud talking about? This is a mystical allusion to the Pearl, which is connected by the fact that the numerical value for the Hebrew word *kol* is fifty, the same as the letter *nun* in *Penina*, and the number associated with *Binah* and wholeness. Thus, the "tree that is all" is the actualization of the completed human soul, the embodiment of "all" the pure Divine qualities.

We are really talking about realizing, actualizing, and embodying the Tree of Life as a human being in the world. But we are not only of this world. As it states in the book of Genesis (28:12), referring to Jacob's dream of the ladder: *Ve-hinei Sulam Mutzav Artza Verosho Magiya Ha-shamayma,* which means, "And behold a ladder set up on the earth and its top reached to the Heavens." This is the kind of thing that we are talking about.

This leads us to the second subcategory of the first primary category of emptiness. Again, there are two subcategories of deficient emptiness. The first is what I call a Tree-Hole, and the second is what I call a Tree-Hollow. Have you ever seen a tree-hollow? It is when the whole trunk looks like it is hollowed out. It is not just a small hole. This is the second category of deficient emptiness, which is much more difficult to work with than the first kind of deficient emptiness. The first kind of deficient emptiness is the feeling that a quality is lacking, one of the Divine Lights. We feel as if we are missing that particular Light, or we are cut off from it. It is not ontologically missing, of course; it is our very nature. It never "goes" anywhere. But, if we are not aware of it, or it is obfuscated in our experience, then it will feel like a hole. So you see, we can experience a deficient emptiness of a particular quality, but all the while still maintain a cohesive sense of a self, a cohesive sense of a self-image or self-identity. That is to say, usually when we experience a hole of deficient emptiness, we have a definite sense of a self that is experiencing this emptiness or this deficiency.

We can work with these deficient feelings directly by moving into the Tree-Hole, and then in due course the space will open. That space will then be colored by the particular color and quality of one of the Lights of Being that was lost to our awareness, be it the red light of *Gevurah*, the white light of *Chesed*, or whichever. While this pure Light is a spacious light, and we have a sense of expansiveness when it opens up, it is nevertheless an experience in which one's self-identity remains intact. That is, it is still one's familiar self-identity that is now having an experience of space, expansion, and a sense of strength in the case of *Gevurah*.

With regard to the red light, perhaps before you felt deficient and now you have the implicit confidence to do what you need to do. You can assert yourself, express yourself, and you do not have self-consciousness around it. If it is the light of will, which is the *sefirah* of *Yesod*, there is a sense that "I will persevere in the process regardless of what comes my way." It is not determined by the thought of it; it just happens this way. It is an implicit sense of will. With the green light—the quality of compassion, which is the *sefirah* of *Tiferet*—the sense is that, "I do not need to fix the other person's pain and can instead feel the raw, sensitive, delicate, compassionate presence." All of these experiences of the Lights have a sense of expansion to them, but still there is a self-identity which feels that "I am experiencing this."

The Tree-Hollow is different than the Tree-Hole in that it has to do with a more fundamental kind of deficiency. It is related to what is called in the Hasidic literature *Bitul Ha-Yesh*. This phrase literally means "nullification of something." In these mystical texts they use this phrase to refer to the "nullification" of one's core sense of self-identity.[8] This process of *Bitul Ha-Yesh* is a necessary step on the journey of true self-realization and enlightenment. I use the term "self-realization" to mean the realization of the True Self, which is the Point of Light, the primordial light of *Chochmah*. I use the term "enlightenment" to refer to the integration and embodiment of the ten primary Lights of Being. Hence the word: enligh*TEN*ment.

There is a particular sense of deficient emptiness that comes up when we rub up against this core sense of being a "somebody" and having a self-identity. The belief that we have a self—that we are a cohesive, organized personality that ontologically exists—is a very primitive psychological structure that is usually taken for granted. However, any true spiritual path will at some point expose that who and what we take ourselves to be is nothing but a collection of mental self-images and identities that fill in a gaping hole at the very core of our soul. The deficient emptiness that lurks beneath the surface of our sense of self is much more difficult to move through and sense into than is the emptiness of a particular quality of Being.

This experience of deficient emptiness is more fundamental and basic than the Tree-Hole, which is why I call it the "Tree-Hollow." This large gaping hole is in the very core of the tree, in the trunk. When the emptiness of the Tree-Hollow is exposed on the spiritual path, one's very self-identity will feel threatened and there will be all kinds of instinctual and primitive defenses that come up to protect its survival. This is usually a crossroads for people on the spiritual journey. Many people cannot take the pain of loss of self and they retreat to some familiar sense of self or to identifying with some religion or ideology. This provides them with a sense of security and safety for their self-identity, which has been subject to the light of exposure.

If we are able to stay grounded in our embodied experience and apply our practice of inquiry, sensing through those difficult sensations, then we may come to a core inner exposure of the sense of self-identity itself. This is usually experienced as some kind of super-concentrated contraction in the body-soul. When we experience this super-contraction it can feel like all the energy of existence is packed into the hard shell of a nut, and this hard-shelled nut is lodged somewhere in our body-soul. Sensing into this hard husk, it can feel like all our defenses and armoring have retreated and concentrated themselves behind a dense shell. This husk can be experienced as a super-concentrated contraction in the body-soul or as a shell that surrounds and armors the entire body-soul.

This experience, which we call in Kedumah the "husk" or the "shell," is what the Kabbalists point to with the Hebrew term *kelipah* (pl. *kelipot*), which literally means "husk" or "shell." The *kelipot* are referred to throughout Kabbalistic literature as the hard husks that cover up and obscure the "sparks of light" from our perception. The purpose of the "shell" is thus to isolate from our awareness the direct perception of the Point of Light, the "spark of light" found in Kabbalah.[9]

If you recall, contractions are what fill in the Tree-Holes; therefore, with regard to the Tree-Hollow, which is a more fundamental kind of emptiness, it makes sense that we would have a more entrenched and profound kind of contraction to compensate for its deep sense of lack. It takes a great deal of development and capacity to work through the husk, specifically integration of *emunah* (trust) and love and the rest of the Divine Lights of Being.

Working through the husk is the core spiritual work of self-realization, and it is alluded to in the Song of Songs (6:11): "I went down to the orchard of nuts, to see the blossoms of the valley, to see whether the vine had budded or the pomegranates had bloomed." The Hebrew terms for "blossoms of the valley," "vine," and "pomegranates" all allude to the awakened self-realized state of enlightenment. As the verse suggests, we have to go down—Wake Down—into the orchard of nuts, which means working through the husks and shells, in order to discover the truth of who and what we are.[10]

We often come up against the Tree-Hollow when we recognize a core character issue that we have in our lives. For example, a person may realize that when they interact with others they feel they are being fake or inauthentic, like they are putting on a show. It could be subtle. It can even just be the sense of trying to be somebody in particular for someone else, of accommodating others. This is a universal phenomenon; probably everybody can relate to this tendency.

But, if we sense directly into this core feeling of being fake, we can then expose this core sense of a self-identity. In fact, if we follow any of the Tree-Holes all the way to the bottom, they can expose this core self-identity structure, the Tree-Hollow. However, there are certain things that tend to expose these structures outright, including fundamental structures of our character. If these structures are challenged they will expose a much deeper, more painful sense of deficiency. You can feel like your guts have been ripped out, like there is nothing to substantiate you. You can feel like completely nothing—empty, parched, dry, lack, and void. Sounds like fun, yes?

In the teachings of the second turning of the wheel of Torah, they refer to this state as the *midbar*, the "desert." The desert is where the Children of Israel went after they left *Mitzrayim*, after they left the land of contraction and moved into expansion. The desert is dry, parched, and empty, and there is no sustenance, no water, and a sense of vast emptiness. There is nothing there.

Interestingly, the word for desert is *midbar*, which can also be read and translated as "speaking."[11] If you remember back to our earlier talks about the centrality of speech on this path and its function in the practice of *drash*, you can see that the function of "speaking" in the journey of transformation is actually very deep. On one level, the journey of emptiness is a journey through the wilderness of the "desert." This is the stage on which the drama of rapprochement between contraction and expansion plays out. It is the ontological backdrop for the Journey of Wholeness. Usually we experience contraction, then open into expansion, and we swing back and forth.

The Journey of Wholeness—the fifty days of *Sefirat Ha-Omer* (counting the *Omer*) between *Pesach* and *Shavuot* that we discussed in an earlier talk—occurs in the Hebrew Bible while traveling in the desert. This process of integrating the Lights of Being is facilitated through the conscious articulation of our speech, which allows the human consciousness to participate in the expressive effulgence of creation. This is not only reflected in the Hebrew word for "desert," *midbar*, which can also mean "speaking," but also in the term *Sefirat Ha-Omer* itself.

The word *sefirat* (usually translated as "counting") can also mean "clarification," "illumination," or it can be a reference to the *sefirot* themselves. Furthermore, the word *Omer* is pronounced the same (and has a nearly identical spelling) as the Hebrew word for "speaking," the only difference being that one is spelled with an *ayin* and the other with an *aleph*. This is similar to the linguistic transformation that we discussed in the very first talk of this series, whereby Adam and Eve's garments of skin are transmuted into garments of light. Therefore, on a deeper level the practice of *Sefirat Ha-Omer* can be understood to be pointing to the Journey of Wholeness and the process of integrating and developing all the *sefirot* through the practice of illuminated speech.

The Journey of Wholeness entails working through all the Tree-Holes, moving into and through each of these holes of deficient emptiness. By moving more deeply into our experience of the holes we integrate each of the particular essential lights, which have been obfuscated by our loss of contact with that light and subsequently displaced with all kinds of psychic and energetic material. The Divine Lights are our birthright; they are our very nature.

The Journey of Wholeness is traversed in the desert. The desert is a metaphor for what I am calling the "Tree-Hollow." It is the core emptiness of our self-identity, of who and what we take ourselves to be. While the Tree-Holes are the feeling of the absence of specific qualities of our essential structure, the Tree-Hollow is the feeling of the deficient absence of the very scaffolding of the structure itself. Upon deep inquiry and investigation into the felt-sense of the Tree-Hollow void, it is possible to make one of the most shocking discoveries. This is the realization that the self-identity actually does not exist. It is a mental construct. The self is simply a projection of the mind. This is the true meaning of the Hasidic principle of *Bitul Ha-Yesh*, "nullification of [one's] somethingness." This, at least, is my experience of it.

In the last session we talked about the Point of Light, the *sefirah* of *Chochmah*. Kabbalists call it the *Nikudah* ("Point"), the *Nitzotz* ("spark") or the *kochav*, ("star"). This primordial "spark" that constitutes the essential nature of the self is revealed to our awareness only once the Tree-Hollow—the core emptiness of self-identity—is experienced and worked through to some extent. This is because the Tree-Hollow state is the condition of deficient emptiness lurking just beneath our sense of self. Our familiar, conditioned self-identity is the psychic material that fills the void of the loss with our real essential self, the Point of Light. It makes sense then that when we allow the dissolution of our familiar self, we will first encounter the feeling of deficient emptiness, followed by the discovery of our original nature that was lost to our awareness—that is the Point.

The *midbar* (desert/speaking) is thus the terrain upon which the journeys of contraction and expansion interpenetrate and cross-fertilize, creating the necessary friction to metabolize our unconscious material into the Pearl. This process—what we call the "Journey of Wholeness"—realizes its fulfillment at the end of *Sefirat Ha-Omer,* on the fiftieth day of *Shavuot*. *Shavuot* reveals the dimension of *Chochmah*, the Point of primordial wisdom, which is symbolized on this festival by marking the revelation and receiving of the Torah, the embodiment of primordial wisdom teaching. Experientially, this is realized as the point of existence, the essential self as the point of dimensionless light, the *Nekudat Ha-Yesh*.[12]

The revelation of this point of primordial wisdom occurs in the vast emptiness of the desert, of the *midbar*. The "wise ones from the East"—the *Masters of Kedumah*—arrive out of the desert to proclaim the Messiah. That is to say that *Chochmah*—the Point of Light, the Star of Jacob—is revealed in that emptiness to be the true self, which could be described as a messianic point of scintillating, dimensionless light shining in eternal space. This soul-spark is what we are. It is our authentic being, our nature. It is what we are, what we always were, and it is what we will always be. Our Starlight never dies, nor was it ever born. On the essential level, we are all the Messiah, anointed with wisdom. This is the messianic state that is alluded to with the *Kochav Yaakov*, the Star of Jacob.

Thus, we see that the process is not linear. We are always moving in, out, and through all the journeys, not necessarily in linear order. The point abides in the space between wholeness and emptiness; realization of both of these truths is required before the point can reveal itself fully. That is, we need to have some degree of maturation of the Pearl and some degree of realization of emptiness—or the space of no-self—in order for the True Self to present itself to us as a permanently available realization.

Now I want to return to our discussion of the different kinds of emptiness. Our messianic nature can only reveal itself to us after moving through the Tree-Hollow, which is the second subcategory of deficient emptiness. However, moving through either a Tree-Hole or the Tree-Hollow can bring us to the realization of the second category of emptiness, which is what I call "beneficent emptiness" or "space." The first category is deficient emptiness, the second is beneficent emptiness, or beneficent space.

This second category of emptiness presents itself to us when deficient lack or void is worked through and its ground is recognized experientially as vast, boundless space. This experience of space is not bound by any concept or structure, or by any physical limitation. When we experience our nature, it is experienced as spacious. Even if our nature is experienced with a density of presence—for example, let's say we are experiencing a dense body of light—the way we know and recognize it as the essential Presence Body is when it has an inherent quality of spaciousness in it, even if it feels dense at the same time. This is paradoxical to the mind, but that is the experience of it. You can feel your body as dense, but it does not have the conventional sense of being bounded. There is an inherent sense of space in the density.

This is a different kind of emptiness altogether, because there is no sense of deficiency in it. It feels real—like boundless open space. I use the term "beneficent" because it feels natural and has a sense of rightness and blessing to it. There is no self-concept or self-consciousness in this space. Many people, when they first feel it, remember feeling this way when they were little children. They think, "I remember this. I remember feeling so light and spacious." As you know, kids are really in their bodies, so there is not that whole dichotomy that is established in the mind between body and soul, as if the body were limited and bounded and the soul were spacious and free. Children are usually not in touch with that dichotomy. They are spacious and free and open and light, and their bodies are dense, earthy, and grounded. Children tend to be very grounded in their bodies. Their bellies hang out and they have their hands on their genitals and up their butts. It is all very real and very earthy and fleshy; and yet, at the same time, they can have this spaciousness about them, like their consciousness is not bound by their body.

We also have this potential as adults. As adults it is a bit different because we usually do not put our hands in our pants—at least not in public. Oftentimes when adults discover who they really are and experience the expansiveness of their nature, they remark that it feels very natural. They are always surprised that their true nature is not out of the ordinary. It feels very, very ordinary, but in a magical way. It is like the magic of remembering our inherent birthright, our freedom, and our true nature. That is what I mean by beneficent space, which can only be integrated by moving through the sense of deficiency.

Our feelings of deficiency are our conceptual and emotional overlays that fill in this spaciousness and obscure our perception of it. When we work through those feelings, it just reveals what has always been there and will always be there—pure open space.

There are two subcategories of beneficent space. The first is called "clear space" and the second is called "black space." The term "clear space" comes from the Hebrew phrase *Ohr Bahir* that is used in many Kabbalistic texts. Literally it means "clear light" and it is used to allude to a particular kind of luminous space. One of the most ancient Kabbalistic texts is named after this kind of space. It is called *Sefer ha-Bahir*, which means "The Book of Clarity." The second kind of beneficent space—the black space—is called in Aramaic the *Botzina De-Kardinuta*, which means "black spark" or "black light." I will discuss the significance of this phrase after we discuss the clear space.

Clear space is marked by an airy, light, fresh, crisp, boundlessness. It is "clear" because there is not a particular color or quality to the light; it is experienced as a clear light or clear space. It has the sense of fresh open vastness that you might experience when you are standing at the top of one of our Colorado mountains: a crisp, fresh, open space. That is the first category of beneficent space. This kind of space typically arises when we work through a deficient Tree-Hole. The Tree-Hole opens into a sense of space and is then colored by the particular light of Being that was displaced by the psychic material filling the space of the hole. A more subtle and boundless variation of this clear space also arises when we work through certain layers of the Tree-Hollow.

The clear space erases the sense of having a conventional body, or a body boundary. Therefore, you might feel that you do not have a physical body, or like wind is blowing through your body. The normal sense of the physical body is altered. It can feel that everything is clear space and this is all there is. But it is important to note that there is awareness of the experience. You are aware that you are aware from the location of your body, even if there is not a sense of limit, like the body is not impeding this clear space. What is interesting is that when our perception opens to the clear space there is often still a very subtle sense of a self that is observing the experience; it can even be just a sense of awareness that has an identity linked to it. Thus, it is possible to have the experience of the erasure of body-boundaries and a sense of spacious, fresh, clean-clear space all over while still maintaining a core feeling of having a self-identity.

The second subcategory of beneficent space—the black space— arises in response to this deeply entrenched sense of self-identity. The black space—or "black light" as it is described in the Zohar—is the most primordial kind of space that can be discussed without sounding completely nonsensical. The Aramaic phrase that the Zohar uses to describe this space is *Botzina De-Kardenuta*. It is one of the most mysterious phrases in the Zohar; it's used to describe the primordial light that precedes the creation of the world.[13]

Black space is experienced very differently than the fresh, clear space. Black space has density to it; it feels like the concentrated substance of spaciousness that saturates the consciousness and completely erases everything. This paradoxical sense of density of the black space does not make sense to the conventional mind because it is simultaneously the most dense substance possible and the most infinitely vast space. It is the most condensed intense light, completely annihilating all concepts of the mind and bringing a kind of cessation to the sense of a self. It is the erasure of all concepts, including the self, the body, and the world. That is how it feels and is perceived. It is the erasure of everything. The black light annihilates all of reality.

If you drop down into the core of your presence right now, you can sense it in the space. The entire room and beyond is saturated in this sublime mysterious black depth. How is it that we're talking and interacting right now and yet this black light saturates our space and the world carries on all around us? There is a sense of this dense, still, silent, deep space that is everywhere and permeates everything. It is a paradox, of course. This black, dense light is impacting us with a profound sense of stillness and silence, yet it is this black space that also allows the possibility of being silent, still, and spacious in the midst of ordinary life. The primordial nothingness of reality thus abides undisturbed in the midst of the hustle and bustle of life.

You can see how this would be an incredible resource in ordinary life, to be able to drop into the black space and disappear. This deep dark space annihilates all friction and agitation in the nervous system—it silences everything and erases all. All that is left is a palpable nothing, deep black night, not a ripple in the cosmos. There is nothing. The Kabbalists call this realm *ayin*, which means, "nothing." This word is one of the code terms for the uppermost *sefirah* in the Tree of Life, usually called *Keter*, which means "crown." This is the dimension of the *Botzina De-Kardenuta*, the primordial black luminosity of absolute nothingness. It is like cessation of all phenomena, except for the palpable truth of nothingness.

STUDENT: Is there a sound associated with it?

ZVI: In my experience, there are different degrees of black space. I am not going to talk about the details right now, but I can talk about it in a general way. There is a level of black space in which there are primordial sounds, but how this will be experienced is unique to each individual. I have heard subtle hums, primordial ocean sounds, and different vowel sounds. However, in one of our earlier talks, I mentioned the journey into deeper and deeper states of silence. There are degrees of black space, just like deeper degrees of silence. At a certain point there is actual cessation, in which you actually go unconscious and do not remember what happened. I would be meditating, going into a deep place, and then I would wake up. I would have no sense or even know how long I had been gone; I would have to look at the clock to know what time and day it was. I would completely disappear. I was not asleep, and as far as I know I did not die.

If you go all the way into the black space then it is possible to fall unconscious. It becomes so silent and there is such a rich nothingness that there is nothing that can actually exist in it. When it is over, you get up and feel that you have slept for a thousand years. It is quite amazing. The body-soul is very refreshed.

At first it can take a while for the usual mind to come back. In the depths there is no mind whatsoever. Some of the meditations in Kedumah invoke this no-mind state. It can be scary because you feel like you cannot produce a thought. Even if you try to think, you cannot. The mind is completely silent. But the strange thing is, that life goes on. Everything still happens, or at least whatever needs to happen, happens. What is striking is that there is nobody doing or thinking; things simply happen. It is very bizarre. The first time I experienced this kind of a thing, I had no context for it, so I thought I must have gone too far and blew a fuse. I was afraid that I might have actually died and that this was what it was like after death. I also thought that maybe I had gone insane in some way, because my mind was not working anymore. I could not produce a thought, yet thinking happened when it was necessary.

So these are the two subcategories of beneficent space, which is the second of three primary categories of emptiness. Before I get to the third primary category of emptiness, I want to say a few more things about beneficent space. The two subcategories of beneficent space seem to correlate in my experience to the two *sefirot* of *Chochmah* and *Keter*, respectively. The experience of the Point of Light, which is *Chochmah*, can also manifest in the consciousness as clear, open, nondual space. It seems to depend on whether or not the light is diffused or concentrated. Because the point is nondimensional, its nondual light can shine in any form, as a concentrated point or as vast clear openness.

It seems to me that *Chochmah* often manifests in the form of a Point when the backdrop of the black space of *Keter* is conscious. The experience of this is like a bright star shining in the deep black silent night sky. However, because the black space of *Keter* is more fundamental and primordial than the point (whether it manifests as a point

265

or as clear nondual space), then it is possible for the point itself to be erased by the black light. So this black light or *Keter* dimension is a deeper level of emptiness that can annihilate even the True Self of the point. This reveals that there are several layers to the spiritual function of the black light. Firstly, it serves to help expose and erase the conventional sense of self, the conditioned self-identity. This erasure then allows the true self, the Spark of Light of *Chochmah*, to arise in the vastness of this black space. This is the primordial seed of our nature, of our soul, the original primordial self.

When a person is in this state and experiencing this kind of expansion, they may feel that this is it—what more can there be than eternal freedom from life and death? The point is not limited by time and space. It is dimensionless. It is timeless. It knows that this is who I am, always was, and always will be. This truth is self-evident. It is not a mental construction; it is not something that you think about it, you just know it. The knowing comes from the experience, without a shadow of a doubt. Even the concept of doubt does not exist in that state. There is the feeling, "Well, this must be it; this must be all there is." This is the messianic condition, a certain kind of eternal freedom.

But then, the black light comes and annihilates even the true self, the Point of Light. When the essential self, our soul-spark, is erased, then we are left with absolutely nothing. This can be terrifying. All that is left is nothingness: black, still, empty, silent. It feels like a black hole; it goes on forever and ever—an endless, groundless nothingness, which contains no light, no person, no self, no essential self, and no existence whatsoever. There is no spirit and no non-spirit, just black intense luminosity.

This is why I associate this dimension with *ayin* and the *Botzina De-Kardenuta*, the "black light" or "black spark" in the Zohar. Another interesting thing is that the black light opens what I call the "central column" or "inner column" of the *merkavah*. We talked about the *merkavah* as the vehicle of consciousness. The inner column of the *merkavah* is experienced as a column of space that extends from our pelvic floor and perineum up our central column, through our head and out the top of our head. I was not aware of this column of space until I experienced the black light and the annihilation of the point. Then I realized that my whole body-consciousness was constellated around this central column of black space that is actually open at the pelvis, at bottom of the perineum, and open at the top of the head. It is a column of simple black space.

Many texts in the second turning of Torah allude to this column of space and the various kinds of emptiness that we have been discussing. These relationships are expressed in the Tree of Life, where the central channel extends from *Keter* (at the top of the head), to *Tiferet* (the heart), and down to *Yesod* and *Malchut*, which are the genitals. They are all connected in a vertical column. In fact, the Kabbalists state explicitly that *Yesod* and *Keter*, the genitals and the top of the head respectively, are intimately connected. They refer to *Keter* as the *Ratzon Ha-Elyon*, the upper will,[14] and *Yesod* as the *Ratzon Ha-Tachton*, the lower will.[15] So *Keter*, *Yesod*, and *Malchut* are all connected through the central column of the Tree of Life.

This central channel of the Tree of Life turns out to be a column of space. There is a verse in Psalms (109:22), for example, where King David states: *Vilibee Chalal Bikeerbee*, which means, "And my heart is empty within me." The word *chalal* means "empty" or "void." There are other verses that point to this inner emptiness-space as well. For example, in the book of Ezekiel (6:7), it states that the true knowledge of God only comes when the "*chalal* falls within you."

Thus, working through the Tree-Holes and the Tree-Hollow exposes both the clear light and the black light, which then bring a sense of complete nothingness. It also opens the central column that seems to support the state of no-mind, which we invoked in our meditation with the practice of thinking more and more about less and less.

There is a strong presence in the room right now. What do you experience right now as I talk about it? What do you notice? What's happening in your consciousness or what do you notice in the space?

STUDENT: I get the sense of a lot of space and it feels similar to being on a sailboat in the middle of a lake, where there's still a rhythm of something underlying it, like the rhythm of the water. It has this undulating, bouncing, steadiness to it, a moving steadiness. And then, all around looking up, there's nothing, there are no trees in the way, nothing obstructing the view, just far horizon.

ZVI: Do you have a sense of the space being more of the clear variety, or black variety, or something else? What's the quality of the light, of the space?

STUDENT: It seems more clear and bright, sort of like the colors of this room but mixed with an image I have of a lake on a sunny afternoon.

ZVI: How does it affect you to perceive in this way?

STUDENT: If I exist just in that perception, it's very calming. When I consider interacting with other humans, then there's a bit of worry and trepidation around that. Some uncertainty of how to bridge that, how to connect that to the content of reality.

ZVI: What's happening in your heart-center as you talk about it?

STUDENT: There's a warmth. It's like a loving, a sense of kindness. It has a quality of emptiness, but it's not like a thing of loving, but it's a space of loving.

ZVI: If you consider the worry that you have about interacting from this space, what's it like from your heart-center? Is your heart worried about that?

STUDENT: No, not at all. The worry's definitely more in the head, in the conceptual.

ZVI: So your heart is not really concerned. It knows it has that capacity to relate.

STUDENT: Yeah, it can hold the content of other individuals and relating to other people. It doesn't feel like I would get in the way of the heart's warmth and steadiness of the spacious perception.

ZVI: Yes. It's amazing that the heart can still relate in a personal way even though it is spacious and not identified with a self-identity. It's the authentic heart, actually. The true heart is an expression of Being, which is space.

In the Hasidic texts they talk about the transformation of the *ani* into the *ayin*.[16] The Hebrew word for "I"—the self-identity—is *ani*. If you rearrange the Hebrew letters that spell *ani*, you get *ayin*, which means "nothingness." This process is the nullification of the *ani* and its transformation into the *ayin*, the nothing.

I am not saying too much here because these processes are very esoteric. It can be confusing, challenging, and possibly disruptive. It is okay to talk about things, but there is a lot more happening behind the words; the actual presence is here. It will, therefore, push up against whatever is in us that has difficulty with these states and expose difficult material.

Oftentimes in spiritual teachings, people are open to transmissions without realizing how open they are. Therefore, they receive transmissions, but there may not be enough healthy structuring of the self to work with it effectively. So you start to talk about emptiness and nothingness and you can feel it in the space. Even if a person is not aware of it, it is still in the space, rubbing up against our consciousness. While this kind of emptiness can be disruptive to some people, it is worth clarifying that disruption in and of itself is not necessarily a bad thing. It is just important that we have the supports in place to work with the things that may come up.

I realize that I have not even talked yet about the third primary category of emptiness. We are still on the second, believe it or not. But I actually think we're out of time.

Student: You can't leave us here.

Zvi: I'm surprised after all that you still want to know what the third one is.

The third kind of emptiness is the most subtle kind of emptiness refracted through this dimension of *Keter* or *ayin*, and it is the kind of emptiness that serves as a transitional vehicle to the Journey of Freedom. In a sense it signifies the portal to freedom. It is difficult to talk about this level of emptiness without sounding completely nonsensical. With the dense, black light and its impact of annihilation and cessation, even though the experience of it feels like nothing whatsoever, we can still talk about it. It is still an experience we can relate to and people can make some kind of conceptual sense out of. Ultimately, it is still an experience that the consciousness has. If it were complete cessation where a person actually goes unconscious, then obviously you cannot talk about that because you were unconscious. But you can talk about an experience in terms of the density, the light, the silence, the stillness, the sense of depth.

This third kind of emptiness is difficult—if not impossible—to talk about because it is a radical nothingness. It is so radical in its emptiness that the word "emptiness" and "nothingness" do not even apply to it. It is not really empty, because the word "empty" is saying too much. We use the word "empty" because we do not know what else to call it; hence the attribute "radical" to signify that it is not akin to the emptiness experienced in the Journey of Vastness or that of the black space. The word "emptiness" means something; it is a concept. However, radical emptiness is so nonconceptual that even the word "nonconceptual" does not apply to it. It does not compute. That is why I say that there is no way to talk about it without it sounding nonsensical.

This kind of nothingness points to the truth of *Ein Sof*, which means "no-end." *Ein Sof* is put in the negative because it is a reality that the Kabbalists intentionally did not talk about. They just say what it is not. They say it is "no-end." There is nothing you can say about it, because actually nothing can be said about it. I am not saying this poetically or metaphorically. There is actually nothing to talk about, because there is nothing there. There is no experience, you could say, to be related.

Usually people translate *Ein Sof* into the English word "infinite" however, the word literally means "no-end." This is a more accurate translation of the term because *Ein Sof* is not really infinite. It is neither infinite nor is it finite. But at the same time it is also not not-infinite nor is it not-finite. It is nothing and everything, you see. And it is also not nothing and everything. It is "neither-nor" and "both-and" as well as not "neither-nor" and "both-and." And even that is not it. Because it is not an "it," you see.

Since it is not an experience, and it is not a thing that exists, then to describe it is impossible. In order to talk about this condition of radical emptiness, it is more useful to discuss the implications of it, to describe its impact on life or on perception. This is how emptiness—on this radical level of which I am speaking—leads to freedom. The impact of it on the consciousness is one of equalization of all experience and of all phenomena. That is to say, there is truly no longer a journey because there is no more spirituality. The word "journey" implies that we are going from a less-spiritual condition to a more-spiritual condition. In this perspective, however, there is nothing more or less spiritual. All that there is is literally what is right in front of your face. That is it. Literally. There is nothing else. This is it. And this "it" is not anything at all.

So you can see that the implications of this kind of emptiness are quite radical. It is radical because it exposes not only that there is nothing relative to something, but that there is also a reality that is so primordial and radical that it is beyond the categories of both "something" and "nothing." It is the truth of hyperliteral reality, where there is no reference point and no directionality. Since there are no coordinates there is nothing outside of the literal factuality of immediate perception.

This radical kind of emptiness reveals the Journey of Freedom, which is not a journey to anywhere, but rather involves the discovery of freedom from all dialectical categories of experience. It is freedom from the dichotomies of conceptual and nonconceptual, of spirituality and materiality, and even freedom from the concept of freedom itself. It is freedom from the fantasy that there is anything other than what is right here in front of our faces in the here and now.

In the Zen tradition, they talk about how on the spiritual journey first there is a mountain, then there is not a mountain, and then there is a mountain again. This teaching is attempting to illustrate how first we perceive reality in a conventional way, then we open up our perception to spiritual truths and nonduality and we appreciate that reality was not what we originally thought. Then, at some point, we again perceive reality in an ordinary simple way, without the bells and whistles of "spirituality"; it is pointing to the very ordinary enlightenment of being beyond categories of "dual" and "nondual" or "spiritual" and "secular."

This is the full fruition of the dimension the Kabbalists called *Adam Kadmon* and it points to the Journey of Freedom. This dimension is really not a dimension at all because it lacks any specific coordinates and has no directionality whatsoever. It is really the non-dimension that points to and allows for the endless unfolding of realization that is *Ein Sof*. This is a condition in which there is no-end to the revelation and realization of truth because each moment and perception contains all of totality. The Kabbalists also call this non-dimensional level of reality the domain of *yechidah*, which means "singularity."[17] It is a singularity in that whatever particular is right in front of your face contains every other particular in reality. Literally everything is in everything. Every particular that ever was, is, and will be is in each and every other particular. Whatever the experience is, it is a singular experience. It is all right here, right now without there even being a here or a now.

The implications of this realization are enormous, because it means that everything that ever was, is, and will be is right here, right now. This is the kind of perception that begins to open up. Basically, the non-dimensional truth of *Adam Kadmon* collapses all concepts of "distance." It erases the concept that there is distance between moments in time or between points in space or between particular people. So, you can have experiences like being somebody else, being animals, or being somewhere else, in a different time and place. But, it is not that you are journeying somewhere else, because it is happening right here. Everything happens in parallel but interpenetrating realities.

At this level of the Journey of Freedom, our understanding of processes like reincarnation begins to change. The processes of birth, death, and rebirth appear differently; it does not make sense from this perspective that we die and are reborn in another body, that we live in a particular body at one point in time, and then live in another body at another point in time. From the non-dimensional perspective, we are living in many bodies simultaneously. All times and places are in the singularity. There is no past or future life that is dissociated from the singularity. It is all just life. It is the one life of reality of which we are each a living cell that contains all cells.

This is why in the very first chapter I quoted from the *Sefer Yetzirah*, the Book of Creation, which says, "The end is embedded in the beginning and the beginning is embedded in the end." At the very beginning we started with the Journey of Freedom. The entire perspective of Kedumah is based on this understanding. That is why, when we do our interpersonal practices together, we are simultaneously two separate and particularized people inquiring together and at the same time we each contain the all and are thoroughly singular. The freedom truth allows for this radical paradox of the particular and the universal simultaneously coexisting.

The journey of emptiness and the Journey of Freedom are, in a sense, not even journeys. They are not really about working on our issues. That is how I experience it, at any rate. The journey simply happens on its own. The concept of choice dissolves in the journey of emptiness. It is no longer that I am choosing to engage the path. It all just happens. I know this contradicts some approaches that emphasize taking personal responsibility for our choices. However, at a certain point there is no choice. You are just on the ride.

Okay, any comments or questions?

STUDENT: I feel like we went through such a journey in these two hours, and now in the end, I feel like I am in a really mundane place.

ZVI: Yes, exactly. That's the impact of speaking to the Journey of Freedom. The Journey of Freedom is radically mundane.

STUDENT: Like we had the most boring conversation and it was awesome.

ZVI: Yes. So you got the freedom transmission. The impact of the Journey of Freedom is that you just become so totally mundane, ordinary, practical. You talk about whatever, the food, the garbage. That is the impact. That is what I mean when I say that the journey is over. It is like there are no more spiritual aspirations on the Journey of Freedom because there is nothing else but just what is right in front of your face. It is about what is most practical.

The non-dimension of freedom also erases the hierarchical structure of spirituality. So what you see is all that you get. There is nothing added and nothing taken away. This is all there is. We could have done this transmission at the very beginning, but without acquiring the tools for practice and discernment then we would be limited in what is possible in our experience and our realization. It is possible that we could adopt the posture of freedom, which is a certain kind of radical equanimity, and be stuck with a very limited range of experience and perception. The Journey of Freedom reveals that having contractions or being identified with a self-identity or an ego-structure is not a problem or somehow less "spiritual." It erases the distinction between things and experiences being "spiritual" or "unspiritual" and that there is something wrong about having a self-identity.

This is what we mean by the "equalization" of experience. Having an egoic reaction from this perspective holds the same value and is of the same singular reality and nature as having an experience of black, dense space. What is usually considered to be enlightenment and the apex of the spiritual journey—eternal life, freedom, space, expansiveness—is exposed in the freedom condition as equalized with contraction, limitation, and suffering.[18] So it is really the freedom to be a human being—an ordinary human being, with all of our holes, contractions, reactions, and all of that.

However, we still engage the spiritual journey because without going through each of the stages and journeys, there is the danger of this revelation of freedom being more of a nihilistic trip. Parts of ourselves that are asleep and have not been illuminated in the journey can use this perspective in ways that are not actually aligned with the truth of it. So we do go through the sequential steps of the journey and we do our practices and our work. The difference is that with this perspective the process is more fun, simple, and ordinary. The freedom perspective takes the romanticism out of spirituality and we can just be real about what is happening, because with the erasure of hierarchy we do not care so much what the particulars are: everything is an expression of the singular truth.

Kedumah comes from this perspective. Kedumah is revealing itself through the lens of this radical emptiness, and is an expression of the freedom condition. Its perspective is what I call the "fourth turning view."[19] In previous turnings, there is a spiritual teacher who is purportedly "enlightened" and everyone is holding this goal of enlightenment, which is not the perspective of this teacher and of this teaching. This teaching holds the freedom perspective, which means we are not seeking a particular kind of enlightenment, nor do we hold a hierarchical attitude toward our experience. Rather, enlightenment for us is a never-ending unfolding of experience and discovery.

So you see, our view of enlightenment is radically different. This is what I mean by the whole "Waking Down" process, which is from my perspective, the teaching of our time, as it turns spiritual hierarchy on its head. My sense is that the nonhierarchical teachings represent the next paradigm of teachings. The Kedumah path not only articulates an orientation and a view that can hold this perspective, but it also presents down-to-earth practices to make this a real path for the next paradigm. This is why it's important that the community develop, because the communal soul will really shape the emergence of this paradigm and this teaching. The next paradigm of teachings will be revealed through the *kehillah* and the *sangha*—through the vehicle of the collective soul that we call in Kedumah the "Soulship."[20]

This teaching is responding to the needs of the emerging generation. The next generation is very different than previous generations in terms of where their awareness and their kind of consciousness are. The capacities of the next generation are very different. So what I see, is that the old paradigm teachings are not so relevant for them. All the structures are different, the orientation is different, and actually, I feel that the biochemistry and the neurology is even different, in the emerging human beings. You could say that this teaching is an attempt to articulate a path for the emerging paradigm, which is about the Waking Down into radical humanness and ordinariness, realized through interpersonal relationships and the awakening of the Soulship, the vehicle of the organismic intelligence of the collective soul.

I probably talked enough about all this. I'm hoping that you—the survivors of this series of talks [Laughter.]—will not take everything so seriously. When I used to practice Rolfing, I often wondered how many people would make it through all ten sessions after I would dig into their *kishkes* with my elbow over and over again. This series feels a bit like that. [Laughter.]

I am attempting to present here just some of the pieces of the puzzle. But you can see how each of these eleven teachings is a whole journey unto itself. It is important that we got through the freedom piece, because it brings it all together. My sense is that some old paradigm teachings also knew about the perspective of this emerging cosmology. They knew about the radical ordinariness that is actually real freedom. It's freedom from spirituality and it's freedom from enlightenment. It's freedom from having to be enlightened. It's freedom from the concept of enlightenment. It's freedom to just be an ordinary person—a broken, messed up person. A person with essential light, a person with a history.

Everything is totally, radically equalized—the most profound experiences of realization and the most mundane particulars of life. Literally equalized. There is no preference or value as one experience being higher or better than any other. This is what I mean by "radical." It is incomprehensible to our spiritually-obsessed identities. Everything is just exactly what it is, just what is right in front of our face. It is all very ordinary.

Other teachings know about this, but it's usually kept secret or it is not talked about very much. Traditionally, there are a lot of concerns about making these teachings available. What are the implications? What would people make of it? There are many questions and concerns. I think that there is something shifting cosmologically and it is actually important to at least put this view out there so that the next generation can actually settle into the emerging spiritual path and paradigm.

When I speak to the Journey of Freedom, what I notice is that folks from the next generation can actually relax and settle into it. They feel, "Oh, okay, now it makes sense. Now I can settle in and trust this work more because I know where it's coming from." The next generation seems to intuit and know the nonhierarchical truth, but they cannot articulate it yet. It is the emerging reality, the emerging generation knows this on some level, the earth knows this. The hierarchies are dissolving.

People come into a spiritual path with all kinds of ideas about what it is. But once I get to the freedom teaching—and describe what I mean by it—then I think it opens up the possibility of this path being real for people in the emerging age, because it erases the pretense of having to accomplish or get anywhere or do anything in particular. And actually, literally and ultimately, all we're doing with the spiritual journey is opening up these dimensions and increasing our range of experience. I don't hold the view that there is a spiritual hierarchy, or that there are good or better experiences to have. They're all just experiences.

STUDENT: If there are no hierarchies then what about people falling into addiction, nihilism, depression, or self-destructive behavior?

ZVI: Yes, it is all the singularity, experiencing itself in that particular location as the sense of nihilism. A person can be depressed or nihilistic, but if they're holding this freedom perspective—which is actually quite an expanded view, even though it's not dimensionally expansive—it divests the psychic investment in the experience of being depressed. So there may be something that looks like depression, but the psychic investment in the experience—which is really where the suffering is—is erased in this state.

The divestment of all energy and charge of self in our experience is the realization of true freedom.

Okay, this formally concludes this first series of Kedumah teachings. The mystery has brought us together in this magical time and place, for this sharing. I want to thank you for joining this journey and for being open to this exploration. Each one of you has brought a great deal to this group.

Appendix:
Kedumah and Judaism

THROUGHOUT THIS BOOK, I use the term "Kedumah" in two distinct ways. The first way I use the term is to refer to the nonconceptual primordial ground of reality itself, the source of all wisdom and all teachings. This first usage is what I refer to as the "Kedumah principle." All authentic spiritual teachings are emanations of this Kedumah principle. The second way I use the term is as a formal name for a specific body of Kedumah teachings, which has its own unique metaphysics and modes of practice that I outline and explain in this book.

In this appendix, I will explain more thoroughly the relationship between the Kedumah teachings and Judaism. Therefore, whenever I use the term "Kedumah" in this Appendix, I am referring to the specific body of Kedumah teachings presented in this book, not to the Kedumah principle more broadly.

The term "Judaism" typically refers to Rabbinic Judaism, which did not become the dominant expression of the Torah lineage until around the fifth century of the common era.[1] That is to say, that the religion that we know today as "Judaism" is really Rabbinic Judaism, which is but one historical expression of the ancient Torah lineage. The Torah lineage has thus expressed itself in various ways throughout history, the religion of Judaism being one such expression. For clarification, the "Torah lineage" refers to all traditions and teachings that trace their origins back to the religion and culture of the ancient Hebrews and Israelites.

However, this distinction that I am making between the Torah lineage and Judaism is a subtle one, and may be confusing for some people. This is because the terms "Judaism" and "Torah" are intimately and inextricably intertwined in common usage. Therefore, for the sake of simplicity, in this appendix, I will utilize the term "Rabbinic Judaism" instead of the more general term "Judaism," to distinguish it from the versions of Torah that preceded Rabbinic Judaism (ancient Hebrew religion) and the versions of Torah that develop out of Rabbinic Judaism (Kedumah being one such version).

Traditionally speaking, Rabbinic Judaism is dependent upon three central principles: 1) the acceptance of Jewish law (*halakhah*) as religiously binding, 2) the authority of sacred texts, and 3) allegiance to Jewish tribal identity. While some contemporary expressions of the Torah lineage—such as Jewish Renewal—forego the binding nature of Jewish law, and thus deviate from the traditional principles of Rabbinic Judaism, they still for the most part hold an allegiance to Jewish ethnic and tribal identity, rely on sacred texts as authoritative, and engage some aspects of Jewish ritual and teaching. In this sense, these versions of Judaism still remain true to some extent to the core principles of Rabbinic Judaism.

Kedumah, however, represents a more radical departure from Rabbinic Judaism because it does not adhere to any of these three core principles. The spiritual path of Kedumah is not dependent on practicing Jewish law or ritual, it does not rely on textual authority, nor does it hold any allegiance to Jewish identity or tribe. In this sense Kedumah is not Jewish, or, more accurately, not Rabbinically Jewish.

Yet, at the same time, Kedumah is an expression of the primordial wisdom of Torah, with the term "Torah" here being used to mean the metaphysical source of Rabbinic as well as pre-Rabbinic forms of Judaism. Torah, in the sense that I am using it here, is thus more fundamental than Rabbinic Judaism, with the capacity to reveal other spiritual teachings that are different than the tradition we know of as Rabbinic Judaism. Therefore, even though Kedumah is an expression of the essential, primordial Torah, it is nevertheless distinct from Rabbinic Judaism, since Kedumah does not accept the core allegiances of Rabbinic Judaism.

On the other hand, to the degree that it utilizes Judaic teachings and texts to express itself (many of which derive from the Rabbinic tradition), Kedumah can also be viewed as offering a new interpretation—or presenting a new paradigm—of Rabbinic Judaism. Kedumah is thus an expression of the primordial Torah that is distinct from Rabbinic Judaism, yet offers a contemplative and universal version of Judaism for the emerging age. In this sense, Kedumah can be seen as a new paradigm of Judaism, an integral part of the Jewish lineage and wisdom stream.

To help illustrate the place of Kedumah among the various paradigms and expressions of Torah that have revealed themselves at different times in history, I will borrow the concept of the Turnings of the Wheel of Dharma from the Buddhist tradition. In Buddhism, this concept serves as a model for categorizing and organizing the different views and practices of the Buddha's teaching that have revealed themselves at different times in history. This same model can also refer to different dimensions of the Buddha's original teaching, representing different modes of engaging the path, rather than an hierarchical progression of teachings revealing themselves progressively over historical time.[2] I will be utilizing both of these ways of understanding the model of the Turnings of the Wheel of Dharma in my mapping out of various paradigms of Torah.

The Hebrew tradition has a model that is similar to the Turnings of the Wheel of Dharma, although it is much lesser known. For example, there is a medieval kabbalistic text called *Sefer ha-Temunah* that outlines the different cycles of Torah that reveal themselves at different stages of history, with each stage corresponding to a different *sefirah* and multiyear sabbatical cycle.[3] Instead of mapping out the various phases of Torah using this kabbalistic model, for the sake of simplicity I will use the model of the Turnings of the Wheel of Torah.

In the historical model of the turnings, the first turning of the wheel of Torah is represented by the paradigms of Torah practiced by the ancient Hebrews and Israelites, with their prophets and prophetesses, kings, queens, priests, and sages. The second turning of the wheel of Torah is Rabbinic Judaism along with the Kabbalah, which established themselves in the first few centuries of the common era and is represented by the rabbis and kabbalists. The third turning of the wheel of Torah is currently in formation and has multiple possible expressions, with Kedumah representing one of these possibilities.

The three Turnings of the Wheel of Torah, as just explained, refer to three distinct historical phases or eras. Each of these three eras is also marked by a distinguished spiritual orientation, a unique metaphysical axis around which the spiritual views and practices of that time period revolve. The three axes around which each of these eras orient represent another way of mapping out the turnings of the wheel of Torah, and they correspond with the second way of understanding the turning of the wheel model in the Buddhist teachings. This approach sees the turnings not only as historical progressions, but also as different dimensions of Buddha's original teaching, each of which tends to be emphasized more in different historical eras but all of which can also be accessed at any point in time, and in any of the historical turnings.

In the Kedumah model of the Turnings of the Wheel of Torah, the first axis is the axis of space, the second is the axis of time, and the third is the axis of person. My understanding of these three axes is derived from the *Sefer Yetzirah*, perhaps the most ancient of all Jewish mystical texts. In Hebrew these axes are called *olam*, *shanah*, and *nefesh*—space, time, and person.[4]

The first turning of the wheel of Torah, which is represented historically by ancient Hebrew and Israelite religion prior to the destruction of the second Temple in 70 CE, is correlated with the axis of *olam*—

space. The emphasis is on sacred space, on creating a spatial vessel for the Divine Presence to dwell. The *mishkan* is the Hebrew biblical term for the sanctuary, the sacred space constructed by the ancient Hebrews for the indwelling presence of God. There is no single topic in all of the Hebrew Bible that occupies as much attention and detail as does the construction and maintenance of the structures of sacred space.

The second turning of the wheel of Torah, which corresponds with Rabbinic Judaism (along with the Kabbalah, which is the mystical dimension of Rabbinic Judaism and inseparable from it) and the historical period following the destruction of the Temple in 70 CE, correlates with the axis of *shanah*—time. Here the attention shifts from sacred space to sacred time. In the Rabbinic tradition the most important religious principle is no longer the physical Temple but rather the Sabbath and the realm of sacred time more broadly. This shift made a lot of sense, given that the Temple had been destroyed and the people were exiled from the land, which made the paradigm of a centralized sacred space and land no longer operative.

Sacred time remains the centerpiece of traditional Jewish life to this day. The central organizing principle of Jewish life and practice is still the Sabbath and sacred time as it is marked through the cycle of the holidays and seasons of the Hebrew calendar. In this paradigm of *shanah*, the emphasis shifts from sacred space to sacred time. Large sections of the Talmud—the great compendium of Rabbinic teachings—deal with the details of sacred time, of how to appropriately perform the obligatory rituals in the realm of sacred time.

The third turning of the wheel of Torah correlates with the axis of *nefesh* in Hebrew, which means "person" or "soul." The shift into the third turning of the wheel of Torah has been unfolding over the last few centuries, beginning with the rise of Hasidism in the late eighteenth century and the advent of the Western psychoanalytic tradition in the late nineteenth century. This shift continues to develop in our time with the ongoing innovations of Western psychology and new spiritual approaches to Torah such as Kedumah. The axis of *nefesh* and its emphasis in the third turning of the wheel of Torah involves shifting our attention to the individual person—the soul—and engaging a deep exploration into the true nature of who and what we are.

To be sure, each of the three axes—space, time, and person—are expressed in various ways in each historical phase of the three Turnings of the Wheel of Torah, but what distinguishes each turning of the wheel from one another is the degree of emphasis placed on the orientation and direction of the inquiry. This correlates with the second understanding of the turning of the wheel model in Buddhism, whereby all the dimensions of the teaching interpenetrate in each of the historical periods, even as one dimension tends to dominate in each of the turns.

The advent of Hasidism, which began in the eighteenth century and flourished into the nineteenth and twentieth centuries, marked a pivotal shift towards the third turning of Torah and its corresponding axis of *nefesh*, which is characterized by a deep interest in the psycho-spiritual nature of the person. Hasidism itself developed out of the Kabbalah tradition, which is the primary mystical teaching of Rabbinic Judaism. Although some contemporary versions of Kabbalah attempt to separate it from its original Rabbinic context, historically speaking it is a wholly integrated expression of Rabbinic Judaism and holds deep commitments to Jewish law, textual authority, and tribal identity.

Like Kabbalah, Hasidism is also aligned with these core principles of Rabbinic Judaism, but it differs from Kabbalah in that it shifts the object of inquiry from the Divine realms to the human realms.[5] In the first few generations of the movement, Hasidism embodied a form of tantric Judaism that openly proclaimed a path of *Avodah She-bigashmiyut*, which means "worship through corporeality," that is, serving God through the flesh.[6] This tantric orientation was coupled with a renewed interest in mapping out the terrain of the soul, the psyche, and human consciousness. This contrasts with the earlier kabbalistic focus on the makeup of the cosmos and the anatomy of the Godhead.

The boldness of the early Hasidic approach was quickly challenged by the Rabbinic establishment and eventually Hasidism was integrated into the more or less normative Jewish community. The traditional Hasidic community today has lost a great deal of the original elan and provocative spirit of the first few generations of Hasidic teachings. Although its tantric elements are less operative now, the vast literature of the Hasidic masters that we have in our possession (mostly untranslated and inaccessible to a contemporary reader) constitutes one of the great untapped treasure troves of psycho-spiritual insight and experiential transmission on the planet. These Hasidic texts serve as part of the contextual background for the emergence of the Kedumah teachings.

Sigmund Freud was another pivotal pioneer of the third turning of the wheel of Torah, which involves inquiry into the nature of self, of person. Freud wanted to know the truth about the self, about the *nefesh*. The groundbreaking path he forged is at this point universally acknowledged as central to our understanding of human psychology.

We also know that Freud deeply identified as a Jew and had some degree of familiarity with the ancient Hebrew mystical tradition, to the point of having a copy of the Zohar (one of the most important texts of the Kabbalah) on his office shelf.[7] His approach to understanding the soul (the more accurate translation of his German usage of the ancient Greek word "psyche,"[8] as well as an alternate translation for the Hebrew word *nefesh*), through the method of *drash* (inquiry), can be seen as an extension of the Jewish approach to inquiry. This can also be said of the psychoanalytic tradition as a whole, since many of Freud's colleagues and followers were also Jewish and were influenced by Jewish approaches to inquiry.

Freud did his best to explicitly divorce his new "science" of psychology from any affiliation with Judaism, and succeeded in large measure to create a completely secular tradition based on the practice of *drash* into the *nefesh*. Essentially, he forged a secular expression of the third turning of the wheel of Torah. He succeeded so much, in fact, that Western psychology performs many of the functions in the modern Western world that used to be performed by religion. If someone in our secular culture suffers from sickness of the soul, they are more likely to go to a psychologist or therapist than to a rabbi or priest.

Kedumah is in one sense an extension of the psychodynamic tradition, as we explicitly integrate knowledge of psychology with mystical perception. Other contemporary systems that utilize knowledge of Western psychology on the path of spiritual realization and development—most notably the Diamond Approach—also inform our teachings and influence some of the ways that we practice inquiry in Kedumah.[9]

In my view, Kedumah is thus another expression of the third turning of the wheel of Torah, and can be seen as a development of both the Hasidic and psychoanalytic approaches. The central practice of Kedumah is what we call Inquiry, the translation of the Hebrew word *drash*. *Drash* is also a central principle in Rabbinic Judaism and is at the root of both Freud's approach to psychodynamic inquiry as well as the Hasidic approach to psychospiritual exploration.

However, like in the Hasidic and psychodynamic traditions, the object of inquiry in Kedumah differs from the object of inquiry in Rabbinic Judaism. Whereas the foremost contemplative practice of Rabbinic Judaism is inquiring into the true meaning of the written and oral dimensions of Torah (a practice called *drash* or *midrash*),[10] the foremost contemplative practice of Kedumah is inquiring into the truth of who and what we are as human beings, and into the truth of reality more broadly.

Therefore, although Kedumah is an expression of my personal experience of the nonconceptual Kedumah principle, my articulation and application of the specific body of Kedumah teachings articulated in this book have foundational roots in multiple wisdom traditions, including Rabbinic Judaism, Kabbalah, Hasidism, Western psychology with its various spiritually-informed derivatives, traditional Eastern somatic and movement practices and their contemporary expressions in the healing arts, and select teachings and practices from related lineages. Kedumah thus represents one contemporary approach to the practice of spiritual inquiry that may be helpful for some people in the emerging age, and it reflects one possible variation of the third turning of the wheel of Torah.

Now I would like to add a few more important details about Kedumah's understanding of the relationship between view and practice, and how it fits into the model of the Turnings of the Wheel of Torah.

As explained above, Hasidism embodies a third turning view in its emphasis on exploring the psychospiritual nature of the individual consciousness. However, although it holds a third turning view, Hasidism still maintains a second turning practice. That is to say, although its orientation toward *drash* (inquiry) is to understand the *nefesh* (the soul), its practice is still deeply rooted in the ritualistic and tribal obligations of Rabbinic Judaism, which for all practical purposes means adherence to *halakhah* (traditional Jewish law) and allegiance to Jewish tribal identity.

Other more contemporary versions of Hasidism, such as Jewish Renewal, also embody a third turning view with a second turning practice. Jewish Renewal is still very much attached to Rabbinic Judaism and its second turning perspective of religion and tribe, even if it dismisses traditional *halakhah* as no longer religiously binding. That is to say, Jewish Renewal still accepts the paradigm of Rabbinic Judaism (*halakhic* practice, textual authority, and tribal identity), along with its central organizing axis of *shanah* (sacred time), even as it attempts to reformat *halakhah*, expand the definitions of tribe and Jewish identity and more generally renew the essential spirit of these core Rabbinic principles.[11]

However, in Kedumah we do not hold any allegiance to the second turning paradigm of Rabbinic Judaism, whether it be in view or in practice. This is because the third turning practice of *drash* has revealed itself clearly in the Kedumah teachings in a manner that does not require Jewish Law, ritual, or identity in order for the practices to be effective and transformative.

To be sure, in Kedumah we do at times utilize second turning practices of Rabbinic Judaism; however, we do not do so out of religious obligation or allegiance to Jewish identity. Rather, we engage such practices in the same way we utilize certain contemplative practices of other traditions: as supports, and not as religious imperatives, for our primary path of inquiry. In this sense, Kedumah is different than Hasidism and Jewish Renewal in that it embodies purely a third turning practice, without reliance on second turning perspectives and methods.

As I mentioned above, although I utilize rabbinic and kabbalistic teachings in various ways throughout this book, Kedumah is not dependent on textual authority for its validity; rather, its validity comes through our direct experience and through the empirical evidence of the path effecting recognizable change in our ordinary life. That is to say, if it's useful and effective as a practice and as a path of awakening, that alone is its validity. I only use texts in this teaching to help explain and clarify, never to validate. This represents another core difference between the Kedumah paradigm and that of the second turning paradigm of Rabbinic Judaism, since the latter requires textual authority to validate its teachings.

As such, Kedumah operates from an altogether different paradigm than does Rabbinic Judaism. However, as I discussed above, the Kedumah paradigm derives from both the ancient Torah lineage as well as from Rabbinic Judaism. In this sense, Kedumah can be understood to be one expression of an altogether new kind of Judaism, one that does not hold any ritualistic, tribal, or textual allegiances.

It is also important to point out that the third turning practices of Kedumah are not incompatible with the practices of the second turning; quite the contrary, a person can maintain traditional Jewish law in the manner of the second turning of the wheel and still utilize the Kedumah perspective to enrich and deepen their personal practice and experience. Since I utilize many concepts and teachings from traditional Rabbinic Judaism (primarily from the Kabbalah) in order to articulate the Kedumah teachings, it is only natural that adherents of traditional Rabbinic Judaism will find Kedumah to be particularly relevant and enriching for their personal practice.

To be sure, the Kedumah approach to inquiry can support practitioners of any religion to deepen into the transformational potential of their path. By honestly exploring one's personal relationship to her or his religious beliefs and practices, and by working through any neurotic issues that may be present, distorted expressions of any religious path will naturally be exposed and in time transformed, ultimately posing less of a barrier to one's inner freedom and awakening.

I mentioned above that Kedumah is different from Hasidism and Jewish Renewal in that it embodies a pure third turning practice, unlike Hasidism and Jewish Renewal that primarily rely on second turning practices. I also mentioned that in Kedumah we utilize a cross-section of practices from other turnings and paradigms of Torah, as well as from various other lineages and spiritual traditions.

This view is one expression of what we call the "fourth turning of the wheel of Torah," which is a more radical perspective that transcends the categories of space, time, and person.[12] As such, in the fourth turning view, practices from any of the first three turnings of Torah—or from any other spiritual tradition for that matter—can be freely utilized if they are useful. This is because the fourth turning is not defined or limited by any specific view or practice, and therefore any practices or teachings from any lineage or path may be engaged if they serve the process of awakening and transformation.

As such, while the Kedumah practice of *drash* is a further development of the Hasidic and psychodynamic traditions (third turning), our view is radically multi-perspectival in that it allows for multiple views and teachings, even when apparently contradicting one another, to simultaneously coexist (fourth turning).

This fourth turning perspective as we understand it in Kedumah has its roots in the Talmudic principle of *Elu V'elu Divrei Elohim Chayyim* ("These and those are both words of the Living God"), which holds that multiple—and even contradictory—views can be equally valid expressions of Divine truth.[13] It is also rooted in our understanding of *Ein Sof*, which is the realization of the truth that is beyond the categories of both infinite and finite.[14] Since this radical nonreferential reality includes everything and nothing at all, it is possible for multiple and even contradictory truths to interpenetrate and coexist without friction.

Kedumah therefore embodies a third turning practice with a fourth turning view. In the Kedumah path we develop the skills to effectively practice our third turning application of *drash*, of inquiry into the truth of our human experience. We hold this practice in a spirit of radical openness that is reflective of our fourth turning view of total inclusivity. This view and practice of Kedumah ultimately has the potential to open up our experience and perception to include more of the mystery and wonder of who we are and of what reality is.

Charts

THE FIVE JOURNEYS AND THEIR CORRELATES IN KEDUMAH AND IN CLASSICAL KABBALAH

	CONTRACTION	EXPANSION	WHOLENESS	VASTNESS	FREEDOM
BODY	Body-Image	Presence Body	Pearl Body	Star-Light Body	Total Body
SCROLL	Words/ Narrative	Individual Letter	Ink	Parchment/ Vowel Points	Totality of Scroll
TEACHING	Myth/ Conceptual View	Practices	Mysticism	Primordial Source	Totality of Teaching
PERSON	Garments	Body	Soul	Soul-Spark/ Point/Star	Total Human
SOUL-LEVEL	*Nefesh*	*Ruach*	*Neshama*	*Chaya*	*Yechida*
OLAM	*Asiyah*	*Yetzirah*	*Beriyah*	*Atzilut*	*Adam Kadmon*
SEFIRAH	*Malchut*	*Tiferet*	*Binah*	*Chochmah*	*Keter/Ayin*
YHVH	Lower *Hey*	*Vav*	Upper *Hey*	*Yod*	*Kotz of Yod*
PARTZUF	*Nukvah*	*Zeir Anpin*	*Imma*	*Abba*	*Arikh Anpin*

THE SEFIROT WITH THEIR ASSOCIATED TERMS IN KEDUMAH

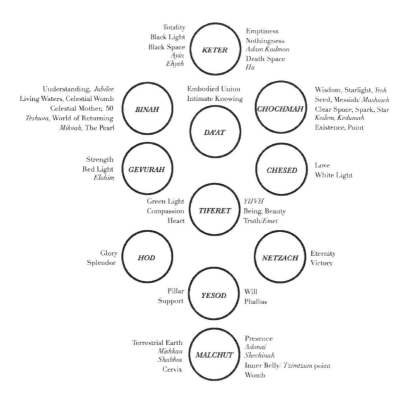

Totality
Black Light
Black Space
Ayin
Ehyeh

KETER

Emptiness
Nothingness
Adam Kadmon
Death Space
Hu

Understanding, *Jubilee*
Living Waters, Celestial Womb
Celestial Mother, 50
Teshuva, World of Returning
Mikvah, The Pearl

BINAH

Embodied Union
Intimate Knowing

DA'AT

CHOCHMAH

Wisdom, Starlight, *Yesh*
Seed, Messiah/ *Mashiach*
Clear Space, Spark, Star
Kedem, Kedumah
Existence, Point

Strength
Red Light
Elohim

GEVURAH

CHESED

Love
White Light

Green Light
Compassion
Heart

TIFERET

YHVH
Being, Beauty
Truth/*Emet*

Glory
Splendor

HOD

NETZACH

Eternity
Victory

Pillar
Support

YESOD

Will
Phallus

Terrestrial Earth
Mishkan
Shabbos
Cervix

MALCHUT

Presence
Adonai
Shechinah
Inner Belly/ *Tzimtzum* point
Womb

Notes

ALL TRANSLATIONS OF HEBREW TEXTS CITED
IN THE NOTES WERE DONE BY THE AUTHOR.

CHAPTER ONE

1. THE ANCIENT HEBREW TEXTS TALK ABOUT A PRIMORDIAL TORAH On the term "Kedumah" and the concept of the Primordial Torah more broadly, see: *Genesis Rabbah* 1:1, 1:4 and 8:2; *Midrash Tehillim* 105:3; *Midrash Tanchuma Genesis* 1:1; *Yalkut Shimoni* 951:13; *Mishnah Avot* 3:14; *Mishnah Kiddushin* 4:13; *PT Shekalim* 6a; *PT Sotah* 37a; *BT Sanhedrin* 111a, *BT Menachot* 29b, *BT Pesachim* 54a and 68b; *Ta'amei Ha-Mitzvot* 3a; *Perush Ramban al ha-Torah, Hakdamah*; *Teshuvot Ha-Geonim, Sha'arei Teshuvah* 351; *Zohar* 1:29b-30a; *Zohar* 1:134a, 1:261a, 3:36a; *Pardes Rimonim* 23:22 c.v. *Torah*; *Maggid Devarim Le-Ya'akov* 50; *Sefer Ba'al Shem Tov, Bereishit* 8.

2. WHAT WE CALL "THE WORLD" CAN THUS BE SEEN AS A CONCEPTUAL OVER-LAY See, e.g., the statement by R. Shneur Zalman of Liadi, the founder of Chabad Hasidism: ואף שנראה לנו העולמות ליש הוא שקר גמור, "Even though it appears to us that the worlds exist, it is a complete lie" (*Torah Ohr* [2001], *Ki Tisa*, p.86c). This echoes the classic understanding in Advaita Vedanta that the world is a projection of the conceptual mind. On the Advaita Vedanta view, see Eliot Deutsch, *Advaita Vedanta: A Philosophical Reconstruction* (Honolulu: University of Hawaii Press, 1980).

295

3. THE THREE *YANAS* CAN BE ENGAGED EITHER SEQUENTIALLY OR CONCUR-
RENTLY On the various ways of understanding the three *yanas* in Buddhism, see Reginald Ray, *Secret of the Vajra World* (Boston: Shambhala, 2002) pp. 13–17 and 66–90; The Dalai Lama, *Essence of the
Heart Sutra* (Somerville, MA: Wisdom Publications, 2015) pp. 54–
55; David Snellgrove, *Indo-Tibetan Buddhism: Indian Buddhists and
their Tibetan Successors*, vol. 1 (Shambhala, 1987) pp. 79–80 and pp.
103-104.

4. WE ACTUALLY BECOME A LIVING TORAH See. e.g., the Chatam Sofer's
comment: אדם ישראל הוי כספר תורה "A Jewish person is like a Torah
scroll" (commentary on BT *Megillah* 26b).

5. HOW THESE DIMENSIONS, IN TURN, ARE REFLECTED IN THE IMAGE OF A
TORAH SCROLL On my use of the metaphor of the primordial scroll and
the four levels of the person and the teaching, see: *Zohar* 3:152a; Also
see Ramban's (Nachmanides) commentary on BT *Moed Katan* 25a:
ולי נראה שהנפש בגוף כאזכרות בגוילין, "It seems to me that the soul in the
body is like the names of God on the parchment." Also see the Maharsha's (R. Shmuel Eidels) commentary to *BT Avodah Zarah* 18a,
where he likewise compares the human essence to the letters on the
Torah scroll.

6. THE INK THAT ANIMATES OUR INDIVIDUAL LETTER On the ink as representing the spiritual essence of the person, see: Abraham Abulafia,
Sefer HaCheshek 1:3 and *Or HaSekhel* 6:2, 10:3.

7. THE PRESENCE BODY IS MARKED BY A SENSE OF SPACIOUSNESS AND EX-
PANSION BEYOND THE USUAL CONFINES OF THE SELF-NARRATIVE The experience of the Presence Body is marked by a distinct sense of being
a completely autonomous individual, free from enmeshment with,
and dependency on, others for self-knowledge. This is reflected in
the Rabbinic principle of *makif g'vil*, which requires that in order for
a Torah scroll to be kosher (fit for ritual use), each letter must be

completely surrounded by parchment; that is, if two letters touch each other the scroll is invalid. See *BT Menachot* 34a.

8. WHAT WOULD IT BE LIKE TO READ THE WHITE SCRIPT INSTEAD OF THE BLACK LETTERS? According to Rabbinic tradition, the Primordial Torah is written with black letters of fire on white letters of fire (*Midrash Tanchuma Genesis* 1:1; *PT Shekalim* 6a; *PT Sotah* 37a). That the white letters are equally as important as the black is reflected in the Rabbinic law that requires that each black letter in the Torah scroll be completely surrounded by parchment to distinguish between the black and the white letters. See, e.g., *Shulkan Arukh, Orach Chayyim,* 32, 36.

9. IT RELATES TO WHAT WE CALL *ADAM KADMON* AND POINTS TO *EIN SOF*... *Adam Kadmon* correlates with with *sefirah* of *Keter* and the prin- ciple of *Yechida*, which means "singularity." See *Etz Chayyim* 4:1; *Sha'ar HaGilgulim* 31. Both *Ein Sof* and *Keter* are fundamentally unknowable and ineffable (see, e.g., *Zohar* 2:239a, 3:225a, 2:42b, and 3:288b). Azriel of Gerona calls *Keter* "that which thought cannot comprehend" and "the annihilation of thought" (*Perush Ha-Aggadot*, ed. Tishby, pp. 40, 104). On the ineffability and incomprehensibili- ty of the nonconceptual nature of *Adam Kadmon* specifically and its coemergence with *Ein Sof*, see *Etz Chayyim* 42:2; R. Moshe Cordo- vero, *Pardes Rimonim* 3:1; Yitzchak Isaac Chaver, *Pitchei She'arim* (Sinai, 1989), pp. 16–49; R. Nachman of Bratzlav, *Likkutei Moharan* 24:1, 8 (R. Nachman refers to this dimension by its alternative name, *Olam HaTzachtzachot*). Adam Kadmon and the corollary principle of *Yechida* represent the totality of all reality. R. Aryeh Kaplan states this point succinctly: "Only the light of *Ain Sof* clothed within *Adam Kadmon* fills the entire Kabbalistic universe" (*Inner Space*, p. 110 and also see his notes and sources there). I will explain these principles more below in Chapters 2, 3, 10, and 11.

10. THE INFINITE MUST HAVE SOME EXPRESSION OF FINITUDE IN ORDER TO COMPLETE ITS INFINITE POSSIBILITIES The narrative that the infinite requires the finite to realize its potential is the central metaphysical view of Chabad Hasidism. See, e.g., R. Shneur Zalman, *Tanya, Sha'ar Hayichud Veha'emunah* 7 (Kehot, 1984) pp. 315–319 and R. Aharon HaLevi, *Avodat Halevi, Veyechi*, 74. Also see Rachel Elior's analysis of these texts in her article, "Habad: The Contemplative Ascent to God" in: *Jewish Spirituality from the Sixteenth Century*, vol. II, ed. A. Green (New York: Crossroad Publishing, 1987) pp. 157–205.

11. *TZIMTZUM* In Rabbinic literature the term *tzimtzum* refers to the concentration of the Divine Presence. See, e.g., *Exodus Rabbah*, 34:1. However, in Lurianic Kabbalah the term *tzimtzum* refers to the contraction or withdrawal of *Ein Sof* into itself, creating a void (*tehiru*) within which creation would manifest (see R. Yitzchak Isaac Chaver, *Pitchei She'arim*, pp. 1-15). For more on *tzimtzum*, see S. Magid, "Origin and the Overcoming of the Beginning: *Zimzum* as a Trope of Reading in Post-Lurianic Kabbalah" in *Beginning/Again: Toward a Hermeneutic of Jewish Texts*, ed. S. Magid and A. Cohen (New York: Seven Bridges, 2002) pp. 163–214, especially the sources he lists on p. 198, note 14. For a non-kabbalistic approach to the principle of *tzimtzum*, see R. Joseph Soloveitchik, *Halakhic Man* (JPS, 1984), Chapter IX, pp. 49–63.

12. IN THE KEDUMAH READING OF THE GARDEN OF EDEN STORY, THIS IS EXPRESSED IN THE TEACHINGS ON THE BODY OF LIGHT According to the *midrash*, Rabbi Meir possessed a variant version of the Torah text that stated that Adam and Eve were given garments of light, not skin (*Genesis Rabbah*, 20:12). On the mystical body of light that Adam and Eve experienced in the Garden of Eden, see *Zohar* 1:36b, 2:229b, 3:261b; Chayyim Vital, *Sefer Likkutim, Genesis* 3. On the capacity of the righteous of any generation to attain such bodies of light, see *Zohar*, 2:210a-b; 1:224a-b.

13. CREATION ENTAILS A SERIES OF CONTRACTIONS AND EXPANSIONS This echoes the Lurianic cosmogenic theory of *Iggul V'yosher*, described by Chayyim Vital in *Etz Chayyim* 1:1–5. Also Cf. *Genesis Rabbah* 1:1.

14. EACH ONE OF US REPRESENTS ONE LETTER On each letter of the Torah representing an individual soul, see: *Zohar Chadash Shir HaShirim*, 74d; R. Nathan Spira, *Megaleh Amukot* on *Va-etchanan*, 186.

15. "THE END IS EMBEDDED IN THE BEGINNING…" *Sefer Yetzirah* 1:7.

CHAPTER TWO

1. "*EIN SOF*, BLESSED BE HE" See, e.g., *Tanya, Sha'ar Hayichud Ve-hae-munah*, 7 (p. 317); R. Menachem Mendel of Vitebsk, *Pri Ha'aretz, Korach*; R. Moshe Chayyim Luzatto, *Kla"ch Pitchei Chachmah*, 1.

2. IT IS DIFFICULT OR MAYBE IMPOSSIBLE TO TALK ABOUT THE PERSPECTIVE OF *EIN SOF* On the impossibility of conceptualizing the nature of *Ein Sof*, see *Zohar* 3:225a; *Tikkunei Zohar* 17a; *Tanya, Sha'ar HaYichud Ve-ha'emunah* 2:9 and 7. Also see my references above in Chapter 1, note 9. One of the ways the kabbalists talked about *Ein Sof* is to distinguish between how things are from its perspective (מצידו) juxtaposed to how things appear to be from our human perspective (מצדנו). See, e.g., R. Yitzchak Isaac Chaver, *Pitchei She'arim, Netiv Hatzimtzum* 3 (p. 5) and *ibid., Netiv Penimiyut Ve-Chitzoniyut* 9 (p. 270).

3. "THE END IS EMBEDDED IN THE BEGINNING…" *Sefer Yetzirah* 1:7.

4. "THE END OF THE DEED WAS FIRST IN MIND" This phrase is found in the kabbalistic hymn *L'cha Dodi*. See R. Kimelman, *The Mystical Meaning of Lekha Dodi* (Cherub Press, 2003) [Hebrew].

5. THE WHOLE POINT IS FOR THE INFINITE TO EXPERIENCE ITSELF AS FINITE...
This is the classical view of Chabad Hasidism. See Chapter 1, note
10. Also see the formulation of this principle by R. Yitzchak Isaac
Chaver, *Pitchei She'arim*, p.16.

6. SOME PSYCHODYNAMIC THEORIES HOLD... For example, Sigmund
Freud acknowledged the possibility of the mystical feeling of oneness
(what he called the "oceanic"), but he explained it away as regres-
sion to the infant's experience of sucking on the breast. See S. Freud,
Civilization and Its Discontents (New York: W. W. Norton, 1961),
pp. 12–14. The principle of nondual perception known in Hebrew
as *da'at* that I will discuss below (see notes 15, 16, and 17) is also
framed in the Kabbalah tradition in terms of remembrance. See, e.g.,
B'nei Yissachar Adar 3:2: עיקר הזכירה הוא בשכל הדעת "The essence of
remembrance is in the intellect of *da'at*." Also see the correlations
with the principle of "mindfulness" in Buddhism below in note 22.

7. THE WAY TO FREEDOM IS *THROUGH* OUR SUFFERING, NOT *AROUND* IT On the
necessity of moving through contraction to attain freedom, see *Zohar*
1:83a; 1:147a-b. These texts demonstrate that the journey into and
through contraction is a central way the Jewish mystics interpreted
the narrative of the descent into *Mitzrayim*. See my discussion of this
below in Chapter 4. On the corollary Hasidic principle of *yeridah
k'tzorech aliyah* ("descent for the sake of ascent") and a description
of how it connects with the descent into *Mitzrayim* and the three axes
of *olam, shanah,* and *nefesh* that I will discuss below in Chapter 3, see
R. David Shlomo Aibeshitz, *Sefer Arvei Nachal, Parshat Lech L'cha*
(Warsaw, 1870) p. 29. Also see see R. Avraham of Slonim's connection of this principle to the holiday of *Pesach* (in *Yesod Ha-Avodah*
2:44), which also echoes my discussion below in Chapter 4. Even
the Messiah is birthed through the process of "descent for the sake of
ascent" (see R. Tzadok HaCohen of Lublin, *Sefer Likkutei Amarim,
Derasha L'siyyum Hashas*). On the Kedumah understanding of the
Messiah, see my discussion below in Chapter 10. On the principle of

"descent for the sake of ascent" in general, see the Ba'al Shem Tov's explanation in *Tzava'at HaRivash*, 64.

8. THIS LIGHT GOES THROUGH VARIOUS STAGES OF MANIFESTATION On the stages of manifestation of *Ein Sof* into the created realm, see: *Zohar* 15a–17a; *Tikkunei Zohar, Hakdamah* 2; *Etz Chayyim* 1:1–5.

9. THE KABBALISTS REFER TO THIS AS *AYIN*, WHICH LITERALLY MEANS "NOTHINGNESS ..." On *Keter* or *Ayin* as the primordial Nothingness, see *Zohar* 3:256b and *Pardes Rimonim* 23:1. Also see D. Matt, "Ayin: The Concept of Nothingness in Jewish Mysticism" in Robert Forman, ed., *The Problem of Pure Consciousness* (New York:, Oxford, 1990) pp. 121–159. On *Adam Kadmon* as the primordial blueprint of the human body, see *Sha'ar Ha-hakdamot* (Jerusalem, 1988) p. 44 and *Etz Chayyim* 5:2.

10. EACH OF THESE NAMES EXPRESSES A DIFFERENT PURE QUALITY On the correlation of the names of God with the *sefirot*, see Joseph Gikatilla's classic *Sha'arei Orah*, which outlines these correspondences in detail. These correspondences are also integral to the terminological system of the *Zohar*, and are implicit throughout the document. See, e.g., *Zohar* 3:257b-258a. Also see R. Moses Cordovero's classics *Tomer Devorah* and *Pardes Rimonim*, both of which address these correspondences at length, and Isaiah Horowitz's *Shnei Luchot HaBerit, Beit YHVH*, 5.

11. IT IS BEST TRANSLATED AS "IS-WAS-WILL BE," OR JUST "BEING" FOR SHORT On my parsing of *YHVH* into "Is, Was and Will Be," see: *Zohar* 3:257b; *Tanya, Sha'ar Hayichud Ve-ha'emunah* 7.

12. THIS NAME ENCOMPASSES ALL OF REALITY—THE GENERALITIES AND THE PARTICULARS See *Shnei Luchot HaBerit, Beit YHVH*, 1: "The tetragrammaton (*YHVH*) is the name that encompasses all of reality—

both the generalities and the particulars." Also see *Zohar* 1:162a and 3:65b. For this reason, I sometimes translate *YHVH* as "Total Being."

13. AS A VERBAL CONSTRUCT, IT ALSO EXPRESSES THE DYNAMISM AND ALIVENESS THAT IS INTRINSIC TO THE NATURE OF BEING See the 46 times the phrase "Living *YHVH*" (חי יהוה) appears throughout the Hebrew Bible. This phrase should be translated as "Living *YHVH*" and not "life of *YHVH*" based on Maimonides' explanation for why this phrase must be pronounced "*Chai YHVH*" and not "*Chei YHVH*":

> And He does not know with a knowledge that is external to Him, as we know. For we and our knowledge are not one and the same, whereas the Creator, may He be blessed—He, His knowledge, and His life are one and the same from every angle, from every perspective, and in every sense of oneness. For were He to live a life and know with a knowledge that is external from Him, there would be many deities—He, His life, and His knowledge ... It therefore says, "*chei Pharaoh*" and "*chei nafshekha*" whereas it does not say, "*chei YHVH*," but rather "*chai YHVH*"—for the Creator and His life are not disparate, as are the lives of the living bodies, or the lives of the angels. (*Mishneh Torah, Hilkhot Yesodei Ha-Torah* 2:10).

Here we see that according to Maimonides, life is not something *YHVH* "has," but it is an intrinsic property of *YHVH*'s very beingness as the singular Divine force in the universe. For this reason I also sometimes translate *YHVH* into English as "Living Being."

14. *YHVH* IS THUS THE TOTAL, LIVING BEINGNESS OF CREATION Maimonides integrates these two principles of Living Being and Total Being in the *Guide for the Perplexed* (1:72):

> There also exists in the Universe a certain force which controls the whole, which sets in motion the chief and principal parts,

and gives them the motive power for governing the rest. With-out that force, the existence of this sphere, with its principal and secondary parts, would be impossible. It is the source of the existence of the universe in all its parts. That force is God blessed be His Name. It is on account of this force that man is called microcosm; for he likewise possesses a certain principle which governs all the forces of the body, and on account of this comparison God is called "the life of the universe;" comp. "and he swore by the life of the universe" (Daniel 12:7).

Also see Shem-Tov ben Joseph ibn Falaquera's commentary on the *Guide for the Perplexed* there (*op. cit.*) where he states that *YHVH* is not just the "life of the worlds" but also the very "form" of the universe; that is to say, it is the living and enduring totality of reality: "נקרא השם בלשונו חי העולמים כי הוא חיי העולם והוא צורת העולם The Name is called in the language of 'Life of the Worlds' because He is the life of the world and he is the form of the world." Maimonides address-es the question of the meaning of the phrase "*chai YHVH*" in all of his major works (in addition to its appearance in *Mishneh Torah* and *Guide for the Perplexed* cited above, it is also addressed at the very end of his commentary on Tractate *Avot* known as *Shemonah Per-akim*). According to R. Yoseph Kapach (in his commentary to *Hilchot Yesodei Hatorah* 2:10), Maimonides' obsession with establishing the correct pronunciation of the biblical phrase "*Chai YHVH*" (and thus, the correct translation) has to do with his recognition of the vital im-portance of preserving the integrity of Divine unity, which is reflect-ed in the correct translation of the biblical phrase "*Chai YHVH*" as "Living Being," not as "Life of *YHVH.*" Also, see the many times the related phrase "Living God," *Elohim Chayyim* (אלהים חיים), appears in the Hebrew Bible: *Deut.* 5:26; *Jos.* 3:10; *1 Sam.* 17:26, 36; *2 Ki.* 19:4, 16; *Ps.* 42:2; 84:2; *Isa.* 37:4, 17; *Jer.* 10:10; 23:36; *Dan.* 6:20, 26; *Hos.* 1:10.

15. WE ARE PART OF THE BODY OF GOD. EACH OF US IS AN EXPRESSION OF
ITS WHOLE BODY On my formulation that we are an expression of God's
body and that the physical body is a microcosm of *YHVH*, see: R. Isaiah Horowitz, *Shenei Luchot HaBerit*, *Toldot Adam*, *Beit Yisrael*, especially sections 16–22; Maimonides, *Guide for the Perplexed* 1:72;
Zohar 2:75b, 2:94b; *Pitchei She'arim*, p. 16. In the Kabbalah tradition
the Divine names and the *Olam HaSefirot*—the *Sefirotic* realm that
serves as a map of reality—are often described in terms of a physical
body. See, e.g., *Zohar* 1:16a, where *YHVH* is described as having a
trunk and limbs. Also see *Zohar* 1:6b, 13a-b, 20a-22a and many more
references throughout the *Zohar*. Also see R. Avraham ben David's
(Ra'avad's) refutation of Maimonides' statement in the *Mishneh Torah* (*Hilchot Teshuvah* 3:7) that all who believe that God has a body
are heretics (Ra'avad's commentary *op. cit.*). Also *Cf.* Moshe ben
Chasdai Taku (the medieval *Tosafist*), *Ketav Tamim*, p. 69. For more
on this topic, see J. Dan, "Ashkenazi Hasidism and the Maimonidean Controversy" in *Maimonidean Studies*, vol. 3 (New York: Yeshiva
University Press, 1995) pp. 29–47. The most explicit description of
God's body in Jewish mystical literature is found in the anonymous
and enigmatic text called *Shiur Komah*, from the Hekhalot and Merkavah period of Jewish mystical speculation. See G. Scholem, *Major
Trends in Jewish Mysticism* (Knopf Doubleday, 2011) pp. 40–79.

16. *ELOHIM ...* REFERS TO CREATION ITSELF, WHAT WE CALL THE BODY OF
GOD On the name *Elohim* representing the body and *YHVH* representing the soul, see *Benei Yissaschar, Rosh Chodesh* 2:1. On *Elohim* as
the manifestation of creation more broadly, see *Kedushat Levi, Chanukah* 5:18; *ibid., Bereishit, Vayeshev* 19. Many texts (e.g. see *Netivot
Shalom* II: 237) point to this principle by noting that the *gematria* of
Elohim (אלהים) equals 86, the same numerical value as the Hebrew
word for "nature" (הטבע). That *YHVH* represents the soul or inner nature of the created realm, see *Shnei Luchot Ha-Berit, Beit YHVH*, 1–6.

17. HUMAN BEING IS A MICROCOSM OF GOD See *Zohar* 1:20a; 1:90b–91a; 2:75b; 2:155a–b; *Zohar Chadash Bereishit* 11d–12a; *Shenei Luchot HaBerit, Toldot Adam, Beit Yisrael*; *Pitchei She'arim*, p. 16. The Zohar expresses the equivalency that humans are microcosms of *YHVH* quite explicitly. See, e.g., Zohar 2:94b: ... יו״ד ה״א וא״ו ה״א דאיהו אדם ואתקרי בדיוקנא דמאריה "*Yud Hey Vav Hey* is the human being and is named in the image of his master." In this statement the Zohar is alluding to the fact that the extended spelling of the *YHVH* (called the *milui*) has the same numerical value (*gematria*) as the Hebrew word for human, *Adam*, 45.

18. GOD IS NOT THE CREATOR BUT RATHER GOD IS WHAT IS CREATED On *YHVH* and *Elohim* being of the *created* realm, not the *creator*, see *Zohar* 1:15a. In this radical reading of the first verse of Genesis, the *Zohar* posits a hidden subject (*Ein Sof*) as the source for the emanation of all the *sefirot* and their associated Divine names.

19. DA'AT ... IS THE CAPACITY FOR BEING TO KNOW ITSELF THROUGH ITS VERY BEING, NOT THROUGH SOME SECONDARY PROCESS. HERE KNOWING AND BEING ARE INSEPARABLE On *da'at* as the nondual property of Being that represents intrinsic Divine knowledge, see Maimonides, *Mishneh Torah, Hilchot Yesodei Hatorah* 2:10 (see the text in note 13 above); *Guide for the Perplexed* 1:68–69, 1:53, 3:20–21; Abulafia's formulation that "knowledge, the knower and the known are all one," in *Sefer HaYashar*, cited by M. Idel, *The Mystical Experience in Abraham Abulafia* (SUNY, 1988) p. 126; Also see R. Shneur Zalman of Liadi's explanation of Maimonides' statement in *Tanya, Sha'ar HaYichud Ve-Haemunah* 7: הקב״ה הוא אחדות פשוט בלי שום הרכבה וצד ריבוי כלל ואם כן מהותו ועצמותו ודעתו הכל דבר אחד ממש בלי שום הרכבה "*YHVH* is a simple oneness without any add-ons or multiplicities whatsoever. Therefore his essence, nature, and knowledge are literally one thing without any addition." Also See *Pardes Rimonim* 8:7 and the comments in *Shnei Luchot HaBerit, Beit YHVH*, 23 (in the long note) and *ibid.*, *Beit YHVH*, 10. The nondual implications of the principle of *da'at*

is the central theme of the Hasidic text *Netivot Shalom* by R. Shalom Noah Brazofsky. See his introduction to *Netivot Shalom*, vol. 1,
pp. 11–35. Cf. the following formulation in the work of Bernadette
Roberts, a Christian contemplative author: "With neither reason nor
provocation, a smile emerged on my face, and in the split second of
recognition I 'saw' and knew I had seen. I knew: the smile itself,
that which smiled, and that at which it smiled, were One—as indis-
tinguishably one as a trinity without division" [Bernadette Roberts,
The Experience of No-Self (Albany: SUNY Press, 1993) p. 72] and
also Cf. the following description by Nisargadatta Maharaj from the
tradition of Advaita Vedanta: "Of course, the knower and the known
are one not two" [Nisargadatta Maharaj, *I Am That* (Durham, North
Carolina: Acorn Press, 1973) p. 424].

20. *DA'AT* ... IS CONTRACTED IN OUR HUMAN EXPERIENCE On the exile of
da'at and its relationship to the state of contraction (*Mitzrayim*), see
Pri Etz Chayyim 21:1; *Sha'ar Ha-kavanot, Inyan Pesach*, 1; *Maggid
Devarav Le-yaakov* 2:1, 7; *Likkutei Moharan* 20:10; *Bnei Yissaschar,
Nisan* 3:11; *ibid., Adar*, 3:3 (2nd *haga*) and 3:6, *Milchamah L'Hash-
em, Derush* 4 and *Derush* 6.

21. MYSTICAL KNOWLEDGE [I.E. *DA'AT*] ON THE OTHER HAND IS DIRECT IM-
MEDIATE KNOWLEDGE OF HOW THINGS ARE On the integration of *da'at*
as the key feature of spiritual liberation, see *B'nei Yissaschar, Adar,
Ma'amar* 3, *Milchamah La-Hashem* 3: החירות היא מן הדעת מי שהוא בעל
דעת נקרא בן חורין "Liberation comes from *da'at*. Someone who is a
master of *da'at* is called a free person." Also see *B'nei Yissaschar,
Ma'amar* 5:19: "In sleep, *da'at* spreads out and the aspect of Messiah
is revealed." In the Kedumah Teachings, the principle of *cheyt* חטא
(usually translated as "sin" but really meaning "missing the mark"—
see Strong's Hebrew Lexicon #2399 and #2398) refers to any state
of being when we are dismembered from immediate contact with our
experience in the Now, which is embodied in the principle of *da'at*.
This is reflected in the Talmudic statement: "A person only sins if a

folly spirit enters him and his *da'at* is interrupted" (*BT Sotah* 3a). For more explanation of the kabbalistic and Hasidic understanding of *da'at*, see my article: Z. Ish-Shalom, "Not-Knowing and True Knowledge – The Essence of Purim." *Spectrum: A Journal of Renewal Spirituality*, Vol. 2, No. 1, Winter-Spring, 2006.

22. DA'AT ... REFERS TO SEXUAL INTIMACY AND PHYSICAL UNITY... That *da'at* represents intimacy and inter-penetration, see *Tikkunei Zohar* 69 (p. 99a); Rashi on Gen. 18:19; *Tanya, Iggeret HaKodesh* 15 (p. 123b). Also see *Bnei Yissaschar, Adar, Ma'amar 2, Derush 4:* דעת מלשון דבקות והתקשרות *"Da'at* is from the language of *devekut* and connection" and *ibid., Nisan 4, Tiyul Be-Pardes Derush* 2). *Cf. Ohev Yisrael, Tetzaveh* (at the beginning): עיקר היחוד והקישור הוא ע"י הדעת "the essence of unification and connection is through *da'at*." Also see R. Zvi Hirsch of Ziditchov, *Sur Me-rah Va-aseh Tov*, p. 56: דעת הוא שורש ומקור האהבה ... כאשר האדם בשלימות הדעת אז היחוד הוא בשלימות "Da'at* is the root and source of love ... when a person is in completion of *da'at* then the unification is complete." On the relationship of *da'at* to sexuality, see *Bnei Yissaschar, Ma'amarei Shabatot* 6:3, where R. Zvi Elimelekh of Dinov discusses how connection and union through the phallus is a function of *da'at*. Also see his discussion of *da'at* as the source of the phallus of Joseph and the *sefirah* of Yesod (*Bnei Yissaschar, Kislev-Tevet*, 4:116). Also see R. Nachman of Bratzlav's statement: כי פגם הברית הוא פגם הדעת "A blemish of the phallus is a blemish of *da'at*" (*Likkutei Moharan* 20:10). He also states (*op. cit.*) that the way to rectify the disconnection from *da'at* and thus achieve redemption from *Mitzrayim* is through the power of one's voice. See my connection to this principle below in Chapter 4, where I discuss using speech as a method to free oneself from contraction. *Da'at* is similar to the principle of mindfulness is Buddhism, although the difference is that in Kedumah by *da'at* we mean an embodied sensing intimacy with our experience in the here and now. It shares with mindfulness the orientation to coming back to the present moment with awareness but adds the embodied element of sensing. Interestingly,

the Tibetan and Sanskrit words for *mindfulness* (*Trenpa* and *Smirti*, respectively) mean "remembrance" (see R. Sharf, "Mindfulness and Mindlessness in Early Chan," in *Philosophy East & West* vol. 64: 4, Oct. 2014 pp. 933–964), which also reflects how the principle of *da'at* is understood by the Jewish mystics (see, e.g. *Bnei Yissachar Adar* 3, *Milchemet La-Hashem* 2: עיקר הזכירה הוא בשכל הדעת "The essence of remembrance is in the intellect of *da'at*").

23. KEDUMAH IS TANTRIC IN ITS VIEW OF PHYSICALITY On the classical tantric view that the physical is the ideal portal for spiritual discovery, see C. Wallis, *Tantra Illuminated* (Mattamayura Press, 2013) p. 50.

24. INNER SENSING ... IS THE MOST ACCESSIBLE DOORWAY TO WHAT WE REFER TO AS THE LIGHTS OF BEING ... THE *SEFIROT* ... That the *sefirot* are the Divine qualities or the essential aspects of reality that can be experienced directly by human consciousness is one of the most basic principles and teachings of classical Kabbalah. See, e.g., *Zohar* 2:42b, 3:257b, 1:103a–b; *Sha'arei Orah*, 1; *Sha'ar HaHakdamot, Hakdamah* 4. That the optimal mode to experience God and the *sefirot* is through the limbs of the body, see: *Sha'arei Orah*, 1: 14a; *Zohar* 1:103a–b; *Likkutei Maharan*, 22:5 (I would add to R. Nachman's comments there that the effect of the *shofar* on the limbs is connected to the embodiment of *da'at*, which is the esoteric meaning of the phrase from the Rosh HaShanah liturgy: אשרי העם יודעי תרוע "Happy are the people who know *teru'ah*.") Also see R. Shalom Noach of Slonim's teachings on embodying "trust of the limbs" (*Emunat Ha-evarim*) in *Netivot Shalom* 1:147, 2:281–284, 2:290, *inter alia*. See especially the Slonimer Rebbe's comment (*Netivot Shalom* 2:239) that "trust of the physical limbs" is the highest level of trust. On the human being as an anatomical microcosm of the *sefirot* and an embodiment of the Divine names, see: *Zohar* 2:75b, 3:48a, 3:201a, 3:238b, 3:335a, 3:341a; *Zohar Chadash* 42; *Sha'areh Orah*, 1 (p. 2b); *Pardes Rimonim* 22:2; *Shenei Luchot HaBerit, Toldot Adam, Hakdamah* 1. On the radical nondual understanding of the relationship between the physical body,

the soul, and the Divine in Lurianic Kabbalah, see Z. Ish-Shalom, *Radical Death: The Paradoxical Unity of Body, Soul and Cosmos in Lurianic Kabbalah* (Ph.D. Dissertation: Brandeis University, 2013), especially Chapter 4.

25. THIS PRACTICE IS ALLUDED TO IN ... SHA'AREI ORAH ... See *Sha'arei Orah*, 1:14a: דע והאמן כי יש ענין בסוד צורת טהרת האברים שאפשר לאדם להדבק בשכינה "Know and believe that there is a secret method involving the purification of the limbs that enables a person to cleave to the Divine Presence."

CHAPTER THREE

1. IN ADVAITA VEDANTA, THE SANSKRIT TERM *AVIDYA*... See Alex Wayman, "The Meaning of Unwisdom (*Avidya*)" in *Philosophy East and West* vol. 7:1–2 (1952) pp. 21–25.

2. IN THE KABBALISTIC TRADITION THERE IS A SIMILAR PARADIGM...AWAKENING REFERS TO ... TRUE KNOWLEDGE One of the most oft-cited biblical verses by Jewish mystical texts is Deut. 4:35: "To you it was shown in order that you *know* that *YHVH* is *Elohim*, there is none but Him." The principle invocation here is to "know" (*da'at*), not to "believe." See, e.g., *Zohar* 2:161b. For a good overview of the principle of *da'at* from a modern day Hasidic master, see *Netivot Shalom*, Vol. 1, pp. 11–35. The centrality of attaining true knowledge of God is also reflected in the major works of Jewish philosophy. See, e.g., the opening line of Maimonides' *Mishneh Torah*: דע שיש שם מצוי ראשון "*Know* that there is a First Cause..." (*Hilchot Yesodei HaTorah* 1:1).

3. TO KNOW MEANS TO KNOW IN THE FLESH ... IN THE BODY See sources listed in Chapter 2, note 24.

4. THE PHYSICAL BODY IS A REFLECTION OF THE DIVINE BODY See sources and discussion in Chapter 2 notes 15, 16, and 17.

5. ON TRANSLATING THE HEBREW TERM *SEFIROT* See *Sefer Yetzirah* 1:2; *Zohar* 2:136b; *Tikkunei Zohar, Hakdamah*; *Pardes Rimonim* 8:2.

6. ON THE NONCONCEPTUAL NATURE OF *EIN SOF* See Chapter 1, note 9; Chapter 2, note 2.

7. GOD IS NOT WHAT CREATED THE COSMOS, GOD IS THE COSMOS See Chapter 2, note 18.

8. WE ARE GOD'S DETAILS See Chapter 2, notes 15, 16, and 17.

9. THESE VARIOUS LIGHTS ... ULTIMATELY CONSTITUTE THE VERY NATURE OF THE PHYSICAL HUMAN BODY See *Ibid*.

10. THE INNER NATURE OF THIS COSMIC BODY IS IN THE CENTER OF THE TREE OF LIFE, *YHVH* See Chapter 2, note 16

11. *YHVH* AS IS, WAS, WILL BE See Chapter, 2 note 11.

12. *YHVH* IS LIVING BEING ... See Chapter, 2 note 13.

13. ALL OF REALITY IS GOD ... INCLUDING US This monistic principle is reflected in the Aramaic refrain "There is no place devoid of Him" לית אתר פנוי מיניה (*Tikkunei Zohar* 91b), an oft-repeated phrase of the Ba'al Shem Tov (*Keter Shem Tov* 1:29:1, 1:39:3) and ubiquitous in Hasidic literature (see, e.g., *Noam Elimelekh, Terumah* 9:3; *Ohev Yisrael, Shelach* 1:2; *ibid., Bechukotai* 3:1; *ibid., Bereishit* 5:1; *Kedushat Levi, Mishpatim* 1, *Devarim* 2). See R. Shneur Zalman of Liadi's discussion of this principle in *Tanya, Sha'ar Ha-yichud*, Ch. 7. The Zohar expresses the equivalency that we are microcosms of *YHVH* quite explicitly. See, e.g. *Zohar* 2:94b: ... יו"ד ה"א וא"ו ה"א דאיהו אדם

ואתקרי בדיוקנא דמאריה "*Yud Hey Vav Hey* is a human being ... and is named so after the image of his master." In this statement the Zohar is alluding to the fact that the extended spelling of the *YHVH* (called the *milui*) has the same *gematria* (numerical value) as the Hebrew word for human, *Adam,* both of which add up to 45. Also see *Zohar* 2:75b: וקודשא בריך הוא כד ברא ליה לבר נש סדר ביה כל דיוקנין דרזין עלאין דעלמא דלעילא וכל דיוקנין דרזין תתאין דעלמא דלתתא וכלא מתחקקא בבר נש "When the Holy One created the human being, He arranged in him all the forms of the upper secrets, of the World to Come, and all the forms of the lower secrets, of the lower world; everything was engraved in the human being." This view of "monistic theism" is also found in the tradition of Nondual Shaivite Tantra (i.e. Kashmir Shaivism). See Wallis, *Tantra Illuminated*, p. 56.

14. *DA'AT IS THE INVISIBLE ELEVENTH LIGHT* See Chapter 11 note 1.

15. "*AS ABOVE, SO BELOW*" See *Zohar* 1:205b.

16. OUR BODIES SERVE AS VEHICLES TO EXPERIENCE THE TOTALITY OF BEING On the physical body as the optimal location of spiritual realization, see Psalms 35:10; Job 19:26; *Sha'arei Orah*, 1:14a; *Zohar* 1:103a–b; *Likkutei Maharan*, 22:5; *Netivot Shalom* 1:147, 2:281–284, 2:290. See also Chapter 2, note 24.

17. KABBALISTS DESCRIBE *DA'AT* AS A FUNDAMENTAL INGREDIENT OF ALL THE LIGHTS See *Bnei Yissaschar, Ma'amar 3, Milchamah L'Hashem, Derush* 1:דעת הוא קיום המדות, "*Da'at* is what maintains all the qualities." Also see his comments *op. cit. Derush* 5:דעת הוא בכל סטרין ואם באתי להאיר לך להתבונן הדבר גם בנשמת האדם יתארכו כמה דפין איך הדעת היא קיום השכל והמדות כולם "*Da'at* fills every side [i.e. all the *sefirot*], and if I wanted to show you to understand the matter with respect to the human soul how *da'at* also upholds the intellect and all of the qualities it would require many pages." Cf. *ibid. Ma'amar* 2:18. This function of *da'at* is reflected in the verse from Proverbs (24:4):

ובדעת חדרים ימלאון "With *da'at* the rooms are filled," which alludes to the *sefirot* (the "rooms"). See *Ohev Yisrael, Tetzaveh* c.v. *ve-hinei.*

18. K*NOWING* [*DA'AT*] IS THE PORTAL THROUGH WHICH WE ARE ABLE TO GO THROUGH A PROCESS OF TRANSFORMATION ... THAT MOVES ULTIMATELY TO FREEDOM See *Bnei Yissaschar, Adar, Ma'amar* 3, *Milchamah La-Hashem* 3: החירות היא מן הדעת מי שהוא בעל דעת נקרא בן חורין "Freedom comes from *da'at*. Someone who is a master of *da'at* is called a free person." Also see *B'nei Yissaschar, Ma'amar* 5:19: "In sleep, *da'at* spreads out and the aspect of Messiah is revealed." I will discuss the Kedumah understanding of the Messiah principle in Chapter 10.

19. O*NE* OF THE CLASSICAL H*EBREW* NAMES FOR G*OD* IN THE R*ABBINIC* TRADITION IS H*A-MAKOM*... EVERYTHING... OCCURS WITHIN THIS SINGULAR M*A-KOM* See, e.g., *Mishnah Pesachim* 10:5; *Mishnah Ta'anit* 3:2; *Mishnah Sotah* 5:5; *Mishnah Avot* 2:9 and 3:10; *Genesis Rabbah* 68:10; *Pesikta Rabatei* 21:10; *Yalkut Shimoni, Vayetzei,* 117: "Why is God called *Makom*? Because He is the place of the world and the world is not His place." Also see Maimonides, *Commentary on the Mishnah, Sanhedrin* 10:3; R. Avraham Leib Schik, *Me'orei Ha'esh* on *Tanna D'bei Eliyahu* 1:8 (*Mosad Li'idud Limud Torah,* 1994). For an alternative reading of the Divine name *Ha-Makom* as deriving from the word *Ha-Mekayem*, "The One who sustains," see *Maharal, Chidushei Aggadot, Sanhedrin* p. 147. The Kedumah view on the mystical meaning of *Makom* is reflected most clearly in *Tanya, HaYichud Ve-Haemunah* 7, where the founder of Chabad describes the light of *Ein Sof* filling all time and space in a non-hierarchical monistic manner: הכל הוא בחי' מקום הבטל במציאות באור אין סוף, "Everything is in the aspect of *Makom*, whose existence is nullified in the light of *Ein Sof*."

20. "O*NE* WHO SAVES A SINGLE LIFE SAVES THE ENTIRE UNIVERSE" *Mishnah Sanhedrin* 4:5; *PT Sanhedrin* 4:9, *BT Sanhedrin* 37a. That the entire universe is contained within the physical form of the human being is a key principle of Kabbalah. See, e.g., *Zohar* 2:75b: וקודשא בריך הוא

כד ברא ליה לבר נש סדר ביה כל דיוקנין דרזין עלאין דעלמא דלעילא וכל דיוקנין
דרזין תתאין דעלמא דלתתא וכלא מתחקקא בבר נש "When the Holy One created the human being, He arranged in him all the forms of the upper
secrets, of the World to Come, and all the forms of the lower secrets,
of the lower world; everything was engraved in the human being."

21. ON THE "TRIADIC CENTERS" IN KASHMIR SHAIVISM See Paul Muller-Ortega, *The Triadic Heart of Shiva* (Albany: SUNY Press, 1988).

22. THE JEWISH MYSTICAL TEXTS ALLUDE TO THIS … *DA'AT* MATURES IN DIS-
TINCT STAGES See *Zohar* 2:97b–98a; *Bnei Yissaschar, Adar, Ma'amar
3, Milchamah La-Hashem, Derush* 6; R. Elijah of Vilna (The Vilna
Gaon), *Barak HaShachar* on Kohelet 1:3: "There are 3 periods for
a man: 1) the days of ascent which are until 20, because then one's
growth has finished as known, and likewise the intellect has finished
[i.e. matured]. Then the primary *neshama* comes to a man from above
if he is worthy, as is known also that at his birth the *nefesh* comes.
At 13 the primary *ruach*, and at 20 the *neshama* which completes his
intellect…." Also see *Sefer Seder Hayom, Perush Mishnah Avot* 5:24.

23. IN THE *ZOHAR*, THESE THREE STAGES CORRESPOND TO THE THREE LEVELS
OF THE SOUL See *Zohar* 2:94b, 2:97b–98a. For this developmental process in Lurianic Kabbalah, see *Sha'ar HaGilgulim, Hakdamah* 2 (at
the beginning). On the inherent unity of these three levels of soul, see
Zohar 1:205b–206a.

24. *CHAYAH* AND *YECHIDAH* … ARE NOT REALLY SUBJECT TO MATURATION
AND DEVELOPMENT … AND ARE TRANS-INDIVIDUAL See *Etz Chayyim* 6:5;
40:10; 40:12; 45:1; R. Chayyim Volozhin, *Nefesh Ha-Chayyim* 2:17.

25. WHEN FREUD TALKS ABOUT SUBLIMATION … See S. Freud, *Civilization
and Its Discontents* (1930) in The Standard Edition of *The Complete
Psychological Works of Sigmund Freud—The Future of an Illusion,
Civilization and its Discontents, and Other Works*, trans. by James

Strachey (Hogarth Press; London, 1961), vol. XXI, 78–80. Also see Marguerite La Caz, "Sublimation, Love, and Creativity" in *Analytic Freud: Philosophy and Psychoanalysis*, ed. Michael Levine (Routledge, 2002) pp. 261–276.

26. BUDDHIST TANTRA HAS ITS ORIGINS IN NONDUAL SHAIVITE TANTRA See C. Wallis, *Tantra Illuminated*, p. 32ff.

27. ON THE *VIJNANA BHAIRAVA TANTRA* AND KASHMIR SHAIVISM See C. Wallis, *Tantra Illuminated*, pp. 242–247; Paul Muller-Ortega, *The Triadic Heart of Shiva*, pp. 42–43. In my study of the *Vijnanabairavatantra*, I used the English translation of this text by Jaideva Singh, *Vijnanabhairava* (Delhi: Motilal Banarsidass, 1979).

28. DIAMOND APPROACH For an overview of the Diamond Approach, see my chapter (co-authored): John V. Davis, Theodore Usatynski and Zvi Ish-Shalom, "The Diamond Approach," in The *Wiley-Blackwell Handbook of Transpersonal Psychology* (Wiley- Blackwell, 2013).

29. THE TURNINGS OF THE WHEEL OF TORAH AND DHARMA See the appendix.

30. ON THE THREE AXES: *OLAM, SHANAH, NEFESH* See *Sefer Yetzirah* 3:3.

31. *TORAH LISHMAH* ... TRUTH " FOR ITS OWN SAKE" See *BT Sotah* 47a.

32. THEY ARE RECOGNIZED TO HAVE EMBODIED THE TORAH TO THE DEGREE THAT THEY ARE THE TORAH See Chapter 1, notes 4 and 5.

33. THE TORAH AND THE DIVINE ARE ONE AND THE SAME, ACCORDING TO THE ZOHAR See *Zohar* 1:24a.

CHAPTER FOUR

1. IN THE TAOIST TRADITION ... On the location of the *tan tien* point in Taoism, see Lu K'uan Yu, *Taoist Yoga* (Rider, 1970) p. 10.

2. TZIMTZUM POINT ... WHERE PRESENCE IS CONCENTRATED AND SOURCED See Exodus 25:22 and *Exodus Rabbah* 34:1, where the term used by the midrash for the "concentration" or "contraction" of the Divine Presence is *tzimtzum*. In these texts, the locus-point of this concentration of Presence is in between the two cherubs that hovered above the Ark of the Covenant inside the Holy of Holies in the ancient Temple in Jerusalem. In Kabbalah texts, the cherubs are thus also associated with the Divine Presence (see, e.g., Abulafia's numerical calculations indicating this relationship in *Chayei Olam Habah*, cited by A. Kaplan in *Meditation and Kabbalah*, p. 10). In Kabbalah, the Divine Presence is called *Shechinah* or *Malchut*, which is typically associated in classical Kabbalah with either the crown of the phallus or with the feet. However, in the Kedumah system I associate it anatomically with the subtle womb center, which is located in the same region as the lower *tan tien* in Taoism. This is also a legitimate location for *Malchut* in classical Kabbalah, since *Malchut* is explicitly associated with the female womb (or the cervix, see *Pardes Rimonim* 23:13 c.v. *mitzvah*; 23:17 c.v. *peter rechem*) which correlates with the cauldron of Presence in the lower belly center. Also, see the diagram and description by M. Cordovero in his commentary *Ohr Yakar* on *Zohar* 2:134a, where *Malchut* is located in between *Tiferet* and *Yesod*, corresponding anatomically with the inner lower belly.

3. MANY TRADITIONAL SOCIETIES DO NOT DISCRIMINATE ... BETWEEN MIND AND HEART For example, in the Japanese language, "mind" and "heart" are represented by the same word, *kokoro,* which means both "mind" and "heart," and refers to both thinking and feeling. See Robert Edgar Carter, *The Japanese Arts and Self-Cultivation* (Albany: SUNY Press, 2007) pp. 9–10.

4. THE SEPARATION OF THE MIND FROM THE HEART IS A MORE RECENT INNO-VATION OF THE WEST This view was solidified by the philosopher René Descartes (1596–1650), who argued for a more radical separation between the mind and the body. See his *Passions of the Soul,* trans. Stephen Voss (Hackett, 1989), pp. 36–37.

5. FOR EXAMPLE, MANY PHRASES FOUND IN THE ANCIENT HEBREW TRADITION PUT HEART AND WISDOM, HEART OF UNDERSTANDING, HEART OF KNOWLEDGE, IN THE SAME BREATH See Exodus 35:10, 36:1; 1 Kings 5:9; Isaiah 6:10; Proverbs 2:2-3; Ecclesiastes 1:16–18, 8:16; On the phrase *Lev Meivin* ("understanding heart"), see *Tikkunei Zohar, Hakdamah* 2.

6. THE PRINCIPLE OF "NOT-KNOWING ..." On the principle of not-know-ing, see R. Zvi Hirsch of Ziditchov, *Sur Me-ra Va-aseh Tov* (Emes Publishing, 1996) p. 94: וזהו ... ידע שאינו ידע אשר זו בחכמה גדול כלל ידע שאינו יודע הדעת תכלית "A big principle in this wisdom is that one should know that they do not know… this is the purpose of *da'at*—knowing that one does not know." The orienting posture of not-know-ing is also reflected in the mystical meaning of the holiday of Purim. See my article, Z. Ish-Shalom, "Not-Knowing and True Knowledge—The Essence of Purim." *Spectrum: A Journal of Renewal Spirituality,* Vol. 2, No. 1, Winter-Spring, 2006.

7. THE WORD *MITZRAYIM* IN HEBREW MEANS "THE CONTRACTED PLACES" See Psalms 118:5; Lamentations 1:3.

8. THE WORD *VE-HIGADITA* IN ARAMAIC ... MEANS "TO DRAW DOWN" See *Netivot Shalom* II: 248, where the Slonimer Rebbe explains that the word *Ve-higateda* from Ex. 13:8 means "drawing down," based on the *Targum's* rendering of the word *Ve-himshichu* in Gen. 37:28 into Aramaic as *Venagidu*. On this interpretation, also see *Tosafot Yom Tov, Ketubot* 4:12. Also see Rashi's commentary on Exodus 13:5. Also see *BT Shabbat* 87a, where the Talmud explains the word *Va-yaged* (Exodus 19:9) as referring to דברים שמושכין לבו של אדם כאגדה

"things that pull on a man's heart like a knot (*aggadah*)." The use of the term *aggadah* here also suggests the language of union. On this theme see *BT Gittin* 78b, where the root of *Ve-higadeta* has the meaning of "connection." Also see *BT Sukkah* 13a, where the same root is used to refer to the binding together of the *lulav*, (אגודה).

9. Pesach ... is read by the mystical sages as two words combined—*pe* and *sach* See *Netivot Shalom* II:249 (at the end).

10. Psychodynamics comes from this very ancient Hebrew understanding ... of speech See my discussion of the Hebrew roots of psychodynamic theory in the appendix.

11. There is a Rabbinic teaching in the *Midrash* that states ... Bi-zchut Ha-emunah... See *Yalkut Shimoni Beshalach*, 240; *Midrash Tanchuma Beshalach* (at the beginning); *Song of Songs Rabbah* 4:18; *Maggid Devarav Le-Ya'akov*, 95; *Netivot Shalom* II: 235, 251. On the applicability of this principle to all times and spaces, see Slonimer Rebbe's comment (*ibid.*, p. 251): וכמו שביציאת מצרים נגאלו בזכות האמונה כך גאולת מצרים שבכל שנה ושנה היא בזכות האמונה "Just as in the exodus from Egypt we were redeemed through the merit of trust, so too redemption from Egypt in each and every year is through the merit of trust."

12. The forty-ninth level of *tumah* see *Zohar Chadash Yitro* 31a; *Beit Halevi, Derush* 2, quoting Isaac Luria; *Netivot Shalom* II: 235.

13. The term "days" is a code word ... that refers to ... the *sefirot* see *Bahir* 57; *Sha'arei Orah*, 2:46; Also see the many passages in the Zohar that utilize the term "days" as a reference to the *sefirot*. See, e.g., *Zohar* 1:36a, 1:224a–b, 2:89b, 3:257a, *inter alia*.

14. The exile into *Mitzrayim* was an exile of *da'at* see Chapter 2, note 20.

15. WHEN WE PRACTICE *DRASH* WITH A PARTNER—CALLED A *CHAVRUTA* In the traditional academies of Rabbinic learning (the *yeshiva* or *beit midrash*), Torah, and especially Talmud, is studied one on one with a designated study-partner, called a *chavruta*.

16. ACCORDING TO THE ZOHAR, *MITZRAYIM* WAS NOT ONLY AN EXILE OF *DA'AT* BUT ALSO AN EXILE OF *DIBUR*—OF SPEECH See *Zohar* 2:25b: דדבור הוה בגלותא "Speech was in exile." Also see *Netivot Shalom* II: 249: בגלות מצרים היה הדיבור בגלות "In the exile of *Mitzrayim*, speech was in exile."

17. TRUTH—*EMET*—IS ACTUALLY ONE OF THE HEBREW NAMES FOR GOD See Psalms 31:5; Jeremiah 10:10. Also see *BT Yoma* 69b, where the Talmud states that God's "seal" is truth. In Kabbalah, the word *emet* is a technical name for the *sefirah* of *Tiferet*, which is also the *sefirah* of the Divine name *YHVH*. See, e.g., *Sha'arei Orah* 5:61bff. See my discussion below in Chapter Five, where I present the equation expressed in the liturgical phrase *YHVH Eloheichem Emet*, "*YHVH* your God is Truth." The Zohar makes explicit the connection between speaking truth and this liturgical phrase. See *Zohar* 2:188a–b.

CHAPTER FIVE

1. AT THE VERY END OF ... THE THIRD PARAGRAPH OF THE *SHEMA*, THE PHRASE IS CHANTED: *ADONAI ELOHEICHEM EMET* The first two words are from the end of the third paragraph of the formal *Shema* prayer (derived from Numbers 15:41). The word "*emet*" is formally the first word of the prayer that follows in the liturgy. The three paragraphs of the *Shema* were understood by the kabbalists to form a sacred unit, as the number of words total 248, the traditional number of limbs in the body and the number of positive commandments in the Torah. See *Zohar* 2:188a–b: יהו"ה אלהינו יהו"ה אחד וכלא איהו אמת ורזא דאמת ומסיימי יהו"ה אלהיכם אמת ודא איהו שפת אמת תכון לעד "'*YHVH* is our God, *YHVH* is

One' (Deut. 4:6): And All is *emet* and the secret of *emet*, and it [i.e. the *Shema* prayer] concludes: *'YHVH* our God is *emet,'* and this is 'True Speech will be established forever' (Prov. 12:19)." See my discussion of this last verse below in Chapter 6, note 18.

2. THE TALMUD STATES ... THAT THE SEAL OF *YHVH* IS TRUTH See *BT Yoma* 69b.

3. AND THE *SEFIRAH* ASSOCIATED WITH THE WORD *EMET* IS *TIFERET*... See *Sha'arei Orah* 5:61b ff.

4. FOLLOWS THE RABBINIC TEACHING THAT *ALEF* IS PAST, *MEM* IS PRESENT AND *TAV* FUTURE ... See *PT Sanhedrin* 1:1, 18a; *Genesis Rabbah* 81:1; *Deuteronomy Rabbah* 1:10; *Song of Songs Rabbah* 1:9. See E. Wolfson, *Aleph, Mem, Tau: Kabbalistic Musings on Time, Truth and Death* (University of California Press, 2006).

5. ACCORDING TO THE ... *SEFER YETZIRAH* ... ALL OF CREATION IS AN EXPRESSION OF THE HEBREW LETTERS AND NUMBERS See *Sefer Yetzirah* 2:1–6.

6. THE NUMBER FORTY, WHICH IS THE LETTER *MEM*, HAS TO DO WITH THE POTENTIAL FOR TRANSFORMATION In addition to the the examples I cited from the Bible, also see the Talmudic teaching that the embryo is formed in the womb over a forty day period (*BT Berachot* 60a); there are forty days between the first day of *Elul* and Yom Kippur, which marks the period of time most auspicious for *teshuvah*, or repentance; at forty years old a person transitions from one level of wisdom to the next (*Avot* 5:22); one does not come to fully comprehend the knowledge of one's teacher before forty years (*BT Avodah Zarah* 5b; also Rashi on *Deut* 29:6); one is not fit to teach Torah until forty years (*BT Sotah* 22b). An interesting passage in the Talmud connects the significance of the number forty with the principle of not-knowing that I discussed in Chapter 4. The Talmud explains that when R. Zeira wanted to learn the Jerusalem version of the Talmud, he first fasted forty

times to forget all he had learned of the Babylonian version (*BT Bava Metzia* 85a). Why would he have to forget his knowledge of the Babylonian Talmud in order to learn the Jerusalem Talmud? In the Kedumah interpretation, the reason is that in order for him to understand the Jerusalem Talmud in a true way, he needs to first adopt a posture of not-knowing, of openness to discovering something radically new and different. Thus, he engaged a process of transformation (fasting 40 times) in order to forget everything in order that he be able to abide in a state of "beginner's mind" (to borrow from the language of the Zen teacher Suzuki Roshi), which is a condition of not-knowing. On the mystical dimension of the inner posture of not-knowing see R. Zvi Hirsch of Ziditchov, *Sur Me-rah*, p. 94 and my article, "Not-Knowing and True Knowledge—The Essence of Purim." *Spectrum: A Journal of Renewal Spirituality*, Vol. 2, No. 1, Winter-Spring, 2006.

7. FORTY IS THE REQUIRED VOLUME OF WATER IN A KOSHER *MIKVAH* See *BT Eruvin* 4b.

8. MAIMONIDES ... STATES THAT IF YOU DO NOT HAVE AN ACTUAL *MIKVAH* AVAILABLE ... YOU CAN ENTER INTO THE "WATERS OF *DA'AT* ..." See Maimonides, *Mishneh Torah, Hilchot Mikva'ot* 11:12. Also see *Degel Machaneh Ephrayim, Mishpatim*, p. 172 and *Bnei Yissaschar*, Adar 3:6.

9. THERE IS AN INNER CHANNEL THAT THREADS THE HEART TO TWO ORGANS OF OUR BEING; ONE IS THE TONGUE, AND THE OTHER IS THE GENITALS This channel is alluded to in *Sefer Yetzirah* 1:3: וברית יחיד מכוון באמצע במילת הלשון ובמילת המעור "A singular covenant (*berit*) precisely in the middle with the circumcision of the tongue and the circumcision of the genitals." The *berit* "precisely in the middle" alludes to the heart-center, which is also the subject of circumcision in the Hebrew Bible (see *Deut.* 10:16). The tongue and genitals in this passage are thus extensions of this singular channel emanating from the heart-center. See *Pardes Rimonim* 1:1:

התת"ת הוא ברית יחיד העולה מעלה מעלה בסוד הדעת וקושר עליונים בתחתונים
ע"י עלייתו בשלש ספירות הראשונות והכרעתו בזרועות ומשפיע בנצחים וביסוד
ובמלכות. הרי כי ברית יחיד במלת לשון ובמלת מעור מכוונת באמצע. פי' באמצע
עשר אצבעות עליונים, המכריע הוא הת"ת שהוא הנקרא מלת לשון כמו שאבאר

"*Tiferet* [i.e. the heart center] is the singular covenant that ascends
high above in the secret of *da'at* and connects the upper realms with
the lower through its ascension to the three first *sefirot*, its balancing
of the arms [i.e. *Chesed* and *Gevurah*] and its influence over the eternities [*Netzach* and *Hod*], *Yesod* and *Malchut*. For behold the singular
covenant [i.e *Tiferet*], with the circumcision of the tongue and with
the circumcision of the phallus is situated in the middle. Meaning
it is situated in the middle of the upper ten fingers [i.e. *Sefirot*]. The
balancing [*sefirah*] is *Tiferet*, which is called the circumcision of the
tongue…."

10. THE ZOHAR AND OTHER KABBALAH TEXTS OFTEN USE THE METAPHOR
OF KISSING See, e.g., *Zohar* 3:250a, 3:223b; *Tikkunei Zohar* 19 (39a),
21 (45b); *Zohar Chadash Shir Ha-Shirim* 64b; Moses Cordovero,
Pardes Rimmonim (Jerusalem, 1962), Gate 8, Chapter 21. For more
sources see Joel Hecker's article, "Kissing Kabbalists" in *Studies in
Jewish Civilization, Vol. 15*: "Love—Ideal and Real—in Jewish Civilization" (Creighton University Press, 2008).

11. *MERKAVAH* … IS DESCRIBED IN THE ANCIENT TEXTS … AS A MYSTICAL WISDOM VEHICLE See *Heikhalot Rabbatei*, especially section 21; *Sha'arei
Kedushah* 3:6.

12. THE PHRASE "FOUR CUBIC FEET …"COMES FROM THE TALMUD, AND IT
REFERS TO THE RANGE THAT CONSTITUTES OUR PERSONAL SPACE See *BT
Baba Metzia* 10a; *PT Gittin* 8:3.

13. THE *MISHKAN* IS THUS A STRUCTURE OF CONSCIOUSNESS THAT HOLDS THE
INDIVIDUAL LIGHT OF OUR SOUL See *Sha'arei Orah*, 1:8a (p.15).

14. HOWEVER, IT IS ALLUDED TO IN THE CLASSIC KABBALISTIC TEXT, *SHA'AREI ORAH*, BY JOSEPH GIKATILLA See *Sha'arei Orah*, 1:5b (p.10).

15. WHICH CORRESPONDS WITH THE TRADITIONAL JEWISH CUSTOM OF RECITING ONE HUNDRED BLESSINGS A DAY See *BT Menachot* 43b.

16. THEY HAD TRUSTED THAT THEY WERE HELD BY THE DIVINE PRESENCE ENOUGH TO MOVE THROUGH *MITZRAYIM* See Maharal, *Netivot Olam, Netiv Ha-emunah* 2:1: שבשכר אמונה שרתה עליהם שכינה "Through the merit of their *emunah* the *Shechinah* rested upon them."

17. TRUST IS ALSO INTIMATELY CONNECTED TO *DA'AT* The principle of *emunah*—faith or trust—is also intimately connected to *emet*, or truth, which more tightly weaves together this web of interconnected concepts. On the relationship between *emunah* and *emet*, see *Magid Devarav Le-ya'akov*, 95:1: נמצא שמדות האמונה נתלבש בתוכו מדת האמת וגורם פעולתו נמצא האמונה נעשה כלי קיבול למדת אמת "We find that the qualities of *emunah* are clothed within the quality of *emet* and causes its action; we find that *emunah* acts as a receptive vessel for the quality of *emet*."

18. SO THE HUMAN SPIRIT IS INTIMATELY CONNECTED TO ... OUR SENSE OF SMELL ... In addition to the sense of smell not being mentioned in the Garden of Eden story in Genesis chapters 2–3, it is also the sense associated with the Messiah. See, e.g., the verse in Isaiah 11:3, classically understood to be a reference to the Messiah: "And he shall smell with the awe of God" (see the discussion of this verse and its messianic interpretation in *BT Sanhedrin* 93b).

19. THERE ARE ELEVEN OF THEM [I.E. SPICES] ... THEY ARE LISTED IN THE TALMUD... the eleven spices are called the *Ketoret Bisamim* (mentioned in Exodus 30:34–38) and are listed in *BT Keritot* 6a.

CHAPTER SIX

1. IN ADVAITA VEDANTA ... *ADYAROPA* ... AND *APAVADA* ... See Sankracharya, *Atmabodha*, trans. Swami Nikhilananda (Vesanta Press, 1947) pp. 53-56. This understanding is also reflected in the Hasidic philosophy of Chabad, which is very similar to Advaita Vedanta in this respect. See above, Chapter 1, note 2.

2. THIS IMAGE IS NOT JUST USED BY SHANKARA, BUT ALSO MORE BROADLY IN INDIAN PHILOSOPHY, INCLUDING IN BUDDHIST TEXTS See A. Sharma, *The Rope and the Snake: A Metaphorical Exploration of Advaita Vedanta* (Manohar, 1997) Ch. 1 and especially p. 14.

3. THE KNOWER AND THE KNOWN ARE ONE ... See Maimonides, *Mishneh Torah, Yesodei HaTorah* 2:10 and the other sources cited above in Chapter 2, note 19.

4. THE ANCESTORS OF THE *MERKAVAH* ARE ABRAHAM, ISAAC, AND JACOB ... see *Genesis Rabbah* 2:6; *Zohar* 1:200b, 3:184b.

5. ABRAHAM IS LOVE, ISAAC IS STRENGTH, AND JACOB IS TRUTH ... See *Sha'arei Orah,* Gates 5, 6 and 7.

6. THE FIRST CHAPTER OF EZEKIEL DESCRIBES WHAT IS TRADITIONALLY TERMED THE *MA'ASEH MERKAVAH* ... for a description of the esoteric techniques based on Ezekiel's prophecy, see Vital, *Sha'ar Ma'amarei Rashbi* p. 58 at the top, the complete text *Hekhalot Rabbatei* and Vital's *Sha'arei Kedusha* 3:6.

7. THE HASIDIC MASTERS SOMETIMES REFER TO THIS PROCESS AS *RATZO VASH-OV*—"RUNNING AND RETURNING"—OR *YARIDAH KITZORECH ALIYAH*, WHICH MEANS "GOING DOWN FOR THE SAKE OF GOING UP." The phrase *ratzo vashov* means "running and returning" and comes from Ezekiel 1:14. In Hasidic literature this phrase was used to point to the principle of the

dynamic process of ascending and descending on the spiritual path. See, e.g., *Keter Shem Tov*, 1:24:2, 1:27:1, 1:59:2, 1:61:1, 1:77:4, and many more; *Tanya* 1:41:3, 1:50:2; *Likkutei Moharan* 4:9, 13:3, 13:4, 65:4, 78:2, 79:3, 269:1; *Kedushat Levi, Exodus, Mishpatim* 3, *inter alia*. In the classical Kabbalah texts there is a different but related principle called *mati velo mati* ("reaching and not reaching"). See *Zohar* 1:16b, 1:65a, 2:268a, 3:164a; *Etz Chayyim* 4:2:2, 7:1:6, 7:2:1–3. For a Hasidic variation on this concept, see *Tzava'at Ha-Rivash* 1:69. On the principle of *yeridah kitzorech aliyah*, see the sources cited above in Chapter 2, note 7.

8. THE SLONIMER REBBE ... EXPLICITLY TALKS ABOUT THE THREE CENTERS ... He comes back to the model of the three centers repeatedly throughout his published works. See, e.g. *Netivot Shalom* 1:147, 2:239, 2:281–284, 2:290, *inter alia*.

9. *ADONAI* IS THE FEMININE PRINCIPLE See *Sha'arei Orah* 1 (p.33); *Pardes Rimonim* 23:1 c.v. *Adonai*.

10. *ELOHIM* ALSO REPRESENTS THIS EMBODIED EXPRESSION OF PRESENCE See Chapter 2, note 16.

11. *YHVH* ... REPRESENTS THE INNER NATURE OF CREATION See Chapter 2, note 16.

12. WE ARE VERBALLY SAYING *ADONAI* ... BUT VISUALIZING AND INTENDING *YHVH* This is one of the most central contemplative practices of classical Kabbalah. See, e.g., the discussion of this technique in *Tanya, HaYichud VeHaemunah* 7, p. 82.

13. PRESENCE IS OUR SPEECH AND BEING IS THE SOUND OF OUR VOICE In classical Kabbalah the *sefirah* of *Malchut*, which is Presence, is associated with "speech" (*Pardes Rimonim* 23:4 c.v. *dibur*) and *Tiferet—*

what we are calling Being—is associated with "voice" (*Pardes Rimonim* 23:18 c.v. *kol*).

14. THE PRIMORDIAL SOURCE OF OUR VOICE IS THE DIVINE NAME *EHYH* WHICH IS ASSOCIATED WITH THE *SEFIRAH* OF *AYIN* The voice (*Tiferet*) comes directly from *Binah*, which has its primordial roots in *Chochmah* and ultimately in *Keter* or *Ayin* (see *Pardes Rimonim* 23:18 c.v. *kol*).

15. OUR BODIES ARE THE OPTIMAL ORGANS ... TO FEEL AND KNOW PRESENCE. THIS IS BECAUSE OUR BODIES *ARE* PRESENCE see Psalms 35:10; Job 19:26; *Sha'arei Orah*, 1:14a; *Zohar* 1:103a-b; *Likkutei Maharan*, 22:5; *Netivot Shalom* 1:147, 2:239, 2:281–284, 2:290. See also Chapter 2, note 15, 17 and 24. On the human being as an anatomical microcosm of the Divine names, see: *Zohar* 2:75b, 3:48a, 3:201a, 3:238b, 3:335a, 3:341a; *Zohar Chadash* 42; *Sha'areh Orah*, 1 (p. 2b); *Pardes Rimonim* 22:2; *Shenei Luchot HaBerit, Toldot Adam, Hakdamah* 1. On the radical nondual understanding of the relationship between the physical body, the soul, and the Divine in Lurianic Kabbalah, see Z. Ish-Shalom, *Radical Death: The Paradoxical Unity of Body, Soul and Cosmos in Lurianic Kabbalah* (Ph.D. Dissertation: Brandeis University, 2013), especially Chapter 4.

16. IN THE *SHEMA* THERE IS A BIG *AYIN* ... AND A BIG *DALET* ... The traditional way of understanding the large letters in the *Shema* is either to prevent a misreading that would change the meaning of the verse (if we misread the word "*Shema*" with an *aleph* instead of an *ayin*, it would mean "maybe" rather than "hear," and if we misread the word "*echad*" with a *reish* instead of a *dalet* it would mean "other"), or as a reference to the word "*Ayd*," "witness," as in to bear witness to God's unity (see *Leviticus Rabbah* 19:2; *Baal Haturim* and *Kli Yakar* on Deuteronomy 6:4). According to Lurianic Kabbalah, the large letters point to higher states of consciousness (e.g. see *Shaar Hakavanot, Kavanat Kriat Shema* 6). Also see R. Zvi Elimelekh of Dinov's

teaching on the nondual implications of the large *dalet* in *Bnei Yissaschar, Adar,* 2:8:10.

17. That the embodiment of the *ayd* principle expresses nondual knowledge of Being is also reflected in the fact that when the order of the letters are reversed the word *ayd* spells *da*, or "know," the imperative form of *da'at*.

18. HOWEVER, THIS VERSE CAN ALSO BE TRANSLATED: "TRUE SPEECH WILL ESTABLISH THE *WITNESS*" As far as I know, this insight does not appear in any prior texts. See the teaching on this verse from Proverbs 12:19 and its relationship to the *Shema* in *Zohar* 2:188a–b.

CHAPTER SEVEN

1. TRADITIONALLY OBSERVANT JEWS MARK THIS FIFTY-DAY PERIOD BETWEEN *PESACH* AND *SHAVUOT* BY COUNTING DOWN EACH DAY IN A PRACTICE CALLED *SEFIRAT HAOMER* See Leviticus 23:15–17; Deuteronomy 16:9.

2. THE RABBINIC TRADITION UNDERSTANDS THE EXPERIENCE OF REVELATION ON SINAI AS A MARRIAGE CEREMONY ... See *BT Taanit* 26b; *Song of Songs Rabbah* 3:2; *Netivot Shalom* 2:334.

3. IN THE TALMUD IT STATES THAT THE MOUNTAIN ... WAS USED AS A *CHUPPAH* See *BT Shabbat* 88a; *Shittah Mekubetzes Ketubot* 7a; *Tashbetz Katan* on *BT Shabbat* 88a.

4. THE TORAH SERVES AS A *KETUBAH* ... See Ibn Ezra on Exodus 25:15 c.v. *ve-natata*.

5. THE KABBALISTS UNDERSTOOD THESE FIFTY DAYS... TO BE THE MOST AUSPICIOUS TIME TO INTEGRATE ALL OF THE *SEFIROT* See *Netivot Shalom* 2:321.

6. THE "LOWER" SEVEN *SEFIROT* ARE CALLED THE "SEVEN DAYS OF CRE-ATION..." "DAYS" IS A CLASSIC CODE WORD FOR THE *SEFIROT*, USED EXTEN-SIVELY IN THE ZOHAR See, e.g., *Zohar* 1:247a, 2:89b, 2:186b, 3:94b, 3:298b. The Zohar also alludes to certain sections of the Bahir as also utilizing the word "days" as a reference to the *sefirot*. See *Zohar* 3:103b–104a and *Bahir* 57, 82, and 158.

7. EACH OF THESE SEVEN IS INCLUDED IN EACH OF THE OTHER SEVEN ... See *Netivot Shalom* 2:321.

8. THESE FIFTY DAYS OF INTEGRATION ... ARE UNDERSTOOD BY THE KAB-BALISTS TO BE THE MOST AUSPICIOUS TIME FOR WAKING DOWN ... *ITARUTA DE-LITATA* ... See R. Shneur Zalman of Liadi, *Likkutei Torah*, *Vayikra* 3:1 and *Emor* 35:2.

9. *ELOHIM* HAS TO DO WITH THE DIVINE QUALITY OF JUSTICE, OF *DIN* ... THE *SEFIRAH* OF *GEVURAH* See *Sha'arei Orah* 6 (p.138).

10. DIVINE RED LIGHT OF *GEVURAH* See *Pardes Rimonim* 10:3: גבור"ה: כלם פה אחד הסכימו שגוונה האור האדום "*Gevurah*: Everyone unanimously agrees that its color is a red light."

11. THE PRISTINE LIGHT OF *TIFERET* WITH ITS SUBTLE GREEN HUE... See *Pardes Rimonim* 10:3. Cordovero points out that in addition to green, there are several other colors ascribed to *Tiferet* in the Zohar, includ-ing purple and a mixture of red and white.

12. THE WORD "PENINA" APPEARS ONLY ONCE IN THE HEBREW BIBLE See 1 Samuel 1:2. The word *"penina"* also appears in Rabbinic literature in various ways. On the etymology of the name *Penina* meaning Pearl, see R. Menachem Azariah de Fano, *Gilgulei Neshamot* 30.

13. "NO ONE CAN SEE MY INNER NATURE AND LIVE" On my translation of *panai* as "inner nature," see *Sha'arei Kedushah* 3:6, where Chayyim

Vital states that "face" refers to the world of Atzilut, which is one of the most "inner" dimensions of the cosmos.

14. METOSCOPY ... WAS THE PARTICULAR GIFT OF ISAAC LURIA See Lawrence Fine, "The Art of Metoscopy: A Study in Isaac Luria's Charismatic Knowledge," *AJS Review* 11 (1986), 79–102.

15. *KAVOD* IS THE WORD THAT IS USED TO REFER TO THE PRESENCE THAT FILLS THE *MISHKAN* See Exodus 40:35 and Psalms 26:8.

16. THE NUMBER FIFTY, THE LETTER *NUN*, REPRESENTS WHOLENESS... The word Torah in singular form appears fifty times in the Torah (see *Rokeach* on *Deut.* 6:7). The redemption from Egypt is mentioned fifty times (*Zohar* 2:85b; 3:262a; *Netivot Shalom* 2:311; also see *Sefat Emet, Shabbat HaGadol* 5634, for how the fifty references to the Exodus correspond to the fifty sabbaths in every year). The number fifty represents the completion of *emunah*, "faith" (*Netivot Shalom* II: 235), and thus *emunah* corresponds with the *sefirah* of *Binah*, which represents the principle of Wholeness and the Pearl (see R. Zvi Hirsch of Ziditchov, *Sur Me-rah Va-aseh Tov*, p. 73, and my discussion of the Pearl below in Chapter 10, note 2). According to the Talmud, creation contains fifty levels of understanding (*BT Rosh HaShanah* 21b, *BT Nedarim* 38a). These fifty levels of understanding, in turn, correspond to the fifty times the redemption of Egypt is mentioned in the Torah (see Vilna Gaon, *Aderet Eliyahu, Balak*). In a reference to the fifty day period between Pesach and Shavuot, the *Midrash* notes that the apple takes fifty days to ripen, representing the principle of wholeness (see *Song of Songs Rabbah* 2:2). There were fifty golden hooks that attached the curtains in the sanctuary, which parallel the fifty times the word Torah is mentioned in the five books of Moses (See *Rokeach* on *Exodus* 26:6). There were a total of fifty letters inscribed on the stones (the *avnei shoham*) attached to the High Priest's vestments, representing the twelve tribes of Israel (*BT Sotah* 36a–b). The letter *nun* (numerical value of fifty) is also considered to be the letter of the

Messiah, based on the verse from *Psalms* 72:17: "Before the sun, his name is *Ye-non* [from *nun*]" (see *BT Sanhedrin* 98b).

17. THE PEARL REPRESENTS THE EMBODIMENT INTO MATURE HUMAN LIFE OF THE TWO SIDES OF THE ONE REALITY WHOSE ESSENCE IS EXPRESSED BY THE PRINCESS PRESENCE My use of the term "Pearl" to signify the maturational process of the Princess Presence is based on: 1) my embodied experience of this Presence, which feels viscerally Pearly; 2) my understanding of the relationship between the Hebrew words *penima* and *penina* (as explained in Chapter 7) and the relationship between the image of the Pearl and the *sefirah* of *Binah* (see the beginning of Chapter 8 and the notes there, and also see below, Chapter 10, note 2) and 3) A. H. Almaas' use of the same term in his book *The Pearl Beyond Price* (Diamond Books, 1988) and my experience of this aspect through my personal work in the Diamond Approach. While many traditions utilize the term "Pearl" to describe various spiritual processes and realizations, the use of this term to specifically denote the maturation of the individual consciousness, including its functional and relational capacities, seems to be unique to the Diamond Approach.

18. THE FIRST TIME I RECOGNIZED THE PRINCESS PRESENCE ... WAS AFTER ENGAGING A PRAYER PRACTICE OF TALKING TO GOD The practice I was engaging at the time was based on R. Nachman of Bratzlov's *hitbodedut* practice. See *Likkutei Moharan* 1:52, 2:11.

CHAPTER EIGHT

1. FORTY IS THE REQUIRED VOLUME OF THE *MIKVAH* See *BT Eruvin* 4b.

2. THE NUMBER FORTY AND THE LETTER *MEM* ALSO REPRESENT THE WOMB See *Etz Chayyim* 39:5; *Sefer HaArachim Chabad, Otiot,* letter *mem,* p. 176 (Kehot Publication Society, Brooklyn, NY).

3. IN THE JUBILEE YEAR ALL PROPERTY WOULD RETURN BACK TO ITS ORIGI-
NAL OWNER, INCLUDING SLAVES ... See Leviticus 25:8–13.

4. THE NUMBER FIFTY IS ASSOCIATED IN THE KABBALISTIC TRADITION WITH
THE *SEFIRAH* OF *BINAH* See *Pardes Rimonim* 13:1; *Nitzotzei Zohar* on
Zohar Chadash, at the beginning of *Parshat Yitro* (*milu'im* 124:72ff);
Etz Chayyim 39:5; Chayyim Vital, *Likkutei Torah, Va-etchanan*, p.
184 (Vilna 1879). On the relationship between the Pearl and *Binah*,
see below, Chapter 10, note 2.

5. SHE IS KNOWN AS THE CELESTIAL WOMB, THE CELESTIAL MOTHER ...
THE CODE TERMS JUBILEE AND LIVING WATERS See *Sha'arei Orah* 8 (pp.
180-181) and *Pardes Rimonim* 43:3. On the womb of *Binah* and its
relation to the Divine name *EHYH*, see *Etz Chayyim* 16:3, 35:2; *Adir
Ba-marom* 90a. On *Binah* as the *Imah Ila'ah*, see Proverbs 2:3; *Zohar*
3:85a, 3:98a.

6. *BINAH* ... IS ALSO ASSOCIATED WITH THE RITUAL OF IMMERSING IN A *MIK-
VAH* The Divine name associated with *Binah* is *EHYH*, which is also
the name associated with immersion in the *mikvah*. See *Shaar Haka-
vanot, Inyan Tevilah Erev Shabbat* (Ashlag, Tel Aviv 5722) p. 25,
Shaar Ruach HaKodesh (Ashlag, Tel Aviv 5723) p. 36, *Shnei Luchot
HaBrit, Shaar HaOtiot, Kedushah* 1:168a, *Sha'arey Gan Eden, Shaar
HaOtiot, Mem* (95a), *Keter Shem Tov* 2, *Sefer Baal Shem Tov, Yitro*
11, R. Menachem Mendel of Vitebsk, *Pri HaAretz* on *Lech Lecha*;
Vilna Gaon on *Tikkunei Zohar* 19 (37a) "Inun;" *Likkutei Halachot,
Yoreh Deah, Melichah* 1:4.

7. FOR A *MIKVAH* TO BE KOSHER ACCORDING TO JEWISH LAW... For the *halakhic* (legal) requirements for a kosher *mikvah*, see *Mishnah Torah,
Hilchot Mikva'ot*; *Shulchan Aruch, Yoreh De'ah, Hilchot Mikvaot*.

8. IN THE HEBREW TRADITION, THE *MIKVAH* IS ALSO ASSOCIATED WITH
YHVH... See *Mishnah Yoma* 8:9: "Rabbi Akiva says: 'How fortunate

are you Israel—before whom are you purified? Who purifies you? Your Father in heaven. As it says: 'I will throw pure water on you and you will be purified.' (Ezekiel 36:25). And it says, '*YHVH* is the *mikvah* of Israel' (Jeremiah 17:13)." Also see *Bnei Yissaschar, Elul,* 1:15; *Tishrei,* 1:3, 3:2; *Adar,* 3:6.

9. ANOTHER TERM THE KABBALISTS ASSOCIATE WITH *BINAH* IS *TESHUVAH* *Zohar* 1:79b, 3:122a; *Sha'arei Orah* 8 (p.171); *Pardes Rimonim* 43:3; *Bnei Yissaschar, Adar,* 6:3; *Avodat Yisrael, Yom Sheni Shel Pesach "Miyom Havi'achem."* Also see the sources listed in the next note.

10. THIS PRIMORDIAL LIGHT IS EXPLICITLY REFERRED TO AS THE *OLAM HA-TESHUVAH*... See *Maor Ve-shemesh, Toldot,* p. 38 (Warsaw, 1859); *Magen Avraham, Chayei Sarah,* p. 27 (Lublin, 1886); R. Avraham HaCohen of Radomsk, *Chesed Le-Avraham, Chukat,* p. 351 (Pietrokov, 1893).

11. TALMUDIC TEACHINGS ON COMMANDMENTS THAT ARE "BETWEEN US AND GOD" AND... See *BT Yoma* 85b, 87a.

12. IT IS A STATE ALSO REFERRED TO IN THE TALMUD AS *TOCHO KE'VARO*... See *BT Berachot* 28a.

13. ACCORDING TO THE RABBINIC TRADITION, WHEN WE DO *TESHUVAH* OUT OF LOVE, ALL OF OUR PAST SINS ARE "TRANSFORMED INTO MERITS ..." See *BT Yoma* 86b; *Etz Chayyim* 49:8.

14. IT IS A TRANSLATION OF THE WORD *CHET*, WHICH MEANS, "TO MISS THE MARK" See Strong's Hebrew Lexicon #2399 and #2398.

15. THIS IS WHY ENTERING INTO THE REALM OF *TESHUVA* IS ABLE TO TRANSFORM REALITY, TRANSFORM THE PAST, IN A MAGICAL, MYSTERIOUS WAY This happens through feeling our remorse deeply and engaging *teshuva* out of love. This awakens our inner messianic light (see my discus-

sion of this principle in Chapter 10 below), which brings us to essential pleasure and wholeness. On this process, see R. Tzadok HaCohen of Lublin, *Tzidkat Hatzadik*, 153:1: ‏וע"י הצער והעג"נ שיש לו בנקודת הלב‎ ‏מעונותיו עי"ז מתעורר תוקף נקודת משיח הגנוזה בו ומאיר לו ... וזהו הסימן על‎ ‏העג"נ שנתקבל לפניו ית' כאשר בא עי"ז לעונג דהיינו ג"ע והיינו שמאיר לו מנקודת‎ ‏משיח דר"ל השלימות‎ "Through the suffering and aggravation that he has in the point of his heart from his transgressions, the Messianic Point that is hidden within him is strongly awakened and illuminates him... and the sign that his aggravation was received before God, is when through this he experiences pleasure, which is the Garden of Eden; that is, that the Messianic Point illuminates him, that is the Wholeness."

CHAPTER NINE

1. KEEP ALLOWING IT TO LAND, LIKE A FEATHER, SETTLING ON A COTTON BALL ... This description and the practice more broadly derive from Father Thomas Keating's instructions for Centering Prayer. See Thomas Keating, *Open Mind, Open Heart: The Contemplative Dimension of the Gospel* (New York: Continuum, 1986) p. 110.

2. IN THE KABBALISTIC TRADITION, IT IS REFERRED TO WITH THE TERM *OLAM HA-AHAVAH*... See R. Zev Wolf of Zhitomir, *Or Ha-Meir, Lech Lecha*, p. 10 (Warsaw, 1883); R. Aharon of Karlin, *Beit Aharon, Likkutim*, pp. 39–40 (Brody, 1873); R. Aharon of Zhitomir, *Toldot Aharon, Bechukotai*, p. 16 (1817).

3. THE WORD *ALL* MEANS THAT EVEN MURDERERS ARE EMBRACED IN THIS LOVE... See R. Aharon of Karlin's reading of the verse in *Proverbs* 10:12: "Love covers all transgressions," in *Beit Aharon, Likkutim*, p. 39.

4. Furthermore, there is a clarity and an objectivity to this love
See R. Zev Wolf of Zhitomir, *Or Ha-Meir, Lech Lecha*, p. 10 (Warsaw, 1883): הוא עולם בהיר ... עולם האהבה, "The dimension of Love ... is a dimension of clarity."

5. This first line of the *Shema* declares the union of dual and non-dual, form and formless ... See the *Sefat Emet*'s non-dual reading of the *Shema*: "The proclamation of oneness that we declare each day in saying *Shema Yisra'el* needs to be understood in its true meaning. It is entirely clear to me... based on the writings of the great kabbalists... that the meaning of "Y-H-W-H is One" is not that He is the only God, negating other gods (though this too is true!), but that there is a deeper truth: there is no being other than God. This is true even though it seems otherwise to most people.... Everything that exists in the world, spiritual and physical, is God Himself. It was only because of the contraction [*tzimtzum*], willed by God that holiness descended rung after rung, until actual physical things were created out of it. These things are true without a doubt. Because of this, every person can be joined to God from any place, through the holiness that exists within every single thing, even corporeal things. You only have to be negated (that is, to transcend the ego-self) in the spark of holiness." See Yehudah Leib Alter of Ger, *Otzar Michtavim U'ma'amarim* (Jerusalem: Machon Gachalei Eish, 1986) pp. 75–76. I am using Arthur Green's translation of this passage from A. Green, *Judaism's Ten Best Ideas* (Woodstock, VT: Jewish Lights, 2014) pp. 90–91.

6. The realm of Divine Love is the realm of grace, the realm of *chayn*... The word *chayn* is often associated with love (*Chesed*) in the sacred Hebrew texts. See, e.g., Esther 2:17; *Pardes Rimonim* 8:16: חן... נשפע מהחסד "*Chayn*... flows from *Chesed*" Cf. *Ibid.*, 9:1. It is also a quality that the scriptures indicate is given as an act of grace from God. See, e.g., "*chayn* and *kavod* are given by *YHVH*" (Ps. 84:12). Also see *Pri Etz Chayyim, Sha'ar Ha-Vidui*, 10:7, where Chayyim Vital associates *chayn* with the *sefirah* of *Binah*: כי חן בא ... מצד הבינה

"*Chayn* comes from the side of *Binah*." This correlates with my discussion associating *chayn* with the principle of *nach*, or "repose," which is associated with the Sabbath. The Sabbath, in turn, is also sometimes associated with *Binah* (when in the aspect of *Shabbat Ha-Gadol* or *Shabbat Shabbaton*)—see *Pardes Rimonim* 23:21 c.v. *shabbat*. Furthermore, both *Binah* and *Shabbat* represent the realm of sensual pleasure. See *Kedushat Levi, Kedushot for Purim, Kedusha Shlishit*, 4, where *Binah* is associated with *Olam Ha-Oneg*—the dimension of pleasure. See the note below titled "*Shabbos* is meant to be ... a day of sensual pleasure."

7. IF YOU REVERSE THE LETTERS ... IT SPELLS THE HEBREW WORD "*NOACH*" See Gen. 6:8:יהוה בעיני חן מצא ונח "And *Noach* found favor (*chayn*) in the eyes of *YHVH*."

8. *SHABBOS* REPRESENTS THE UNION OF *MALCHUT* WITH *TIFERET* See, e.g., *Zohar* 1:175a–b and many more. For more sources and a thorough analysis of this topic, see Elliot Ginsburg, *The Sabbath in Classical Kabbalah* (Albany, NY: SUNY Press, 2012).

9. IN THE HUMAN REALM, THIS UNION IS PERFORMED THROUGH SEXUAL INTERCOURSE ON *SHABBOS* EVE ... See R. Meir Ibn Gabbai, *Tola'at Ya'akov* 49b. On the contemplative methods of this sexual practice, see *Zohar* 2:11b and especially R. Avraham Azulai's commentary on this passage (see *Or Ha-Chammah*, ad loc.): "He focused on *Tiferet*, and his wife on *Malchut* [*Shekhinah*]. His union was to join *Shekhinah*; she focused correspondingly on being *Shekhinah* and uniting with her husband *Tiferet*." This passage is also cited by Daniel Matt in his compilation Zohar (Paulist Press, 1983), pp. 236–237.

10. ACCORDING TO JEWISH TRADITION, SEX IS PARTICULARLY ENCOURAGED See *BT Ketubot* 62a and *Baba Kama* 82a.

11. THE ROOT OF BOTH OF THESE WORDS FOR "REST" [*MENUCHA* AND *VAYANACH*] IS *NACH* OR *NOACH*... See *Tikkunei Zohar* 55a:5 and 140a:2 where *Noach* is explicitly compared to *Shabbat*: נח דאיהו שבת "Noah is *Shabbat*." Also see the *Sefat Emet's* interpretation of this passage *Sefat Emet, Parshat Noah*; *Likkutei Moharan* II, 2:5: בחינת שבת שהיא בחינת נח... "The aspect of *Shabbat* is the aspect of Noah."

12. *SHABBOS* IS MEANT TO BE A DAY ... OF SENSUAL PLEASURE ... See Isaiah 58:13; *BT Shabbat* 118a; *Zohar* 2:47a-b; *Likkutei Moharan* 57:6. The principle of sensual pleasure also connects to the principle of *da'at*, sensual intimacy. *Shabbat* is thus also recognized as a day of *da'at* and of the magnification of *da'at*. See *B'nei Yisaschar, Nisan,* 4:6 c.v. *al derekh haremez*; *ibid., Nisan* 3:11. *Da'at* in turn is also the source of the essential quality of Love. See, e.g., R. Zvi Hirsch of Ziditchov, *Sur Merah Va-aseh Tov*, p. 56: דעת הוא שורש ומקור האהבה "*Da'at* is the root and source of Love."

13. SIMILAR IN FORM TO THE CENTERING PRAYER PRACTICE AS TAUGHT BY FATHER THOMAS KEATING See his book, *Open Mind, Open Heart: The Contemplative Dimension of the Gospel* (New York: Continuum, 1986).

14. A SIMILAR PRACTICE ALSO APPEARS IN THE HASIDIC TRADITION See, e.g., R. Kalonymus Kalman Shapira's meditation instructions, translated and cited in Kalonymus Kalman Shapira, *To Heal the Soul,* trans. by Yehoshua Starrett (Oxford: Rowman and Littlefield, 2004) pp. xxix–xxx.

15. THE MYSTICAL TEXTS STATE EXPLICITLY THAT *SHABBOS* IS THE DAY OF DIVINE LOVE See, e.g., R. Elimelekh of Lizhensk, *Noam Elimelekh, Ki-Tavo* 1:1: שבת היא בחינת אהבה "*Shabbos* is the aspect of love." Also cf. *ibid., Vayigash* 1:3 and *Vayeshev* 5:2.

16. THE ZOHAR STATES IN ARAMAIC, *RAZA DE-SHABBAT* ... *Zohar* 2:135a–b.

17. THE TALMUD TEACHES THAT ON *SHABBOS* THE SOUL IS ENDOWED WITH... AN "ADDITIONAL SOUL ..." See *BT Beitzah* 16a and Rashi's commentary there; *BT Ta'anit* 27b; also see Nachmanides' commentary on Genesis 2:3 and Exodus 31:13.

18. WE ARE TRAINING FOR THE "DAY THAT IS ALWAYS *SHABBOS* ..."A TRADITIONAL REFERENCE FOR THE MESSIANIC AGE ... See *BT Sanhedrin* 97a; *Midrash Tehillim* 92:1; *Noam Elimelekh, Yitro* 5:1; *Kedushat Levi, Ki Tisa* 10, *Va-etchanan* 28.

CHAPTER TEN

1. I CHOSE DEATH See the similar description by Abraham Abulafia, which accurately reflects my personal experience:

ודע כי כל מה שיתחזק אצלך השפע השכלי הנכבד, יחלשו איבריך החיצוניים
והפנימיים, ויתחיל כל גופך להשתער שערה חזקה עד מאד, עד שתתחשוב בעצמך
שעל כל פנים תמות בעת ההיא, כי יתפרד נפשך מגופך מרוב שמחה בהשגתה
ובהכרותה מה שהכרת. ותבחר מות מחיים בדעתך כי זה המות קורה לגוף
(בלבד), ובסיבה זו תחיה הנפש תחיית המתים לעולמי עד. ואז תדע שהגעת אל
מעלת קבלת השפע

"Know that as the glorious ethereal influx strengthens, your external and internal limbs will weaken and your entire body will begin to tremble intensively, until you will begin to think that you are about to die ... and you will choose death over life ... and then you will know that you have arrived at the level of receiving the Divine influx" [Abulafia, *Chayei Olam Habah* (Jerusalem, 1999) p. 147].

2. THE EXPERIENCE OF THE PEARL WAS REALLY THE INTEGRATION OF *BINAH* INTO THE PRESENCE BODY ... In some texts the image of the Pearl is associated with *Binah*. See, e.g., R. Pinchus HaLevi Horowitz, *Sefer Hafla'ah* (Offenbach 1787) on *BT Ketubot* 2a, commenting on Prov-

erbs 31:10: רחוק מפנינים מכרה שאי אפשר לקנות אותה אפילו בעולם הבא
שנקרא פנינים "'Her price is far above pearls'; for it is impossible
to acquire her even in the World-to-Come [*Olam Ha-bah*], which is
called 'Pearls' [*peninim*—plural for *penina*]." The phrase *Olam Habah* (the "world-to-come" or the "world-that-is-coming") is a common
code-term for the *sefirah* of *Binah* in Kabbalah texts (see, e.g., *Zohar*
3:290b, 1:92a-b; *Sha'arei Orah* 8, p. 174). Also see R. Dov Baer of
Mezeritch, *Or Torah, Likkutim*. In his reading of Kohelet 12:12 he
describes the Pearl as being located in the "Sea of *Chochmah*," an
allusion to *Binah*, which is the "Sea" that flows out of *Chochmah*
(ולמצוא פנינים מים החכמה). This last text can also be translated as defining the word "pearls" as the "waters of *Chochmah*," which can also
be understood to be an allusion to *Binah*, commonly referred to in the
Kabbalah texts as various kinds of water. She is the water that flows
from *Chochmah* (*Be'er Sheva, Rechovot HaNahar, Yam Ila'ah*, etc.
See *Sha'arei Orah* 8). The Pearl is also understood to be a reference
to beginnings (see *Numbers Rabbah* 6:1; *Shnei Luchot HaBerit, Naso,
Torah Ohr* 10), which correlates with *Binah* since she is situated at
the beginning of the emanation of the Tree of Life, emanating out
of *Chochmah*, the primordial "beginning." Furthermore, the *Midrash*
describes the Pearl as illuminating the belly of the fish that swallowed
Jonah. See, e.g. *Pirkei Derabbi Eliezer* 10:1: "R' Meir said: there was
a single pearl suspended in the belly of the fish which gave light for
Jonah like the sun at its strength in the midday and Jonah could see
everything that was in the sea and the deeps as it says (Ps. 97:11):
'A light is sown for the righteous...'" Also cf. *Yalkut Shimoni, Nach*
550:2; *Ein Yaakov, Baba Batra* 8:22. The Hebrew word for "fish,"
dag, yields the numerical value of 7, which represents the seven lower
sefirot from *Chesed* to *Malchut* (these seven are called in Kabbalah
the "Children of *Binah*"). Thus, in this text, the Pearl that illuminates
the *dag*—the seven *sefirot*—can also be an allusion to *Binah*. Furthermore, see the description of the formation of *Binah* outlined in
Zohar 1:15a–b, where *Chochmah* is likened to a silkworm forming
a cocoon around itself. This cocoon encases the seed of *Chochmah*

(The Point of Light) and the womb of *Binah* is formed out of the essential substance of *Chochmah*. This cocoon serves as the primordial source of the human body and soul (as well as for the seven "days" of creation, the *sefirot*), and its developmental formation is similar to the developmental process of a Pearl, which is constructed as a gradual layering of its own substance upon itself. See Matt, *Zohar*, p. 209, note titled "The silkworm…." Finally, see the parable of the "good, pleasant, pretty and *whole*" princess in *Bahir* 54, where the King places a window between himself and his daughter. The phrase שם חלון בינו לבינה "He placed a window between himself and his daughter," can also be read "He placed a window between himself and *Binah*," referring to the "whole princess," (בת מלך שלימה), i.e. the Pearl. Cf. *Bahir* 63, where *Binah* is again referred to as the "Princess" that contains all.

3. IN THE ANCIENT TEXTS THEY CALL IT THE *NEKUDAH*, WHICH LITERALLY MEANS "THE POINT" The term *Nekudah*—point—appears in the Zohar as a reference to *Chochmah* over 100 times, making it a central descriptor of this essential aspect. See, e.g., *Zohar* 2:239a. The term also appears often throughout later kabbalistic and Hasidic texts. See, e.g., *Etz Chayyim* 5:5:3, 43:3:1: נקודה חדא הנקרא עדן שהוא חכמה "A single point that is called *Eden*, which is *Chochmah*;" *Pardes Rimonim* 4:2:2; *Magid Devarav L'yaakov* 127:3; *Tanya, Iggeret HaTeshuvah* 4:3; *Ibid., Iggeret HaKodesh* 5:1. A similar term is *Nitzotz*, which means "spark." While this term does not exclusively refer to the *sefirah* of *Chochmah*, it is an alternate designation used by Kabbalists to refer to the essential identity of the soul. See, for example, the *Sefat Emet*'s usage of this term above in his letter to his children (see Chapter 9, note 5), where it clearly denotes the essential self, revealed once the ego-self is nullified. The term *Nitzotz*, or spark, is also the preferred term used by Isaac Luria, the meaning of which I examine in great detail elsewhere. See Z. Ish-Shalom, *Radical Death: The Paradoxical Unity of Body, Soul and Cosmos in Lurianic Kabbalah* (Ph.D. Dissertation: Brandeis University, 2013).

4. In Kabbalistic code, it is also called the Beginning See Psalms 111:10: *Reishit Chochmah* "*Chochmah* is the *Beginning.*" Also see *Zohar* 1:15a–b, *inter alia*; *Pardes Rimonim* 23:20 c.v. *Reishit*.

5. It is called the seed. This Point of Light ... impregnates *Binah* See *Zohar* 1:15a-b. For a list of more sources describing this process, see Matt, *Zohar* (Paulist Press, 1983) pp. 208–209.

6. This seed is birthed into manifestation which are the lower seven *sefirot* See *Zohar* 1:15a.

7. The souls are born and created in *Binah* See *Zohar* 2:95b; *Pardes Rimonim* 8:22. Also see the following statement attributed to the kabbalist Isaac the Blind: "I heard in my master's name that the place of the souls is in *Teshuvah*, which is in the *sefirah* named *Binah*. They originate there and then move down to the *Cause* (*Malchut*), and then they go forth and attach themselves to the human body" [*Perush Ha-aggadot Le-Rebbi Ezra*, cited in I. Tishby, "The Doctrine of Man in the Zohar" in *Essential Papers on Kabbalah*, ed. L Fine (NYU Press, 1995) p. 132]. Also see Nachmanides' commentary on Genesis 2:7.

8. Kabbalists use the Hebrew term "*Yesh*" to refer to *Chochmah* See *Sha'arei Orah* 9 (p. 185); *Pardes Rimonim* 23:10 c.v. *Yesh*.

9. *Chochmah* is the first expression of reality that can be called "existence" It is thus also called in the texts the *Nekudat Ha-Yesh*, the "Point of Existence." On the use of this phrase, see R. Abraham Isaac Ha-Cohen Kook, *Shemonah Kevatzim* 4:121:1 and 4:122:1: נקודת היש הנשמתית של האדם "The Point of Existence of the human soul." Also see *Ma'or Einayim*, *Kedoshim*: התחלת היש שהוא הגבול נרמז ונקרא נקודה "The beginning of existence ... is called a Point." There is an interesting correlation between my experience of the Point and its association with *Chochmah* consciousness, and with what A.H. Almaas also

calls the point of Existence [see A. H. Almaas, *The Point of Existence* (Shambhala, 2000)]. In his book, Almaas points out what he feels are similarities between his own experience of the Point and descriptions of experiences found in the works of Nisargadatta Maharaj and Bernadette Roberts (See *ibid.*, pp. 439–455). My own experience of the Point correlates most closely with the following description by the Christian mystic Thomas Merton:

> At the center of our being is a point of nothingness which is untouched by sin and by illusion, a point of pure truth, a point or spark which belongs entirely to God, which is never at our disposal, from which God disposes of our lives, which is inaccessible to the fantasies of our own mind or the brutalities of our own will. This little point of nothingness and of absolute poverty is the pure glory of God in us. It is so to speak his name written in us, as our poverty ... It is like a pure diamond, blazing with the invisible light of heaven. It is in everybody, and if we could see it we would see these billions of points of light coming together in the face and blaze of a sun that would make all the darkness and cruelty of life vanish completely ... I have no program for this seeing. It is only given. But the gate of heaven is everywhere [Thomas Merton, *Conjectures of a Guilty Bystander* (Image Books: 1968), 158].

10. CHOCHMAH IS THUS THE FIRST LIGHT THAT EMERGES OUT OF NOTHINGNESS OR EMPTINESS See *Zohar* 1:15a–b.

11. WHICH IS TRANSLATED BY THE KABBALISTS AS "CHOCHMAH COMES FROM AYIN" See *Tikkunei Zohar* 135a:1; *Zohar Chadash, Sifra Tanina* 62; *Pardes Rimonim* 1:8, 5:1.

12. EXPERIENTIAL CONTACT WITH THE ... DIMENSION OF NOTHINGNESS PRECEDED... THE POINT OF LIGHT... See Dov Baer of Mezeritch, *Or Torah, Likkutim* (Lublin, 1909) p. 105: כי אין להשיג החכמה אלא אם כן עשה עצמו

כאין מוחלט "It is not possible to attain *Chochmah* unless he makes himself like an absolute nothing."

13. ONE HASIDIC TEXT—*NETIVOT SHALOM* BY THE SLONIMER REBBE ... See *Netivot Shalom* 2:257, *inter alia*.

14. THE HEBREW WORD FOR "STAR," *KOCHAV*, AND ITS MYSTICAL SIGNIFI-CANCE See *Zohar* 3:282a; *Zohar Chadash Balak* 98-102. On *Kochav* as the Messiah, see Maharal, *Netzach Yisrael* 61:5: קרא מלך המשיח כוכב "He called the King Messiah a star." For more sources see below, Chapter 10, notes 20 and 22.

15. SUCH AS A KING OR A PRIEST... See Exodus 30:22-25; Leviticus 4:3; Numbers 35:25; 1 Samuel 24:6. The term *Mashiach* also appears several times in the Hebrew Bible to describe someone endowed with a sacred mission, such as the non-Jewish king Koresh (Isaiah 45:1) or the prophet Isaiah (Isaiah 61:1).

16. THE MESSIAH ... REPRESENTS THE REALIZATION OF *CHOCHMAH* CON-SCIOUSNESS ... See R. Tzadok HaCohen of Lublin, *Tzidkat Ha-Tzadik*, 153:1: ונמצא בכל נפש פרטי נקודת השתדלותו אל התכלית האמיתי הוא נקודת משיח "In every individual soul there is a point [i.e. *Chochmah*] of aspiration for the true purpose—this is the messianic point." This description seems similar to the principle of *bodhicitta* in Buddhism, which is the intrinsic aspiration for awakening that is latent in all beings [see Norman Fischer, *Training in Compassion: Zen Teachings on the Practice of Lojong* (Shambhala, 2013) p. 11]. Also see the quote from Khedrup Norsang Gyātso cited below in note 19 correlating *bodhicitta* with the flow of *amrita*, which also correlates with *Choch-mah* consciousness. Also see Tanya, *Iggeret HaKodesh* 4:1: ולכן משיח בא ... לכללות ישראל והיא גילוי בחינת נקודה פנימית הכללית "Therefore the Messiah comes... to the totality of Israel and it is the revelation of the aspect of the collective inner point."

17. I WAS AMAZED HOW THE SUBTLE SENSATION IS FELT SO DISTINCTLY FLOW-
ING DOWN THE HEAD, FACE AND OVER THE ENTIRE BODY Abraham Abulafia describes an experience very similar to my own:

ויתחיל כל גופך להיותו נרתע ורעדה נופלת על כל אבריך, ואתה מפחד פחד
אלהים ויראת יי תכסך, ותרגיש בעצמך רוח נוסף מעורר אותך ומחזקך ועובר
על כל גופך ומהנה אותך, ונראה לך בו שש[ופע] עליך מראשך ועד רגליך שמן
אפרסמון פעם אחת או יותר, ושמחת ונהנית

"And your entire body will begin to spasm and all your limbs will
tremble … and you will feel an additional spirit arouse and strength-
en you and it will pass over your entire body and give you pleasure.
It will seem to you that a fragrant oil is flowing upon you from your
head to your feet, one time or more, and you will rejoice and take
great pleasure" (Abraham Abulafia, *Otzar Eden Ha-Ganuz,* section
9).

18. THE CHANNEL OF OILS CAN ONLY BE OPENED ONCE THE DIMENSION OF
CHOCHMAH IS ACCESSED Aside from signifying messianic consciousness, the word "oil" (שמן) is also a code-term for the ethereal fluid that
flows from *Chochmah* (and originates, according to some texts, from
Keter) through the rest of the *sefirot*. See *Zohar* 3:34a: שמן עלאה דנגיד
ולא פסיק לעלמין דשריא בגו חכמה עלאה "The celestial *Oil* that flows and
does not cease forever, that dwells within the celestial *Chochmah,*"
and Cf. *Zohar* 3:39a; *Pardes Rimonim* 7:2: וכן ע"י הצינור הזה נמשך
השמן הטוב על הרא"ש יורד על הזקן זקן אהרן … שעיקר השמן הוא מהכתר ע"י
החכמה אל הכהן איש החסד "And therefore through this channel the
good *oil* flows onto the *head* [i.e. *Chochmah*], descending to the
beard, Aaron's beard… because most of the *oil* is from *Keter* by way
of *Chochmah* to the priest, [who is called] man of *Chesed;*" Cf. *Noam
Elimelekh, Likkutei Shoshana* 12, where he alludes to the celestial oil
flowing down from the head to the beard. These last two passages in
Pardes Rimonim and *Noam Elimelekh* are clearly echoing the verse
in *Psalms* 133:2 ("It is like the good oil upon the head, coming down

upon the beard; even Aaron's beard, that comes down upon the collar of his garments"), an older Midrashic interpretation of this verse (see *Otzar Midrashim, Eileh Toldot Aharon Ve-Moshe*, 4), and a passage in the Zohar that mentions *oil* descending from the head down to the beard (*Zohar* 3:209a). Also see *Pardes Rimonim* 8:19: שמן הוא מצד החכמה "*Oil* is from the side of *Chochmah*," and the extended explanation of the flow of *oil* in *Ibid.*, 20:1, and his discussion of the difference between a "Son of oil" and "Son of Freedom" and how *oil* derives from the "right" side of the Tree of Life in *Ibid.*, 23:2 c.v. "*Ben Shemen*," and ultimately descends into the testicles where the *oil* is "cooked" and released through the phallus, or *Yesod*, see *Ibid.*, 23:7, c.v. "*zeitim.*" The principle that the *oil* and the semen are one in the same substance is also mentioned by Cordovero in *Ibid.* 23:11 c.v. "*ketuvim stam.*" Also see *Magid Devarav Le-Yaakov* 127:1: שמן הוא חכמה כנודע "*Oil* is *Chochmah*, as is known." Cf. *Ibid.*, 134:2; *Kedushat Levi, Vayetzei*, 2: ויצק שמן על ראשה רצה לומר שהמשיך למעלה ההוא שמן כינוי לחכמה עליונה "'And *oil* was poured on his head' (Gen. 28:18)—this means that he drew down from above that *oil* that is a moniker for the celestial *Chochmah*." For similar formulations as the above texts, see Vilna Gaon on *Sefer Yetzirah* 1:7:2 (Warsaw 1884); *Kedushat Levi, Kedushot Chanukah* 5:18; *Tzidkat HaTzadik* 147:1; *Likkutei Moharan, Likkutei Tinyana* 5:2; *Sichot HaRan* 261:1; *Divrei Emet, Tetzaveh* 2; *Ohev Yisrael, Bereishit*, p. 5 (Zhitomir, 1861); *ibid.*, *Tetzaveh* (at the beginning). The *oil* itself is ultimately an ethereal fluid-like substance that flows through all the *sefirot* in the Tree of Life (originating in *Keter* and the "right-side" via *Chochmah*) and manifests in different ways in our consciousness and experience depending on the *sefirah* it is flowing through. The particular quality of *oil* that descends down the head via *Chochmah* is termed the "Good oil" (*shemen ha-tov*), whereby the term "good" signifies "light" or "luminous." See *Pardes Rimonim*, Ch. 23:21 c.v. *Shemen*.

19. SIMILAR TO THE TEACHINGS ON *AMRITA* IN THE VAJRAYANA TRADITION... See, e.g., the following passage from Khedrup Norsang Gyātso that

correlates the flow of *amrita* from the crown *chakra* with *bodhicitta*: "From this action [a meditative action] the nectar stream of the *bodhicitta* fluid descends from the crown to the sixteen petals of the forehead *chakra*. The resulting bliss divides into the joys of body, speech, mind, and gnōsis." [Khedrup Norsang Gyātso, *Ornament of Stainless Light: An Exposition of the Kālacakra Tantra* (Somerville, MA: Wisdom Publications, 2004) p. 257]. This correlates with the text cited above by R. Tzadok HaCohen that frames *Chochmah* consciousness and the Point in a manner similar to *bodhicitta*. See above, note "The Messiah...." For similar expressions in Vajrayana texts, see Adrian Snodgrass, *The Symbolism of the Stupa* (Delhi, India: Motilal Banarsidass, 1992) p. 300; Anyen Rinpoche, *The Union of Dzogchen and Bodhicitta*, trans. Allison Graboski (Ithaca, NY: Snow Lion Publications, 2006) p. 196; Khedrup Norsang Gyātso, *Ornament of Stainless Light: An Exposition of the Kālacakra Tantra* (Somerville, MA: Wisdom Publications, 2004), pp. 258–259. I am indebted to Igor Guisti for pointing me to these sources. See his forthcoming doctoral dissertation on the topic of *amrita* for more sources and also for an analysis of similar descriptions in other Buddhist lineages.

20. THE ANCIENT COMMENTARIES UNDERSTOOD THIS VERSE [NUM. 24:17] TO BE AN ALLUSION TO THE MESSIAH See *Or HaChayyim* on Numbers 24:17; *Otzar Midrashim, Midrashei Mashiach* 3–4. *Otzar Midrashim, Perek R. Shimon Bar Yochai* 7; *Netzach Yisrael* 61:5; *Noam Elimelech, Vayigash* 6–7.

21. *HAMEIVIN YAVIN* A common phrase found in the mystical texts meant to allude to a secret teaching.

22. STAR AND KING ARE BOTH ALLUSIONS TO THE MESSIAH... For sources referring to star as the Messiah, see above, note 20. For sources referring to king as a reference to the Messiah, see *Da'at Zekenim* on Genesis 49:10; *Rashi* on Isaiah 28:16; *Lamentations Rabbah* 1:51; *Midrash Mishlei* 19:3; *Pesikta Rabbatei* 36:1; *Mishnah Torah, Kings*

and Wars 11:4; Maharal, *Gevurot HaShem* 18:2; Maharal, *Netzach Yisrael* 22:6, 29:6, 38:2; 44:3, 47:12; *Zohar* 1:237b; *Etz Chayyim* 29:5:1. Also see Maharal, *Netzach Yisrael* 61:5: קרא מלך המשיח כוכב "He called the King Messiah a star." Cf. *Likkutei Moharan* 6:7: דרך כוכב מיעקב בחינת מלך "A star goes forth from Jacob—[this is the] aspect of king."

23. *KEDUMAH* ... IS ALSO A TECHNICAL REFERENCE TO THE SEFIRAH OF *CHOCHMAH* See *Tikkunei Zohar* 117b: תרין יודין ... אינון חכמה קדומה וחכמה תתאה "Two *yud's*... are the *Chochmah Kedumah* and the *Lower Chochmah;*" *Pardes Rimonim* 1:7, where Cordovero distinguishes between the *Avir Kadmon*, the "Primordial Ether" that is *Keter*, and the *Chochmah Kedumah*, which is *Chochmah*. Also see *Ibid.* 23:22, where the Torah Kedumah is associated with the *sefirah* of *Chochmah* and Cf. *Chesed Le-Avraham, Breichat Avraham* 15:2: סוד חכמה -- תורה קדומה "The secret of *Chochmah* is the *Torah Kedumah*." On a more fundamental level, the term *Kedumah* points to the interpenetration of *Keter* and *Chochmah*. See *Pardes Rimonim*, 3:8, 11:7 and 23:8 c.v. *Chochmah*, where Cordovero discusses how *Chochmah Kedumah* represents the most primordial and hidden aspect of *Chochmah* that is within *Keter*. Also cf. *Tikkunei Zohar* 117a. It seems that for Cordovero the term "*Kadmon*" in general refers to *Keter* and *Chochmah Kedumah* refers to the aspect of *Chochmah* that is embedded within *Keter*. See Ibid., 23: c.v. *Keter*. This understanding also makes sense to me experientially, since in my experience the Point of Light literally emerges out of the black nothingness of *Keter*. Ultimately Cordovero acknowledges that there are divergent traditions of how to understand the technical meaning of the root word *Kedem*; one tradition associates it with *Keter* and a second with *Chochmah* (see *Pardes Rimonim* 23:19 c.v. *Kedem*).

24. THE GREEK PHRASE "FROM THE EAST ..." ALLUDES TO THE LIGHT OF *CHOCHMAH*, THE MESSIANIC POINT OF LIGHT See *Otzar Midrahim, Midrashei Mashiach*, 3-4 (New York, 1915): ויצמח כוכב במזרח ... והוא

כוכבו של משיח "And a star will sprout in the East… and it is the star of the Messiah." Also Cf. *Otzar Midrashim, Midrashei R. Shimon Bar Yochai*, 7. Also Cf. *Etz Chayyim* 5:5:3 and 43:3:1: נקודה חדא הנקרא עדן שהוא חכמה "A single point that is called *eden*, which is *Chochmah*." Cf. Yogananda's understanding of the "wise men from the East" and his description of the "brilliant star of light" in Paramahansa Yogananda, *The Second Coming of Christ* (Self Realization Fellowship, 2004), p. 60.

25. *EDEN MI-KEDEM* This biblical phrase can also be translated as "Primordial Point," since the word *eden* is also a technical term for the point of *Chochmah*, and *kedem* can mean "primordial." See, e.g., *Etz Chayyim* 43:3:1: "A single point that is called eden, which is Chochmah."

26. "JESUS OF NAZARETH …" DOES NOT REFER TO A PLACE-NAME, BUT RATHER TO A MYSTICAL MESSIANIC TITLE THAT WAS KNOWN TO FIRST CENTURY JEWS My analysis of the ancient Greek epithet Ναζωραῖος used to refer to Jesus in Matthew 2:23 in conjunction with specific Rabbinic texts, leads me to the conclusion that the enigmatic and non-existent biblical reference "he shall be called a Nazarene" in Matthew 2:23 does not refer to a place called Nazareth at all, but rather to a messianic title known to first-century Jews. I intend to demonstrate this through an analysis of these texts in a future publication. It is also interesting to note that the main Hebrew term used in Rabbinic literature to refer to Jesus, *Yeshu*, can be broken up into *Yesh* (*Chochmah*) and *Hu*. *Hu* literally means "he," which would render *Yeshu* as *Yesh-Hu*, meaning "He is *Yesh*." The name *Yeshu* can thus be seen as a messianic embodiment of the *sefirah* of *Chochmah*, also known as *Yesh* (meaning "existence")—the messianic star or Point of Light. Cf. the book of John (8:12): "I am the light of the world." Alternatively, *Hu* can be a mystical reference to the Divine name "Hu" referring to the *sefirah* of *Keter* or *Ayin*. See *Sha'arei Orah*, Gate 9, p. 187: הוא סוד הכתר "*Hu* is the secret of *Keter*"; also see *Pardes Rimonim*

23:5 c.v. *Hu.* This reading would situate Jesus (to his first-century Jewish followers) as the embodiment of the integration of *Keter* and *Chochmah*, which is also the full expression of the Kedumah principle (see above, Chapter 10, note 23). For an academic review of the etymology and meaning of the name *Yeshu* in Rabbinic literature, see P. Schäfer, *Jesus in the Talmud* (Princeton University Press, 2007).

CHAPTER ELEVEN

1. THAT IS HIDDEN AND INVISIBLE See *Pardes Rimonim* 1:4:במציאות נעלם בסוד הדעת "in a hidden reality in the secret of *da'at;*" *Etz Chayyim* 23:5, 23:8, 25:6.

2. NOT USUALLY INCLUDED IN THE COUNTING OF THE TEN *SEFIROT* See *Pardes Rimonim* 2:3; 3:3, 3:5.

3. ACCORDING TO LURIANIC KABBALAH ... THE TREE OF LIFE INCLUDES ALL ELEVEN *SEFIROT* AS A SINGULAR UNIT AND SERVES AS THE ULTIMATE RECTIFICATION OF ALL DISTORTION AND EVIL IN THE WORLD This applies in the dimension of Atzilut. See *Etz Chayyim* 48:1.

4. THESE ELEVEN *SEFIROT* ALSO PARALLEL THE SECRET BLEND OF ELEVEN SPICES See *Etz Chayyim* 9:2, 48:1, 49:3.

5. WE WILL EXPERIENCE THIS HOLE AS A LACK OF THAT QUALITY My formulation of the teachings on the "Tree-Holes" echoes A. H. Almaas' "theory of holes" described in his book *Diamond Heart: Book One* (Diamond Books, 2000), pp. 17–34. My experiential understanding of this process has deepened through my encounter with Almaas' teachings on this subject.

6. THIS IS ALLUDED TO IN ONE OF THE MOST ANCIENT KABBALISTIC TEXTS CALLED *SEFER HA-BAHIR* See *Bahir* 22:

אני הוא שנטעתי אילן זה להשתעשע בו כל העולם ורקעתי בו כל וקראתי שמו
כל שהכל תלוי בו והכל יוצא ממנו, והכל צריכים לו, ובו צופים ולו מחכין, ומשם
פורחים הנשמות בשמחה

"I am the one who planted this tree that the whole world would take
delight in it, and I established in it everything (kol) and I called its
name 'all' (kol), because all depends on it and all comes out from it,
and all need it and gaze upon it and wait for it, and from it all the souls
fly out in joy." See E. Wolfson, "The Tree that is All: Jewish-Christian
Roots of a Kabbalistic Symbol in *Sefer Ha-Bahir*" in *Journal of Jewish Thought and Philosophy* 3 (1): 31–76 (1994).

7. THE *BAHIR* ECHOES THE TALMUDIC TRADITION THAT ABRAHAM HAD A
DAUGHTER WHOM HE NAMED "*KOL*." See *Bahir* 78 and *BT Bava Batra*
16b.

8. *BITUL HA-YESH* See *Tanya, Iggeret HaKodesh* 20:1; *Sefat Emet, Be-
har* 13:3; *Ohev Yisrael, Bishalach* 7:8, 7:11; *Netivot Shalom* 1:298.

9. *KELIPOT...* COVER UP AND OBSCURE THE ... POINT OF LIGHT... See *Sefat Emet, Devarim* 18:4: שבכל קליפה יש בתוכה נקודה גנוזה "Within every *kelipah* there is a hidden Point." Also see *Zohar* 3:246a; *Chesed
L'Avraham, Even Shetiyah, Maayan* 1, 25:5; *Ohev Yisrael, Vayetzei*
3:4; *Sefat Emet, Miketz* 4:3, *Vayechi* 1:3.

10. WE HAVE TO GO DOWN ... INTO THE ORCHARD OF NUTS... See *Zohar*
1:19b, 1:44b, 2:233a; *Pri Etz Chayyim, Sha'ar Tikkun Chatzot* 2:14.

11. *MIDBAR ...* CAN ALSO BE READ AND TRANSLATED AS "SPEAKING" See
Noam Elimelekh, Bamidbar 3:3.

12. THE POINT OF EXISTENCE... THE *NEKUDAT HA-YESH* On my use of this
phrase, see R. Abraham Isaac Ha-Cohen Kook, *Shemonah Kevatzim*

4:121:1 and 4:122:1. For more sources and a discussion of A. H. Almaas' use of the same phrase, see Chapter 10, note 9.

13. Bᴏᴛᴢɪɴᴀ Dᴇ-Kᴀʀᴅᴇɴᴜᴛᴀ... See *Zohar* 1:15a; *Pardes Rimonim* 4:7:2. On the etymology and meaning of this phrase, see the discussion and sources cited by D. Matt, *The Zohar: Pritzker Edition,* Vol. 1 (Stanford University Press, 2004) pp. 107–108.

14. Tʜᴇʏ ʀᴇꜰᴇʀ ᴛᴏ Kᴇᴛᴇʀ ᴀs Rᴀᴛᴢᴏɴ Eʟʏᴏɴ See *Pri Etz Chayyim, Sha'ar Ha-Shabbat* 22:1; *Maggid Devarav Le-yaakov* 72:1; *Tanya, Iggeret HaKodesh* 29:3.

15. Aɴᴅ Yᴇsᴏᴅ ᴀs ᴛʜᴇ Rᴀᴛᴢᴏɴ Hᴀ-Tᴀᴄʜᴛᴏɴ See *Kedushat Levi, Vayera* 7.

16. Tʜᴇ ᴛʀᴀɴsꜰᴏʀᴍᴀᴛɪᴏɴ ᴏꜰ ᴛʜᴇ ᴀɴɪ ɪɴᴛᴏ ᴛʜᴇ Aʏɪɴ See *Noam Elimelekh, Vayeshev* 5:3.

17. Aᴅᴀᴍ Kᴀᴅᴍᴏɴ ... "sɪɴɢᴜʟᴀʀɪᴛʏ" ... ᴀɴᴅ ᴛʜᴇ Jᴏᴜʀɴᴇʏ ᴏꜰ Fʀᴇᴇᴅᴏᴍ On the nondimensional and singular nature of *Adam Kadmon*, see the sources cited above in Chapter 1, note 9 and Chapter 2, note 9. My formulation of the teachings on the Journey of Freedom echoes in some respects A. H. Almaas' oral teachings on the "Freedom Vehicle," which I received from him on several occasions. I am grateful to my teachers A. H. Almaas and Morton Letofsky for helping me appreciate more fully the nuances and implications of this particular mode of experiencing reality.

18. EQᴜᴀʟɪᴢᴀᴛɪᴏɴ ᴏꜰ ᴀʟʟ ᴇxᴘᴇʀɪᴇɴᴄᴇ ᴀɴᴅ ᴏꜰ ᴀʟʟ ᴘʜᴇɴᴏᴍᴇɴᴀ See Isaac of Acco, *Meirat Einayim, Ekev*; *Maggid Devarav Le-yaakov* 68:6; *Tanya, HaYichud VeHaemunah* 7.

19. Tʜᴇ Fᴏᴜʀᴛʜ Tᴜʀɴɪɴɢ ᴠɪᴇᴡ The term the "fourth turning" was used by R. Zalman Schachter-Shalomi over a decade ago in some of his

oral teachings, the principles of which were later published in Z. Schachter-Shalomi and N. Miles-Yepez, *Foundations of the Fourth Turning of Hasidism* (Albion-Andalus, 2014). While my use of this phrase does not correspond with Schachter-Shalomi's usage, it does echo in some respects A. H. Almaas' use of the same phrase in his book *Runaway Realization* (Shambhala, 2014). In particular, Almaas associates what he calls the "View of Totality" with the fourth turning of the Diamond Approach. While Almaas' View of Totality appears to be similar to concepts found in some ancient wisdom traditions (for example, the Talmudic principle of *elu v'elu divrei Elohim chayyim* reflects this concept—see the note 13 below in the appendix—and it is also is a key component of the view of Kashmir Shaivism—see e.g. C. Wallis, *Tantra Illuminated*, p. 297), linking the View of Totality to the terminology of the fourth turning is Almaas' unique usage and I have adopted a similar model in Kedumah.

20. THE NEXT PARADIGM OF TEACHINGS WILL BE REVEALED THROUGH THE *SANGHA* Cf. the statement by Thich Nhat Hanh: "It is possible that the next Buddha will not take the form of an individual. The next Buddha may take the form of a community, a community practicing understanding and loving kindness, a community practicing mindful living. And the practice can be carried out as a group, as a city, as a nation" (Thich Nhat Hanh, *"The Next Buddha May Be A Sangha"* in *Inquiring Mind Journal*, Spring 1994).

APPENDIX

1. RABBINIC JUDAISM ... DID NOT BECOME THE DOMINANT EXPRESSION OF THE TORAH LINEAGE UNTIL AROUND THE FIFTH CENTURY OF THE COMMON ERA See Jacob Neusner, "Varieties of Judaism in the Formative Age" in *Formative Judaism,* Second Series (BJS 41; Scholars, 1983), pp. 171–197.

2. In Buddhism, this concept [of the Three Turnings] On the two primary ways of understanding the model of the turning of the wheel in Buddhism, see David Snellgrove, *Indo-Tibetan Buddhism: Indian Buddhists and their Tibetan Successors*, vol. 1 (Shambhala, 1987), pp. 79–80 and pp. 103–104; see Reginald Ray, *Secret of the Vajra World* (Shambhala, 2002), pp. 13–17 and 66–90.

3. Sefer Temunah See G. Scholem, *Origins of the Kabbalah* (Princeton University Press, 1990), pp. 460–475

4. Olam, shanah, and nefesh See *Sefer Yetzirah* 3:3.

5. Hasidism... shifts the object of inquiry from the Divine realms to the human realms See G. Scholem, *Major Trends in Jewish Mysticism* (Schocken, 1995), pp. 325–350.

6. Hasidism embodied... Avodah she-bigashmiyut, which means "worship through corporeality" For a selection of Hasidic texts translated into English that expresses this principle, see N. Lamm, *The Religious Thought of Hasidism* (Yeshiva University Press, 1999), pp. 323–337.

7. We also know that Freud deeply identified as a Jew and had some degree of familiarity with the ancient Hebrew mystical tradition, to the point of having a copy of the Zohar See David Bakan, *Sigmund Freud and the Jewish Mystical Tradition* (Dover, 2004) pp. Xix-xx and Joseph Berke, *The Hidden Freud: His Hassidic Roots* (Karnac, 2015) p. 39.

8. His [i.e. Freud's] approach to understanding the soul See Bruno Bettelheim, *Freud and Man's Soul: An Important Re-Interpretation of Freudian Theory* (Vintage, 1983).

9. The Diamond Approach For an overview of the Diamond Approach, see my chapter (co-authored): John V. Davis, Theodore Usatynski and

Zvi Ish-Shalom, "The Diamond Approach," in *The Wiley-Blackwell Handbook of Transpersonal Psychology* (Wiley- Blackwell, 2013).

10. A PRACTICE CALLED *DRASH* OR *MIDRASH* On the definition of the Hebrew word *drash* and the practice of inquiry in Rabbinic Judaism, see D. Weiss Halivni, *Midrash, Mishnah, and Gemara* (Harvard University Press, 1996), p. 73.

11. JEWISH RENEWAL STILL ACCEPTS THE PARADIGM OF RABBINIC JUDAISM See S. Magid, *American Post-Judaism: Identity and Renewal in a Post-Ethnic Society* (Indiana University Press, 2013), pp. 125–132.

12. THE FOURTH TURNING OF THE WHEEL OF TORAH See above, Chapter 11, note 19.

13. *ELU V'ELU DIVREI ELOHIM CHAYYIM* ("THESE AND THOSE ARE BOTH WORDS OF THE LIVING GOD") See *BT Eruvin* 13a.

14. OUR UNDERSTANDING OF *EIN SOF*, WHICH IS THE REALIZATION OF THE TRUTH THAT IS BEYOND THE CATEGORIES OF BOTH INFINITE AND FINITE See above, Chapter 1, note 9 and Chapter 2, note 2.

Works Cited

Biblical Sources

Genesis 1:3, 1:27, 2:24, 2:7, 2:8, 3:4-5, 4:1, 5:1, 6:8, 28:12, 28:16, 28:18, 37:28

Exodus 13:8, 17:12, 20:11, 25:8, 25:15, 25:22, 26:6, 30:22-25, 30:34-38, 31:13, 33:20, 35:10, 36:1, 38:27, 40:35

Leviticus 4:3, 23:15-17, 25:8-13

Numbers 15:41, 24:17, 35:25

Deuteronomy 4:6, 4:35, 5:26, 6:4, 6:5, 6:7, 10:16, 16:9, 20:19, 29:6

Joshua 3:10

1 Samuel 1:2, 17:26, 24:6, 36

1 Kings 5:9

2 Kings 16, 19:4

Esther 2:17

Job 19:26, 28:12

Psalms 1:3, 26:8, 31:5, 35:10, 42:2, 45:14, 72:17, 84:2, 84:12, 109:22, 111:10, 116:10, 118:5, 119:18, 133:2

Proverbs 2:2-3, 10:12, 12:19, 20:27, 24:4, 31:10

Ecclesiastes 1:16-18, 8:16

Lamentations 1:3

Song of Songs 6:3, 6:11,

Isaiah 6:10, 11:3, 17, 37:4, 45:1, 58:13, 61:1

Jeremiah 10:10, 17:13, 23:36

Ezekiel 1:14, 6:7, 36:25

Daniel 6:20, 12:7, 26

Hosea 1:10, 2:20

Malachi 3:6

Matthew 2:1-2, 2:23
John 8:12, 8:32

RABBINIC SOURCES

MISHNAH

Avot 2:9, 3:10, 3:14, 5:22
Kiddushin 4:13
Pesachim 10:5
Sanhedrin 4:5
Sotah 5:5
Ta'anit 3:2
Yoma 8:9

BABYLONIAN TALMUD

Avodah Zarah 5b
Baba Kama 82a
Bava Batra 16b
Bava Metzia 85a, 10a
Berachot 28a, 60a
Eruvin 4b, 13a
Gittin 78b
Keritot 6a
Ketubot 62a
Menachot 29b, 34a, 43b
Nedarim 38a
Pesachim 54a, 68b
Rosh HaShanah 21b
Sanhedrin 37a, 93b, 97a, 98b, 111a
Shabbat 87a, 118a
Sotah 3a, 22b, 36a-b, 47a

Sukkah 13a
Ta'anit 26b, 27b
Yoma 69b, 85b, 86b, 87a

Gittin 8:3
Sanhedrin 1:1, 4:9, 18a
Shekalim 6a
Sotah 37a

MIDRASH

Deuteronomy Rabbah 1:10
Exodus Rabbah 34:1
Genesis Rabbah 1:1, 1:4, 8:2, 20:12, 68:10, 81:1
Lamentations Rabbah 1:51
Leviticus Rabbah 19:2
Midrash Mishlei 19:3
Midrash Tanchuma Beshalach 1
Midrash Tanchuma Genesis 1:1
Midrash Tehillim 92:1, 105:3
Numbers Rabbah 6:1
Otzar Midrashim, Eileh Toldot Aharon Ve-Moshe 4
Otzar Midrashim, Midrashei Mashiach 3-4 (New York, 1915)
Otzar Midrashim, Perek R. Shimon Bar Yochai 7
Pesikta Rabbatei 21:10, 36:1
Pirkei De-rabbi Eliezer 10:1
Song of Songs Rabbah 1:9, 2:2, 3:2, 4:18
Yalkut Shimoni 951:13
Yalkut Shimoni Beshalach 240
Yalkut Shimoni Nach 550:2
Yalkut Shimoni Vayetzei 117

KABBALISTIC, HASIDIC, AND OTHER HEBREW SOURCES

Abraham Abulafia. *Sefer HaCheshek.* 1:3

——. *Chayei Olam Habah.* Jerusalem, 1999. 147

——. *Or HaSekhel.* 6:2, 10:3

——. *Otzar Eden Ha-Ganuz.* sec. 9

Abraham Azulai. *Chesed Le-Avraham, Breichat Avraham.* 15:2; ibid. *Even Shetiyah, Maayan* 1. 25:5

Abraham Ibn Ezra. on Exodus 25:15 c.v. *ve-natata*

Abraham Isaac Ha-Cohen Kook. *Shemonah Kevatzim.* 4:121:1, 4:122:1

Abraham Joshua Heschel (Apter Rav). *Ohev Yisrael.* Zhitomir, 1861. *Bereshit,* p. 5; ibid. *Tetzaveh* c.v. *ve-hinei; ibid. Shelach 1:2; ibid. Bishalach* 7:8, 7:11; *ibid. Vayetzei* 3:4

Aharon HaLevi. *Avodat Halevi, Veyechi.* 74

Aharon of Karlin. *Beit Aharon, Likkutim.* Brody, 1873. 39-40

Aharon of Zhitomir. *Toldot Aharon, Bechukotai.* 1817. 16

Avraham Gobiner. *Magen Avraham, Chayei Sarah.* Lublin, 1886. 27

Avraham HaCohen of Radomsk. *Chesed Le-Avraham, Chukat.* Pietrokov, 1893. 351

Avraham Leib Schik. *Me'orei Ha'esh* on *Tanna D'bei Eliyahu* 1:8 *(Mosad Li'idud Limud Torah,* 1994)Avraham of Slonim. *Yesod Ha-Avodah.* 2:44

Azriel of Gerona. *Perush Ha-Aggadot.* Edited by Isaiah Tishby. 40, 104

Baal Shem Tov. *Keter Shem Tov.* 1:24:2, 1:27:1, 1:29:1, 1:39:3, 1:59:2, 1:61:1, 1:77:4, 2
——. *Sefer Ba'al Shem Tov, Bereishit* 8; *ibid. Yitro* 11
——. *Tzava'at HaRivash.* 1:69, 64

Bahir. 22, 54, 57, 63, 78, 82, 158

Bezalel Ashkenazi. *Shittah Mekubetzes. Ketubot* 7a

Chayyim Ibn Attar. *Or HaChayyim* on *Numbers* 24:17

Chatam Sofer. *Commentary on the Talmud. Megillah* 26b

Chayyim Vital. *Etz Chayyim.* 1:1-5, 4:1, 4:2:2, 5:2, 5:5:3, 6:5, 7:1:6, 7:2:1-3, 9:2, 16:3, 23:5, 23:8, 25:6, 29:5:1, 35:2, 39:5, 40:10, 40:12, 42:2, 43:3:1, 45:1, 48:1, 49:3, 49:8
——. *Likkutei Torah, Va-etchanan.* Vilna 1879. 184
——. *Pri Etz Chayyim,* 21:1; *ibid. Sha'ar Ha-Vidui,* 10:7; *ibid. Sha'ar Tikkun Chatzot* 2:14; *ibid. Sha'ar Ha-Shabbat* 22:1
——. *Sefer Likkutim, Genesis* 3
——. *Sha'ar HaGilgulim, 31, Hakdamah* 2
——. *Sha'ar Ha-hakdamot. Jerusalem, 1988.* 44, *Hakdamah* 4
——. *Sha'ar Ha-kavanot, Inyan Pesach,* 1; *ibid. Kavanat Kriat Shema,* 6
——. *Sha'ar Ha-kavanot, Inyan Tevilah Erev Shabbat* (Ashlag, Tel Aviv 5722), p. 25
——. *Sha'arei Kedushah.* 3:6
——. *Sha'ar Ma'amarei Rashbi.* p. 58
——. *Sha'ar Ruach HaKodesh.* Ashlag, Tel Aviv 5723. 36

Chayyim Volozhin. *Nefesh Ha-Chayyim.* 2:17

David Shlomo Aibeshitz. *Sefer Arvei Nachal, Parshat Lech L'cha.* Warsaw, 1870. 29

Dov Baer of Mezeritch. *Maggid Devarim Le-Ya'akov.* 2:1, 7, 50, 68:6, 72:1, 95, 127:1, 127:3, 134:2
——. *Or Torah, Likkutim.* Lublin, 1909. 105 on *Kohelet* 12:12

Ein Yaakov, Baba Batra. 8:22

Elijah of Vilna (Vilna Gaon). *Aderet Eliyahu, Balak*
——. *Commentary on the Zohar. Tikkunei Zohar* 19 (37a) *"Inun".*
——. *Commentary on Sefer Yetzirah.* Warsaw 1884. 1:7:2

Elimelech of Lizhensk. *Noam Elimelekh. Terumah* 9:3; *ibid. Ki-Tavo* 1:1; *ibid. Vayigash* 1:3, 6-7; *ibid. Vayeshev* 5:2-3; *ibid. Yitro* 5:1; *ibid. Likkutei Shoshana* 12*; ibid. Bamidbar* 3:3

Haggadah Shel Pesach

Heikhalot Rabbatei

Isaac of Acco. *Meirat Einayim, Ekev*

Isaiah Horowitz. *Shnei Luchot HaBerit, Toldot Adam, Beit Yisrael,* 16-22; *ibid. hakdamah* 1; *ibid. Beit YHVH* 1-6, 10, 23; *ibid. Shaar HaOtiot, Kedushah* 1:168a; *ibid. Naso, Torah Ohr* 10

Jacob ben Asher. *Baal Haturim* on *Deut.* 6:4

Joseph Dov Soloveitchik. *Beit Halevi. Derush* 2

Joseph Gikatilla. *Sha'arei Orah.* 1, 1:5b, 1:8a, 1:14a, 2:46, 5, 6, 7, 8, 9, p.2b, p.33, p.138, p.171, p.180-181, p.185

Joseph Kapach. Commentary to *Hilchot Yesodei Hatorah* 2:10.

Joseph Karo. *Shulkan Arukh, Orach Chayyim.* 32, 36; *ibid. Yoreh De'ah, Hilchot Mikvaot*

Judah ben Eliezer. *Da'at Zekenim* on *Genesis* 49:10

Judah Loew (Maharal). *Chidushei Aggadot, Sanhedrin.* 147
——. *Gevurot HaShem.* 18:2
——. *Netivot Olam, Netiv Ha-emunah.* 2:1
——. *Netzach Yisrael.* 22:6, 29:6, 38:2; 44:3, 47:12, 61:5

Kalonymous Kalman Epstein. *Maor Ve-shemesh, Toldot.* Warsaw, 1859. 38

Levi Yitzchak of Berditchev. *Kedushat Levi, Exodus, Mishpatim 3; ibid. Chanukah* 5:1, 5:18; *ibid.*

Mishpatim 1, *Devarim* 2; *ibid. Kedushot for Purim, Kedusha Shlishit,* 4; *ibid. Ki Tisa,* 10; *ibid. Va-etchanan,* 28; *ibid. Vayetzei,* 2; *ibid. Vayera,* 7

Maharsha (R. Shmuel Eidels). *Commentary on the Talmud. Avodah Zarah* 18a

Maimonides (Rabbi Moshe ben Maimon). *Commentary on the Mishnah, Sanhedrin* 10:3
——. *Guide for the Perplexed.* 1:53, 1:68-69, 1:72, 3:20-21
——. *Mishneh Torah, Hilkhot Yesodei Ha-Torah.* 1:1, 2:10; *ibid. Hilchot Teshuva* 3:7; *ibid. Hilchot Mikva'ot.* 11:12; *ibid. Kings and Wars.* 11:4
——. *Shemonah Perakim*
——. *Ta'amei Ha-Mitzvot.* 3a

Meir Ibn Gabbai. *Tola'at Ya'akov.* 49b

Menachem Azariah de Fano. *Gilgulei Neshamot.* 30

Menachem Mendel of Vitebsk. *Pri Ha'aretz, Lech Lacha; ibid. Korach*

Menachem Nachum Twersky of Chernobyl. *Ma'or Einayim, Kedoshim*

Moses Cordovero. *Pardes Rimonim.* 1:1, 1:4, 1:7-8, 2:3, 3:1, 3:3, 3:5, 3:8, 4:2:2, 4:7:2, 5:1, 7:2, 8:2, 8:7, 8:16, 8:19, 8:21, 8:22, 9:1, 10:3, 11:7, 13:1, 20:1, 22:2, 23:1 c.v. *Adonai,* 23:2 c.v. *Ben Shemen,* 23:4 c.v. *dibur,* 23:5 c.v. *Hu,* 23:7 c.v. *zeitim,* 23:8 c.v. *Chochmah,* 23:10 c.v. *Yesh,* 23:11 c.v. *ketuvim stam,* 23:13 c.v. *mitzvah,* 23:17 c.v. *peter rechem,* 23:18 c.v *kol,* 23:19 c.v. *Kedem,* 23:20 c.v *Reishit,* 23:21 c.v. *shabbat* & *shemen,* 23:22 c.v. *Torah,* 43:3
———. *Ohr Yakar* on *Zohar* 2:134a
———. *Tomer Devorah*

Moshe ben Chasdai Taku. *Ketav Tamim.* 69

Moshe Chaim Ephrayim of Sudilkov. *Degel Machaneh Ephrayim, Mishpatim.*172

Moshe Chaim Luzzatto. *Adir Ba-marom.* 90a
———. *Kla"ch Pitchei Chochmah.* 1

Nachmanides (Rabbi Moses ben Nahman). *Commentary* on *Gen. 2:7; BT Moed Katan 25a.*
———. *Perush Ramban al ha-Torah. Hakdamah*

Nachman of Breslov. *Likkutei Halachot, Yoreh Deah, Melichah,* 1:4
———. *Likkutei Moharan.* 1:52, 2:11, 4:9, 6:7, 8, 13:3-4, 20:10, 22:5, 24:1, 57:6, 65:4, 78:2, 79:3, 269:1; *ibid. Likkutei Tinyana* 5:2
———. *Likkutei Moharan II.* 2:5

Nathan Spira. *Megaleh Amukot* on *Va-etchanan*. 186

Nosson of Breslov. *Sichot HaRan*. 261:1

Pinchus HaLevi Horowitz. *Sefer Hafla'ah*. Offenbach 1787. on *BT Ketubot* 2a

Rashi (Rabbi Shlomo Yitzchaki). *Commentary* on *the Torah*. *Gen.* 18:19, *Ex. 13:5, Deut.* 29:6, *Isa.* 28:16
——. *Commentary on the Talmud. Beitzah* 16a

Reuven Margolies. *Nitzotzei Zohar.* on *Zohar Chadash, Parshat Yitro (milu'im 124:72ff)*

Rokeach. *Commentary on the Torah. Exodus* 26:6, *Deut.* 6:7

Sefer HaArachim Chabad, Otiot. Kehot Publication Society, Brooklyn, NY. letter *mem,* 176

Sefer Yetzirah. 1:2, 1:3, 1:7

Shalom Noah Brazofsky. *Netivot Shalom.* 1:11-35, 1:147, 1:298, 2:235, 2:237, 2:239, 2: 248, 2:249, 2:251, 2:257, 2:281-284, 2:290, 2:311, 2:321, 2:334

Shalom Sharabi. *Rechovot HaNahar*

Shem-Tov ben Joseph ibn Falaquera. *Commentary on Guide for the Perplexed.* 1:72

Shimshon ben Tzadok. *Tashbetz Katan* on *BT Shabbat* 88a *Shiur Komah.*

Shlomo Ephraim Luntschitz. *Kli Yakar* on *Deut.* 6:4

Shneur Zalman of Liadi. *Likkutei Torah. Vayikra* 3:1, *Emor* 35:2.
——. *Tanya, Sha'ar Hayichud Veha'emunah* 7 (Kehot, 1984) 1:41:3,
    1:50:2, 2:9, p.82, p.315-319; *ibid. Iggeret HaKodesh.* 5:1, 15
    (p.123 b), 20:1, 29:3; *ibid. Iggeret HaTeshuva* 4:3
——. *Torah Ohr, Ki Tasa.* 2001. 86c

Teshuvot Ha-Geonim, Sha'arei Teshuva. 351

Tikkunei Zohar. 17a, 19 (39a), 21 (45b), 55:a:5, 69 (p.99a), 91b, 117a-
    b, 135a:1, 140a:2, *Hakdamah 2*

Tzadok HaCohen of Lublin. *Sefer Likkutei Amarim. Derasha L'si-*
    yyum Hashas
——. *Tzidkat Hatzadik.* 147:1, 153:1

Yaakov Kopel. *Sha'arey Gan Eden. Shaar HaOtiot, Mem* (95a)

Yaakov Yitzchak of Lublin. *Divrei Emet. Tetzaveh* 2

Yehudah Aryeh Leib Alter of Ger. *Otzar Michtavim U'ma'amarim.*
    Jerusalem: Machon Gachalei Eish, 1986. 75-76
——. *Sefat Emet. Shabbat HaGadol,* 5634; *ibid. Parshat Noah; ibid.*
    Behar 13:3; *ibid. Devarim* 18:4; *ibid. Miketz* 4:3; *ibid. Vayechi*
    1:3

Yisrael of Koznitz. *Avodat Yisrael. Yom Sheni Shel Pesach, "Miyom*
    Havi'achem"

Yitzchak Isaac Chaver. *Netiv Penimiyut Ve-Chitzoniyut* 9. 270
——. *Pitchei She'arim.* Sinai, 1989. 1-15, 16-49
——. *Pitchei She'arim, Netiv Hatzimtzum* 3. 5

Yom-Tov Lipmann Heller. *Tosafot Yom Tov, Ketubot.* 4:12

Zev Wolf of Zhitomir. *Or Ha-Meir, Lech Lecha.* Warsaw, 1883. 10

Zohar, 1:6b, 1:13a-b, 1:15a-17a, 1:19b, 1:20a-22a, 1:24a, 1:29 b-30a, 1:36a-b, 1:44b, 1:65a, 1:79b, 1:83a, 1:90b-91a, 1:103a-b; 1:134a, 1:147a-b, 1:162a, 1:175a-b, 1:200, 1:205b-206a, 1:224a-b, 1:237b, 1:247a, 1:261a, 2:11b, 2:25b, 2:42b, 2:47a-b, 2:75b, 2:85b, 2:89b, 2:94b, 2:95b, 2:97b-98b, 2:135a-b, 2:136b, 2:155a-b, 2:161b, 2:186b, 2:188a-b, 2:210a-b 2:229b, 2:233a, 2:239a, 2:268a, 3:34a, 3:36a, 3:39a, 3:48a, 3:65b, 3:85a, 3:94b, 3:98a, 3:103b-104a, 3:122a, 3:152a, 3:164a, 3:184b 3:201a, 3:209a, 3:225a, 3:233b, 3:238b, 3:246, 3:250, 3:256 b, 3:257a-258a, 3:261b, 3:262a, 3:282a, 3:288b, 3:298b, 3:335a, 3:341a-b

Zohar Chadash Bereishit, 11d-12a*; ibid. Shir HaShirim,* 64b, 74d; *ibid.* 42*; ibid.* Yitro 31a; *ibid. Sifra Tanina* 62; *ibid. Balak* 98-102

Zvi Elimelech of Dinov. *B'nei Yissachar. Adar,* 2:4, 2:8:10, 2:18, 3:1, 3:2, 3:3, 3:4, 3:5, 3:6, 5:19, 6:3*; ibid. Rosh Chodesh* 2:1; *ibid. Nisan* 3:11, 4:6 c.v. *al derekh haremez*; *ibid. Nisan* 4:2; *ibid. Ma'amar* 5:19*; ibid. Ma'amarei Shabatot* 6:3; *ibid. Kislev-Tevet,* 4:116; *ibid. Elul* 1:15; *ibid. Tishrei* 1:3, 3:2

Zvi Hirsch of Ziditchov. *Sur Me-rah Va-aseh Tov.* Emes Publishing, 1996. 56, 73, 94

Sources in English

Almaas, A.H.. *Diamond Heart: Book One.* Diamond Books, 2000.
——. *The Pearl Beyond Price.* Diamond Books, 1988.
——. *The Point of Existence.* Shambhala, 2000.
——. *Runaway Realization.* Shambhala, 2014.

Anyen Rinpoche. *The Union of Dzogchen and Bodhicitta.* Translated by Allison Graboski. Ithaca, NY: Snow Lion Publications, 2006.

Bakan, David. *Sigmund Freud and the Jewish Mystical Tradition.* Dover, 2004.

Berke, Joseph. *The Hidden Freud: His Hassidic Roots.* Karnac, 2015.

Bettelheim, Bruno. *Freud and Man's Soul: An Important Re-Interpretation of Freudian Theory.* Vintage, 1983.

Carter, Robert E. *The Japanese Arts and Self-Cultivation.* Albany: SUNY Press, 2007.

Dalai Lama. *Essence of the Heart Sutra.* Translated and edited by Geshe Thupten Jinpa. Somerville, MA: Wisdom Publications, 2015.

Dan, Joseph. "Ashkenazi Hasidism and the Maimonidean Controversy" in *Maimonidean Studies*, vol. 3. New York: Yeshiva University Press, 1995.

Deutsch, Eliot. *Advaita Vedanta: A Philosophical Reconstruction.* Honolulu: University of Hawaii Press, 1980.

Elior, Rachel. "Habad: The Contemplative Ascent to God" in: *Jewish Spirituality from the Sixteenth Century*, vol. II, edited by Arthur Green. New York: Crossroad Publishing, 1987.

Fine, Lawrence. "The Art of Metoscopy: A Study in Isaac Luria's Charismatic Knowledge," in *AJS Review* II, 1986.

Fischer, Norman. *Training in Compassion: Zen Teachings on the Practice of Lojong.* Shambhala, 2013.

Freud, Sigmund. *Civilization and Its Discontents.* New York: W.W. Norton, 1961.

——. *Civilization and Its Discontents* (1930) in the Standard Edition of *The Complete Psychological Works of Sigmund Freud – The Future of an Illusion, Civilization and its Discontents, and Other Works* vol. XXI. Translated by James Strachey. Hogarth Press; London, 1961.

Ginsburg, Elliot. *The Sabbath in Classical Kabbalah.* Albany, NY: SUNY Press, 2012.

Green, Arthur. *Judaism's Ten Best Ideas.* Woodstock, VT: Jewish Lights, 2014.

Gyātso, Khedrup Norsang. *Ornament of Stainless Light: An Exposition of the Kālacakra Tantra.* Somerville, MA: Wisdom Publications, 2004.

Halivni, David Weiss. *Midrash, Mishnah, and Gemara.* Harvard University Press, 1996.

Hecker, Joel. "Kissing Kabbalists" in *Studies in Jewish Civilization* vol.15: "Love – Ideal and Real—in Jewish Civilization". Creighton University Press, 2008.

Idel, Moshe. *The Mystical Experience in Abraham Abulafia.* SUNY, 1988.

Ish-Shalom, Zvi. "Not-Knowing and True Knowledge – The Essence of Purim", *Spectrum: A Journal of Renewal Spirituality*, Vol. 2, No.1, Winter-Spring, 2006.
——. *Radical Death: The Paradoxical Unity of Body, Soul and Cosmos in Lurianic Kabbalah.* Ph.D. Dissertation: Brandeis University, 2013.

Ish-Shalom, Zvi, John V. Davis, and Theodore Usatynski. "The Diamond Approach" in *The Wiley-Blackwell Handbook of Transpersonal Psychology.* Wiley-Blackwell, 2013.

Kaplan, Aryeh. *Inner Space.* Edited by Abraham Sutton. Moznaim Publishing, 1991.
——. *Meditation and Kabbalah.* Red Wheel/Weiser, 1978.

Keating, Thomas. *Open Mind, Open Heart: The Contemplative Dimension of the Gospel.* New York: Continuum, 1986.

Kimelman, Reuven. *The Mystical Meaning of Lekha Dodi.* Cherub Press, 2003.

La Caz, Marguerite. "Sublimation, Love, and Creativity" in *Analytic Freud: Philosophy and Psychoanalysis*, edited by Michael Levine. Routledge, 2002.

Lamm, Norman. *The Religious Thought of Hasidism.* Yeshiva University Press, 1999.

Magid, Shaul. *American Post-Judaism: Identity and Renewal in a Post-Ethnic Society.* Indiana University Press, 2013.
——. "Origin and the Overcoming of the Beginning: *Zimzum* as a Trope of Reading in Post-Lurianic Kabbalah" in *Beginning/Again: Toward a Hermeneutic of Jewish Texts*, edited by Shaul Magid and Aryeh Cohen. New York: Seven Bridges, 2002.

Matt, Daniel. "Ayin: The Concept of Nothingness in Jewish Mysticism" in *The Problem of Pure Consciousness,* edited by Robert Forman. New York: Oxford, 1990.
——. *The Zohar: Pritzker Edition,* vol.1. Stanford University Press, 2004.
——. *Zohar.* Paulist Press, 1983.

Merton, Thomas. *Conjectures of a Guilty Bystander.* Image Books: 1968.

Muller-Ortega, Paul. *The Triadic Heart of Shiva.* Albany: SUNY Press, 1988.

Neusner, Jacob. "Varieties of Judaism in the Formative Age" in *Formative Judaism,* Second Series. BJS 41; Scholars, 1983.

Nisargadatta. *I Am That: Talks with Sri Nisargadatta Maharaj.* Durham, North Carolina: Acorn Press, 1973.

Ray, Reginald. *Secret of the Vajra World.* Boston: Shambhala, 2002.

Roberts, Bernadette. *The Experience of No-Self.* Albany: SUNY Press, 1993.

Sankracharya, *Atmabodha.* Translated by Swami Nikhilananda. Vesanta Press, 1947.

Schachter-Shalomi, Zalman and Netanel Miles-Yepez. *Foundations of the Fourth Turning of Hasidism.* Albion-Andalus, 2014.

Schäfer, Peter. *Jesus in the Talmud.* Princeton University Press, 2007.

Scholem, Gershom. *Major Trends in Jewish Mysticism.* Knopf Doubleday, 2011.
——. *Origins of the Kabbalah.* Princeton University Press, 1990.

Shapira, Rabbi Kalonymus Kalman. *To Heal the Soul.* Translated by Yehoshua Starrett. Oxford: Rowman and Littlefield, 2004. Xxix-xxx

Sharf, Robert. "Mindfulness and Mindlessness in Early Chan" in *Philosophy East & West* vol. 64: 4. University of Hawaii Press, Oct. 2014.

Sharma, Arvind. *The Rope and the Snake: A Metaphorical Exploration of Advaita Vedanta*. Manohar, Jan. 1997.

Singh, Jaideva. *Vijnanabhairava*. Delhi: Motilal Banarsidass, 1979.

Snellgrove, David. *Indo-Tibetan Buddhism: Indian Buddhists and their Tibetan Successors*. Vol. 1. Shambhala, 1987.

Snodgrass, Adrian. *The Symbolism of the Stupa*. Delhi: Motilal Banarsidass, 1992.

Soloveitchik, Joseph. *Halakhic Man*. JPS, 1984.

Strong's Hebrew Lexicon. #2399 and #2398.

Thich Nhat Hanh. "The Next Buddha May Be A Sangha" in *Inquiring Mind Journal*, Spring 1994.

Tishby, Isaiah. "The Doctrine of Man in the Zohar" *in Essential Papers on Kabbalah*, edited by Lawrence Fine. NYU Press, 1995.

Wallis, Christopher. *Tantra Illuminated*. Mattamayura Press, 2013.

Wayman, Alex. "The Meaning of Unwisdom (*Avidya*)" in *Philosophy East and West* vol. 7:1-2. University of Hawaii Press, 1952.

Wolfson, Elliot. *Aleph, Mem, Tau: Kabbalistic Musings on Time, Truth and Death*. University of California Press, 2006.
——. "The Tree that is All: Jewish-Christian Roots of a Kabbalistic Symbol in *Sefer Ha-Bahir*" in *Journal of Jewish Thought and Philosophy* 3 (1), 1994

Yogananda, Paramahansa. *The Second Coming of Christ.* Self Realization Fellowship, 2004.

Yu, Lu K'uan. *Taoist Yoga.* Rider, 1970.

Index

Abraham Abulafia, 296, 305, 315, 336, 342, 356

Abraham Azulai, 334, 356

Adam and Eve, 44, 55, 62, 115, 183, 258, 298

Adam Kadmon (primordial human), 17, 41, 272-273, 293, 297, 301, 349. *See* Journey sub sec. Freedom

Adanim (sockets; *Adonai* pl.), 110-111

Addiction, 207-208, 210-212, 278

Adonai/ ADNY (divine name), 99-100, 110-111, 114, 117, 119, 122, 131-132, 135, 138, 201

Advaita Vedanta (nondual school of Vedanta), 55, 125-126, 295, 306

Adyaropa (superimposition), 125

A.H. Almaas, 329, 339-340, 347, 349, 350, 363

Ahavah (love), 193-195, 197. *See* Love

Alef (Hebrew letter), 104, 319

Alienation, 17, 19, 39, 55, 84, 170, 187, 221

Alignment, 11, 27, 36, 63, 68, 79, 86, 102, 141, 143, 146, 177, 179, 181-182, 198, 220, 275, 286

Aliveness, 2, 16, 31, 42, 43, 54, 58, 139, 164, 225, 240

Amalek (biblical figure), 111

Amrita (ambrosia), 232, 343-344

Ancestors, 84, 86, 88, 109, 127-128

Anger, 69, 163, 220

Ani (I), 269

Annihilation, 263-264, 266-267, 270, 297. *See* Black Light, Black Fire

Apavada (removal of superimposition), 126

Arbah Amot (four cubic feet), 108

Arica Tradition, 76

Aryeh Kaplan, 297, 315, 366

Attachment, 101, 148-149, 209, 213

Attunement, 68, 149

Atzilut (one of the kabalistic worlds), 293, 328, 347
Authenticity, 14, 23, 96, 102, 146, 152, 156, 166, 173-174, 181, 184-185, 188, 241, 248-249, 257
Avidya (ignorance), 55
Avodah she-bigashmiyut (worship through corporeality), 286, 351
Awakening, xviii, 13, 45, 55, 66-67, 79, 84, 98, 152, 176, 208, 213, 246, 291, 309, 341
Awareness, 3, 20, 30, 42-44, 53, 69, 77, 85, 135, 141, 197, 207, 213, 246-247, 254, 256, 259, 262-263, 276, 307
Ayd (witness), 135-137, 325-326. *See* Witness
Ayin (nothing/nothingness), 41, 228-229, 264, 266, 269-270, 293, 301, 325, 340, 346, 349. *See* Black Light, Black Fire, Emptiness, *Keter*, Nothingness, Space sub sec. Black

Being, 7, 40, 42-44, 46, 55-56, 58-60, 62, 68-69, 71-72, 75-76, 78, 85-87, 99, 103-104, 109, 112, 120, 122, 124, 128-129, 131-138, 146-147, 150-153, 156-157, 160, 167, 171, 173, 176, 178, 181-182, 185, 189, 191-193, 196-197, 199, 201, 203, 205-206, 213, 216, 221, 226, 231, 236, 246-248, 253-256, 258, 262, 269, 301-303, 305, 308, 310-311, 324-326. *See YHVH*, Lights of Being
Being-Self, 226
Belief, 68, 80, 107, 111, 125-126, 148-149, 206, 233, 249, 255, 291, 304, 309
Belly-Center, 60, 62-65, 75-77, 98, 100, 106-107, 111, 119, 124, 128-130, 134, 153, 164-166, 243, 315, 337. *See* Head-Center, Heart-Center, Three Orienting Postures
Bernadette Roberts, 306, 340, 367
Bible, Hebrew, 6, 9, 41, 44, 58, 72, 83, 85, 94, 99, 103, 109-110, 158, 172, 194-195, 231-234, 253, 258, 285, 302-303, 319-320, 341, 353. *See* Deuteronomy, Exodus, Ezekiel, Genesis, Hosea, Leviticus, Numbers, Samuel, Torah
Binah (understanding/a *sefirah*), 60, 151, 176-178, 188, 192, 221, 227-228, 253, 293, 325, 328-330, 333-334, 336-339. *See* Lights of Being, Pearl, *Penima, Penina, Sefirot, Teshuva,* Tree of Life, Wholeness
Birthright, 146, 258, 261
Bisamim (incense), 116, 322. *See* Spices of the Temple
Bitul Ha-Yesh (nullification of one's somethingness), 255, 259, 348. *See Ani,* Annihilation

Rolfing, xvi, 90, 130, 277
Royalty, 163, 173
Ruach (level of soul), 63-64, 115, 293, 313

Safety, 112, 121, 131, 220, 255
Samuel, Book of, 158, 303, 327, 341, 353
Sanctuary, 40, 71, 109-110, 159, 285, 325. *See Mishkan*
Sangha (spiritual community), 16, 276, 350
Scroll, 9-15, 21, 72, 74, 135, 231
Second-Turning, 70-71, 73, 88, 95, 110, 257, 267, 284-285, 289-291
Seder (ritual Passover feast), 82-83, 88. *See Pesach*/Passover
Seed, 227-230, 266, 337, 339
Sefer Ha-Bahir (Book of Clarity), 253, 262, 317, 327, 338, 347-348, 357
Sefer Ha-Temunah, 283, 351
Sefer Yetzirah (Book of Creation), 36, 104, 273, 284, 299, 310, 314, 319-320, 343, 351, 361
Sefirat HaOmer (Counting of the Omer), 150, 258-259, 326. *See* Omer
Sefirot, 46, 56-59, 84-85, 103-104, 120, 128, 132, 151, 154, 157, 172, 176-178, 201, 227-229, 233-234, 245-246, 254, 258-259 264-265, 283, 293-294, 297, 301, 304-305, 307-308, 310-312, 317-319, 321, 324-330, 333, 337-339, 342-343, 345-347. *See Ayin, Binah, Chesed, Chochmah, Da'at, Gevurah, Hod, Keter,* Lights of Being, *Malchut, Netzach, Tiferet,* Tree of Life, *Yesod*
Self, 4, 35, 38, 69, 84, 131, 135, 138, 147-148, 163, 195, 197, 204, 223, 226-227, 229, 249, 254-255, 259-260, 263, 266, 269, 287, 333, 341. *See* No-Self, True Self
   Awareness, 42-43
   Concept, 39, 261
   Consciousness, 155, 163, 254, 261
   Encapsulated, 39
   Entity, 148
   Evolution, 87
   Extinguished, 229
   Identity, 80, 94, 147-148, 223, 225-226, 248, 254-257, 259, 263, 266, 269, 275
   Images, 35, 147, 174, 248-250, 254-255
   Knowledge, 38, 42, 44, 296

The Kedumah Institute

THE KEDUMAH INSTITUTE is a 501(c)(3) nonprofit organization that supports and disseminates Kedumah, offering classes, retreats and training programs. For information about upcoming events please visit: www.kedumah.org.

Photo by Netanel Miles-Yépez 2016

ZVI ISH-SHALOM is the guiding teacher of Kedumah, the founder of the Kedumah Institute, and is an Associate Professor of Wisdom Traditions at Naropa University in Boulder, Colorado. An ordained rabbi, he also holds a B.A. in Classics from McGill University and a Ph.D. in Jewish Thought from Brandeis University. To learn more about Zvi or to join one of his upcoming teachings, visit: www.zviishshalom.com.